Finally Florida

a love story

Lynn Monahan

Finally Florida

for Philip

Prologue

Had I but known...

Prior to life with Peter, I managed my life somewhat successfully. Depending on your measure of success. Some years better than others. I made ends meet, barely, always having just enough. I simply adjusted my needs to fit the circumstances. With Pete, it was the illusion of having just a little more, a pedicure every payday did not seem too extravagant. A pair of shoes from a discount store, no questions asked. Financial extravagances were not by any stretch unlimited, but for once I was just above par, above survival. Pedicures, a loving man, living in the Florida sunshine. This was my version of making it. Finally, happy. I thought it would last.

Mom treated us to pedicures for Christmas. The mere mention of a pedicure made me anxious. It had been months since leaving Florida and I had managed to shut out most of the memories. At least that was the goal. I wanted nothing familiar of that time. Pedicures were the number one reminder. I knew I'd have to adjust to a new routine. A routine that included the word lack. Lack of funds, lack of dates, lack of Florida sunshine. Being financially challenged came as no surprise but I no longer had reason to be ready for summer at all times. There was no justification for keeping up with pedicures. And so, I'd settled back into the life of closed-toe shoes, not a new experience for me. Nervousness came over me, reliving those foot soaking memories, anxious about letting myself remember a happier time. Mom and my sister were oblivious to my inner turmoil. They didn't notice how I approached the massage chair with trepidation. Once I assumed the position in the chair, feet in the tub, slightly too cold, all the memories came flooding back. Closing my eyes, I held back tears, not successfully, a few came streaming down my cheeks, quite a few. In the last two years, prior to moving to Virginia, I had gotten a hundred or more pedicures. It was a way of life for me, a small indulgence, for date nights, for peace-of-mind time, a necessity of Florida living, a joke of my extravagance shared with Peter. So many emotions attached to those pedicures. It's the muscle memory of that experience, of a time and a person I used to be.

When we walked out of the salon, I noticed an unusual sighting of seagulls in the parking lot. With the Virginia sun on my face, I paused, closed my eyes and briefly allowed myself to remember Finally Florida. My name is Victoria Bench, and this is our story.

Tampa house? That was my hook, or was it his hook and I took the bait? When I was 19 years old, I lived in Miami for two years. Lucky to make it out alive I returned to Pittsburgh in one piece and vowed to return to Florida one day. It took me another 33 years but here I am. Hot and happy.

Peter brought me here. We met online. The picture of the Tampa house, with the Porsche and Range Rover in the driveway piqued my interest but more than that, it was the picture of him with his four children. He looked extra handsome in his tux. His stance told me he was confident, sure of himself. The children, ages ranging from 10 to 20, looked nothing like him. All dark hair, all exotic. Their father with his red hair and pearly white skin stuck out like a sore thumb. The picture-perfect loving family. All of my friends told me to *run*, do not get involved with a man with that many kids, but he mesmerized me. There was something about this family picture that drew me in.

I sent him my comment. *Tampa House?* He responded to my comment. I'm cute! Why wouldn't he? My profile picture was one of those rare pictures where I actually liked how I looked. A summer day, blonde hair glistening, sunglasses (made me look cool) and my signature smile. We communicated through emails for a while until he gave me his phone number and said whenever ready I should call. He wrote that if I turned out to be a crazy stalker, he would simply change his number. He was cute in his prose. Good grammar, no spelling errors. I called. He talked, non-stop, for three hours. I didn't mind. Non-stop. I'm not making that up.

Those were the days. Thinking back on them, even now, even after what happened, I still smile. I think of that picture of him and the kids and our early conversations. I still get butterflies remembering how smitten I was. As my friend Diane insists, I jumped all in on date two. I argue with her, just because I don't want to admit it, but maybe she's right. At least I didn't sleep with him on the first date. But at our age why wait? Second date is long enough. Besides with these things, life being as short as it is, romance at a distance (he lived in Charlotte at the time - long story, it will unfold). Who knew if I would ever see him again. Oh, here's another really peculiar but endearing thing he did. During our second date, watching a movie, he narrated the entire movie. "He's looking around the corner, she sees him, he has on blue pants, she has a knife." I was thinking, *is he going to talk through the entire movie?* It's no wonder I was quick to have sex. He wouldn't shut up. I miss that too. Movies are boring without hearing his narrations. Funny what you get used to.

Since his parents lived in the Pittsburgh area, he used them as an excuse to drive up from Charlotte for the weekend and while he was seeing his parents why not come and meet me in person? Sounds reasonable right? I mean internet dating is about "dating" is it not? We had talked so much on the phone, okay *he* talked so much on the phone, that by the time we met, I felt I already knew him. Our initial meeting was like meeting an old friend. He was nervous. He was fidgety. I dismissed the sports jacket that was too big. I dismissed how nervous he was. I dismissed the stupid jokes he made with the waitress, and I looked in his eyes. When he smiled his eyes crinkled on the sides. He looked both like a little boy and a mischievous man. I was drawn in. Up to this point in my life, it was hard for me to be drawn in, to fall in love, to even *like* anyone. I was picky. I am picky. I should have been pickier. I went with my heart, not my head. It was the eyes. I could "see" him in there. I said to him often during those days. "I *see* you."

After our initial meeting/weekend he returned to Charlotte. Not knowing if he was a womanizer or a con artist, I accepted the possibility it was just a weekend fling. Weekend flings are okay, aren't they? A little cosmopolitan, a little hip. No longer worried about unwanted pregnancies I could handle a weekend fling. My previous relationships up to this point had not been fun. He was different, he was fun. No, I take that back. *I* was fun. All my walls came down and I let him woo me. I let him lie, I didn't know they were lies, but I didn't question. I didn't care. I wanted to be wooed. And to my surprise, and unexpected delight, he did not disappear from my life. He kept in touch.

There were questions though; I asked a lot of them. He wasn't at all forthcoming. He did talk a lot but seemed to leave out key points. I would dismiss this by justifying to myself our relationship was new. All would be revealed in time. I didn't need to know everything up front. I wanted to enjoy a relationship, with a man. Go on some dates, have sex, be happy. My rules were no alcoholics, no drug addicts, no married men. Not overly confident about the drug addict part, but he didn't appear to be an alcoholic, and I knew for sure his wife was dead. Google. That's what Google is for. Researching facts about people you meet on line. That's exactly why it was created, right?

To keep the relationship alive, we would Skype. I needed to see the eyes. I can't believe how in control of my feelings I thought I was at the time. It was okay with us not lasting in the long run at this point. Steps were taken to make sure I didn't open myself up too much into a situation that would not last. I had drawn a line (in my head) that it was okay not to know everything. I was protecting myself by letting the relationship evolve slowly. I would not share everything with him either. I didn't even know him. Why would I tell him deep secrets? That's how I justified not learning all his secrets. It was okay. We were just dating. I focused on the eyes. I felt like I could see through all the baggage, all the hurt, all the walls and heartache. In his eyes, I could see his soul and I liked it. I liked it a lot.

He had moved a year earlier from Tampa to Charlotte, North Carolina with the thought he would relocate his family there after the death of his wife. He thought maybe they'd get a fresh start. But three of the four children refused to move. After a month on the phone Skyping with each other, a couple of weekend visits with me, and visits to his parents, he abandoned his attempt of reuniting his family in Charlotte and moved to Pittsburgh.

He moved to Pittsburgh because of me, at least that's how I remember it, that's what he said anyway, and he thought maybe moving to his hometown would be healing, plus he wanted to help with his aging parents. Who wouldn't fall in love with that? We would get to know each other now. This was too exciting. In the beginning, I thought I was meeting a man who lived in Florida, that was the hook, Florida was the hook. But this was even better, a man in Pittsburgh. Florida was not on top of the list now. He was.

From the beginning there was mystery. Mystery about his ex-wife, mystery about an ex-girlfriend (was he or wasn't he still dating her?) Where were the daughters? Where was everyone living? Where was the Tampa house he posted on his dating site? Where was the Porsche? The answers came, slowly. Typical hardship stories, wife dying sad stories, him trying to find himself again stories. Stories that make your heart melt even if you're not a romantic. But I'm not gonna lie; there were still big questions. But, the big "but", the fun continued, and the sex was unbelievable and to be honest I didn't want to know. I wanted to keep the relationship alive. I think (I know) I was afraid of the answers.

New relationships...they're the best, aren't they? My friend Sandy will want me now to give sex details, but I am just going to say what I said then, *four hours*. Yes, four hours was a typical night. I thought it was incredible stamina, energizer bunny stuff, blamed it all on new love and blocked out the Viagra commercial going through my head. I focused on the incredible abs and glutes I was about to develop with all the sexercise, never questioning how he could go that long. Is it a lie to keep the fact you are taking an enhancing drug a secret? Would that have been a deal breaker? I think not. I was smitten. I was in love.

For the first few weeks after Pete moved to Pittsburgh it was just the two of us, and the dog. His son, who had been staying with an aunt in Texas for the summer, would join him in a month. The daughters said "no" they would not be moving there to Pittsburgh either. They wouldn't move to Charlotte and they would not move to Pittsburgh. Too cold. So, it was just us.

We dated. We went to nice dinners, a couple of concerts; we did a lot with his family, his mom and dad. Everyone got along. His mom loved me, his dad said I was good for him. Everyone approved of everyone. We stayed in, I cooked, we watched TV, we settled in very quickly as a couple. It was comfortable. We talked a lot, he talked a lot, he talked *a lot* about his deceased wife, but he also listened. We snuggled, a lot. I am not a fan of verbalizing the importance of "snuggling". He, on the other hand, would talk about that incessantly. It was annoying. I like doing it, I didn't like talking about it. It was kinda weird.

I would push him sometimes to get more answers on issues like, where are your children? Why aren't you all together? Why did you start dating three months after your wife died? Didn't you like her? Do you miss her? Although the incessant talking of her should have clued me in to the answer to that question. Why did you break up with this last girlfriend? Why don't you spend more time with "my" family getting to know my sister, my sons, my nieces? Okay I never asked that last question, but I wondered. I dismissed it concluding that he was just getting back into town, reuniting with his parents, his siblings, dating a new girl; maybe introducing my whole group of family and friends was too much. Maybe it was going too fast. Although he didn't seem to have any qualms about moving fast when his son Jasen came to town. Pete had not yet found his own place, opting to live with his mom in the interim. Pete and Jasen (and the dog) would stay with me most weekends. Wonder why that wasn't too fast?

Soon Pete found and rented an adorable little country home for him and his son with a very big yard for his very big dog. I spent most weekends there with them. I loved the country. I loved hanging out with them. Having already raised two boys, I felt very comfortable with Jasen. That said, I took it slow on the mom front. There were obvious emotional scars from his mom's death. Deep emotional shit. He wouldn't even mention her. I was his dad's new girlfriend that he seemed to be perfectly ok with. One who did stuff like cooking and cleaning (his dad's last girlfriend didn't know how to cook.) Once we went through clothes to see what still fit. That's a mom thing. I made sure he had new tennis shoes for his first day of school. That was a mom thing. I went to his school's open house. Another mom thing. Jasen was very appreciative and accepting of it all. His main concern was that his dad was happy. But he liked the attention too.

The three of us were a little family going to movies, eating together, working around the house, playing with the dog. We planted a vegetable garden, we planted flowers, we had bonfires, we hiked in the woods.

After dating six months I got an apartment in the city, downtown Pittsburgh. It was farther away from the country home, but it was one where if we ended up living together, I could get out of the lease easier. We agreed it was too early in the relationship to move in together but weren't sure we wanted to wait another year. Had I signed a new lease where I had been living it would have been hard to break that lease. I moved to an adorable apartment, in the city where transitions are common occurrences. Since I had downsized when I moved into the city, Peter ended up using my extra furniture for his bedroom in the country house. It made me feel at home to be with him, in his house, with my stuff. Like we were joining forces. I stored quite a bit of my extra stuff in his basement. We were entwined. It seemed very natural.

We had our issues. Well, *he* had issues, I guess. I was pretty drama free at this point in my life and open to helping him with his issues, resettling his family, helping him get back on his feet. Loving every minute we spent together, I beamed. All my friends noticed. When they finally got to meet him, they all thanked him for making me happy. And I *was* happy. I couldn't believe I was having thoughts about how happy I was. For years my life was just mundane. Besides my children and the roller-coaster of single parenting ups and downs, my life revolved around my friends and family. There's nothing wrong with friends and family but I was ready for a different experience. I wanted a relationship with a man. A man that liked me. I'd even go so far to hope that he would "love" me. And here I was with this man who seemed to like me *and* made me happy, even with those unanswered lingering questions. Even though I still didn't know everything, I thought "I could marry this guy." I was just so sure.

And then we broke up. I know, right? He lost his job, there was a strain in the relationship, he clearly wasn't happy, but I thought this was what relationships were about. I would be there for him through it all. Wasn't that my place? Isn't that my role? We can get through this together, right?

Wrong.

He said he needed a time out, was depressed, yadda yadda, didn't want a girlfriend, this he says after I decided to myself just weeks earlier I'd never been this happy. Ever. And he wanted a break. Guess we weren't on the same page.

Interestingly at first, I handled it pretty well. I went back to my old "it's my fault" scenario. I'm not good enough. I can't sustain a relationship. You know, all those feelings we women tend to have throughout our entire lives, ok just some of us women have those thoughts. I have had those feelings all my life. It was easy to feel them again. I had a couple months of happiness, why expect more? Plus, there were new questions he never seemed to answer. Like, where did this cutesy Hallmark card come from? Who sent you this Christmas card that looks like it's from a secret girlfriend, unsigned, in a drawer, not from me? What about these homemade cookies? Why did you look petrified when I said I accidentally was on your Facebook account? Why do I have these feelings that go unanswered? Well, doesn't matter now. Might as well put that all behind me and move on.

But I couldn't move on. He had my furniture. It was literally the tie that bound us. He was "using" my furniture and I was storing things at his house that didn't fit into my apartment. I wasn't going to just give those to him. It kept us connected. Furniture. Who knew?

Less than 2 weeks later I see his picture on Facebook with *her*. Yes, there was a *her*. Apparently, she didn't count in the "I don't want a relationship" category. From the moment he moved into town, she started calling him all.the.time. In the beginning, he tried to fend her off, really, he did, but knowing what I know now, I'm pretty sure he encouraged the attention when I wasn't watching. He not only encouraged it, he relished it. He loves flirting, he loves attention, there's something wrong with him. But I'm jumping ahead. The homemade cookies, the Facebook scare, the unsigned card. It was all coming together in my head. Those nagging questions answered.

Maybe people want to hear the gory details of this not so cut-and-dried indiscretion. Maybe that would be interesting to some, but I can't relive it. My emotions were at that time all over the place. He lied. Then he didn't lie, which hurt worse. He chose her over me. Over *me*! I was his girlfriend. She was married. None of it made sense. We were close, weren't we? I could not wrap my head around this. I couldn't even blame myself. Was this happening to me...again? I thought I had left this kind of man behind. I thought I had finally found my "one." Do all men cheat? Is this just the nature of the beast?

Then he tells me he's got a new job back in Florida. *Seriously*? We're broken up. He's dating a married woman. Is she moving to Florida with him too? Isn't moving to Florida *my* dream? *Our* dream? What in the world is going on?

I sucked it up and started to get back into my single groove. He could use the furniture I didn't need, at least for now. Then the texts started. When he was in Florida, attempting to get resettled with this new job, he started to text me. "Wish you were here." "It doesn't feel the same without you." "You should see the moon." There was even one that said, "I found a house I think you should look at." What did he want from me?

I have this theory. When in a relationship and you find yourself going back and forth, in and out of the relationship and you want to decide once and for all, the best thing to do is go all in. That's right –

all in. Do or die. After a few weeks of these texts, I took a deep breath and asked him. "Do you want to do this? Do you want to go all in? Do or die kinda thing?" He said yes. He said a lot of things. He said:

1. We were on a break
2. He said he was sorry
3. He came completely clean about the whole affair

There is something extremely sexy about a man who admits the truth, although sexier when they tell the truth to begin with. Nevertheless, it's sexy to admit mistakes, say I'm sorry and mean it. I could feel the sincerity in his apology.

The truth made us stronger, made me love him that much more. I forgave him. We all make mistakes. People have setbacks. He's hurting. He lost his wife, he lost a job, Pittsburgh is cold, he didn't feel good about himself. He felt good about himself when he was with me. That's what he said. I believed him. Couples can be stronger after something like this right? It's not a sign. It's just a thing. A thing that couples go through. We're a couple. It's okay. He got it out of his system. Now we can move on, literally move on to Tampa! A man *and* Florida? Could God like me now?

The move to Tampa, *with me*, was on. I refused to be left behind. I didn't want to wait. I didn't want to be an afterthought with the kids. I wanted there to be an "us" when we started this adventure together, a solid couple, madly in love, headed to *our* forever home, happily ever after. We picked out the house we would live in together. *Our* home. We were on the same page. I was ready for it. I thought he was too. At least he said he was. He said many things, words I clung to for reassurance.

I left everything and everyone behind. Two sons, now adults, but still the apples of my eyes. Zachary, my oldest son in his 30's and Jimmy, my baby (well, baby is relative; he would be graduating from college that year). To this point in my life, my life revolved around them. As a single mom they were my everything. With them out of the house, the house sold, I felt it was okay to have this new adventure. We would visit often. They would come to our Florida house. Mom is happy, it's going to be great. Right? I had this covered, confident it was going to be okay.

I left behind countless numbers of friends and family. You don't live in your hometown for 50 years and not know everyone, their parents, their children and pets. I left my sister, my nieces and nephews, and great nieces and great nephews. I left my beloved Bunko group. We had just celebrated our 10-year anniversary. It was hard leaving them all, but I was in love. I was moving to Florida. Florida was my dream!! They had their own lives. It was my turn.

I left a decent job, a job I had a love/hate relationship with. I was ready to leave that job but was leaving eight years of work friendships. One week before I gave my two-week notice, I was offered a substantial promotion. I didn't give it a second thought. I quit on a dime.

I left my adorable apartment in downtown Pittsburgh. It was fun living there.

I gave up my independence.

I gave up control of my life.

Two-week notice, with no job to go to (although I did have an interview lined up), with promises from my new man that everything was going to be okay, *we* would be okay; I left everything and everyone behind. He was worth the risk. *They* were worth the risk. Plus, I was getting to Florida, finally.

Birth of the Blog

I have this friend, Diane. We met in secretarial school. Actually, we went to high school together, but I don't remember her from there which is only important when we attend our high school reunions together and everyone comments "you two weren't friends in high school". It is a little odd that I didn't know her since we went to a small-town high school, where everybody knows everybody. Although I do have one memory of her from those days. I used to go to school, late, *all* the time. One day when going in late I saw her walking away from the school. I remember commenting "that girl is never in school." We are the opposite sides of the same coin! Years later, we ended up going to the same business school. It was there we became fast friends.

Through the years Di and I would talk long, long hours on the phone. My older son Zachary remembers it well. He claims he lost half of his childhood to me talking on the phone with Diane. I don't think he's wrong. I'm a communicator. What can I say?

Diane and I both had office jobs. We would talk to each other on the phone while at work. Remember when we used to do that? Anyone else remember the days before emails? After the invention of emails, we would then email each other. I referred to them as updates, or "Di" breaks. I would work a while and when I got a breather I'd email her an update on my day...*i.e., Rose stopped by to say hi, I didn't know she was getting divorced. Susie got passed over for a promotion again, she's pissed. Cordelia asked me out to happy hour, I can't decide if I'm going.* ...stuff like that. Little did I know I was practicing being a blogger.

I know I am a wordy person. Someone who likes to share every blessed moment of their life, that's me. Well, seemingly every blessed moment. I don't really share them all, it just seems like I do. My friends who I left behind in Pittsburgh wanted me to keep in touch, wanted my updates, suggested I start a blog.

There are friends who *say* they want to hear from you but maybe don't really mean it, and there are friends not as familiar with my wordiness and rambling nature and surely don't want an unwanted email that they feel obligated to read. I turned to the blog idea. Easy fix. I wouldn't worry about clogging up anyone's email inbox. Thus, after moving into the new Bench/Clark household in Florida, getting settled and finding my computer, I figured out how to start a blog.

The blog became my "thing". The "thing" I did every day that was about me, not about the Clarks, to both entertain and present this new life in a positive way to entertain and amuse my friends.

Pete was super supportive of my blog. He helped get it set up, helped me figure out how to buy a blog name, helped with the design. He told his work colleagues I was a blogger, you know, like it was a thing. It was fun. He was great. I loved this boyfriend who was so supportive. He looked forward to the blogs and commented if I didn't post one or if I posted late. He missed reading about my day.

My days were scheduled around making the time to blog, posting pictures, sharing new adventures, both proud and excited. I was everyone's hero. My friends lived vicariously through me. I don't want to call it fiction because I really was happy, but let's just say I stuck with the positives, a "fake it till you make it" approach. Mainly I was pretty much there, making it, at least I believed I was.

There were a lot of transitions going on in the beginning. I had to get accustomed to living with and being part of this new family. For one thing, our family of three grew to a family of four. His youngest daughter Zoë, reluctantly (on her part) moved in with us. The family routines of cooking and cleaning came naturally, dog problems were not unfamiliar to me, but the way the kids treated each other was definitely new. There was no love-lost between them for sure. My kids never talked to each other the way those two did and if they would have, there would have been some smacking going on (not abuse but certainly consequences) It was difficult for me to say the least.

There were many attempts to correct their interactions. Some of it, I decided, was normal sibling behavior, some of it was downright unacceptable. Peter was not the most consistent disciplinarian which was an added challenge. Often it felt I was fighting an uphill battle. They were used to the dog on the couch, they were used to screaming at each other saying really hateful things. But, I was dedicated and had taken on this family and truly loved them.

My friendship with Zoë grew quickly. Jasen was starting to rely on me for more "mom" types of things. They all loved my cooking, having consistent dinners together at the table like a family, and my famous chocolate chip cookies (famous in my home town after making them for years for my boys and their friends). I even made their beds every day, I don't think I ever did that for my own kids. We had dinners together, the house was clean, I decorated, we were a family. I was all in.

There was also a transition going on with my not working outside of the house. I had never been supported in my entire adult life by a partner or spouse. I was not finding a job (the interview didn't pan out) and depended on Peter for everything, and I was uncomfortable with that. It was a new experience for me. I applied daily for jobs. Daily. It was very stressful. Nothing was coming through for me. I had to recreate myself. The family chores and the chauffeuring kept me busy, really busy. It didn't take long to realize that the new life of managing this household and this family was more than full time.

Financially, we seemed to be making it work. I was used to being poor. I kept that frame of mind. I didn't immediately start buying Jimmy Choo shoes, instead sticking to $20 shoes from Ross Dress for Less. I was respectful of his money and of my position, which I really never knew what it was; nanny, housekeeper, cook, concubine? Still, even though on paper it was working out, I was giving up my independence.

But I'm getting ahead of myself. I'll start from the top, from the first blog post and you can decide for yourself:

JUNE 2014

MONDAY, JUNE 2- THE MOVE – YOU CAN'T MAKE THIS STUFF UP

We have been here in Palm Harbor, Florida a little over a week. Get a cup of tea. I have a lot of news. Some of you have already heard about our trip down. It was awful. We had gotten separated on the road on Saturday. He was stuck in West Virginia and I had kept going into Virginia, because I didn't know he was stuck in West Virginia, cell signals being what they are (or aren't) in the mountains. Our trip did *not* start out well. During that late-night phone call, he sounded sweet, honest, and concerned about all the mishaps. I wasn't sure where he was going in the conversation. I just listened. As it turned out he was concerned that I would think it was a "sign" that all the calamities were happening. "I love you" he said. I melted. It didn't cross my mind at all that it was a "sign." It was just a setback. A lot of setbacks but we were headed south, that's all I cared about. Seriously, though, we could not have made up all the mishaps.

First of all, our original plan to leave Pittsburgh was delayed by a day because the truck broke down. On Friday as Pete was coming to my apartment to load my stuff, he was only able to load *my* stuff on Friday - as opposed to both houses – we had planned to leave early on Saturday. Since both of our homes were packed up, I ended up staying at my sisters in Sewickley Friday night. My brother was there, visiting from California. On Saturday, Jimmy and my brother and I went to breakfast - then onto Memorial Park to play with those grandbabies (or in my case, grandnieces and nephew) who all lined up to give me a hug when it was time to go. I had originally planned to leave town on Friday. That delay, in retrospect, was a godsend. I loved spending that time with my family. Jimmy went off to meet up with friends after breakfast and I didn't say my final goodbye as I was sure I would see him before I left. I had said my final goodbye to Zachary after he loaded up the moving truck the day before. I spent the rest of the day driving around with my brother visiting all the houses we used to live in. We walked around our old hangouts, then I sat in the backyard with my sister trying to get some sun. A perfect ending to my 50+ years in my hometown. It was a really nice day.

I got the call from Peter at 4:00 pm to head on out. A *really* late start. I didn't get to see Jimmy; he was still golfing. I sobbed like a baby on the phone when I called him to say goodbye. I continued sobbing saying another goodbye to Zachary on the phone. My sister and I hugged and cried, and I was off. Sobbing aside, I was excited. I have never been this excited, *ever*!

Somewhere in West Virginia, I got stuck in a two-hour traffic jam. Pete luckily had the heads up and was able to miss the traffic jam, finding a way around it. For a while I was behind him in traffic but then I caught up because he was broken down on the side of the road. I mean, I "saw" him on the side of the road. Sheesh. I stopped of course, but he assured me that help was on the way and he would catch up. Onward I went. He had tried calling me, several times apparently, to tell me that after waiting for help, he learned that the truck was unusable and he had to stay overnight where he was--all the way back where I had seen him broken down. But I didn't get the message. The mountains have no cell phone signal. At some point, I heard the message and even then I just kept driving because I needed to find a place to stay for the night...alone.

The first hotel I tried was sold out. Being that it was Memorial Day weekend the hotels were all filled. Didn't think about that. I had to drive another hour before I found a vacancy. At this point we're about four hours apart. Penske (the truck company) said since the truck he had was unusable they would send another truck the next morning which got there at 7:30 am. They kindly said they would send a professional crew to unload the original 26-foot truck and reload into the new 26-foot truck. The truck arrived at 7:30 am – yay - the movers arrived at noon. NOON. Pete didn't get out of wherever he was until around 3:00 pm.

I took my time in the morning leaving my hotel, but my only option was to keep going. We hoped to make it to Savannah and meet up there, but by now he was far behind. I ended up stopping in Orangeburg, South Carolina around 5:00 pm and waited for him. He got in around midnight. Needless to say, we were both cranky. Not the romantic "We're on our way to Florida" first night.

We reached Florida, finally, on Monday, Memorial Day, around 8:30 pm. I saw the house, *our* house, for about 20 minutes before dark. Did I mention the torrential rain and hail we drove through? We arrived at our house, our very, very cool house, and slept on the floor in a sleeping bag. All our stuff was still in the truck. It was dark (no electricity). We camped out in our new home. No kids, no dog, no furniture, just us. *That* was very romantic.

The movers (two young buff guys) arrived to unload the truck on Tuesday around 11:00 a.m. They were a blessing, truly. There is no way we could have unloaded that truck ourselves. It took them about three hours to unload. I showed them my prized possession (my antique buffet with the marble top) and said out of everything in the truck it was the only thing of value. And then, they broke the marble top, in four pieces. I couldn't talk for hours. The buffet and several of my framed pictures were also broken in the move. Just *my* things broke. A lot of my things.

Turns out Pete has soooo much shit, I'm ready to turn him into hoarders anonymous. I didn't see the living room until yesterday. It's been very, very stressful but I will say at no time did I want to move out. Not even close.

The pool is lovely. It is kidney shaped with ceramic tile around the top and single ceramic tiles set in the cement on the steps and floor of the pool. It does need resurfaced but it's a pool! I met Steve the pool guy already. He comes on Mondays. Our number one pool rule, we learned quickly, is no glass around the pool which the last tenants must not have observed as I got glass in my foot the first day. There are glass shards all over the patio area which we are still finding, in our feet.

Our kitchen is sort of small for the amount of stuff we have together, but we are almost getting the items down to a manageable size and put away. The bedrooms are all a decent size but it's really a three-bedroom house, not four as advertised. The fourth bedroom is more like a den or study. It's right off the front door. I'm not sure what we'll do about that. Maybe a sleeper sofa instead of a bedroom.

Thursday I already had my interview. I loved the sounds of the job. It's an Operations Administrator. There are four openings. Hopefully they will consider me for one of them. I assumed they got my name because I interviewed there before but the interviewer did not seem to know that. Remember how she called me the day I gave my two-week notice at Point Park. Remember that? I mean could there have been a better sign? But now, I have no idea how they got my name to call for that interview which is really weird. I'll just have to wait and see what happens but hopefully it will take a while before I need to start. I need a couple weeks to settle in. Who knows job interviews can go either way.

On Friday night we went to dinner where Pete's oldest daughter works and is the executive chef. It is the coolest place ever. We had a lovely time and the food was delicious. His daughter, Nina, was very happy to see us and very, very welcoming of me.

Saturday was spent unpacking (okay, every day is unpacking) and then on Saturday night we went to a high school awards night for his youngest daughter Zoë. I thought my own kids' banquets were long. Imagine when you know nobody and have to sit there for four hours. But actually, it really was okay. I got right back into the swing of things. Zoë, in 9th grade (well just finishing 9th grade) will be moving in with us on Friday after school is out. She says she is looking forward to hanging by our pool all summer. How great is that?

I ordered two floaters for the pool from Amazon. They should be here by Tuesday. I got my last paycheck right before the move, I have been buying things for the house. I trust I will be working soon, therefore; I can afford to buy pool floats for us, right? I bought a Dollar Store blow up raft to use in the meantime. Today was the first day Pete and

I floated, although by the time we got in the pool it was time for the afternoon thunderstorm. We stayed in anyway. Thunder be damned! Everyday there is a thunderstorm late in the day. There is something about those late day thunderstorms, that is soo cool.

Our yard is a tropical secret garden kind of place, complete with snakes and lizards galore. Lots of palm trees and vegetation. We have gardeners that come on Tuesdays. I've met them too. They are scary looking, one guy looks like Charles Manson, and I don't think they actually do anything. But I met them this week, through a crack in the front door.

Early today, before pool floating, we discovered some great consignment type stores and bought ourselves a new bedroom set. The one we had (which were my two dressers from the boy's room) doesn't fit all of our combined stuff. Luckily, we both loved the same dresser set at the store and have bought our first purchase together for the new house.

The house is in a very quiet neighborhood. One of the neighbors who lives across the street, came over with cookies. She actually took a step back when I answered the door. She apparently had no idea Pete had a "me." Actually, took a step back. I believe she was very disappointed to see me. Once she regained her composure and I invited her in (she declined) she became talkative. I found out that she's been living here 28 years on this street. She said no one has ever moved on the street except for the house we're in. Everyone knows we're renting, right? Anyway, it's a very quiet nice street, but we are very close to whatever we need store-wise. We can ride bikes to the Pinellas Trail (I wonder if we ever will) and everything else is a short drive. Nothing is walking distance - but nothing is more than 3 minutes away by car.

Last Friday, I got my hair cut - love it - and a pedicure. I'm feeling human and like a native more and more. Already finding my spots. Plus, there's even a PNC, my hometown bank, right on the corner! More signs!

When we stopped for our new furniture we bought our Pink Flamingo - he's made of iron. I can't wait to junk up the yard, Florida style. Pete calls it "Floridafying."

I absolutely love it here; I'm feeling very at home. It's almost like a honeymoon. I'm happy. This past week our routine has been Pete goes to work and I make dinners for when he comes home. We have spent time getting the house fixed up and buying stuff for it. After he went to work on Friday it was quiet. No kids have moved in yet which means the sex flows freely and often. I don't know how I'll manage the kid-friendly transition. I purposely did not bring men home during my tenure as a single mom to avoid this very issue. How do married people manage? Well anyway, I made myself a nice breakfast, sat at our dining room table overlooking the pool and teared up. I couldn't believe I'm sitting in *my* house looking at *my* pool in Florida.

Later that evening we uncovered the living room, sat on the couch and did that cuddling thing and watched a movie together (after I made a delicious dinner.) We are finally feeling normal. We are happy together. I can't believe my good fortune. God is good.

TUESDAY- JUNE 3 - WELCOME TO FLORIDA

There are A LOT of bugs in Florida. I knew that I would have to get used to the palmetto bugs (luckily, I haven't seen any since our first night here – and the ones I saw were outside) – Pete calls all bugs crickets. The lizards are little and surprisingly I don't mind them, although one night while driving to the store I noticed I had a little lizard on my windshield wiper hanging on for dear life. That was unnerving. Thankfully he was on the outside of the car. Oh, and get this.. last night in four lane rush hour traffic, this HUGE spider ran up from under the dashboard INSIDE the car – on the passenger side headed towards me – I screamed a blood curdling scream and looked for something to hit it with – like a baseball bat (it was really big) –I think I scared it with my scream. It ran back under the dashboard. Thank God it was bumper to bumper slow moving rush hour traffic, or I would have wrecked for sure taking everyone near me out as well.

Last night Pete fixed my broken driver's side window (love men who can fix things don't you?) and then we opened the hood to see if we could see anything that would resemble a spider's nest. We came in the house and completely forgot to go back out to shut the hood until the morning. The hood was open all night. Either all the critters have found their way out – or I will have a plethora of new ones. Needless to say, I haven't gotten in my car today.

Then last night I started seeing these ghost ants in the kitchen. Teeny tiny prolific little creatures! All anybody says when I ask them about it is "welcome to Florida". I'm thinking they should say something more helpful.

I have a new land line. The phone constantly rings. As soon as it was turned on, I got a call from the police looking for a donation. I hung up on them. Pete is afraid we'll be targeted now.

The new bedroom furniture was delivered today. Looks Florida-ish. But they didn't polyurethane it. I'm afraid to put anything on it or in it because it will scratch. I am going to add a coat of polyurethane to the tops only. Now the bedroom is all junked up again because there are double dressers and I can't move the extra dresser into the extra room because the extra room is still full of boxes. Did I mention he was a hoarder?

Our home is really starting to look like a home. *Our* home. Although Pete says to be patient and let things come together, I can easily get overwhelmed. Everything needs cleaning including the floors. I bought a new Shark floor cleaner yesterday – woo hoo! – but don't feel like putting it together. The kitchen now has ants that I'm trying to get rid of, the bedroom is a mess and there's no room for towels in the bathroom. So, eff it all. After this blog I am going to go float in the pool.

This is the first day I don't have to pick up Pete from work. I've been taking him and picking him up every day, but he decided to rent a car for the rest of this week. I'm not gonna lie. It made me sad. I really liked the routine and togetherness of that time in the car. I really like being with him. Not to mention, he has thrown off my routine of dropping him, shopping, coming home and putzing, making dinner and going back to get him. Today I stayed in bed way too long, made no progress and told him we're going out to dinner. Probably because I missed our alone time too. Hey, if I don't get it during the car ride, I've got to get it in there somehow. Maybe he'll take the car back if this is going to be how it is. Although we are saving money by me not stopping to shop on my way home.

I've been making good dinners – it's been fun for me, first to have someone to cook for and second, to have the time to do it. I've been enjoying being the pseudo housewife, spending money (although the money I'm spending is from my own last paycheck...I'm in trouble very, very soon) and making food for my man. Today I'm just stuck and can't seem to move forward (still blogging though and not in the pool, am I?) Tomorrow, I believe a daughter is coming to dinner. I shall hopefully get re-motivated.

Pete is flying to Pittsburgh on Friday and then planning on driving Jasen and the dog down. Poor Pete having to do that trip again. He left his 16-year-old Range Rover in Pittsburgh. The one with no air conditioning, no radio and a muffler that is falling off. God bless them all having to make that trip. I'll be here, floating in the pool.

WEDNESDAY - JUNE 4 - QUESTIONABLE WEDNESDAY

I'm up – dressed and ready for action! Today's jobs are polyurethane the top of the new furniture – just the tops should be enough, right? Just so all our stuff doesn't scratch the paint. Then we have a dinner guest coming. Although it's a child (not a young child but - you know - an offspring child), and they tend to cancel for various reasons. Just ask my Jimbo. Zachary is better at making the commitment. Wonder when I'll get them to Florida?

Based on emailed questions I'm getting, today is Question and Answer Day – then I must get to work:

How many children does Pete have and are they all there with/ by you?

Pete has four children. Three girls; ages 23, 21 and 15. And one boy age 13. Jasen (the boy) has been living with him in Baden (15 miles north of Pittsburgh) this past year. Jasen has been staying with his grandma (Pete's mom) in Baden until he finishes out the school year. Pete's going to go get him next weekend and bring him down. Zoë is 15 and she's been going to school here in New Tampa (about 25 miles north of Palm Harbor) living with her Godmother. She will be moving in this weekend. Her last day of school is today. The older two, Nina (23) and Monica (21) have their own places but threaten to move in occasionally. Everyone is welcome of course but we're really not set up for everyone to live here permanently unless there's some doubling up. But as parents, we are always open to house whoever needs housed. I think I'm a little more open than their Papa. We shall see. I'm hoping these girls with their own places take half of the leftover stuff that we can't fit that we are trying to unpack. Heck I want them to take all the stuff we can't fit.

Will they pay for the damages to my marble top?

The thing about that is Penske only provided the help to unload as a courtesy for all the truck trouble. We (Pete) put on the paperwork the breakage and then followed up with a letter. We haven't heard anything yet. Not one word. He said they sent him a satisfaction survey yesterday. HA! Not sure how we're covered in this case. But I hope we are.

Why the pink flamingo?

Because it's FLORIDA!! And pink flamingos are a must...probably not for the true Floridians but for us (really both of us) we had to have one. I did go with the more "artsy" flamingo in the iron form. Pete picked where to place it in the yard and it's quite perfect as I can see it when I pull into the driveway. Although I'm not pleased with the view of him from the porch. He needs to be turned so I have a better view of him from the porch. And yes, he's a he (because he's made of iron – plastic flamingos are she's. Everybody knows that.) I haven't named him yet though. Nothing has come to me. Freddy the Flamingo?

What does the house look like?

The house has a living room/dining area combo, not separate rooms but they are separated by carpet and tile floor. A not particularly big kitchen – not a good design -- but certainly sufficient. There are two bedrooms upstairs, they are both big rooms with a bathroom in between them. Downstairs off the kitchen toward the back of the house we have made into our bedroom. It looks like it was originally an office because it has a built-in counter type desk with built in desk-style drawers. The best feature of the room is the sliding glass door that opens to the pool! How cool is that?

When you walk in the front door the living room is on your left. Steps to upstairs are directly in front of you. There is a long hallway that goes back to the kitchen, pool and our bedroom but directly to the right of the front door is this fourth room. It has a fireplace. It's not a typical bedroom. Not sure why they advertised this house as four bedrooms it's just false advertising. But he (Pete) fell for it (and the house) and here we are. I have plans for that room, to use it as a guest room, library room (he has tons of books...have I mentioned the hoarder thing?) and extra TV room. The room is private enough for guest room reasons. Not sure if we can fit a piano in there though because of the books.... and books...and books. I might start selling

them on Amazon. I wonder if Pete would notice if they're gone. Probably be able to buy a baby grand piano with the sale of the books.

And that's it for the question-and-answer period. It is time to get polyurethaning. Signing off while looking at the pool.

MONDAY - JUNE 9 – PAYING FOR SUNSHINE

Big sticker day today! I am now an official Florida resident with my new Florida driver's license. The license picture isn't even that bad although my necklace was crooked. Good news/bad news is that the license is good for eight years, bad news it's eight years of that crooked necklace. I asked about the process for registering my car and the lovely civil service agent walked me through the process and highlighted the fee of $412. FOUR HUNDRED AND TWELVE DOLLARS!! To which he commented "you pay for sunshine". No shit. I fear my car will never be a Florida resident. Have I mentioned the no job/no income thing?

This weekend was full of sticker days. I picked up Zoë on Friday. It takes almost two hours, one-way, to get to her Godmother's house (where she's been living). *One way.* It's the red lights. There are many and they stay red a long time. Then there are accidents, always. I'm thinking they are all "bug" related. I am sure everyone is distracted by spiders, lizards, and snakes in their cars. But there are a lot of cars on very big highways. Anyhoo, we had a lovely weekend. Just the two of us (Pete is in Pittsburgh, remember?) To recap; Zoë and I found the beach - with a bonus of a little beachy cafe, on the water, at sunset. We had fish tacos and then walked on the beach at sunset. Then stopped at Winn-Dixie and did some grocery shopping. Groceries are cheaper here. Much cheaper than Giant Eagle. And everyone was friendly. We figured they must train them like the Ritz Carlton to greet everyone. Then we came home and sat with our feet in the pool for a couple hours just chatting. Just the two of us. It was really, *really* nice. On Saturday, we headed into our little village and went to the Parrot Head festival – which was just a bunch of vendors selling stuff (found a new Mary Kay rep). Then we had lunch, came home and I taught her the art of floating (in the pool). I warned Zoë that I was a professional (at floating) and not everyone is as astute as me in this art, but she caught on quickly; although didn't want to get wet. Go figure. Then we went and saw the movie *Fault in our Stars*. We found a nice theater very close by. There were about 20 people total in the movie theater. We had plans for Sunday, but they were thwarted because....

Pete, Jasen and Sam (the dog) are home already!! Pete drove straight through and got here Sunday at around 2:00 pm. He was almost incoherent, but still cute. He was awake on Saturday morning (the day before) at 6 am but had to cut the grass at the Baden house (which he is still renting until September) It took him four hours to cut the grass. His landlord there is an ass. He got a late start and then got stuck in a traffic jam somewhere near Pittsburgh for another two hours. No air conditioning in the car helped make the decision to drive through the night.

I am now living with a man, a girl, a boy and a dog. Of all the additions, the dog is the hardest for me. And I love dogs. But this dog, Sam, is very unpredictable, and very big and makes me very nervous. The 110-pound black lab has already dragged me through the woods once when I was trying to walk him when he went after another dog. I don't worry about him with people but if there's a cat, a dog, anything not human moving I fear he's off and there's no stopping him. Not to mention I have those white ceramic tile floors that will no longer be without that dog's black hair. Labs shed a lot. Sam almost immediately jumped in the pool. Now there's dog hair in the pool. I must get used to that. Steve (the pool guy) must get used to that too; although he seems less concerned than I am.

And then there's the eating thing. I can't remember if I taught my kids not to eat all over the house but I'm more worried about it here because of the cat size crickets (palmetto bugs) I am a bit on edge with all the crumbs. Speaking of food, I must think about meals again. I made salmon again last night – it was freakin delicious. In the Dutch oven, with a nice honey glaze, asparagus, mushrooms, and I threw in a peach just because – it was delicious! I'm thinking some sort of pasta for tonight. Maybe a casserole.

And lastly, I'm concerned with working full time and leaving these kids all day alone. Just doesn't seem right. Also, it's rather odd that I am back to worrying about that. I thought I was done with that particular worry. It made me sick to leave my own kids back in the day, and now I must relive that. But I need a job, and I needed one then. I guess it's a little full circle. Maybe I'll try for part time (mornings while they're still sleeping) or work at home. Lots more to think about now, and again.

I will think about all of that tomorrow – today we're off to the beach.

TUESDAY - JUNE 10 - GOING TO HELL

Is it me? Does anyone else feel like they're going to hell if they throw out old photos? In an attempt to make more room for "junk" in the kitchen, I went through one of my plastic drawer bins stuffed with photos. Getting rid of doubles is an easy choice, but what about pictures of people you don't even remember? What about a 40-year-old picture of my then boyfriend Bobby rolling a joint? How about my friends, Jean and Larry, wrapped in towels coming out of the bathroom? Do I need either of those? There are lots of pictures of my brother Scott with various old girlfriends. Should I keep them because Scott is in them? There are the ones I absolutely must keep, like my sister Kerry and Tommy in Colorado from 1981. I have kept a Christmas card from an old college crush, Burney, from 1976. What is wrong with me? I have pitched a few, put others in boxes, marked the boxes and now those boxes are in the closet.

Let's see what else... Yesterday, we did not make it to the beach. Zoë ended up wanting to go back to her godmother's (Leslie). I admit I cried. I don't know why. Well, yes, I do. I really like her company already. I love our family. I think I was afraid she was not feeling it, not feeling the same "love" that I do, and I wasn't sure how long she was going to stay there (turns out only for a week). I mean I not only love my man (that would be Pete) but I just love us all being together. Well, all that and I didn't want to do that drive. Ha! Anyway, after I collected myself we had a lovely drive to New Tampa. It was long but no traffic. We ran into this ridiculously heavy rain storm and suddenly, I could see *nothing*. Thankfully, we were minutes away from Leslie's. Zoë will be back here next week (which means I'll have to go back and get her.) Jasen went with me for the ride to keep me company, and we chatted on the way home. Remember those captured times with your kids? You learn a lot in those car rides. I appreciate the one-on-one time.

And now we're going to the beach (Jasen and I). We are going to Honeymoon Island to see what we can discover. I think there might be boating classes over there. In my pretend head (the one where I don't have to work) I'd like to take kayaking lessons with Jasen and horseback riding with Zoë; although it's *really* hot. I'm guessing horseback riding is not a summer time sport here. Maybe we'll just stick to water sports for the summer. I was on that Meetup site last night looking for sailing clubs. I think I need a more structured place to learn to sail though. The meetups seem to be for people that already know what they're doing. Another "job" for me. Find boating classes. True, we don't have a boat, but doesn't mean we can't learn to sail anyway.

No word from my job interview, but I have enough money for gas and the beach, and maybe even a boogie board making today a good day.

WEDNESDAY - JUNE 11 - HAPPY BIRTHDAY TO ME

It's my birthdayyyaygetting a lot of birthday texts and phone calls. Jasen was great and did a countdown on his phone last night to midnight when he could wish me happy birthday, "the best day of my life" he said. And I got a very nice card under my pillow from the boys who are now Pete, Jasen and Sam (the dog), as opposed to Zach and Jim. Should I read into the fact that I've always been surrounded by boys? Probably why I was very sad to see Zoë go the other day-finally a girl. But boys are nice too. And Pete and Jasen have been extra wonderful to me.

Speaking of boys, I miss mine extra more today (yes, I know that's not proper grammar, but I like it). Everyone who knows me, knows that my birthday has traditionally been my favorite day of the year (besides Christmas morning and Mother's Day). I have always taken the day off from work and forced my boys to spend the day with me. There were some bad birthday years early on until I made the decision to take control, put my foot down and declare "boys, you are spending the day with me, mandatory, and you have to do what I want!"

In the beginning, they would whine about me dragging them to the Arts Festival, however, in later years it became a day to look forward to. Of course, not every year was Arts Festival worthy due to weather. Those years we would end up at the movies. That's how I fell in love with *Thor*. I remember the year Zachary said he was taking me to that movie for my birthday. I was very skeptical at the choice for *my* birthday but figured it's something he likes so I'll go along because it's time with him. Turns out *Thor* is now my favorite movie of all time. Okay one of my favorite movies of all time but still up there.

I'm sad that Pete didn't think to take the day off work and spend it with me. I *know* that is selfish and someone has to work in this house, but I think it's a testament that I just like his company and, well, I'm used to making my birthday special and now I want special time with him. Maybe next year we can start that routine. Maybe I need to ask him to do that. I mean I had to make my boys do that too. Nothing like strong-arming the men in my life to spend time with me.

However, all is not lost. Pete and two kids are taking me to dinner to a restaurant of my choice, which will be lovely. I will probably get Jasen used to being dragged around with me to do whatever it is I can make him do. He's 13. Still young enough to mold right? Onto corrupting another family with art festivals and spending time with me. Today it might just be a Yogurt store stop. Better start slowly. Jasen just mentioned he wanted to go to this place called Mosi. Said it's like the Carnegie Science Center. Maybe it won't be hard to corrupt him after all.

One thing that has changed, for sure, is parenting/childcare after 50. When we were at the beach yesterday, in barely knee-deep water, Jasen said, "Did you know that most shark attacks occur in shallow water?"

"Thanks for that. Don't get bit. Don't drown."

Jasen sees me struggling, "You okay?"

"Yea, just stepping on these rocks. Why does Dunedin have all these rocks in the water?"

"Want my sandals?" (that I was smart enough to wear and will sacrifice my feet for your comfort?)

"Yes"

Jasen asks again, "You okay?"

"I just lost my glasses...Got em"

Jasen asked a third time, "You okay?"

"Yea, just lost your shoe...got it. Jasen I'm going in to sit on the towel. Don't drown."

"Okay"

I guess we know who's taking care of whom here. But that was parenting when I was 55. Now I'm 56. I'm going to give him the keys to the car, a pillow to reach the pedals, a beer and a pack of smokes. Tell him to come home whenever he feels like it.

I still miss the Arts Festival but thanks to Di for telling me it's raining there today. It would not have been a good Arts Festival Day anyway.

THURSDAY - JUNE 12 - EATING BON BONS

Update on bday... Lots of calls, texts, emails. Nina came over with a card and flowers. They were just beautiful! I had a nice dinner of Mahi Mahi encrusted in coconut with jalapeno aioli and pineapple salsa, Jamaican greens and coconut rice. Yum. Received a certificate for a massage treatment over at Safety Harbor Resort plus the promise of a bicycle of my choice. Not to mention a delicious cake, chocolate ganachethat cake sure does give Prantl's a run for its money. In the end, Peter did a great job with the birthday celebration.

Speaking of Nina Clark, she is now a superstar. She was interviewed for the South Tampa magazine. I feel honored to be in the presence of a celebrity. She talked about going on one of those cooking shows, *Chopped*. Until then, I just want her to cook for us! Unfortunately, she has a job. I'll have to keep doing the cooking, I guess.

This morning, Pete said "do you want to do something for me to-day?" Maybe it wasn't "for him" but it wasn't presented like a chore. In my pretend head I'm thinking he's going to say something like the following: Why don't you go online and order some stuff for the house – don't go over $500 or Why don't you go online and order some new clothes for yourself – don't go over $500. Or maybe Why don't you go to the corner and look at the Ferrari's and see which one you like (we really do have a Ferrari show room at the corner). Why don't you take Jasen to lunch and go to the stores – don't go over $500.

See? I'm being practical right? Limiting my thoughts to $500 (Ferrari store a stretch). Isn't that what stay-at-home people get to do? But no, he says, will you measure the walls and get the square footage, and estimate how much paint we need. What? *What*? High math? How is this fun? I said what you do is look at the walls and guess. Measuring, calculating, adding? What is *that*? He may or may not have made some crack about me lazing around all day. Yeah right. I mean I work my ass off around here. Like today, I woke up. Stayed in bed and sent Gina a long email, tried to get my massage appointment, looked around the room, made the bed, made some tea, talked to Jimmy. I think I moved a box. See? Busy! I'm going to have Jasen measure the walls. He needs the math practice. We'll just write down a lot of numbers on a piece of paper and say we did it. I'm going to walk around and guesstimate. Bet I'm right too. He'll never know the difference.

FRIDAY - JUNE 13 - RAIN RAIN, COME AGAIN ANOTHER DAY TOO!

The only thing better than a sunny day in Florida is a rainy day in Florida. There are not many full days of rain here (from what I re-member and understand) but today it's dark, it's pouring and thunder rumbling. I love it! A perfect day to catch up on inside stuff. Emails, phone calls, dusting, laundry, maybe even looking for a job. There's a lot of pressure that comes with constant sunshine. Being from Pittsburgh,

I feel like when it's nice weather I must take advantage of it and do something outside. I've been pushing myself to be productive in the mornings, then I can get outside in the afternoon.

Today however, I'm looking forward to taking it slow and having an excuse to stay inside. Of course, if the house blows over or a tree falls on my car I don't know if I'll be happy anymore. It is *really* coming down out there. It is hurricane season. The dog's not real happy about the thunder but we haven't needed a thunder cape.

Yesterday, Jasen and I spent our Ferris Bueller day off. We did not measure walls, although we tried. Once he started talking about subtracting doorways, taking off for this and that, I just wrote down two gallons here, two gallons there, buy more if needed. Done. Off exploring we went.

We drove to Dunedin Marina and looked at boats and took a picture in front of our favorite yacht. We saw a seahorse which was the coolest thing ever. Just a little lone seahorse traveling along the wall. We sat on the pier for a while. Both of us content just to sit by the water. There was a fisherman, but he didn't catch anything. The water was choppy, and we noticed all the sailboats in the water had their sails down. See how observant we are to our new marine living? We hung out there for a while, came back over this way and stopped on our way home to try out the yogurt store.

We downed our yogurt and then went to the local pier where we saw all these crabs. They are cool and gross at the same time. These kinds of crabs have holes in the sand and when you walk towards them they all go back into their holes, but these crabs were just swarming under the pier. Sort of like a horror movie. Jasen liked chasing them. I stayed above ground on the pier. Also, there were a bunch of kids jumping off the pier. That looked like fun and maybe something Jasen will partake of in the future. The younger mom in me probably would have said it was too dangerous. Yesterday I just thought it looked like fun.

The weekend is upon us and who knows what we will do? Pete assures me we will have fun. I am planning my birthday massage on

Father's Day, and he can stay home and bond with his brood. Decent of me don't you think? Maybe we'll go look at bikes too. I realize I haven't been reporting on our sex life. Do you know why? Kids. And the fact that I don't want to rub it in necessarily or even talk about that kind of thing. But I will say I always look forward to the weekend mornings. Those kids sleep in and we typically stay in bed until noon. It's our alone time. We tend to talk a lot in the mornings.

I have discovered another thing we have in common; we are both professional loungers. It is nice for me, and well, hopefully for him too. It really makes the weekends great. The addition of the kids in our lives makes it busy but we have been able to find time for just us. It's pretty wonderful.

MONDAY - JUNE 16 - THERE'S NOTHING TO EAT AROUND HERE

Apparently even when you make a decent income, payday is still something to be celebrated. Friday was payday and celebrating was had by all. Nothing super crazy, just Costco, but we all know "just Costco" can get out of hand too. Although on this particular day, on this blog, I want to address food. I am thinking about my kids and if they could see the amount of food in this house, I'm not sure how they would respond. We never had an abundance of food in our house when I was raising them. I don't mean like starving people-no food, but only the staples. Peanut butter, jelly, white bread, milk (although Zachary would disagree about the milk), apple juice, never pop/soda, and the only junk food was if I baked. Obviously, cookie ingredients were staples.

I remember trying a couple different food items occasionally, like chipped ham. I think we tried turkey once. Potato chips were sometimes a staple because they are perfect with peanut butter and jelly. We'd have grapes--I remember that. Well, the point is, this house I live in now has sooo much food.

When we go grocery shopping and Jasen or Zoë ask, "can I have this?" I'm like "Sure, throw it in the cart". I never say no. Mostly because I don't have to, except for the soda, that still gets an "it'll stunt your growth" no. And not only do we have snack food, we have Costco snack food, which means a lot of everything. We have an assortment of Sunchips, Peanut butter stuffed pretzels, dried apricots (okay those are for "me"), chocolate coconut bark (these might be a "me" too) crunch rice rollers, a case of V8 fusion drinks, a case of Capri Suns, four other kinds of bottled juice--Clarks are big juice drinkers--a cheese drawer overflowing. Is this how real people live? Maybe I helped my boys in the long run by not giving them too many choices or maybe by not giving them too much processed foods? I feel a little guilty living a life without them with all these choices. I didn't feel the real impact of it until I thought about (and had to put away) all the food.

In other news, Pete's kids came and made him a big breakfast on Father's Day. I went and had my massage. Then we had a delicious steak dinner on our new grill. Payday, remember? After dinner we all stretched out together on the couch, all together, and watched a movie. Even with all this food in the house, and all these choices to be made, what did everyone wait for last night? My chocolate chip cookies. Things aren't that different after all.

TUESDAY - JUNE 17 - LIFE'S A BEACH

My typical day is made up of something productive in the morning, then my blog, then play time (or errands). However, today it was juggling beach day and the Brazil US World Cup game at 3:00 pm. Juggling children's interests is a blog for another day, one that will be filled with heavy sighs and possibly cryingbut not today.

Today, after figuring out how to register Jasen for school for next year, we left for the beach. Beach life is rather similar to pool life. In the days when we used to go to the pool, I'd drag the pool bag, lunch, and stuff to keep the kids busy. Going to the beach today was similar dragging but more--the beach bag, bottles of water, sunglasses, skim board, four beach chairs, phone (we didn't have cell phones when we went to the pool back in the day), keys, money, Go. The beach is only about 10 minutes away. It's close. We played, lounged, I walked, and a great time was had by all. We made it home by 3:00 for the game (it ended in a tie). I took advantage of the fact that I was already wet and floated in the pool until dinner time. Getting wet is a commitment. Getting wet with sand is even more of a commitment but somehow easier to say yes to.

Here are some of my living-at-the-beach observations:

I am now wearing a hat at the beach, in the sun. Yes, I know I should have always worn one, but in Pittsburgh I couldn't get sun every day, I needed to soak up as much as I could, when I could. Today I sported my Dollar Store floppy hat. I probably look super cute, but I felt stupid asking Zoë to keep taking pictures of me to post. Regardless, I look forward to getting more hats to add to my collection (or start a collection.)

I will never again have a car that is sand free. I wonder if I should get another more beach friendly car, but that would entail getting a job. For now, I had Pete hook up a hose near where I park the car to immediately rinse off all the beach paraphernalia. I need to add a vacuum to that hook up as well. I certainly see why beach houses have outside showers.

Also, beach chairs, that have been outside, need to be inspected for spiders and hiding lizards *before* putting into the car.

Lastly, I have observed that many of the "old" people down here float in the Gulf. I think they live here on the Gulf side because there are virtually no waves which makes it perfect for floating. Also, the water is like bathwater. This is my kind of life. I love floating, I love my new family.

WEDNESDAY - JUNE 18 - THINGS THAT MAKE ME GO HMMMMM

A funny thing happened when I tagged along to register Jasen for school this morning. Actually, a couple of funny things. Firstly (is that an actual word?) I put my tennis shoes on for the first time since moving here. I drove over with Pete but then walked back home. That was exciting. Almost exercise. We live about ½ mile from the school, it was a nice little walk. You would think all the unpacking, swimming, etc., would count for exercise but according to my snug clothes it does *not*. I'm looking forward to longer walks in the future. Might have to wait until it cools off just a tad.

The secondly funny thing that happened (ok I know secondly is not a right word) is I had a pang of missing working, and more importantly work friends. The woman we met with at the school was very nice and I thought, I could be her friend. The school is very close to home, I could walk there, and I thought hmmm, I could work here. Tomorrow is this woman's last day until July 28. Ten days off! I thought even more hmmm, *I could work here*! The school day for the middle school is 9:30 – 5:00. Really? Jasen will be super thrilled about that (since last year in Pittsburgh he caught the bus at 7 am, in the dark and cold) I could work 9:30 – 5:00. Although we all know that my actual work day would be longer, but still. I came back home and went online to look for a job at Pinellas County schools. Who would have thought I would actually miss work?

Although I have many friends, I'm not particularly an outgoing person. The last two apartments where I lived in in Pittsburgh, I did not meet any neighbors (mostly by choice). I've been here now almost a month, I met a neighbor, but she never came back. Remember the one that seemed particularly upset that I wasn't Pete? One day the guy next store tried to say hi but I was running inside to use the facilities. Ya know? Just bad timing. I haven't felt like I'm missing having new friends just yet. I have my back home friends, right? But something about sitting in that office talking to that woman this morning made me miss having friends nearby, and this morning I was missing work friends.

My neighborhood is very much a Wisteria Lane by the number of houses (eight) and the layout of the street. I go between not wanting to meet anyone and wanting to start a new Bunko group in the neighborhood. We shall see which side of me prevails in the long run.

Tomorrow night I will be making the trip back to Pittsburgh for the weekend for my niece's high school graduation party. Hopefully I'll get a friend fix while I'm there. All this family time I put in with my "new" family, I wish Pete would come with me to see my "old" family. He doesn't feel like he can leave the kids, the dog, work. I get it. But it still makes me sad.

Last night we put a table up on the patio by the pool for dinner. This is where I'm writing my blog today. Nice huh?

MONDAY - JUNE 23 - I'M BACK

I'm back, which today has many meanings.

- I'm back to blogging
- I'm back from home
- And I'm back home

One of the questions that I was asked a lot over the weekend was how it felt to be back "home". There's a familiarity about Sewickley that you don't find anywhere else. I know I can go "upstreet" to get supplies at Thrift Drugs (still what we call the drug store even though Thrift has been out of business for years); I know where to get my watch batteries replaced, where to pick up my contact lenses and I can get a Starbucks and sit on the park bench (before the town drunk gets there).

The trouble with going home is there is never enough time. There are people I didn't get to see and there are many friends that I would have liked to have seen but didn't. But that just means I'll catch them next time.

When I left Pittsburgh to fly back to Florida today, I was coming "home". I was excited to get back, excited to see my boyfriend, excited to even make the drive from his office (something I do often) excited to see the dog (well he was a little more excited than me) excited to see the kids, the house, our room, excited to go get my toes done. Tonight, I'll make some sort of dinner that's sure to be a masterpiece (knock on wood) followed by me making my welcome home cookies.

In conclusion, and on a completely sappy note, the saying goes "home is where your heart is" and well, my heart is in each and every one of my friends and family. I am home with my boys no matter where we are. I am home with my friends no matter where we are. Every one of my friends and family have a piece of my heart, every place I've "hung" has a piece of my heart, and now my heart is here as well. I think that must be why it feels like "home" here, because my heart swells when I'm here, and I'm just taking it (Florida) and them (the Clarks) all into my heart. And well you know, once you're in, you're in.

TUESDAY - JUNE 24 - SHOULDA COULDA WOULDA

This is what I SHOULD be doing today:

- Eating a healthy breakfast
- Cleaning the upstairs bathroom
- Looking for and/or applying for jobs on line
- Hanging pictures and other decor in our bedroom
- Unpacking a box of books and putting them on the shelves in the living room

This is what I'm GOING to do today:
Go to Tarpon Springs. Tarpon Springs is about 20 minutes from our house. It's this cool little old world Greek village where they fish for

sponges. Someone asked me recently if there is a big Hispanic speaking population here and surprisingly there is not. But there is a great big Greek population, instead of the Spanish/Mexican/Cuban accents we get a lot of Greek accents everywhere.

Today I'm going to wake those little angels up and drag them up there to do some adventuring. I know there's a good restaurant, cheap sponges and where the fudge store is. There is a place where you can buy jewelry for $1.49.

It's great being back from Pittsburgh. Peter met me at the airport with roses. Did I mention that before? I now have these beautiful roses to look at all day. I should be working (an added should) but in the meantime I'll just admire my roses. Even the kids seem happy to see me. Jasen accompanied me on my trip to pick up Pete after work yesterday. He was protecting me from the snake I ran over but then didn't see.

So, get this, I'm driving down the road, a black snake is on the road, and I drove over it. Not on purpose. I thought my tires missed it but honestly, I didn't really care if they didn't. Does that make me a bad person? A serial killer? I looked in the rear-view mirror to see the dead carcass on the road and nada. I turn the car around to go find it and nada. Where is the snake? I am convinced it jumped up to save itself and is now hiding under my hood. I wonder if it likes spiders and will eat the families living there that I didn't get with the bug bomb. I explained to Pete that he is the man, therefore his job to find the snake. He's put it on his to-do list. Hmmm.

As for the rest of my shoulds:

- I'll think about that bathroom later, I'm going to just block it from my mind for now.
- I'll wait for Peter to hang pictures; he has a better sense of balance (see how I did that?)
- Jobs/schmobs – ya know when I die will I say, gee I wish I would have worked sooner when I moved to Florida? Or will I say, gee

wasn't it fun spending all of Pete's money and uncovering adventures? I know what I would say, wonder what Pete would say.

- Unpacking a box of books is something you do when watching mindless television, at night, or during a rain storm, and that's not today.
- Eating a healthy breakfast. I just got the yogurt out of the fridge and ate a chocolate cookie on the way to the fridge. Will the yogurt get opened or will I just go for another cookie and call it a day?

Stay tuned to tomorrow for the results of my breakfast quandary.

WEDNESDAY - JUNE 25 - GOOD THING I SPEAK PARSELTONGUE

It's the end of the month and bill paying time. A stressful time anyway because of my no job thing. This is how the day has played out thus far:

My day started with Steve, the pool man, coming early (early is now before 10, the no job thing has me sleeping way too much) –– anyway, we have this sand and dirt in the pool that came from somewhere. Steve doesn't know where it came from but just turned the Kreepy Krawley vacuum thing on and said it should clean it up. No sooner did he leave then the Kreepy Krawley vacuum thing stopped working. So, I'm leaning over the pool to try and get the vacuum working, pop myself in the face with the hose, the phone's ringing, the dog's tripping over me, and hours earlier spent on the phone with Verizon idiots and I'm thinking I should go back to bed and start over.

I guess it doesn't matter where you live, even in Paradise you must put up with Verizon idiots, broken pool equipment, and snakes. I learned there are lots and lots of snakes in paradise when I visited the aquarium in Tarpon Springs with those kids the other day. Thank God for that screened in pool.

THURSDAY - JUNE 26 - I FORGIVE MYSELF AND THEN I MOVE ON

Last night was date night – we've chosen Wednesday night as date night. I love date night no matter when we go. Don't get me wrong, I love this family, I really do, but I'm here for Peter. That sounds selfish, doesn't it? Well after all I did fall in love with him first. The family is an extension of him, naturally I love them too. But it was and still is the time Pete and I spend together that keeps me here, keeps me grounded in why I moved here and left everything behind. Now it's like *they* are my everything. I forgive myself for sounding selfish and move on.

So, date details, Peter was looking extra handsome in his blue shirt and I was looking very Florida casual cute in my CVS dress. We had a lovely dinner and then went to the Hard Rock Casino and Hotel. It's a huge place with some very *very* cool memorabilia and lots and lots of slot machines. Much bigger than our Pittsburgh Casino. You can smoke in the whole place except for one very small room designated as the no-smoking room. It will be my go-to room in the future. We gave ourselves a $20 limit each and I'm happy to say we stuck to it. I was on a winning streak and got it up to $60+, BUT I wanted to win $400 or go home broke. We managed to probably stay close to 2 hours with that limit, but you guessed it, we went home broke. I forgive myself for blowing money. There is a lot I am forgiving myself for these days.

I am tired today, probably from being out late and all the excitement at the Casino. I am going to be a slug and watch TV. I'm allowed slug days. I forgive myself and move on.

I haven't found a job yet although I do look daily, I don't apply daily, but I do *look* daily. I forgive myself and move on.

I bought a $5 dress the other day at Tarpon Springs, but it doesn't fit. I've wasted money. I forgive myself and move on.

I ate fudge for breakfast; I forgive myself and move on.

I am making roast beast in the crockpot with French Onion soup – the soup packet has no nutritional value, is processed and certainly not organic. I turn on the crockpot, forgive myself and move on.

I am being told that I have had some typos in my posts, I forgive myself (but cringe nonetheless) and move on.

The dog was on the couch this morning, I sort of forgive him (I just gave him that look) and move on.

I found candy wrappers under the couch, uh no,

MONDAY – JUNE 30 – WEEKEND UPDATE

Don't think for one minute that I don't enjoy, or think I don't deserve, down time now that I'm not going to an office every day. Actually, sometimes I feel like I do more. I *know* I do more. Different more, but I'm pretty much hopping all the time, and/or thinking about what to do next. Laundry? Dusting? Planning an outing? Cooking? Dishes? I mean seriously I'm always doing something. Add this blog and well it's a full day. Friday, I made sure I cleaned those bathrooms and had the laundry caught up because I was planning on doing *nothing* over the weekend, and I was most successful.

Friday night Pete, Jasen and I drove 20 miles to go to Sloppy Joes, a restaurant on the beach in Treasure Island. We got there right at sunset and then it *poured* down rain. We didn't get to see the sun setting. Sunset here on the Gulf coast of Florida is quite the event. If you are near the beach or even in our little town (a mile from the beach), at sunset people move to see the sun setting and wait for it to go down. While at Sloppy Joes, 5 minutes before sunset, people were starting to move over to the railing to watch but then with the rain the ritual was over. It really is something to see. It must be in our DNA to stop and watch it. Although we here in the Clark/Bench household have not been consistent sunset watchers. We've only caught a couple of them. In our next house we will have a better view (JK...remember I'm never moving).

After a not-so-good dinner we went miniature golfing. Not to focus on money but it really was expensive for miniature golf. Nice course though. Their gimmick or draw is you can feed the alligators. I walked by them quickly with my eyes shut. The rain had stopped, and it was late (10:30) but we got a round in. Have I mentioned how competitive Peter is? This makes it all the more fun and even *more* fun to report that I beat him (he's not the only competitive one.) We drove home, up the coast, and then I was informed by both Peter and Jasen that it was way too far and we won't be going there again. Fine...

On Saturday we didn't bother to wake up Jasen, so we could lounge in the pool, alone. Nice huh? I'm usually a much better parent but I struggle with my selfish side that wants that alone time. And what did we do with that alone time? We slept on the floaties, in the pool, without sunscreen and Peter, the fair redhead, turned bright red with sunburn. For those of you that asked, "can you get sun through the screened- in pool?" the answer is a resounding yes!

We decided to go to an early movie before going out to dinner. We went to *22 Jump Street*. The "F" word was every other word and although at times I was in stitches laughing I wanted to cry at all the sexual references with the 13 and 15-year-old sitting beside me.

Then we went for Pizza at a local place. Only thing notable about this, other than the very good crust, is that every time someone walked in the door I looked up. At some point I realized I don't know *anyone* here. Not one single soul. I don't know why I look up as I will never see anyone I recognize. Maybe not "never" but certainly not yet.

Sunday, we didn't start our day until very late. We had planned on going to the beach later in the afternoon, with lots of sunscreen. But Zoë, in a surprise move, jumped into the pool. After one month of not wanting to get wet she jumped in and that decided our day. Continuing with the competition Peter donned his Speedo and came out for swimming races. He was on the swim team in High School. Not very fair odds for me, but we had much family fun racing, squirting each other with water guns and playing P.I.G. with the basketball hoop. Pete and I both lost in P.I.G.

I made a delicious dinner and then topped it off with a game of Scrabble. In another show of good parenting, exhibiting good sportsmanship, after I naturally won, Peter told me I had to sleep in another room. Can a round of billiards be far behind? We need a white board, to keep track of my victories.

The night ended with poor Jasen slipping in the kitchen and breaking a plate. One of my Pier One plates. I was very calm and was immediately reminded of how I scarred my oldest son for life when I yelled at him for breaking a plate back in the day. Did I yell at someone recently too for breaking a water goblet? Since I buy all my stuff either at the Dollar Store or on some clearance sale, they are usually not replaceable. In the past I have made this huge deal about it. What is wrong with me? I did not make a huge deal last night. I have learned from my past mistakes. He certainly didn't throw the dish down on purpose. Poor kid. I realized that now we have 7 plates and 7 goblets. In a dinner of 8 Jasen will get the paper plate (JK) – or better yet I think I'll just buy a new set.

JULY 2014

TUESDAY - JULY 1 - IT MIGHT AS WELL BE TUESDAY

Had I still been working at PPU in Pittsburgh today would have been *my* payday. It's the first time in eight years that I have not had a paycheck on the first day of the month. I am having trouble with this unemployment business.

However, in other news it has been brought to my attention that there is a storm brewing here in Florida. Hurricane Arthur is brewing on the east coast. I will continue to keep the weather channel on and watch ad nauseam to keep track of my east coast brothers and sisters (figuratively) at least until Zoë comes down and puts the World Cup on.

Yesterday was uneventful. Besides unpacking a couple of boxes and making an adequate dinner not much went on. Peter and I finally went for a walk after dinner. Finally, a minute alone and finally some exercise. We are hoping to make it a habit, both alone time and exercise, but we only made it to the mango tree at the end of the block and it poured down rain, accompanied by lightning and thunder. At least we ran back. Neither of us could breathe after our short run and were convinced it was at least a mile. On my errand this morning I checked the mileage with the car...02 miles. We're pathetic. But it's a start. Perhaps tonight we will run again from the mango tree and before you know it we will be entering our first 5K. I've been this pathetic before and have overcome. One day this week I was convinced I would do yoga on my own. I know how to do it and I've had a home practice before. I did one downward dog and called it a day.

I'm continuing to try and think of constructive things to do with these kids, but it's hot. It really makes it hard to want to leave the air conditioning. It's hard. Both thinking of things to do and thinking about what I'm doing in the big picture. I mean I know I took on this family package deal but sometimes it's all consuming. I don't mind the mom part, I really don't. The mom side of me is what's ingrained in me. It's the new boyfriend side that I want to do more with though. In addition to thinking of things to do with those kids I make it my 'job' to think of ways for us to be together too. I really struggle with leaving the kids out and leaving them in too much. Ugh!! I should just go back to work outside the home.

I applied for an outside job yesterday at Eckerd College. I thought I'd get back in the swing of applying for jobs. The whole practice of looking and applying is a mix of hope and rejection. Not sure I'm ready to continue with that roller coaster.

For now, I'll just look at the pool (from inside in the air-conditioning) and see what comes up next.

WEDNESDAY - JULY 2 - WHY YOU DIRTY RAT

Where do I start?

I was making very healthy snacks and a delicious dinner yesterday afternoon, I look out the window, you know like all people do when they have a window over the sink, and what do I see? A rat. Yes, a *rat*. Walking, tottering I should say, along the pavers as if on an afternoon stroll. Why yes, I guess he/she *was* on an afternoon stroll. And so, I screamed. Not the same scream when I had the cat sized spider in the car but a scream that said, "KIDS WE HAVE A RAT!" Actually, this was the first time I've ever seen a rat. At least a live rat. I've seen a dead river rat and that was much grosser than this rat. It looked a little like a small squirrel, not really threatening, but when I realized it was a rat, well my reaction was typical of new rat experience for sure.

Jasen immediately thought to tape up our cat door (we have one of those doors where a cat could come and go). Honestly, I don't know why we didn't think of taping it shut before. But leave it to Jasen to think of that first. Then he asked if he could get his BB gun and go hunting. Yea, baby. My money is on Jasen in the event of a zombie apocalypse. Where was the dog you ask? Sleeping in the AC. But I have a confession to make. I feel slightly bad about all of this. First of all, the rat wasn't that menacing. My brother, who also lives in paradise on the west coast (L.A.), often talks of rats. It must be a tropical thing. Although we don't have any citrus trees surely there are citrus trees in neighboring yards and perhaps this rat was just passing through on his way to the neighbor's lemon tree. And it was outside. Inside is fair game but I wonder if the proper response to Jasen would have been to let it alone because it's outside but to block the exits to make sure it doesn't come inside. I don't know. Could have been a lapse in parenting judgement...again...

That was yesterday's excitement and today all the kids are gone. Just for the day. The older girls took them for an outing which they are very excited about and I'm excited for them to go do something fun and be all together. I don't know what to do with myself. I'm excited and yet it doesn't feel too different. Jasen usually sleeps until 3 pm anyway. Zoë is so good and quiet, and I like her company. Pete is always at work. He needs a stay-at-home job, one where I can bug him during the day.

One difference is that I'm watching movies instead of the World Cup. I've watched two movies so far. I'm also washing Jasen's sheets because he can't breathe, I'm thinking it's dog hair overload. Doing laundry doesn't seem too different. But I'm trying to make it like a Woo Hoo day and celebrate that I have all this time to myself. I thought about floating in the pool to finish my book but it's soooo hot and I really don't want any more sun. Maybe I'll just keep watching movies and finish laundry. That will be some nice alone time. Watching a movie I want to watch without getting up to do something. I think we need a bigger TV.

The day is going to end great because tonight is date night!!! I love dressing up for date night instead of dressing for work. My whole focus on what's important has changed (as well as my outfits). We're going to go *up* the coast. We're going to go up to New Port Richey and see what we can discover. But right now, I'm going to focus on this movie while all the kids are gone. I thought it was a funny movie, but I have a feeling it's going to be a tear jerker.

THURSDAY - JULY 3 - I'M NOT MYSELF

I'm not myself...who am I? Sounds like one of those riddles.

Yesterday, with my free time, remember how I thought I was going to lie on the couch all day, watch movies and finish laundry? I ended up cleaning floors. I cleaned my white tile floors. Got all the dog hair up, put the dog in the other room, got the Shark cleaner out and away I went. I kept the TV on all day and watched movies while doing that. I was right – *The Family Stone* was a tear-jerker. And I cried and cried all by myself. That was nice. But I cleaned with my time off. I did not lay in the pool and get more sun. Who am I? I don't even recognize myself anymore. The sun/pool used to always come first.

I don't have one girlfriend down here. Not one.

I have no income. I have no job where I leave the house and sit at a desk and type some nonsense and get paid for it. None of my own income.

Pete and I have a rule. Well, it's mainly Pete's rule. I'm not allowed to say I'm fat or make negative remarks about myself. I totally get it. Who wants a girlfriend, (or boyfriend) that is down on themselves? Makes you wonder why you're with them if they are so bad. I will not be negative, but I sure don't feel like myself. You would think that my weight might be a little under control because I'm always doing something. Cleaning, cooking, laundry, whatever, I'm mostly on my feet and moving all day. I am not sitting for 8+ hours a day. So why am I gaining weight? I am definitely not myself and getting further and further from myself all the time.

I am not anywhere near my family. Not with my boys, not with my sister Kerry, niece Evan or the babies. Not with anything or anyone familiar.

I had this wonderful psychology teacher at Carlow who talked about deconstructing to reconstruct. I am certainly in a deconstructing mode. It's like everything familiar has been stripped from me. I'm not complaining but I am floundering.

I don't mind protecting my skin from the sun and staying inside. I have probably regained years of lack of Vitamin D already. I like living in a clean house and I'm able to keep it up. I like crying at movies all by myself. I like what I did yesterday.

I love my girlfriends but without them I have Pete to lean on. I love our time together and honestly; I love not to have to juggle time between him and with friends. I'm able to be with him all the time. That's another "who am I" for sure as I've never wanted to be with anyone this much before. Better not question it too much. I think the balance will come later and I will plan more trips up north to Pittsburgh than I originally thought I would. I need my friend and family time too.

However, without that income I have no way of making plans like visiting my friends and family. I am not struggling to survive, as has been my typical status, although I now must rely on someone else. To let go of that control is definitely a new experience. And I am thankful every day to my benefactor that I have the opportunity to see what is unfolding in my life. I am letting go of control and letting the job find me. I feel like anything can happen now. I hope "anything" does happen…soon…very soon.

My weight has always been a struggle. I just need to exercise and quit eating everything I bake. I know that only too well. I just hope I remember to do it.

I miss my boys. There's just no getting around that. And I miss my family.

Pete says I have to give it time. When I ask him how much time he doesn't have that answer. Guess he's a lot of things but apparently not a psychic. In a weird way the more comfortable I get here the harder it is. I think it's being far away from the familiar of any kind that is hard. Like I'm abandoning myself. I have my things (broken as they are) but I don't have "me" yet. I don't know if that is a good thing or a bad thing. It is definitely a hard thing. I've been wanting a change and well I am getting that for sure. Guess I have to give it more time.

MONDAY - JULY 7 - PLANNING AHEAD

I have come to expect to *not* have any expectations when it comes to the Clark/Bench family making plans together.

On Friday, the 4ᵗʰ, we had big plans to go get massages and hang out at the spa where the fireworks would be held later. But the spa changed their policy for that day only and we weren't allowed to hang out there (any other day we would have been allowed) We cancelled our appointments (I know who does that?) Also, my man was sick. Caught some sort of something and was in bed most of the day. He woke up for the delicious hot dog dinner.

Our plans to attend Fireworks in Safety Harbor (a town nearby) were thwarted by thunderstorms. We went out anyway and found another location away from the storm. We parked along the causeway and saw about 50 different fireworks displays all up and down the beaches. It was pretty darn cool. Not what we planned but I think it was better!

Saturday, I stayed in bed all day. I caught Pete's cold. It was lovely to stay in bed but our previous plans we had made for that day were cancelled by me not getting up. At dinner time, instead of our plans to go out to a fancy dinner the kids ended up getting Chick Fil-A, me eating soup, and Pete having left overs.

On Sunday we were both back to feeling normal. We planned to go to the mall and look for stuff for the house. But what really happened? Pete ended up making an eye appointment for Jasen at the mall and they took him on Sunday (who knew you can get an appointment on a Sunday?) I went to Macy's while they were at the eye doctors and found nothing. *Nothing.* And then we ended up going to the movies and saw *Earth to Echo,* which I was sure I was going to hate. But surprise, I really enjoyed it.

Anyway, turns out our weekend plans turned out perfectly. Dinner on the 4ᵗʰ and last night were lovely, we both got some much-needed rest, Jasen got new glasses, I enjoyed a movie that I would have never picked for myself, the mall is awesome, and I didn't spend any money.

(Wait maybe not "any" money, but I didn't spend "much" money) Can't get much better than that.

WEDNESDAY - JULY 9 - PYTHONS, AND LIZARDS AND SPIDERS OH MY

I believe I've mentioned the heat once or twice. The weather channel keeps talking about a cool front affecting the southeast. Our temperatures have dropped from 90's during the day to 88° during the day but all the way down to 77° at night. When they say "southeast" I don't think we're included in that. Every time I say "it's hot" to Pete his immediate response is "I love it!" and he's right, I love it too. I don't really want to be out in it all day, but when I walk outside into the heat my immediate thought is "I love it!" After walking across a hot parking lot with the asphalt reflecting onto my being for 5 minutes, do I want to get to my air-conditioned car? You betcha, but before then I love it.

Oh wait, did I mention we were working in the backyard? Didn't I mention once or twice that we have gardeners? Why I believe I have. Why, you might ask, are "we" working in the back yard? Well, first Pete loves to putter around, which is a great quality. Second, it's because our gardener is useless. I helped drag all the cuttings to the road last night. I risked life and limb by dragging piles of brush that COULD have been inhabited by pythons, lizards, and cat sized spiders, but I was a trooper. I am embracing my environment and diving in with my devil may care attitude. Hiding pythons? Come and get me (Jk,,,,really,,,,jk)

The gardener told me this pathetic story yesterday that would be perfect for a Jerry Springer show, explaining his absence these past few weeks. I dare not repeat it because if it's true then surely God will strike me down for poking fun at it but really it was hard for me to not smile. He's scary. Believe me I did my best to act interested.

Speaking of diving into my environment, I dragged Jasen on a how-do-we-learn-to-sail/boat adventure yesterday. We stopped at the local Dunedin Yacht Club. Not a person to be found to ask questions. We continued on to the Clearwater Community Sailing Center where it was manned by people to question. I found out that Jasen does not care about learning to sail but they have Adult Learn to Sail options. Pete and I will put that on our to-do list. I want to immerse myself in my new environment, therefore I will continue my quest into water sport knowledge. I need to learn to drive a motorboat as well.

Tonight is date night. We're going to try the Salt Rock Grill. It looks a little fancy. I think a new outfit is called for. Don't you? The kids are starting to get both cute and annoying when it comes to date night. I think it's cute that they look forward to getting pizza when we go out. Pete finds that annoying. I think it needs to be his battle although I don't see what's wrong with shelling out $20 for pizza (they both want their own pizzas) – a small price to pay for alone time.

THURSDAY - JULY 10 - I'M LYMING

Lyming is the Caribbean art of doing nothing—without feeling guilty about it. (copied from Bottom Line's 5-minute Cures & Overnight Miracles) According to the pamphlet, Lyming gives your brain time to process all the information it receives over the course of a day. Therefore, you should take a 5-minute mental vacation every few hours. I'm going to try Lyming. All day....

Today, I tried to sit by the pool and lyme. Got bit by a mosquito. Brushed the dog. Took something out of the freezer for dinner. Thought about what to write on my blog update and wondered how long I should Lyme before I try to finish reading my book. I'm happy to say this is a new book and not Owen Meany. I finally finished that last week. Phew...

Maybe I Lyme too much? Maybe I need to do more unlyming. Every now and then I'll work for 5 minutes and Lyme the rest of the time. Maybe I'll become a professional Lymer. Wonder if there's any income in that?

With all this absorbing I've decided to declare Thursday as Lyming day, and not feel guilty about it, which is good because the dreaded bathroom cleaning Friday is right around the corner. I would clean today but today is Lyming day. I can't veer from my schedule.

MONDAY - JULY 14 - THE 50 DAY ITCH

I'm itchy. I keep telling Peter that I'm getting bit by bugs. He's not getting bit. He thinks it's in my head. Zoë is getting bit too. She's getting bit on her arms and I'm getting bit on my legs. However, as I just sat down now I felt something crawling on me and I thought "let it go, it's in your head" but just to be sure I went to the mirror and saw the bug crawling down my neck AFTER biting me. Looked like an ant before it fell into my top. "In my head" my ass. This bug was different though because it stung me, which is different from these bites that I'm getting. It's clear I need to bug bomb. Anyone that has done that knows what a huge pain it is. I am reluctant but it's going to have to be done. I also ordered Skin So Soft Avon products over the weekend and will slather up as soon as it gets here. Getting bit and always scratching is ruining paradise.

I'm also itching, still and again, for a job. I've been here 50 days. I originally thought about a month off would be nice and it's a month plus. It's time. I hope to spend a good part of the day applying to at least one job. I was told about a part-time job, driving a snow cone truck. I was told that it would be a fun job and very flexible. I just have to put ice in the cone and the kids (or whoever) put their own syrup on. Easy peasy; except I can't see myself doing it. I'll follow through anyway cause usually the things I don't think are for me tend to be exactly for me.

The weekend was nice, as usual. Thursday's Lyming day spread to Thursday night and then I took myself to a movie. It was a sticker day as I believe I became more of a native when I wore my jeans and long sleeve T-shirt, in Florida, in the summer. Under 85 degrees and now I'm cold. It was my first night out alone. Felt kinda good and kinda sad. Okay there was a small argument that led to that alone time, but I don't know, maybe it's something (alone time, not arguing) I need to add into my life.

Friday was the dreaded bathroom cleaning day although not as bad as usual as Peter and family put a big dent it in it when I was at the movies (a result of said small argument and a habit I hope to keep up – both my alone night AND their cleaning night – but not the arguing) Zoë and I went to the mall then Peter came home and we headed to the beach for fish sandwiches (no one got fish sandwiches) combined with sunset at the beach. It was the first time we were there at the beach during low tide. It was really low. The beach is extremely rocky, and I couldn't get out in the water past the rocky shore. At sunset the bugs came out and ate us alive. We couldn't get to the car fast enough.

On Saturday Pete and I got up early and rode bikes to our little town. The Pinellas Trail is right by our house. We got on the Trail and rode about 10 feet (I'm exaggerating...but not much). First time I've been on a bike in a while and although you may think Florida is flat I saw a sign that said elevation 17 feet. And we live up from there. Maybe another foot. The ride down to town was great. It was the ride back I was concerned about. Don't laugh. We putzied the rest of the day, burgers by the pool, Pete went on another bike ride with Jasen and then later that night we went bar hopping. Yep bar hopping!!! It was fun, even for me, the nondrinker. Lucky for me my Pete is not a professional drinker and getting him to drink a beer at the different places was challenging which is such a plus for me. He didn't realize we were going to bar hop. Thought he'd be sipping all night. We ended up getting a hemp brownie at the last stop. Fortunately (or unfortunately, depending on your point of view) there are no side effects from eating something with hemp in it. We decided it's a good cancer preventative and went home. Without the munchies. A very nice night for sure.

TUESDAY - JULY 15 - ON THE RUN

I have submitted one more application to McKinsey. Maybe the third time's a charm. And I have an interview with the Ice truck company tomorrow. She mentioned needing office help. So, see? You never know.

I see my life going two ways; which means that it'll go a completely different way than either of these two. But I see me either getting some part time job that is purely fluff and low paying enabling me to keep the home cooking/caretaking thing going, or I'm going to get a high-powered traveling long hour job with McKinsey paying the big bucks and never be here. What I don't want is a job where I'm working long hours, never home and not making any money. Like what's the point in that? But for now, it seems like I'm just a blogger who must leave NOW to go pick up Zoë.

WEDNESDAY - JULY 16 - I'M IN A QUANDARY

You may be asking yourself, just what does one wear to a sno-cone truck driver interview? I asked the same question myself. $100 later spent at Ross Dress for Less and well I came up with quite a few possibilities. My friend and former work colleague Judy would be proud. I was complimented on my outfit at my interview today and complimented on my accessories. I was able to go through each item and tell her where I got stuff (she asked? Can it get any better than that?) Some of the new stuff will double as an outfit for date night. Ya know? Can I make a buck stretch or what? Those of you that know me the best (or even a little) will say, but Victoria, you have no income, how can you go shopping? HA! This is true. But I have this boyfriend who will put money in my account. I know, right? Although there are questions at times as to what this money is actually for, I took advantage yesterday and bought myself some new clothes. I consider it an investment since now I have the possibility of getting some of my own income. Of course, a week of my new income will most probably equal what I can spend in a day but still, it's something.

Not ever having been in this "income" type position it's hard to know how to justify someone putting money into your account, consistently, and not feel guilty. It's not like I don't pull my weight around here (and then some). I mean if I was being paid to be a full-time nanny, I wonder what that would pay. I wonder if I should do that part-time in the a.m. in someone else's home and then come home and do it here in the p.m.? Honestly, I'm not a nanny as no one here *really* needs me, but you moms know it's always nice to be here anyway, just to say, "need anything? Want a grilled cheese?"

On Monday I cleaned three area rugs with that new Shark cleaner (not sure if it's worth it as no one noticed), went grocery shopping, and made this delicious spaghetti with meatballs dinner. I think it's the day I cleaned the bed, head to toe, because of the "itch". I had it all cleaned up, bed remade, dinner ready and waiting by the time Pete got home. I have to say it's fun. This is the most fun I've had in a long time. I like the challenge of getting it all done and believe me it's a challenge. It's very retro but I still think it's fun. I do stop short of getting up early and handing him his lunch as he walks out the door; although he needs me to do that because he never remembers to make his own lunch. I mean really, I'm having fun even getting ready for date night. Like it's all a "job".

This morning I had my sno-cone interview, got gas in the car, put air in the tires and got slammed with a rain storm. Like someone dumped a bucket of water on me. Unbelievable...I came home to put on dry clothes and then went and got a mani-pedi for date night. I still have lots I should do today. Like I'm thinking about dust. It's already 2:00 – do I start that today? Or do I wait until tomorrow? Maybe I'll do some today and finish tomorrow. There's no food in the house. Do I wait for my man and do power shopping, or do I go and get jelly? I had peanut butter on bread. Zoë is having carrots. Jasen probably won't even wake up until pizza time. I mean these are the decisions I make every day.

It's not like I haven't worked all my life and had to make dinners and clean a house but at least now it's fun. My stress level is like soooo down.

THURSDAY - JULY 17 - NISSAN ALTIMA FOR SALE

It's a slow day. Except I may have to move back to PA since I can't seem to get my car transferred to the state of Florida or get insurance coverage (jk). The insurance quotes are double what I paid in PA. On the plus side, gas and groceries are cheaper. But to have a car seems a little cost prohibitive. Especially without a job. Greer, my niece, is going off to college in August. Wonder if I could rent out her room back home. I'm never quite sure when Peter is going to give me the boot and send me packing. It makes me sick to my stomach that I have none of my own income.

Two very nice things that happened this week. At Ross Dress for Less there is a Tuesday "club". Over 55 years of age you get 10% off on Tuesday. During check out last Tuesday I told her I'm eligible. She carded me! No kidding. She told me to be sure to bring my I. D. with me on Tuesday's because I don't look like I should be in the "club". I mean I LOVE her. Although in the back of my mind I bet they are paid to say that. But then this morning, my neighbor Linda was at her garbage can at the same time I was at my garbage can, we were chatting. Like neighbors. Nice! Anyway, I told her my insurance woes and she said to try AAA. Then she said something about AARP but didn't think we were old enough for that. HA! HA! What a young-looking couple we are. A plus for the ego. But the minus to the pocket-book is still no good.

Date night was nice. A little different from some. Dinner out as usual. There are many places to eat here, but I'm sure the same can be said for Pittsburgh. I *know* the same can be said for Pittsburgh. Just got to get in the car in Pittsburgh as well as down here. And we are not averse to getting in the car. After dinner we went to the local Bingo place. There are no drop-ins, just so you know. You have to show up at like 4:30 or

5:00 and play all night. So, we shall have to schedule for another night. Then we went grocery shopping. We were alone at the grocery store. I guess it still counts as dating; that and I had mascara on.

The sun is coming out. I'm going to sit by the pool and try not to think about my car registration and insurance dilemmas. Lyming day is about escaping and not thinking. I need to get at it. Right after I go to the grocery store for dinner supplies.

MONDAY - JULY 21 - DISNEYLAND DAD'S WEEKEND

Blogging needs a sick day. But before I go back to the bathroom, perhaps I can get you all caught up.

Except I can't remember. I'm trying to remember back to Friday and my mind is blank. Did I shop? Maybe that's what it was. Someone in this house is having a 53rd birthday today and I found time to bday shop in a store next to Old Navy. So, listen to this, in Old Navy at checkout she says I can save 46% if I open a charge. 46%! That's huge isn't it? But I say no. After she checked me out she said she admired my resolve. I admire my resolve too. Pete would admire my resolve more if I just didn't go in at all, but to know me is to love me. (or not)

You know the expression Disneyland Dads? How moms do all the work-work and dad's get the kids and do all the fun? I think I'm getting to benefit from the Disneyland Dad thing. And it's working for me...and it doesn't really count in the negative sense cause it's not part-time but anyway, here's "some" of our weekend:

Friday night, Zoë and I met Peter at Costco. Then to Panera and topped it off with a game of mini golf. Pete won but Zoë and I suspect foul play. The two mini golf places we have visited both have feeding the alligators as a side show. Not sure what the connection is between alligators and mini golf. But they really are kind of interesting to watch.

Saturday, we packed up the fam and went to Bradenton (about an hour plus away) and went to the DaVinci Machines Exhibit. Very *very* cool. Then onto a quick run through of the museum next door (very quick) and an animated planetarium show at the Bradenton observatory. It was cute. I learned (or relearned) quite a bit about the planets.

Then the four of us walked around the Pier and dreamed about what boats we want. We ended the night watching sunset at Pass-a-Grille beach. A wonderful family day for all.

On Sunday I spent an hour in the pool and then cleaned, laundry etc. and THEN I got my new bike! Happy Birthday to me! We didn't get back from the store until late. I only got to do a quick spin, but I love it. AND I have sunglasses to match. Oh, and we joined the YMCA too. It is very close – we can ride our bikes there. I made sure to check out the visitor pass situation. When my sister comes to visit she can keep up her treadmill addiction. (not a bad addiction to have.. perhaps I can work on one myself)

Today I have errands to run and birthday dinners to make. The cranberry juice seems to be taking effect. I should take advantage and run to the stores (and get more cranberry juice). I'm not sure what I have but I don't feel good, I'm in the bathroom a lot and cranberry juice is what Peter has prescribed. It is nice to have someone in your life that cares about you enough to prescribe and buy you cranberry juice when needed. So many things a boyfriend is good for!

P.S. – the ice lady called. I start on Wednesday, thus the trip to Old Navy for shorts (that fit). I ended up moving all my old work clothes from my bedroom closet to the winter closet. I don't think I'll be needing any suit jackets or pants for that matter any time soon. Those suit jackets might just go to the Goodwill. But not yet...

TUESDAY - JULY 22 - COUNTDOWN TO SCHOOL DAZE

It's quiet. No one is home, except Sam (the dog) and myself. Not that when they are home it's noisy. Jasen sleeps all day. Zoë couldn't be quieter, but it's the guilt thing. Do I wake them? Do I cook something? Should I be taking them somewhere? That kind of thing. Today their

Papa (that would be my Peter) took a vacation day and has taken them to the doctors. It's quiet and guilt free!

School starts August 18th. That's less than a month away. Hard to believe it's coming right up and hard to believe that I'm back looking at school calendars (at least middle school and high school calendars). I printed off the school calendar yesterday. Pretty normal calendar other than the hurricane make-up days. Although we always looked forward to snow days I'm not particularly looking forward to hurricane days; unless they are false alarms. Once school starts that's going to be a whole different experience for me too. First experience of moving away from home and everything and everyone I know, then inserting myself into this family, and now when everyone is gone off am I going to go stir crazy? OR will I be driving ice trucks to the schools? I am scheduled to go out with the Ice Lady tomorrow. She told me that if I end up going to the schools I will have to get the background check and fingerprint thing and then I can have access in any Pinellas County school.

Zoë and I drove over to the high school. There are 2500 kids at this school, which sounds huge. Zoë's comment was that it looks like a school you see on TV or in the movies. It kinda does.

We stopped in the office and asked about looking around (the gate was wide open, but I asked anyway) they said no. The fact that we are new to the neighborhood and not even allowed to look at the school just kinda left me speechless. Which is another new thing for me. I wouldn't have cared about embarrassing my own kids. I would have spoken right up and said "this is the stupidest thing I ever heard". Pete thinks the secretary just wanted to go home for the day. He may be right; it was late in the day. Even with that not-so-welcoming experience I am looking forward to going to football games. I'm kinda excited for school to start. I mean I might as well get back into it right? Pete has to fill out something for me that gives me the right to go into the schools and act like an official pain-in-the-ass parent/guardian. Too bad I didn't have that official status the other day or I would have said something to that not-so-helpful school secretary.

THURSDAY - JULY 24 - WHAT A DIFFERENCE A DAY MAKES

I'm freezing. But will get to that in a minute.

I made it through day 2 as an Ice Lady. I was so *so* close to quitting this morning. I didn't ever want to go back. It's supposed to be fun and I was dreading it. Peter said he would not hate me if I quit. I was prepared to tell her it wasn't working for me. My body was sore. My feet swollen last night. But it was Debbie's comment about how everyone hates the first day that made me get my ass out of bed. I thought I would give it one more day and confirm that I hate it. And well, I didn't hate it as much today. I wore different shoes today and found a stool in the truck that I sat on for much of the 2 hours and I got to make the ice and serve the cones. We went to an assisted living place and the ice cups were prepaid. I didn't have to make change. Old people are darn cute. Everyone got the same size and I'm getting my ice scooping rhythm down. I ran out of ice a couple of times (in the ice machine, not in the cooler). I have to get used to the sound it makes so I know to refill it before I burn it out. And pouring on the flavors was simple. I'll go back tomorrow. I only worked one event today as that's what we agreed on yesterday. I don't hate it today. I will keep going I guess, and that first paycheck will possibly go for some new Merrill's (sandals) for my poor *poor* feet.

But back to the fact that I am cold. I have the chills. I don't know if it's because it's only 82° out there or I'm getting a fever. I almost pulled out my space heater. Almost. But that's a slippery slope as once I turn it on I'll be back to using it every day and our electric bill is high enough. I think I'll just get a bath or maybe sit outside. but Brrrrr...

MONDAY - JULY 28 - DON'T JUDGE ME

Here's what went down. Remember way back on Thursday, when I was cold? Yea, it was a fever. Over 102°. It was bad, I was sure I was dying. I was ready for it. Bring me home, Lord. Fortunately (or unfortunately depending on your point of view) the Lord is apparently not ready for me. I went to one of those urgent care places on Friday (temp was down to a manageable 101°) and they gave me a prescription for an antibiotic to treat a UTI. I am not dying...I have a UTI....it just feels like dying. I started the antibiotic on Friday and slept most of the day and night. On Saturday I got up kind of normally and I was out of bed until around 4:00 pm (sitting by the pool, in the shade) when the fever shot up again, all the way back up and over 102° and it stayed up until about 9:00 at night. And then, like magic, it went away, and I was starving.

I didn't do much over the weekend, other than think about my life. What I focused on was my current employment status. When I woke up today I quit the Ice Lady job. Don't judge me! It's just not me. I mean, I'm 56, I want to be able to go pee when I need to pee. Did the not being able to pee cause the UTI? Or did the UTI cause the miserable experience? It's hard to know which came first. Sure, it's a workout but I just joined the YMCA and I want to go to yoga with Zoë over lunch time, or swim laps with Pete, or go for a bike ride. I don't want to lift 20-pound bags of ice and 50-gallon syrup jugs. Nor do I want to sit in a hot truck for hours at a time. It's not fun, it's not me. So there, I said it. At least I tried it and I know what I do NOT want to do. Right? I don't think I feel like a quitter. I think I feel like a smart-er. I am just adding it to the list of "I forgive myself and move on." There is no time in my life to be unhappy. I mean I could have died this weekend from my illness (ok *ok* I'm exaggerating) but it *could* happen. All because I couldn't pee? *Come on*...Anyway, I'm happy again. I'm home. I'm blogging. I'm coming up with some plans to produce income. I mean I'm back to myself. And hey maybe in the art of finding myself I really am finding myself. How about that? Not to mention I confirmed that I have a really good supportive boyfriend. When I asked him if I could quit he just laughed and hugged me. He really is the best boyfriend ever. It's not like I'm a lawyer quitting a $100,000 annual salary. He just is worried about what I might try next. Snake charmer perhaps? I do speak parsel tongue.

I decided today that I will unplug my computer in the a.m., go to the dining room table and work on the computer until the battery runs out. That's all I'm going to allow myself. Whether it's blogging or applying for a job once the battery is out it's time to do something else. Like today as soon as this battery dies I'm running the sweeper. (is that Pittsburghese? Running the *sweeper*?) I know I do that often but today I'm doing it because we bug bombed last night. We had one too many crickets (you know, *crickets)* and well most of you know how much I hate bugs. I forced my new family to go to the movies and we bug bombed. We went at night, so the dog could stay outside when it wasn't hot. Anyway, I have found a few dead bugs. I'm happy there are only a few, but honestly not sure if I wish there were more or wish there were none. But listen to this.... There was a *cricket* upside down on the kitchen floor and when I went to sweep him up those legs started moving. I tried smashing him with the broom and that did nothing. They are really big to squish with your shoe. I went to get the Borax bug stuff that kills them on contact. Well, this mo fo, I poured that stuff on him and he effing jumped up (they are bigger when right-sided) and ran like a bat-outta-hell under the fridge. MO-FO. I just swept more of that poison under the fridge. He sure didn't look as big when he was laying upside down. I may have learned a valuable lesson about them playing possum and next time I WILL use my shoe.

I know this is Florida and I know Florida has bugs and don't let anyone be fooled that Florida is anyone's paradise in the summer. But there are ways to limit them in your house even in Florida and I want them OUT. I am getting much better at not freaking out, well I'm not screaming anyway. I do take advantage of the fact that I have a boyfriend now and I will call him when I see one. I think I've been doing that so he knows how many we have. He pretty much has the attitude that this is Florida and you just have to live with it. NOT I say. NOT NOT NOT! I mean within reason anyway.

Enough about that. Even though I was bed ridden for the weekend the "fam" had fun without me and then on Sunday I arose from the dead. Just like Jesus. The third day. Well anyway, after an hour of a *Joan of Arcadia* marathon (thanks for the heads-up Di), appropriate for the occasion, I then helped build a model. All four of us worked on it. This was not an IKEA piece of furniture. It was a model called a Strandbeast. The box said for ages 7 and up. I don't know any 7-year-old that would have been able to figure this out. Anyway, Pete was the brains of the group and I must say I'm more than a bit attracted to that intelligence. Although that attraction made me want to do it right then and there (you know *do it)* I had to refrain as it was a nice *family* project.

Zoë is up and wants to make candied bacon. See? This is the stuff that life (and cholesterol) is made of. And this is why I really need to get to the Y.

TUESDAY - JULY 29 - TUE-BLAH DAY

I finally made it to yoga at the YMCA. No fever, no ice lady job and Zoë and I were both in the mood, so we went. Woo hoo! It was an intro class and very good. I always like the intro classes better. Zoë liked it too. I think we're on to something.

It's actually a gray rainy day. Like *all* day (so far). According to the weather we are supposed to get a cold front pass though, but what that means for Florida is that it just dries up (according to the Weatherman on the news). He said once it passes through, the temperatures will become "almost" pleasant. "almost" – I thought that was funny. I am watching the hurricane currently forming in the Atlantic with a different appreciation, that's for sure.

And now here's a question for the day. Why don't peaches grow in Florida? They grow in Georgia and that's only like 5 hours away. Shouldn't Florida be able to grow peaches? I want a peach tree.

I have no plans for the rest of today. Jasen wants Taco pie for dinner. I must go get a doctor recheck, so I can quit taking my UTI meds (they're making me crazy). Maybe it's the weather but I think it might be a lay low/read a book kind of day. After all I am still recovering from my near-death experience (UTI).

THURSDAY - JULY 31 - DOG DAYS OF SUMMER

For those of you who are concerned that I've lost my mind; rest assured that even though I live in my head I also have a tiny foot in reality, only when I have to. This morning I got up early and applied for two "real" jobs on line. Not that I haven't applied for real jobs before but I'm hopeful for either of these. Those applications tend to take forever, especially this one county job. Holy heck.

On other notes: I don't want to belabor the fact that I bought my couch and furniture for *after* my kids were grown, and my dog gone, but I am trying to keep it somewhat nice. Ya know? And even when I had kid furniture I didn't want the dog on it. I mean, the dog gets hair all over the couch and then people get hair all over their clothes, it stinks, and the dog's oils spoil the fabric. You know? I just don't want it on the furniture. It's not that I don't like our dog, I love this dog, but he smells (which is not his fault) and he's smart. We put bean bag chairs on the couch to keep him off. He now knows how to take the bean bag chair off the couch and climb up there. The other day I put a basketball and pillow on the chair and moved the ottoman blocking his access. Do you know he moved the pillow and the ball and this huge dog cuddled up in the chair? It's a white sort of chair. Ya know? Why? WHY? I realize these are only "things" but seriously, why? Now I must wash blankets and pillows (cause really, he smells) and then I'll probably break the washing machine again because of the pillow and well it's not my fault Peter!

I don't yell at Sam (the dog) but I do give him a look and he knows. Now we have TV trays on all our furniture, but I will NOT give in. Suzanne and others know how I agonized over picking that couch. Maybe I could get just a couple more years out of it? Is that too much to ask. Is it?

Last night was date night and we went to Tarpon Springs. I was disappointed because most of the stores were closed. I thought we'd stroll around stores all night. But no. We went back to the same restaurant we went to on Thanksgiving last year. There were about 5 people in there.

The food is delicious, we were not unhappy. I asked the waitress why all the stores are closed, and she said they don't stay open at nights until the season starts which is around Thanksgiving until about March. But we know from last year, because we were here Thanksgiving Day that they don't open until after Thanksgiving. However, after dinner, even though it's not the season, we found a couple of stores opened. We didn't go home empty-handed. New soap for everyone. Sponges and soap, what else would you expect to find in Tarpon Springs?

AUGUST 2014

FRIDAY - AUGUST 1- WHO KNEW?

Yesterday turned out to be a whirlwind of activity. Luckily, I got a wonderful yoga class in first. Then to Zoë's new school to ask about registering her; then to the post office where there was a short line but a lot of stoopid questions asked by the woman before me; then home to grab Jasen's papers to drop off at the middle school to register him; which I was going to do quickly as I still hadn't eaten or been home from yoga; then ended up waiting an HOUR AND HALF – yes 1.5 hours - and after all that time sitting there, I found out I had forgotten the immunization records. I practically broke down in tears. It's now 4:45 and I'm supposed to leave for the mall at 5:00 to take Zoë to her eye doctor appointment (contact recheck) – I haven't showered or eaten. But I manage to get home and get a 10-minute shower, grab a power bar, and then left for the mall pretty much on time. Peter, who is meeting us there, gets stuck in traffic and doesn't get there until after the eye appointment (which is no big deal) and because I am starving the first thing I do is drag him to eat. We ate "crap" food in the food court. I don't think I've ever eaten in a food court.

After dinner we took the kids for new tennis shoes. Both Jasen and Pete said that Jasen didn't need new. I said there is no way you are not buying this kid new tennis shoes for the first day of school. Jasen is a new kid and the last thing he needs is someone pointing out his old tennis shoes. Watch, at schools down here they will probably get made fun of for *new* tennis shoes. Interestingly they have a dress code that says no flip-flops and no slide shoes. I would think flip-flops would be a staple at Florida schools. Who knew?

At some point while in Champs, and simultaneously I might add, as I looked at the shoes and thought "I'm too old for this crap" I looked up and saw a basketball shirt, thought of my son Jimmy, and immediately started crying. I know, I know, I know. They are grown anyway, but I miss them and their school days. Even though I was glad when they were over. There's probably a good lesson in there about enjoying the moment(s). I know I enjoyed the moments and remember quite a few fun ones. I remember parent/teacher meetings with my older sons' Zach's teachers where they would say "why do you come, he's so good?" And of course, I had to say "because it's my job, just talk..." Stoopid teachers. Meetings with Jimmy's teachers were another story. Not good stories, but looking back now how can we not laugh? I'll be reminded of Jimmy's sports games soon, but that won't be until later in the fall when basketball starts and then I will cry again. At school time, the start of fall, all those school memories come rushing back. Who knew it would be this hard to move on? WHO KNEW?

After the mall trip I came home – we drove separately. I let them go on their own to the book store. Clark bonding time and all. Jasen brought me home a Yoga book they bought for me at Barnes & Noble. He's a good kid. While at the mall Zoë and I broke out in dance in some dress shop (she started it!) Really, I am having fun. It's just I have a hard time wrapping my head around school days again. I think I'm supposed to be moving on to "other" things now, not going through them again. That's how you get over it – you move past it. But *nooooo*, I have another opportunity to have fun and get all caught up in these kids' lives. I guess I'll just embrace it.

I can't wait to yell at my first teacher.

MONDAY - AUGUST 4 - IN THE MOOD

Does anyone ever think about *why* you wake up in a "mood"? Is it the dreams you have the night before? The weather? A movie/TV show you've seen before bed? Is it the food you eat the day before? The moon? Today I woke up and ran my school errands. Got Jasen's paperwork all turned in. Got Zoë as settled as I can. But now? I just want to lie on the couch, eat Hostess cupcakes and Ho-Hos and watch TV. I've watched *Sliding Doors* and now onto *Love Actually*. I had one cupcake and two Ho-Ho's. I'm not depressed. I love my boyfriend. All is well. I just want to do nothing. I don't feel like vacuuming although this house needs it. This house *always* needs it (the dog) ...I am doing laundry and I did take chicken out to thaw for dinner. I mean I'm not totally useless. But I am in a mood. We'll call it a quiet mood. Guess it doesn't matter where you live. Even in Florida there are down/quiet days.

TUESDAY - AUGUST 5 - JUST SAY "NO"

Today was our orientation day at the high school. There's a lot of silent drama going on as our girl does not want to go there. I've watched her through the kitchen window with a broken heart, both mine and hers. My heart is broken watching her cry and her heart is broken having to go to this new school. I know with every fiber of my being that this will be a good move for her in the long run but there's no convincing her of that. I'm not even going to try. Pete has been especially kind and compassionate when it comes to this. He's been firm about it though. She has asked once or twice about moving back in with her Godmother and he answers with the perfect Papa answer of "absolutely not" – we are all together now and that's the way it's staying. I know she'll be okay, but my heart breaks for her. And although begrudgingly, she was up and dressed for orientation and off we went. Us parents went into the auditorium. We had 20 minutes of introductions and then almost 2 hours of a NOPE presentation. I can't remember what it stands for but it's some drug abuse awareness program focusing particularly on prescription drugs. There were about 20 pictures of kids who have OD'd, and I assume rather recently. Extremely heart-breaking stuff. I was not prepared for this type of presentation. These prescription drugs are all the rage. This police officer giving the presentation said every single overdose death started with marijuana use. Every single one. There was more talk about parents hosting keggers or buying beer for the prom and honestly, I just wanted to cry and curl up in the fetal position when I came out of there.

I have often been made fun of for my zero-tolerance policy or "nervous Nelly" attitude. But doesn't the gamble scare you? Although the percentage is high for not becoming an addict; do you really want to think of that gamble? Do you want your kid to be the one that the odds are against? How do you know it will stop there? How do you know? These are the things that go through my mind. I think maybe it's because of my past and the fact that I'm thankful that I didn't end up dead in some canal in Miami that I go overboard on the fear factor. It was sheer luck on my part to survive or I had a guardian angel for sure. Unfortunately, it appears that not everyone has a guardian angel, or the luck of the draw as evidenced at our presentation.

I really don't have zero tolerance. I say I do but I don't even know what that means. In "my" house there was a no drinking party policy – so Jimmy went to his dads. Ya know? I mean years of praying nobody died up there or after leaving there. Cause praying was my only recourse (so far so good) It was years of stress, for all of us. And Zachary? Who knows where he went. And I'm not a great parent either – I bought a case of beer one time for Jimmy at college for Mom's weekend. They were going to get it anyway with a fake I. D. and I just went and got it. I hated myself for it. I told them it was for the "moms". But they're going to get it anyway. Right? It's hard to know what not to do.

And now? These kids, in *Florida*, drug capital of the world, in big schools, where at least one of them doesn't want to go. And I know nobody? I honestly don't know how I'll get through it.

I came home from that presentation and threw out all my pain pills (left over from teeth problems) I don't take them anyway. I didn't take them when I supposedly needed them. Why do we hang onto them?

Tomorrow is Jasen's orientation. I'm sitting close to the exit and if those NOPE people are there again, I'm cutting out, running home and going back to bed. Just like the good guardian I am.

WEDNESDAY - AUGUST 6 - GO PANTHERS!!

We're Panthers (and Hurricanes) But today we're Panthers. What a difference a day makes. Today's Orientation at the middle school for Jasen was organized. Today we were in the gym, we got a folder, a lock for his locker, gym clothes and a ½ hour presentation that was actually informative about school stuff. Then Pete and I got to leave and get breakfast, all alone, while the kids stayed and did their thing. What a great morning. Even though we live 2 minutes from the school I picked Jasen up after his orientation. The car line was down the street around the block but by the time I got there he was already with a friend. And now he's being nice to his sister. I am hopeful! It is a good day.

I am going to sign up to volunteer at Jasen's school. It's a way to meet people, stay on top of Jasen's school stuff and maybe get an "in" at the school district. Maybe someone knows someone who knows someone who will want to hire me. You just never know. They told us yesterday at the high school that they don't "need" volunteers. They said they have 900 volunteers for the high school. The schools are different. They even have different mascots. Isn't that weird? Jasen is a Panther and Zoë is a Hurricane. Sounds like the hoodie companies are making money on us. And yes, they sell hoodies here too. I can't wait until it's cool enough to wear one.

Another thing both schools have is a dress code. No short shorts. Shorts and skirts must be mid-thigh. I don't think Zoë owns a skirt or shorts mid-thigh. Everything she owns is short *short short*... we'll have to see how that goes. Hopefully it'll just be another fun shopping outing.

And in other news – the gardener showed up. He cut the grass and took the clippings from three weeks ago. It's a good day. I'm going to make cookies.

FRIDAY - AUGUST 8 - A FLORIDA FRIDAY

I'm having a hard time blogging. I don't have anything new to say and it really can't be that exciting to follow my eating habits. But on date night last night we really did hit the dessert jackpot. We went to this place called Lucky Dill's and they had a full bakery in the restaurant. REALLY nice and a great local discovery. I don't report too much on the actual details of date night, but I will say they never get old. We are making the night a priority. Although this family/mom thing really sounds like it's taking over I'm glad for the family distraction during the days since I can't find a job. Do I wish there were no kids in this picture? No, I love these kids already just as much as Peter. I love them all. It's just a balancing act now between all of it. I guess it's good there's no job yet in the long run. I don't know how I would manage that too.

Speaking of managing, I spent my last $40 on scallops to make for dinner. Not sure it was worth it although they were good. But that's two pedicures. And I'm in need of one of those. But as usual we sacrifice for the family.

We have no weekend plans. Maybe I'll dedicate an entire day to job hunting. Lock myself in my room and search the internet. Or that might have to wait until school starts. I'm counting down the days, both to school starting and a job starting.

It's raining at the moment. Complete with thunder and lightning I'm waiting until it passes to go to the library and try to get Zoë her reading requirements (books) for school. She has one week to read two books. I'm confident she can do it.

MONDAY - AUGUST 11 - MONDAY, MONDAY

It's raining, it's pouring, and I love it. First, we don't have to water plants when it rains so that's nice (and a savings on the water bill). Second, I feel like doing "inside" work when it rains and the house loves it. And it both cools things off and then makes it muggier. As the "weather girl" (as some of you know me as) I do like a nice change of weather. I don't know if that change will happen in October or when. But whenever it happens, it will be a welcome change of pace. It's still summer hot. When is that autumn fall cool weather going to start?

As I have mentioned, I am mesmerized by the sky here. It can be pouring down rain inland and sunny at the beach. That happens a lot. Last weekend Zoë didn't come to the beach with us because when we left it was thundering; however, true to Florida form it was pure sunshine 5 miles away at the beach. I got the sunburn to prove it. Today though seems like a total gray day, quite unusual, quite Pittsburghish.

As for the weekend we did a lot of unpacking and more settling in kind of stuff. Pete cleaned the shed/studio. It's air-conditioned out there and has electricity. Now I know where to find him when he goes missing. He uncovered (and organized) about 10 hammers and maybe 5 ratchet sets and drill bits out the wazoo. Every size nail or screw imaginable (but no "S" hooks...I was looking for one to hang a birdhouse...I improvised) And the shed is filled with mostly empty storage bins. It's a lovely thing. I need some projects so I can hide out there too. He told me the other day that it fills his heart to see me through the kitchen window while I'm making dinner. I don't think he's excited about my cooking. He likes the "family" down-home simple lifestyle and there's something about me being in the kitchen that is very endearing to him. Which is good because I do spend a lot of time in there.

We are developing a habit of a Sunday bike ride, alone, before anyone is awake. I donned my Steeler jersey and got a woot woot at our breakfast restaurant that's on our bike trail. I am feeling very out of touch without my Pittsburgh sports. I have to figure out how to stay on top of things. There must be a Steeler bar nearby

WEDNESDAY - AUGUST 13 - THE POWERFUL PLAY GOES ON AND YOU MAY CONTRIBUTE A VERSE...WHAT WILL YOUR VERSE BE?

It's hard to write today without mentioning Robin Williams. Hearing the news last night was shocking. Even my son Jimmy texted me to see if I heard the news. It seemed like a family member died or at least a close acquaintance. The posts on Facebook were sad and personal. When Mark Hannigan posted how much he'd miss Robin Williams I cried. It's surprising how these celebrity figures affect our lives. Apparently, Robin was open about his problems with addiction and was proud of his 20 years of sobriety. A lot of other posts today on Facebook are "rehab" and addiction related. One post hit close to home. Craig Ferguson did a monologue a few years ago on his own struggles with alcohol addiction. Craig Ferguson points out that addiction is not cured by a "rehab" stint and boom after 28 days you're magically cured. It's a lifelong commitment. *Lifelong.*

We often hear of these comedic celebrities, such as Robin Williams, who have a very dark side. What we see is a comedic nut case but perhaps what they are doing is hiding their dark side. And really who wants to know about other people's dark side? Even with these posts of mine I always try and post the positive and when I can't be positive I either make something up or I post nothing. Nobody wants to hear about the bad stuff. And I don't want to focus on it either. (not that there's a lot of bad, but you get the idea.)

All of this has made me think about my own quitting issues. I'm thinking of the Robin Williams' of the world that put on that brave face, make people laugh and then commit suicide. Isn't there always a drug and alcohol connection too? I admit there are times I think of drinking, but the bad memories of hangovers and lost days are stronger than any drink could ever taste. A beer would taste great. But then what? Another? Next thing you know, well I don't want to think of the next thing. I don't want to think of those next things ever again. They had their place and time in my life but I'm not that person anymore. However, if I don't think about those times then I might lose perspective on their importance in my decision to not drink. Maybe I'm more mature now. Maybe I could drink a drink or two. Maybe I could, but what if I couldn't. It's a balance. It's a commitment to make that decision, over and over again.

These days when I want to escape, I think about going to an ocean-front hotel, alone (or preferably *with* my boyfriend), for a weekend, perhaps with a spa treatment or three. Not drinking a bottle of whiskey or taking pills. That doesn't even sound fun to me anymore. However, it's never far from my mind that drinking or something similar is an escape option. All of us quitters are just one drink, one sip away of a setback. Therefore, I must never forget my decision to quit.

I am a quitter and I'm proud of it. I pray that I'm committed to it for the rest of my life. I am proud to make being a quitter a verse in my life.

Nanu nanu

THURSDAY - AUGUST 14 - AN ANNIVERSARY OF SORTS

Yesterday was my 50th post. 50th!! Who knew I could ramble on 50 times about nothing. It was my 50th post and my 80th day in Florida. Seems like I should do a recap or something. Both 50 and 80 are milestones, aren't they? So, let's review...

My brother recently asked me how I liked Florida now that I'm "finally" here. I answered that with all the changes in my life, living in Florida is the least of it. When I thought about moving to Florida for the past 5 years it was a vision of living in a 2-bedroom condo on or very near the beach, alone. Not a 4-bedroom house looking at middle and high schools. Peter and I will on occasion say to each other "Hey, we're in Florida, *together*!!" It was something we talked about a lot during last year's cold *cold* winter in Pittsburgh and now we're really here. If I had time to take it all in it would probably seem a bit surreal. But honestly these other changes take precedence over the geography of Florida, at least for now. For instance:

1. I no longer sleep alone. I have slept alone for the past 24ish years. Except for the last year on weekends (with Pete), I have had that bed to myself. Not only do I not sleep alone I now sleep all intertwined with another human being of the same age (I am not counting the years of my children sleeping in my bed). However,

at 7:30 am when he is out of bed getting ready for work, I am back to spread eagle, middle of the bed, big smile on my face remembering my alone years. I loved my bed when I lived alone, loved sleeping alone, I wouldn't even let Max the dog on the bed because he hogged too much of the bed. Now look at me (us) and I love it.

2. I live with strangers. Although I was with Pete and Jasen for a year (Jasen about 9 months) before all of us living together, they really are strangers. They don't feel like strangers, but I think in the big scheme of things they are. We somehow are managing to surpass any awkwardness and are a family. It seems like we all have been together for a long time. Jasen the other day had a bottle of soda on the table at dinner and he went to pour himself a glass and he looked at me and said, "I'll get water." I replied "What? I didn't say anything." His reply, "I know the *look*" ...HA! That didn't take long. He can now commiserate with my boys on the "look". However, the look may have been more about the plastic on the table than another drink of soda...but I'm weaning myself of certain expectations.

3. My parenting has taken a 180. I was very vigilant with my kids on certain things but with these kids, you want to sleep until 4:00? – go ahead...more quiet time for me. Want a fudgsicle for breakfast? Sure, get me one too. McDonalds? Ok (but just once a week). I think seeing that it doesn't matter a whole lot what you do during these years on certain battles, well I just pick different battles, which I typically make Pete fight. Plus, I have a girl! I never had a girl before. The biggest difference there is clothes shopping. And although I think I know her "look" I still never pick out the right thing. Some things aren't that different. Jimmy used to wear whatever I bought him. Zachary *never* wore what I bought him (unless it's a superman T-shirt). Zoë likes superman T-shirts too.

4. I have a dog that I *can't* walk. I have had dogs for 30 years. Daily walks were part of the routine of having a dog. Walking in the parks, being in nature, seeing them run through the fields. This dog can't be walked because if he runs after something he's going to kill it. Not people but other dogs and/or cats, especially cats. I tried walking him one time and he dragged me across the sidewalk and practically separated my arm and attacked my neighbor's new dog by the throat. I've been traumatized ever since. And as I've mentioned several times on this blog my pretty new furniture is covered with items to keep the dog off. I've had my share of dog hair, but this black hair is something else. He's a nice dog though, with people, but the no walking thing is very different.

5. I don't work...outside the home...yet. I now know why people add "outside the home" because I tell you I'm hopping most days. HOPPING. Pete will occasionally make fun of the time of day that I wake up (I'm a late sleeper) and give me that look (to which I say "shut up") but I'm telling you I run a lot of errands, I clean a lot, and I cook pretty often...although right now I'm thinking Thursdays should be leftover night don't you? Goes along with Lyming day. My stress level is soooo down from not "going" to work. I'd take "these" days over "those" days any day...if only it paid better. I love my life right now. I'll love it more when school starts but even then, I'll only have 4 hours with everyone gone. I blog everyday(ish) that's a little like work. I'm busy, it's just different. Very different.

6. I have a boyfriend. I know this should have maybe come first in the review and is the reason for ALL the changes but bottom line is *I have a boyfriend!!* And I think he really *really* likes me! We have fun together. We have our date night. We've been sneaking out Sunday mornings on our bike rides before anyone gets up. We like being together. I mean who would've thunk it? This is definitely a new experience for me. One day I was having a particularly bad day, (yes, I still have them) and found myself

wondering what the heck I'm doing, worrying about work, stuff like that and I came home from the store and he came out on the porch to greet me and I just smiled and smiled. And I thought to myself "this is why I do it...I just love him"... Nice huh? Just nice.

7. So, living in Florida? The geography of Florida? It's hot. Really hot. I have to say of all the changes it's my least favorite. I know can you believe I'm saying it? It's not that I hate the heat, but it does make it hard to do things. And it's too hot to go to the beach, at least very often. And the bugs. I'm constantly bit. Constantly. I don't know who scratches more. Me or the dog. I don't like it. I don't like it one bit. (Get it? Bit?) Pete says I'm going to love it here in the fall, winter and spring and I believe him. Kinda like Pittsburgh. Not a great place to be in the winter, especially this past winter, but the rest of the year it can be pretty nice. I would rather live through a hot summer than a cold winter so in general I like it, but right now I miss Pittsburgh. Yes, I do. I miss the summer weather, I miss the Pirates, I miss the Steelers. I miss my friends and family, and I really liked living downtown. Do I want to move back? Heck no. Probably never. I'm sure once I learn more things around here, make friends, get on a better *visit* Pittsburgh schedule, get Pittsburgh visitors here in the winter months, and when we get involved in water sports and enjoy the beach more I know I'll come around. Right now, we're getting settled. I just have to be patient. (a common theme) I enjoy our bike rides, and the flatness of the terrain, the sky, the water, the big trees and Spanish moss, and looking up at night and seeing the moon through the palm trees. Sandy asked me before I moved down here, as a test to my commitment, if I would move to Idaho with Pete. Luckily, I didn't have to make that decision then. Now, the answer is "yes" – but probably only during the summer – then we'd have to move back here.

FRIDAY - AUGUST 15 - IT WAS A DARK AND STORMY NIGHT (AND DAY)

Thank you for all the complimentary comments over these past 51 posts. Right when I think nobody wants to read these anymore, I get a comment that says to keep going. So, I'll keep going with my nonsense as long as someone wants to read it. Maybe if I can get through another 50 posts I'll start the book. *It was a dark and stormy night...*

Pete took a vacation day today in anticipation of a family weekend. However, this is what's happening. Him and Jasen are going to Orlando; Disney we hope – Magic Kingdom I hope – because I don't really care about going to Magic Kingdom and Jasen's never been there and since I'm not going I don't want them to do something I want to do too. Does that make me selfish? I think not. Zoë has been to the Magic Kingdom twice (at least). She's going to stay with her Godmother for the weekend which she is thrilled about and me? I'm staying home...ALONE...I'm so excited I can't stand it. Not that I don't love my family. Pete was saying "are you sure, I feel bad...blah blah." And I responded "are you kidding me? It'll be like HEAVEN. HEAVEN I tell you!" I'm staying with the dog. I can't wait to sit by the pool and read my book (now reading *What Alice Forgot*) and maybe I'll even take myself to the beach. Maybe I'll watch some girlie movie. Maybe I'll stay on the phone all weekend, I mean the options are endless.

Not only am I getting ready for my alone weekend it's payday and Pete says I'm taking over the budget. Scary I know. But I'm up to the challenge. I think I might be a little more vigilant than him but since I overdrew my account yesterday I'm not totally sure this is the right move. I hope he's going to keep a secret stash in the event I fail. With my alone weekend maybe I'll even go shopping. I don't know what I'm going to give myself in the budget department, but I mean this weekend is getting better all the time. We're starting to decorate a little more. We need to pick a theme though and stick with it. Our living room is kinda dark and wood theme. But I'd really like to go to a beach theme someday. White, flowy, airy. But not yet. First, we need to finish unpacking.

And when I say "we" I mean "he" needs to finish unpacking. He is making great headway. But we still don't have a guest room. Soon, certainly in time for the season (I hope).

Have a nice weekend. Can't wait to blog about my alone time. Hope it's a boring blog because I'll have done nothing!!

MONDAY - AUGUST 18 - MONDAY AND MY NEW ROUTINE

Happy First Day of School. Woot whoop whoop! I say again, whoop!! I loved getting up early and getting going with the day. We will see how long it lasts but day one I'm feeling productive. Pete and I took Zoë to school at 7:00 a.m. She seemed perfectly fine. If she was nervous she did not show it. Typical me I've already texted her, no response yet. I hope that's not a bad sign. Jasen was next and got himself up and showered and was ready at like 8:00 am – he doesn't start until 9:30 but I took him around 9:00. He wanted dropped off about a block from the corner, so he could walk in. He said he'll walk home. I'm planning to meet him half way. If I see him walking with someone I'll hide. He doesn't have a cell phone yet (well he does have one, but it only works for texts and games), but I still asked him if he knows the home phone number, his dad's number or mine in case. He said no. I said "okay." Eh, if we lose him we lose him. After I dropped him off I went to the grocery store (again and always) – got stuff to make for dinner – came home figured out how to make what I'm making for dinner – applied for 2 jobs online – and now writing this blog all before 10:30! I'm usually just rolling out of bed around this time. I have laundry to fold, and have to go get Jasen a phone charger and Zoë a bike lock and by that time it'll be time to pick Zoë up and then I'll have all this time and won't know what to do with myself. Maybe I'll wait and take her with me to get the charger and bike lock.

Backing up - on my alone-time weekend, here's the universal question I thought about. Not where do we go when we die? Not should I be taking this family to church? No, what I came up with? Should I start getting manicures? I mean is that important? I've never had finger-nails. Sometimes they grow and then as soon as they start looking good they peel and break. When we first moved here I had good-looking nails. After this weekend they are now looking like Pittsburgh nails; which is to say broken and weak. Should I do it? I have added pedicures to a "have to" routine. The toes are always out. Pedicures are a must. With my day to myself that was the universal question that I came up with.

Otherwise after the troops left Friday I was mixed with both excite-ment and a "now what do I do?" attitude, and so, I assumed the position on the couch which I am familiar with in my pre-Peter life and proceeded to call my brother. He used to call me on a Friday and make sure I was in my chair watching TV, my typical Friday night routine. With this new boyfriend/family I have I'm never in the TV watching/vegging position. Pete drags my ass all over the place. It's fun but down time is nice too. The dog made me a little nervous as he was guarding the front door for a good part of the time. I don't know if he was miss-ing Pete or there was suspicious activity out there. Either way he's good to have around when alone.

I woke up Saturday and found that a mosquito had found its way into the bed and enjoyed a drunken evening at my poor legs expense. Mother effer. I got him though. Then I put on my swimsuit certain I was going to treat myself to the beach, set off a bug bomb (again) in the bedroom, sat out by the pool with the dog for a couple of minutes and it started to thunder. So much for the beach. It remained cloudy and rainy the rest of the day. I was thinking about how the beach I want to go to is about 30 minutes away. And you know what I was thinking? "that's a long way away!" Can you believe it? I would drive 8 hours to get to the beach all my life and I'm sitting there thinking a ½ hour is too far. I hope I shake this attitude soon. I think it was just the fact that I had a lot to do on my big day off. I wanted to relax and not drive. Well anyway, I missed the beach but promised myself I would go on Sunday. I did enjoy my day by the pool (under cover from the rain), talked to my mom on the phone a long time, read a little and then did my errands. Went to Home Depot and Wal-Mart, being ever vigilant since I'm now in charge of the funds. I actually put stuff back. And I stayed out of Michael's. Maybe next pay. Saturday night was spent again on the couch, TV on, talking on the phone to Di. Just like the old days.

Sunday, the plan was to clean the kids' rooms, get their beds made, you know something nice to come home to and the night before school and all and somehow fit in the beach. Thought I had until 7 pm but they came home early so there went that. They all got home around 4:00 and then Monica (#2 child) and boyfriend came for dinner, we whipped up a delicious impromptu dinner for the 6 of us. We're good at this meal thing (team work). In conclusion about my weekend alone, I was productive, but I missed my boyfriend and he missed me (isn't love grand?) We decided the break was nice because it's nice seeing each other again. I haven't talked about sex lately either have I and that's because it's none of your business, but just for the heck of it, it's always great after time apart. This Thursday I'm planning on going to Orlando to see Marissa (remember her? My work-study at PPU). Could be the start of something. (leaving and coming back) – I really wish he was coming with me though. I would love an entire alone weekend with this man.

Oh, I know the biggest thing that happened this weekend. I bought Jasen and myself fishing poles AND I got my very first fishing license. I can't wait to post pictures of the fish I catch and of course blog about the ones that got away.

TUESDAY - AUGUST 19 - GO ASK ALICE

When you read a book do you think you're the character? I do. I totally get into the character. Movies too. I'm reading *What Alice Forgot*. The gist of the story is that Alice has hit her head and she's lost 10 years of her memory. She thinks it's 1998 when it's 2008. She doesn't remember her 3 kids. It's an interesting premise, isn't it? I mean what if I did the same thing and I thought it was 2004? Jimmy is 13, Zachary still at Penn State? Well, the point is if I woke up now thinking it was 10 years ago how shocked I would be to find myself living here with the strangers. With a couple of days to myself, and reading the book, I'm thinking about the strangers I live with. I wonder when or if that feeling will ever stop. I don't *really* feel like they're strangers all the time and especially not when we're all busy doing stuff, but 10 years ago they sure would be. I really do feel like I've been plopped into the middle of a story. I know very little about these people's past or when they were babies, and what I hear is like I've read it in a book. It's not real cause I wasn't there. I mean think about it, the only people I married or dated (with a few exceptions) were all from my hometown. Even from the same high school. Anyway, I know I've mentioned my new family as "strangers" before and I don't want to keep calling them that, but I'm getting sucked into that book. I told Zoë that I keep forgetting if it's the character that has lost 10 years or if "I" have lost the 10 years. Surprisingly she gets me (thank God!) At least I think she does. Although she does run and hide in her room...a lot.

Better day for Zoë today at school as she was able to change her schedule to what she wants. THREE sciences. Sheesh. And she's excited! Go figure. Plus, she's in Chorus and they might go to Disney over Christmas (if they make the cut). How fun is that? Jasen went to school early today on his bike. Today, he's a happy camper. He said he liked his school up north (last year) better though. That's based on one day. We can't even use the winter to convince him, he says he liked the winter. Dam kids. He's not unhappy though, just an observation. There's an awful lot of kids on bikes that live around here. All boys, this could be a good thing.

I had a slow morning, read my book and then to yoga. I can tell this is going to be a great transition with these kids in school and these quiet mornings. *Honest Pete, I'm looking for a job. Really, I am.*

Better get back to my book. Pete says when he reads a book he thinks the characters in books are waiting for him to get back to it so they can finish their story. I better get back to Alice and help her remember her kids. Best if I help her remember reading by the pool.

THURSDAY, AUGUST 21- THE GOOD, THE BAD AND TODAY I'M UGLY

I'm miserable today. I read the "general" horoscope I get in my Inbox every day. Today it says:

Anxiety floats around today, yet we can't seem to put our fingers on the source of the unrest. Finding our center of gravity is tricky business. Meanwhile, complexity builds as an annoying Venus-Pluto aspect reveals a deeper layer of feelings. Fortunately, an insightful Mercury-Pluto trine brings enough wisdom to manage the emotional intensity.

Mostly it's like "what?" But there are words in there that I'm feeling today. Anxiety, annoying, complexity, emotional intensity. I threw something (soft) across the room today I was pissed off that the dog was on the couch. I didn't throw it *at* the dog, but I just wanted to cry...and I did...again. (and then the dog came over and gave me kisses because he knew I was sad) At some point I know I need to give up on that. I think the choice is live with this family or be alone and have my things. I know the couch is just a thing but sometimes I can't separate knowing how long it took me to finally get something nice for myself. It really is an insightful, emotional kind of day. I skipped yoga today because I lost track of time, instead I decided to do one of those 20-minute meditation things with Oprah and Deepak. Today's message is "Living Kindness – being kind to all" ...yea, no... I skipped it and went back and did yesterday's meditation. I don't want to be kind today. That's how bad it is. Pete is probably reading this ever thankful that I'm off to Orlando for the day/night.

I'm off to Orlando today to see "my Marissa" in a play. She's in the musical version of *The Big Fish*. I'm excited to see her and I love the Big Fish story. I had no idea there was a musical version and no idea Marissa could sing. I'm staying in a hotel for the night that I found on Groupon.

I didn't think about checking the reviews before booking. BIG mistake... maybe. Pete thinks Groupon wouldn't sell a flea-bag place. We'll see. I hate to go from being bit in one place to being bit in another. Not a good day to test the anxiety, annoying, emotional intensity thing I have going on. But if all is okay, I'm looking forward to sitting by the pool in the morning. There's something different about sitting at someone else's pool. No laundry to do, phones to answer, emails to check. I can just unplug. Which reminds me to take my IPOD cause I'm not really going to unplug that much.

To end on the positive side.... I went to the beach yesterday morning after dropping Pete at work. We went to a network thing last night (ugh) I drove him to work and picked him up. The beach was nice and was most definitely "pinch" worthy. Sue always asks me if I'm pinching myself out of disbelief that I'm finally in Florida. When I'm at the beach I feel like I'm in Florida. It was nice. Even the network thing wasn't that bad. And of course, a night out with the BF (boyfriend) is always nice. Love him more than the couch. Guess I better keep that in mind.

FRIDAY - AUGUST 22 - HAVE I MET YOUR NEEDS?

First, I'm in a much better mood today. Even though I ended up driving home from Orlando last night at midnight arriving home at 2:00 a.m. After my third cockroach in the hotel room, I decided I'd had enough. Thank God for the coffee mocha milkshake Marissa and I split at midnight. The caffeine got me home safe and sound and I was happy to be in my own bed. Marissa and the whole production was/were excellent. She did a great job – singing and dancing – looking as cute as ever. She had about 8 wardrobe changes. A lot of the talent was from Disney, the voices and acting were great. There was a live orchestra. All for $10. You just can't beat it. And great to see her. I can't wait to go back. But never, ever, ever stay at a place called Roomba in Kissimmee. Ever.... *ever....*!

MONDAY - AUGUST 25 - STILL HERE

I'm still here. Both on this blog site and in Florida. But I am packing to go up North. I'm packed.... mostly. I'm looking forward to wearing a sweater, and long pants. I am already acclimated to this Florida climate as when it's in the 80's I'm wearing jeans and long sleeves.

My crisis of the day is trying to get a pedicure before leaving. Also trying to figure out how open house works tonight at Zoë's school. Do we go to her first period when we get there? I called the school just to confirm and the main number rang for 3 minutes and then they picked up the phone and hung it up. I love her school. I tried again, and they did the same thing. Is it me Lucille?

This past weekend was nice. Always are but I usually can't remember what I did other than the day before. I'm going to try here now. Let's see, Friday night we went to a new place for dinner – Peggy O'Neills – right in our little neighborhood. We decided we like it and will go again. It was loud but the food was good. A band started to play as we were leaving and they sounded good, but did I mention loud?

Saturday, ummmm, I think there was reading by the pool and honestly, I don't remember much else. We had Chinese food though. I do remember that. Oh, wait was this the day when it started to thunder when we got out of the pool and Pete decided it was time to clean out the gutters? You know, with a metal pole, on the roof, with thunder. Doesn't everyone do that? Next thing you know we were all out there (the storm passed). The most important discovery is what is right in our neighbors back yard. A pond. Yep, standing water. Do you know what's in standing water in Florida? ALLIGATORS and mosquitoes. This could explain the feeding frenzy on my legs at dusk if I'm out side. Hopefully someone will decide that it's a good piece of real estate and fill it up. I'm NOT a fan of standing water, in Florida.

Sunday was our bike ride and this time Zoë joined us. It was hot. Like throwing up and passing out hot. I think the heat index was something like 105. And I got a flat tire. Do you know how hard it is to ride a bike with a flat tire? I was able to put air in it after breakfast and almost made it home before it went flat again. The last mile or so was brutal. Then I went in the pool with my clothes on (no shoes). I made a pretty good salmon dinner and that was our weekend. Today is back to school and well, like I said, packing and pedicure, laundry and open house. Perhaps I will leave them with some cookies to remember me by. Hopefully they will want me back.

SEPTEMBER 2014

TUESDAY - SEPTEMBER 2 - AND I'M BACK!

I'm home again, from being home, and now I'm home...again...home. It was a long visit but not. Know what I mean? I got to Pittsburgh last Tuesday – met my sister and niece for lunch, ran downtown to Point Park University (PPU) and got to see a few old work friends for like a minute each and then *didn't* see a lot of people that I wanted to see. Zachary and I had a lovely evening out, even ran into another work colleague at Target (picking up another hello) – On Wednesday I hit the road and went to Virginia. I absolutely love that drive.

The visit with mom was one day driving, one day visiting, and one day driving back. Phew. Then got to see all the babies, all my sister's grandchildren (there's 5 of them) at Mya's 2-year-old birthday party. She is the cutest thing ever.

Then a quick game of Scrabble with the girls (Di, Jer, Jan and Kerry). Wonder why I didn't take any pictures there? Especially of my winning score?

On Saturday I was able to hit the farmers market which is such a big deal for me because it's "off" season down here in the great tropics. Seeing all those fresh vegetables and bustling morning activity was quite the rush of homesickness. I managed to smuggle apples onto the plane. I am enjoying my northern apples as we speak (or as I type).

Saturday afternoon in Pittsburgh was spent at the pool with the babies. It was quite a sight to see my sister with 5 grandbabies in tow. My how times have changed. We still hit the water slide, my sis and I. The old broads coming down the slide. It was fun, but that pool water sure was cold. The late afternoon and evening was spent with my boys – a pizza in Shadyside and a walk around the Point State Park fountain. LOVE that fountain in Point State Park.

Then I came back home home, here to Tampa, yesterday morning. My boyfriend met me at the airport with roses and a new look. He's got a little scruffy beard thing going. I couldn't stop looking at him. I like it. Makes him look younger, not that he looks old without it, but I don't know, kinda sexy I'd say. We went right to Indian Rocks beach, had a lovely breakfast in a French cafe joint and then proceeded to get stupid sunburn as we were floating in the Gulf from 10:30 am to 2:30 pm. Honest we put on sunscreen, I'd hate to see what we'd look like if we hadn't. Best welcome home ever! I love that boyfriend of mine.

Pete had the house all clean, yard work done, a new basket on my bike and fixed flat tire on my bike and then showed me the junk room/music room/guest room and it was all cleaned and I started to cry!! Then I dragged him to the furniture stores so we can redo that room. I'm excited. We can have visitors now! Well not now, now, because Jasen decided he wanted the bed that we had in there. Now we have no bed but we're shopping for one. And I think I might paint first. I wonder who our first visitor will be? And should they get a prize?

This has been fun writing this update, remembering what's been happening. I'll have more to say another day when I don't have to pay bills, go grocery shopping, get some paint chips and look at furniture before making dinner. Maybe I'll apply for a job in there too.

WEDNESDAY - SEPTEMBER 3 - FALL IS IN THE AIR...SORT OF

A few weeks ago, I was in Michael's, in the 95-degree heat, and they had all the Fall decorations out. I gave them some mental slack since, well, it's a crafts store and perhaps it was time to be working on Fall decorations. I was in full summer mode though. I'm still in full summer mode and it's September. I think in Florida it's going to be full summer mode until October when it becomes "bearable" summer mode. When I got off the plane in Pittsburgh last week the first thing I did was take a deep breath in. That day, in Pittsburgh, the air was refreshing. It felt like I could breathe again. I made sure I slept with the windows open all week (although many fans still going). I talked with a couple of women yesterday who have lived here for years, one of them her whole life (believe it or not, I did not know they made native Floridians), and they both said that this has been the hottest summer they have ever experienced. Which is good to know because other than a few days it hasn't been *that* bad. I mean it's bad, but it's Florida in the summer so I was expecting that. But I miss Fall. I'm hoping by October we will be able to open windows. To me that will indicate Fall. The sun also seems to be looking a little different. Like shining in our room at a different time, or around the pool differently. There are indications of something going on that's slightly different. Open windows will signify Fall and then of course we will display Marcus the Carcass. I'm sure all of you don't know who Marcus the Carcass is, and well let's just keep that as something to look forward to closer to Halloween.

And then the big question, what does one wear in Florida in the Fall? During July I was in the mall (down here) looking in Macy's as I was walking by and I thought something was off. Something was just not right. And what was it? Fall clothes. In Florida? Fall colors, sweaters, I mean who will wear those? I have the same t-shirt dress on that I always wear and am assuming I will wear it year-round until it either falls apart or Pete burns it cause he's sick of seeing it. Of course, I'm not working. I don't need work clothes, but it is date night tonight. I need to dress appropriately, right? Do I wear white still? So many things I have to learn, and buy. I saw some Uggs in Plato's Closet also in July. Uggs down here will make more sense as they won't get salt stains and be nice and toasty for when it drops below 70. My sister-in-law who lives in California wears her Uggs and a parka when it's under 70. It gets colder there in California than here, I think. We shall see. It will be something for me to do. Follow the weather.

I'm trying to figure out what to do with myself today. I've putzied a little, did some dishes, doing some laundry, making some chicken soup, now writing this. My new blog page is kinda fun. Lots of buttons to figure out. I added a "follow" button last night – it's at the very bottom of the blog. I guess I could work on that more. OR, I have a pile of catalogs that I want to go through then I can pitch them. Do you have that problem? Do you get all these catalogs that you're never going to order from but then you save them because you "think" someday you might order something from them so you keep them, and then they just accumulate until you throw them away? Never ordering anything and even if you did want to order something wouldn't you do it online anyway? Sheesh...if only I ran the world.

I'm going to sit by the pool and go through those magazines/catalogs. One of them is about weekend trips. Perhaps I will plan a weekend trip with my boyfriend and then pick out a new wardrobe from the other catalogs to pack for the trip. Maybe we could take the trip in a new car that I will pick from the Land Rover catalog. I think this trip we should go North. Just drive until we see yellow and red leaves and can sleep with the windows open. I'm sure there's some cabins to rent in the Smoky Mountains in one of those catalogs. This seems like a good use of my time.

THURSDAY - SEPTEMBER 4 - I'M SUCH A SELL-OUT

Check me out. I've been reading the Amazon tutorial this morning (on what is supposed to be Lyming day) on how to put advertising with Amazon on my blog page. There are all these gadgets called widgets. I don't want to junk up my site cause really, I just like to ramble, but this is fun to see all the different options and experiment with all the buttons. You will all have to bear with me while I experiment. Seems like if I tell you for instance, that I'm reading this book, *The Boys in the Boat*, and then you buy the book I guess I get credit.

Anyway, It's fun. I'm playing and really I'm working, right? Perhaps that's a "job" for tomorrow, figuring out how to manipulate these widgets.

My boyfriend, who've I mentioned once or twice, is the *best boyfriend ever*. We had date night last night and I was telling him how happy I am blah blah and mentioned I'd like to contribute financially, more blah blah, and he said we're making it without me working so not to worry and just do what I want. Today I'm doing what I want...which is learning about this blogging and advertising stuff. Can I sell enough products through Amazon and buy a boat? Or just make my car legal?

Speaking of "making it" (monetarily) and my boys, here's a weekend story from my visit last week with my boys. I think I mentioned the three of us, went to this restaurant in Shadyside, Mercurios, a nice pizza place, not horribly expensive, and after dinner we all agreed that now that everyone (except me) is employed and able to contribute that we would all guess the amount of the check – the one closest does not have to pay – we added the caveat "closest without going over" – well we were all over and then somehow I ended up paying for the whole thing. How does that work? Dam kids.

I'm missing Lyming day. I have dishes to do. Fish to marinate and soup to eat all before dinner. I need some serious cleaning time but I think that might be tomorrow. Before I sign off though, last night my boyfriend suggested that I write a "beard blog" in honor of his facial hair growth. Although I will not be writing a beard blog I will post a picture of his face. I like it. Both his face and his beard. But no beard blog honey...sorry.

FRIDAY - SEPTEMBER 5 - THE WEEKEND IS UPON US

And I'm ready for my weekend. It was a short week but the weekend approaching always makes me excited. Even though I'm not leaving the house everyday I'm still excited to have Pete home all weekend. Saturdays, I usually do absolutely nothing but lounge around with him, sometimes in the pool, or just sleeping late. It's nice. Zoë just left with her Godmother, Leslie for the weekend. Since Leslie came to pick her up I was a maniac cleaning all morning. Meanwhile it looks pretty much the same as before I started. I'm sure she can't tell that I washed the area rugs in our bedroom, you know? Or the fact that I dusted. . but there's nothing like company or the threat of company coming over to get your house good and clean. We need some motivation, right? I remember when my kids were little and my mother would come to stay with us I would kill myself cleaning. Zachary told me once that I shouldn't expect him to do that for me when he gets older. I think that's why I'm never invited into his house. I don't think I actually clean for the people who visit, I just clean because it needs done. Who 'my kidding? I wanted Leslie to like the house and be happy for Zoë. She complimented us on the hominess – said the house is nice. I didn't clean Zoë's room but I did make her bed. Okay here's a question, do you mom's make your kids beds every day? I've been doing that. Jasen's bed is a little more work since I have to get the dog hair off every day but I just think it's a nice thing for them to come home to. I don't clean in there – although I will clean Zoë's room this weekend before she comes home.

I did not get to Lyming yesterday, I got caught up in the Amazon link madness, as I consider that my new job. Today I've spent time learning about the "voting" button. It's too big. How do I get it smaller? Most of the time I don't do what I say I'm going to do on this blog. If I don't start out first thing in my day on the "thing" whether it's cleaning, lounging, blogging, then I have a hard time getting to it. Something always comes up. Yesterday instead of blogging I tried to teach myself how to build a website. There are lots of things I want to do and I have NO idea what I'm doing. I didn't get very far and then it was dinner time. Maybe now that the house is 1/2 clean, and I'm out of the mood to finish cleaning, and it's Friday (which I think should be eat out night shouldn't it?) maybe I'll work on learning this website stuff a little more. I want to be able to put things on my page where I want them ya know?

And by the way dear, we need to buy more bathroom rugs – guess I shouldn't have put them in the washer/dryer. Sorry...

MONDAY - SEPTEMBER 8 - HERE WE GO STEELERS!

There are no words for how much I missed Pittsburgh today while watching that Steeler's game. I could tell it was a beautiful day there. Sunshine, blue sky, I could "smell" the fall air. I was almost in tears. But then I ran an errand during half time and it felt a little fall-ish to me here too. I can feel it. Even though there's no Steeler vibe there is still a vibe here. I hope I'm going to be okay. It's amazing how I'm taken back to years of high school football games. There are many memories coming back this fall. I am out of my element. And my element is Pittsburgh in the fall.

To compensate for my homesickness, I practiced getting fresh air into the house. I ended up opening the patio door in our bedroom which does not have a screen, to practice getting air in the house. I sprayed the heck out of the surrounding areas outside on the patio and the door frame with bug spray. Then I put down that roach powder everywhere I could see. Of course, that won't keep the mosquitoes out but I don't plan on keeping it open at night. I attempted to open more windows around the house. Some I was successful with, others not so much. But for a little while I actually had windows open until the kids complained it was hot. I think they're crazy but whatever. All kids are crazy.

Other weekend events included my very first fishing outing. I was excited. We don't have any real bait so I Googled it and seems like any-thing goes and really there's a lot of luck involved. I took some very unique items to use as bait; fruit jems, spinach, tomatoes, celery, cheese, dried mangos. I was hoping to be the genius with some unique magic bait but alas only the small fish were biting. Pete found a dead fish on the shore and cut it up for bait. You can imagine the stink and the flies. Gawd. But I was the trooper. I could sit there all day and maybe I will start doing that. Just sitting on the causeway with my fishing pole and chair. Although not sure what I would do if I caught one. I don't even know what we're allowed to keep. We had an old-timer on the pier when we were fishing talking about the opening of Snook season. Would I know a Snook if I caught one? What if I caught one and it wasn't Snook season? Do I get arrested? But in any event I loved it. Now I need a boat.

Speaking of boats, I actually made $2.00 on Amazon from your clicks and purchases. Can you believe it? Well on my way to my boat purchase. Pete says I can now call myself a "paid" blogger. I've been working all night on seeing if I can update my page. There are (no kidding) at least 14,000 themes to choose from. First, I pick a theme and then I have to customize it and as some of you can tell I don't know what I'm doing. It's very tedious. I am such a work in progress, in many ways. I hope I live up to my $2.00 benefactors.

My family probably hates me as I've ignored them all night playing, I mean *working,* with this. I typically write these in the mornings/days but since I'm experimenting with new themes thought I'd get a jump on it. Cause I think I'm going to switch to a different theme tomorrow.

TUESDAY - SEPTEMBER 9 - A BUNCH OF NOTHIN'

Have you ever wondered what you'd be like if you were in high school today? Not like knowing what you know now, but given your same circumstances how you'd fit in with today's high school kids? Kids today don't seem like kids at all. The girls in particular seem years beyond their age. At least down here when I pick up Zoë after school that's what I'm seeing. Grown-ups. It got me to thinking, what would I be like if I was in high school today? Would I still be on the hippy side? Would I play sports? Sports was just not that big for girls back then. Band was such a big part of my life, and it was cool, wasn't it? Band today isn't cool like it used to be. What would I do? The focus on college is different today than in my day. I mean either you went or you didn't but it wasn't a "given" like it is today. Hopefully I would finish college the first time around if I had to do it again. But we sure couldn't afford it at today's prices. I know one thing, given the same family circumstances, I would not be able to keep up with the clothes. The fashion back then didn't seem to be such a focus as I recall. There weren't even very many stores to choose from. Or at least not in my world, i.e., the hip huggers, smoking in the bathroom, waiting for Howard to pick me up after school world. I wasn't really paying attention to too much back then, other than my high school boyfriend. He came to our high school as a junior. He was already through the dorky nose picking stage. Today it seems like the boys are a little dorkier longer (not my children granted). Maybe dorky is not the right word, maybe it's immature. Today's boys don't seem as sophisticated as the girls; unless they're in sports, then they look like they're 30 years old. Just something to think about cause that's what I do, think about stuff.

Know what else? Daytime TV is horrible. I've been fighting with my blog theme design trying to get a "good" one and I just turned the TV on to keep me company. I think it's the first time I've had it on during the day since moving here. How weird is that even? And other than *The Price is Right* it's just stoopid. Drew Carey looks unbelievably good though, doesn't he? I mean all that weight off. I wish *The Guiding Light* was still on. I've tried to get hooked on another daytime drama but I just haven't been able to. I think that's probably a good thing. I watched *Ellen*. She's cute and funny. I guess her show is okay. I prefer her over *Dr. Phil* anyway. Apparently, it's the season opener. Fall is here, isn't it? Can't wait for my night-time shows to start. Then I'll really have something to blog about!

Do I sound like a bored housewife or what? I'm scaring myself...where are those bon-bons?

I think the Gods were hearing my homesick prayers and they have given me two completely grey, dreary days. Those days are very unusual here. I remember how many grey days there are at home, in Pittsburgh. Really, I don't miss those days. They, those Gods, have been nice enough to cool it off a bit. This morning taking the girl to school it was almost refreshing. Refreshing is a bit of a stretch but we actually turned the air off in the car, and at the moment I have two windows open. (Sticker day!) One in the back of the house (without a screen) and one in the front of the house (with a screen), you know to get that cross breeze. The window thrill is very similar to the thrill you get in Pittsburgh after a cold winter and you can finally open the windows to get air in the house. Same thing, only it's after a long hot summer. I still prefer the long hot summer over a long cold winter. I know that for sure. Pete pointed out that I have the windows open *and* the AC on, to which I responded, "what's your point?" Then I looked around for ghosts as he was obviously channeling my dad.

I am a bit of a workaholic. That term doesn't apply to just working outside of the house. When I get onto something, especially on the computer, it is very hard to pull away. Like those stupid blog themes. I have been sitting for hours trying to get the right one, then getting frustrated and wanting to throw the computer into the pool (jk honey...jk) I remember when I was working from home back in the day, Jimmy would come to my desk and beg me to just turn the computer off. I'd be like "just one more thing honey, just one more..." It's a great attribute for employers, not so much for your family. I ended up apologizing to Jasen the other night as I promised to make cookies and then got stuck in PC blog theme hell. I finally dragged myself away to make the cookies and they were closing up going to bed. It's bad.

To keep balanced, I'm imposing a Tuesday lyming afternoon. Although now it's thundering, the breeze feels like heaven out there. I need to get away from the computer and read my book.

Tomorrow is volunteer orientation at Jasen's school. I'm very excited.

WEDNESDAY- SEPTEMBER 10 - THE NEVER-ENDING GUILT TRIP

Volunteer orientation is over...it was painful. I had quite the furrowed brow trying to follow along. As Janice would say I had the eleven's (think double lines in the forehead). I'll just say this. . there were a lot of very competent mothers in attendance willing, begging, to help with communication. We introduced ourselves. Most everyone has small children, a couple still had some in grade school, a couple with just middle school and/or high school and there was one other like me with grown children and then 2 step children who are twins in the 6th grade. I'm just grateful Jasen is in 8th grade and I didn't go back that far. I noticed I'm getting better as today's meeting didn't make me want to cry. I didn't miss my own boys and I didn't miss the retired life I thought I was going to have. I actually liked being at his school and hope to spend more time there. The school "halls" are outside. It's just different enough for me not to get homesick. It helps that it's a freakin GORGEOUS day here. I mean gorgeous. Today's day is why people love Florida. The school needs front office help. I can help in the mornings but I have to pick up the girl at 1:30. I can't do afternoons. But that's what I signed up for, morning office work.

Listen to this...yesterday it was pouring rain, POURING. I left what I thought was a couple of minutes early to pick up Zoë, you know, so she wasn't in the rain. I ran out without my phone but no big deal, right? Cause every day it's the same thing, I pick her up in the same spot. Except yesterday. She was not in the spot. I had to park so I wasn't that person holding up the line looking for her. I waited 45 minutes, got out of the car twice to look around, I mean it was really pouring, and then I just had to come home to find my phone so I could get her text messages (and phone calls). Ya know? I mean what are the chances? She had been waiting in a different spot and we just missed each other but really...the one day I leave my phone because I wanted to get there early and I didn't get her until 45 minutes later. Good grief...

Speaking of children; this whole work or stay at home mom thing, it's a familiar theme and certainly one that has permeated throughout my life. I'm still looking for full-time jobs, as even though I'm up to $6 on Amazon clicks it just doesn't seem like enough ya know? I mean I should contribute even if it's just for the trifecta (Judy's term for the cable bill), I want to have my own money, I need to pay for my plane tickets, but in no way are we starving and I have been home to Pittsburgh twice already and I have a free ticket (in points) for my next trip. It's not like I'm a prisoner here or anything, I have gotten back when I want to. But I do need insurances, I mean I do need some things. I don't know, it almost is a necessity on one hand. This morning before I left for the school meeting, I opened an application for a job at USF in St. Petersburg. It's a haul, like 25 miles, but whatever, thought I'd apply after the volunteer meeting. But at this meeting at one point, they became focused on the importance of stay-at-home moms and if you don't have to work you really shouldn't so you can be there for your kids and middle school and high school are really more important to stay home than grade school and blah blah blah. I mean really? REALLY? Is this a sign? Or is the sign that I get no response to my resumes "the" sign. Pete often says "get a clue" and perhaps my clue is to just stay put because it doesn't matter how many resumes I send out, I still get nuthin'. I was just flabbergasted at the familiar guilt over stay at home or working.

Back in "my" day I didn't have the choice but still managed to have that gut wrenching guilt over the issue anyway. I was able to be home many years when Jimmy entered middle school and Zachary was in high school. I used to say I was determined to be the first stay-at-home single mom and thanks to being able to work at home I was able to do it for a while. I didn't start working full time again, out of the house, until Jimmy was in 10th grade. Jimmy never could get the hang of me having to go to work and not being able to pick him up at a moment's notice for whatever reason. It still made me sad not to be there full time even though we all know he was fine. Zachary had very little stay at home time with me except when he was in high school – and then he probably wished I wasn't there all the time. I always had to work while raising him, but he had his grandma to watch over him. He is the smartest and wisest person on the planet. Apparently, me working out of the house didn't hamper him. Obviously, many many MANY children turn out fine when their parents work, but I don't know, these Clark kids have been through so much. Maybe since I *want* to be here maybe I should just wait and see what happens. Maybe I should close that USF application window. It is such a dilemma. I mean *really* a dilemma.

Maybe I can get that volunteer coordinator's position at the middle school. She only works ½ days (mornings)...that would be perfect for me. Whether the argument for working moms is right or wrong it has been a constant guilt trip for me since I was 24 years old (just a few short years ago). I thought at least those guilt days were over. Sheesh, I say,,,,sheeshh...and why?

That's my day today. I never got to lyming yesterday. I got stuck in blog theme hell again. I might run the sweeper later but I really do think I'm going to get outside and read today. I have some community stuff I can read that I found at the Middle School office. There's even a couple of advertisements for riding stables. Now how cool would THAT be? Maybe I can drag Zoë along and rope her into being a riding partner. (get it, rope her?)

K...gotta make beds (yes I'm still doing it). I even cleaned Jasen's dresser drawers yesterday. I started thinking to myself that I would clean my own kids dresser drawers so I should do his too right? Until he tells me to keep out, but right now he's thanking me. My thinking was and still is if they get used to things being nice then maybe they'll keep it up. I know it didn't work with my kids but whatever, I can dream.

THURSDAY - SEPTEMBER 11 - A DAY TO REMEMBER

And what does September 11 mean to you? First of all, it's 108 days since I moved here. Broken down 108 days can be converted to one of these units:

- 9,331,200 seconds
- 155,520 minutes
- 2592 hours
- 108 days
- 15 weeks (rounded down)

Pretty meaningless statistics. But a fun fact nonetheless. I don't know how many posts I have now since I've changed to this new blogging site. The old program would tell me, congratulations you've just posted your blah blah post. This one just says "done".

Although this is not a holiday the day does give me pause and I do remember vividly hearing the news on September 11. Undoubtedly that incident has changed our lives drastically. At the airports, going to sports event, I mean kids get thrown out of school for terroristic threats now while in the past that same infraction would have either been overlooked or they would have just been sent home. I remember running through the old Pittsburgh airport to catch my plane back to Miami in 1980 at the last possible second. Now if you change your flight plans at the last minute you get sent to "that" line. And remember when people used to greet you getting off the plane? That was nice (or embarrassing if you were being greeted by my brother and his wife.) I don't want to wallow in the event but I do remember it, tearily.

Its Thursday, supposed to be Lyming day. I think it was a one-time thing. I have been trying daily to get out there to no avail. I know I talk about it a lot but I never get to quite actually *do* it. Today was going to be *the* day, but between my niece Evan calling (she's a talker), the pool pump Kreepy Krawley thing not working, working with PNC to reduce those service charges since I don't have direct deposit anymore, and now it's time to get the girl. I always think I'll have time in the day but I never do. You working women, don't ever ask "what do you do all day? " to someone like me because the day just goes. Of course, maybe I should get up and stay up when I take Zoë to school at 7 am, but I'd be napping by 11...hmmm, well there's an idea anyway. Naps are good.

I'm still loving my new family. Yesterday Zo and I went to lunch after I picked her up from school. The weather was nice, I wanted to do something outside. We sat inside, (dam kids) but didn't matter, we were just girls chatting away. It was very nice. Date night was very nice last night. We took a picnic to the beach. Chipped ham on white bread and chips. Does it get any better than that? On the way to our beach picnic the heavens opened up and it poured, and I mean poured. We sat in the car and ate our sandwiches, chatting away, then once it stopped we sat out on a deserted beach and watched the lightning in the distance. Since we didn't get electrocuted, it was like heaven. Hopefully this will be a date night staple; although dinner out is nice too!

Both kids have tests today. I try not to care, but I do. Maybe we shouldn't have gone out the night before Jasen has a test. He needs help studying and we know he didn't crack a book without us here. Zo is ridiculously motivated. She wouldn't even know if we were here or not. We left them food; no one ate. Dam kids.

PS – I did apply for a job yesterday.

FRIDAY - SEPTEMBER 12 - MOVING ON

It's probably best that we don't even talk about it. It's just as well I'm not going into an office in Pittsburgh today; although historically the depression over a Steeler loss usually only lasts through the morning and then it's business as usual. I will just add that the officially signed Rocky Bleier terrible towel has been taken down.

Let's just move onto the weather shall we? It is getting cooler at nights here – down to like the high 70's. We need to get a solar cover if we want to continue using the pool for a month or two more. I think it would be nicer to have the pool in the cooler weather. Yesterday Pete asked if I was "in" the pool and I told him it was too hot. Ya know? It's more about the sun, when that sun is too hot I just don't want to be baking in it.

I'm watching the newest hurricane that is currently going over southern Florida. I'm not sure what effect it's going to have on.

Zoë and I followed through with our YMCA orientation last night. We go again tonight. Do you know they now tell you to do three reps of 10-12. Didn't it used to be two reps? WTF? Zoë has it all worked out, how fast we'll go on the treadmill each time and the percentages of the incremental increases. The downfalls of living with engineers, everything is in percentages. I'm not going to tell her yet that I'm old. Even the trainer last night was talking about how the machines are geared towards the "old" people, like I wasn't standing there. I decided he must think I'm not old, and well, I'm just going with it.

Both Florida kids are doing well at school. Jasen is doing really well in comparison to last year, and really well in general. Like mostly A's, so far. That's a relief and very encouraging. Zoë is doing well. She really has hard courses (or is it she has really hard courses?) She seems to be having fun though and talking more and more about friends. Maybe we'll even try going to a home football game tonight. She says the high school band is good. Pete and I, both old-time band members, will be the judge of that.

My northern boys are doing well too. Zachary is hard at work finishing his degree at Point Park. He works hard. Wish I still had the ability to view his grades, not that I expect anything less than an A, still. Jimmy is really excelling at his job. I don't want to jinx him though. Let's just say he's doing well and he's very happy. Jim is still pursuing the idea of visiting us here in Tampa and working out of the Tampa office while here. That way he doesn't have to take any vacation time. We need to get that guest room ready. I'm hoping after he does it once (visits and works) it'll seem easy and then he can visit more often. Florida kids will love that as they'll get more cookies; although there might be more fighting over them. Hmmm... Zachary won't be able to come for who knows when. Between going to school and working every blessed weekend who knows. I'll just keep going up there too. I hope I didn't miss all of fall and it's now winter up there. If that's the case we really do need to finish that guest room as I plan on and hope to get many phone calls from friends wanting to thaw out.

Well, I think that's enough blabbing for the day. It's a nice sunny day out there, not a whole lot planned. I cleaned the upstairs bathroom just a couple of days ago. I'm thinking maybe I really will get to that book.

Have a good weekend.

MONDAY - SEPTEMBER 15 - BLAH… PINCH ME…BLAH

Blah. Blah blah blah blah. . and then blah and more blah. That's what it sounds like in my head. I've gone from being boring, never doing anything, to being boring always on the go. We went out to eat, we went shopping, I applied to jobs. It's hot, it rains. . it rains hard, it's very hot.

However, there are moments recently when I do feel like pinching myself. I think it's finally sinking in that I'm here. I'm feeling it. One day while watering the flowers I was like "wow, look where I am" (to myself of course). At dinner the other night with the kids playing hangman on the paper placemat (and me losing terribly) it felt like I've been here forever and that was sort of a pinch-me moment too. Those moments, sort of like "aha" moments, seem to be creeping in more and more. Not that I don't still wonder if I'm going to end up moving back to Pittsburgh, or San Diego (I know, random, but after all it is beautiful in San Diego and not quite as hot), but the pinch-me moments seem to be becoming more frequent. And they're good pinch-me moments. Like "get outta town…look at me" moments.

Other updates include we are painting. As typically happens the paint on the walls looks nothing like the paint chip we picked out. It's not bad but not what we envisioned.

Zoë has been dragging my ass to the YMCA. We've had two orientations and tonight we get our full weight routine. We've been running on the treadmill for 20 minutes. Tonight, we might increase to 25 minutes. It's a start, and all I need. I'm running at a 4.1 pace. She's running at 5. I'm wearing a knee brace, an ankle brace and those Dr. Scholl's shoe lifts. Dam kids.

Zoë wondered if I ever talked about Sam (the dog) in my blog and sent me a picture to post. I'm glad she's interested in the blog.

Peter has taken the day off which is both very nice and sort of annoying. Annoying is not the right word because it is *very* nice, but he is certainly interrupting my flow, but only because I'd rather spend time with him than do my usual chores. I've slept in much too late, got nothing accomplished this a.m. and now he wants to go shopping. I'm picking up Zoë at 2 and then going to the YMCA at 4. We are looking at pianos. We went yesterday afternoon, had to drive pretty far away and then they weren't home. They want us to come back tonight. But I don't know, maybe we can wait until someone who lives closer is selling one. We did have a delicious lunch yesterday at a place on the water, after the rain, and it wasn't too hot! Love that.

Gotta run. Peter has a list. Tomorrow is volunteer day at the school (rescheduled from today due to his vacation day, see what I'm saying? My schedule is all off).

TUESDAY - SEPTEMBER 16 - STICKER DAY AND OUR NEW ADDITION

Sticker Day*... I put on work clothes and went to an office. I volunteered at the middle school from 10-1. Next week I'll go at 9:00 but today I didn't want to show up when all the action happens, it's too confusing. I think I have some new possible friends. I like the front office women. They're all my age-ish. Turns out I don't really have to wear "work" clothes. My new bff, Joan, also a volunteer, had on jean shorts, tank top and tennis shoes. I guess I do not have to adhere to the no sleeveless rule. I mostly observed what everyone was doing today. I dropped a call on the telephone. Put them on hold and had no idea where they went or how to get them back. Oh well. See? And I'm one of those mom's that blog about the incompetence of those people. But hey! I didn't really have proper training on the freakin switchboard. Yes Di, me on a switchboard. I hate phones, and I'm unclear about voice mail. They must have it right? I mean who doesn't have voice mail? But it's going to be okay. There are students that come every period (all day) and they are the ones that are supposed to check in guests at the front desk AND get the phones. It's an actual class for them. They get graded so we let them (make them) do it. There's one phone that if it rings no one is supposed to answer, we are just supposed to yell "WHITE

PHONE, WHITE PHONE". It doesn't seem like I'll have to deal with faculty. Just parents and staff. I think I can handle it for one half-day a week. I think... but you know how us crazy parents can be. I'll be begging to work with faculty again.

The biggest news is we have an addition to the family. Meet our newest flamingo, Frances. (Using an "e" is the proper female form of Francis/Frances) She came to live with us yesterday. We got her to not only give her a good home but to keep Fred company. I'm not sure if she's a bit loose; she has her leg up in the air, permanently. Is it a mating call? Not sure. Floozy. I'll talk to her about it later. Thanks for pushing us on the "mate" for Fred, Ja Nel. We think she is a grand addition. I know I said only males were "iron" and females were plastic but I was wrong. Clearly Frances is a female and made out of iron.

On the way to "work" (haven't said that for a while) I saw this bird in the neighbor's yard and thought perhaps they got their own Ethel. However, Ethel proved to be real. Sure looked fake, until she started crooning her neck. Strange birds here in paradise that's for sure. Although we have our share of normal birds too. We have a couple of blue jays and I saw a red cardinal the other day. We had this really cool bird feeder that I carried all the way from Virginia from the last time I was home. It's a bird house covered in birdseed. The birds can eat right off of the house. It was down on the ground and every last seed gone within 2 days. Dam squirrels. I don't know why we try. It's a nice thought to think we can feed birds but really we have only fed squirrels both here and in Pittsburgh.

Guest room/music room/den painting is coming along nicely. It would take just a little bit of time to put the second coat on the trim but I think it's going to wait for tomorrow. I have a pedicure appointment at 2:30 – and then tonight is Jasen's open house. Tomorrow is a better day to get the paint clothes on. It looks very very nice, even if the color is not what we expected. I'll be sad when all the furniture (i.e., boxes) go back in there.

*Sticker Day – think baby calendars and how you put stickers on big item days, like first time they roll over, first steps, first words, etc. Sticker day....

WEDNESDAY - SEPTEMBER 17 - THINGS I MUST COME TO TERMS WITH

I'm not really a good painter. I mean I can paint and I can paint a window without tape on the glass and do a pretty decent job, but I rush and I make mistakes. YES, there, I said it, I make mistakes. And sometimes they cause us all more work.

I am a messy painter. I get more paint on myself then one might think humanly possible. I guess it's better that it gets on myself than on the walls in the wrong spot but I wonder, how do I get it all over myself? I must come to terms with the mystery of the messy painter. I suppose it makes me more interesting to have a certain mystery about me. Probably not "this" mystery but it's a start.

Also, I can't make hardboiled eggs. I make really good deviled eggs, but I can't make them without the shell pulling off the egg and making the white part a mess. I have tried everything. Ice water, sitting for 20 minutes, I mean you name it I've tried it. I have to come to terms with I can't make hardboiled eggs. But if someone else can do the actually boiling part, I can handle the deviled egg part. I have been making really good deviled eggs. My secret ingredient? Celery seed. Yum, and now not secret.

I will never keep up with the dog hair, or Jasen's room. Mostly I can't keep up with Jasen's room because I haven't tried, he's 13, the dog sleeps in there and well he's 13. And I guess the #1 reason is,,, I don't want to. Is that bad? I think it should be the Papa's job. Don't you? I mean boys do boys room and I'll do Zoë's room. I think that's just the way it has to be. I have to come to terms with if that's the way it's going to be than that's the way it's going to look. I don't have to go upstairs.

And last but not least, I will never be 5'7 and weigh 120.

Other than that, I tried to finish painting the guest room/music room/den this morning, which went into the afternoon. I think I've done a bad enough job that Pete won't expect me to do it again. I'm just like the kids. The paint wasn't going on very well. I don't know if it's the paint or the 9000% humidity today. But it was very sticky. Still looks lovely though.

We had a good night at Jasen's open house last night. Very crowded. I like all the teachers. He had a lot of acknowledgements from different friends throughout the night. Seems like he's fitting in quite nicely. And his grades are still good. How about that? I had to punch Pete in the arm cause he was going to say something bad about one teacher. Doesn't he know that kids pick up EVERYTHING the parent says? I feel bad though. I think I hit him pretty hard. Does that make me abusive? I mean I didn't really *mean* to hit him hard but I wanted him to shut up before he said too loudly that the teacher was stupid. It's all that working out at the YMCA and my new-found strength. Maybe I need therapy. Well, I know I need therapy, that's a given.

Tonight is date night. We're going to look at a piano and then out to dinner back near our favorite beach. I'm not sure if the rain will stop long enough for us to walk on the beach but nevertheless we are headed that way. Hopefully we will get a game of billiards in as well. It's been awhile since we've had a competition.

And that reminds me, something that Peter must come to terms with…. I AM NOT A PIANO MOVER. There I said it. I am NOT moving a piano, but I do hope we get one tonight for the new room!

Okay that's it. Gotta run. Gotta get the girl, make Jello for the boy (I've been promising) clean up myself and various drop cloths used in painting. It's garbage night…I mean the chores are endless. There's a lot to be said for hired help.

THURSDAY - SEPTEMBER 18 - MEET THE CHAIR

We have a new addition! A new chair. And because we bought this chair we got a Piano to go with it!!

We're pretty happy. It looks good. Needs tuned but really that's it. We hope. Pete has to pick it up this weekend, rent a truck and hopefully recruit some neighbors to unload. The people we bought it from will help load. Please refer to yesterday's post, which I will restate: I AM NOT A PIANO MOVER.

But, apparently, I am a cleaner. I have been cleaning up the new room all morning. You might think it's easy but that's because you didn't see all the paint splatters on the wood floor. I Googled the solution and luckily came up with using rubbing alcohol, which I happen to have a plethora of. I have mint rubbing alcohol now the room smells good too. I vacuumed, then I dust mopped, then I scraped up paint, then I washed with the Shark thingy and I'm waiting for that to dry then I can dry mop again and pick up loose paint chips that the alcohol got up then I'm going to try polishing with my Shark cleaner.

All this on what is supposed to be Lyming day. My boyfriend turns out to be a task master. I'm not sure what part of "I'm a prima donna" he doesn't get. I must be in the wrong house because I'm pretty sure that's what I was promised. If not promised it was at least implied. I'm not only living with strangers; I'm living with liars!! (Everyone knows I'm teasing right? Tongue in cheek stuff? Since only people I know read this I'm assuming I don't have to explain...but just in case...)

FRIDAY - SEPTEMBER 19 - ST. ANTHONY ARE YOU LISTENING?

You know that feeling you get when you lose something that you just saw a minute ago? I have spent the whole morning...practically the whole morning...looking for this index card with the name of a website on it. I put the index card ON my computer the other day. I knew exactly where it was and today I thought I had time to look at the site.

Instead of spending my time looking at the site I have spent the entire morning looking for the card with the address of the website. I've gone through the garbage twice, I've gone through papers on my desk at least three times, another basket three times, my desk drawers, the floors, under my bed, my purse, and I've prayed to St. Anthony. *PLEASE St. Anthony something is lost and can't be found, please St. Anthony look around.*

St. Anthony has never let me down, except when the thing is lost for good. I know how important that card was to me. I can't imagine throwing it away, but I think sometimes I am on such auto pilot and I do a swipe and things end up in the garbage that shouldn't be there. I am inundated with papers again. Kids and schools tend to do that. We've already discussed magazines. I hope to become closely acquainted with the paper shredder this weekend.

Speaking of St. Anthony, I'm not Catholic; however, I do like a Catholic church. Sometimes you just have to hit-your-knees and a Catholic church is a good place to do that, for me. Other churches are typically locked during the day. Plus, in the Catholic church (in my experience) nobody bugs you. You just go in. Between my Carlow Catholic theology education and taking Jimmy through the Catholic system (is it called a system?) I do feel a little affinity towards the Catholic faith. I'm nothing like my hard-core Catholic friends and I don't go up for communion. I believe you burn in hell for that don't you? If you're not Catholic? At least that's what my dad used to say. Anyway, we have a lot of churches down here. There seems to be a church on almost every block but none are Catholic. I Googled Catholic churches and there is one a few miles away that I might try to find someday. But until then I'll just have to wait to hit-the-knees, which is a good thing because I can't kneel on that left one anyway. Hopefully St. Anthony is not holding that against me.

Gotta take Zoë back to Leslie's today after school. It's a haul and it's supposed to rain, hard. I hate driving in the rain. I think I hate it more than the snow. The hard rain down here ponds along the road. It's just a mess and scary. I believe we are getting remnants of some hurricane that has been coming all along the southern states, like Arizona, Texas and back into the Gulf and it's going to hit as soon as I'm on the road. Anyway, I have that to look forward to. Jasen is still home. Says he's throwing up and whatnot. Stomach flu sounding. OR he has a test. Whatever the reason he's upstairs sleeping. The Maze Runner movie is out this weekend. If he is miraculously cured at movie time we shall probably know for sure.

We started to put the new room together, okay Pete started putting the room together last night. Our house is looking nice again. We (okay "he") moved some things around. It looks *really* nice. I started a little fall decorating this morning. I actually found my fall/Halloween decorations. I got started but then distracted with that index card and then figured I'd blog just to distract myself even further. It's such a nice gray soon to be rainy day. Would be great to sit on the couch in our nice clean house and look at that website. Stupid card.

MONDAY - SEPTEMBER 22 - IT'S STARTING. . THE NEW FALL LINEUP

If I thought I was busy before, I need to think again. All my shows are back on. And with the Steelers playing Sunday well I'm already behind. GO STEELERS!!! And wasn't that a great game? The boys donned their Steeler garb. Apparently, this was the magical arrangement to ensure victory.

Today I have to catch up on *The Good Wife*, and did *Once Upon a Time* start? And now there's a new show that they are all waiting for me to watch, *Scorpion*, but I'm trying to write a little of this blog and finish last night's *Good Wife*. I'm actually almost a day behind on the blog. I thought I'd catch up tomorrow but I have to "work" at the school and then Zoë and I are supposed to start our regular YMCA workout routine after school, then it's time for dinner. I'm just behind.

The weekend was productive. We bought some new things for the house. Like palm tree pillows for the couch, new everyday silverware, and he brought the piano home. Do I have pictures of these items? Not yet. Why? Because if I go out there to the living room to take pictures, well I'm just not going to do it. It's nice family time for them without me. Everyone fights to sit next to their Papa. It's better if I stay out of it.

I'm settling in more and more. It feels like home more and more every day. I still call Pittsburgh home but now when I say it I think about it. Like it almost doesn't sound right. Jimmy sent me a text the other day and said he would call me on his way home. I thought he meant Sewickley; he was referring to his apartment in Columbus. Look at that, we're all getting settled.

I'm not gonna lie though – I do need some alone time. I mean I LOVE my Pete time and I never tire of spending time with just him but I do need a break from the bickering of the family. There's a lot of dynamics going on. The combo of just Me and Pete is a great dynamic. Me and Jasen are mostly good. Me and Zoe are great. Jasen and Pete can be tense. Zoe and Pete are usually great. Zoe and Jasen are HORRIBLE. And the four of us are somewhere in the middle. Pete will get mad when I remove myself from them and hide back in the bedroom but seriously, I know myself. And I know I can't handle that Clark dynamic all the time. Well anyway, all is well I'm just giving you a report.

TUESDAY - SEPTEMBER 23 - I'M DMV OFFICIAL – FINALLY FLORIDA GIRL

Such a big sticker day today! I got up (that's always a good sign), put on "work" clothes, which is kinda nice since I still have them, went to the DMV and didn't even have to wait, got to sit right down AND, I have a new Florida license plate! GO ME! I'd take a picture but I don't know if that's a smart security move on the web and all. But I will say this, it's the same style as Pete's (I know, cute huh?) and the first three letters are FFG –Finally Florida Girl. I mean really.... is that meant to be or what? AND, the fee was about $80 less than I expected. She said the rates went down September 1. See that? How fortuitous of us to procrastinate. Now I just need a Steeler border thingy-do. Really is there anything that Amazon does NOT sell?

Then I went off to work. It was an observing day today because there was yet another volunteer Joan was training. It's anti-bullying week and everyone was supposed to wear black today. Luckily, I had on black. Chances of wearing black to work on any given day are pretty high. Even here in Florida. Which is another question...can I wear linen year-round? I'm going to go with a yes. But do I hear any opposition out there? I still don't think I can do white after Labor Day. It's just too far in my blood to not do it. However, I will observe my colleagues and students and see what is acceptable here but it's not feeling very "white" these days with all this rain.

The rain has not let up. The weatherman is saying rain for another TEN days! I do hope they are wrong but I'm not sure if they will be. If not I will have my space heater at the ready. I already am sitting in front of it with it on. I am known for always having my heater on.

Here's a cute story, when I was moving here and worried about my kids and their mom not having her own home Jimmy assured me that the only thing that made him feel at home was me...and a space heater. Obviously, I will always have a space heater.

My brother sent me an email this morning saying he was all cozy in front of his heater and taunting me saying I wouldn't get those chilly mornings...ha,,,,think again. Actually, I'm surprised this is the first it's been on. Of course, now I'm having a hot flash, but none the less, it's on.

I'm going to have to start coming up with something interesting to say. With getting settled in here there's not a whole lot new to talk about. I clean (usually) I pick up kids, now going to the Y, I cook (sometimes), I blog, I run errands.... it rains.... I love my boyfriend, the kids are good, the dog is hairy, I mean I need to step it up a little. I will give it some thought.

Oh, I know, I do have a *paying* job, October 11. I got called for Jury duty! I lived in PA 50+ years, called to Jury duty once in my entire life, down here 3 months and wham gotta go. It's okay though. It'll give me something to blog about. Changing the names to protect the innocent and all. Hey, maybe I'll start a book (like write a book) about the case. Or I'll just read a good book while I wait and get sent home at noon. For one day it's $15 – more than three days it's $30 a day. There ya go. Something to look forward to. Gotta go get the girl.

WEDNESDAY - SEPTEMBER 24 - TO HONE OR NOT TO HONE

Ok let's pretend for a minute that I wanted to be a writer, I mean I do write, but what if I wanted to officially be a writer. They kinda do what I do. Write during the day. They probably have better content but hey, ya know, we all start somewhere. I joined this Aspiring Writers Group on LinkedIn and spent a couple of minutes reading some of the posts, because honestly I *hate* sitting at the computer all day. I'd do better to print all those posts and take them outside and read them. But then that's not eco-friendly is it. In reading one of the articles about being a better writer it said something like "one must *read*, as well as write, to be a good writer" and I listened. In my attempt to be a better writer I went outside this morning and sat by the pool and read my book! Yes I did! There's a lot of great things about that.

1. It's not raining. It has now clouded up but there was some sun-shine out there this morning
2. It's not hot. It's like, how do you say it. . *nice*, and,
3. There's plenty of inside work to be done, but really when isn't there plenty of inside work to be done. When? And I am guilt free about my decision.... almost.

Unfortunately, between being on hold cancelling my PA car insurance, waiting for Sam to be settled (I believe he was trying to get out of the fence so then I had to find a rock to make it more secure) then I needed a cup of tea, THEN I thought I better eat something, THEN I read about 5 pages and fell asleep. But I did get to read, by the pool. Three cheers for me.

Depending on the girl I might even go back out there this afternoon. She may want to drag me to the Y again. It's pitiful because I should be the one dragging her, but believe me if she doesn't want to go I'm not going to push it. She had me do 125 sit-ups with her yesterday. I hung but OMG. We were talking about some sort of measurement of our progress. I still refuse to get on a scale and I thought twice about measuring myself before and after. She suggested before and after pictures. At that horrifying thought I said I'll just wait and see if I can get in a smaller pant size to measure my success. I think the best measure would be to try to keep running some 5K's. But for now, I'm struggling getting through one mile on the treadmill. She says I motivate her to keep going on the treadmill but unfortunately it's not working the other way around. I convince myself there is no way I can keep up with a 15-year-old and then immediately give up and starting walking on the treadmill. I know, it's bad.

Zoë needs some things at the mall. She's such a girl. This is totally out of my element, but much fun. She needs some makeup and a couple of things, at the mall. And then what's really different is I get money to take her! I mean it's all good. Seriously if I had a daughter I would hope she was like Zoë, super smart, motivated, ambitious, musically talented, and of course pretty, with minimal makeup. She has the nice balance of wearing jeans and a t-shirt and looking adorable in size 4 dresses, which she never wears but owns anyway. I'm thankful that she's not one of those Kim Kardashian girls that I wouldn't have any idea what to do with and who would certainly be embarrassed by me and my daily t-shirt dresses. I am hoping the mall trip trumps the YMCA but maybe we can do both. Should I be the leader and tell her we can do both? I hate being the leader.

Then tonight is date night. Not sure what we're doing. But I will attempt to look cute.

And this (all this running around) is why I feel no guilt when I take some time to read by the pool, honing my craft (which is either napping or writing). I am awaiting inspiration from the Gods as to "what" to write about. In the meantime, whilst I wait, I shall ramble on about nothing, because apparently I'm good at that. Rambling comes very easy for me (unlike sit-ups).

THURSDAY - SEPTEMBER 25 - ANOTHER DAY IN PARADISE

Now I'm pissed. Ya know, I am typically a pretty calm reasonable person...to a point. But once I reach that point that reasonableness goes to the back burner. So, you know, I'm emailing Jasen's teachers to make sure he doesn't fall through the cracks. Sometimes as a parent/guardian you need to stay on top of it you know? Especially when they need it. I've been nice but now I'm done being nice. I am getting one-word answers. I ask three questions; I get one short answer to one of the questions. Now I'm pissed and straight to "enough of the one-word answers, when can we meet. " I should add "don't piss me off" – but she seems to be a formidable woman. I'm not a 'scared of her though. I can be formidable too. This is where working in the front office might just help me out if I can't get a meeting with this woman. Anyway, that's the start to today. The adrenaline is pumping, which should make Peter happy because now I will probably clean the bathroom.

I'm having a bad living-in-Florida day today. There was a bug in our bedroom last night and I just killed another. Doesn't it seem like I bug bomb ad nauseum? This bug was seen in broad daylight. . which made it easier cause they are slower in the daytime. But still, that's two too many. I thought my Moon Township apartment and its plethora of bugs would have prepared me for this but these bugs are just big.

Luckily the adrenaline built up by the stupid teacher made it easy to smash it but the fact that it's here at all is annoying to say the least. I looked at an article on the web that said "You will not enjoy your life in Florida if you can't stand these insects. Palmetto Bugs are just an inescapable part of Florida lifestyle". I guess the good news is they are not harmful, they don't bite, just nasty. They like hair, which mine is everywhere as is Sam's and they like paper. Three fourths of our house is books. I guess they find our house a slice of heaven. To which I say, *heavy sigh.*

And about these frogs.... Zoë was sitting at lunch – at an outside table – and a fellow student tapped her on the shoulder and suggested she move herself as there was this monstrous frog by her foot. Turns out these frogs are called Cane frogs. They are not native to Florida but were introduced in 1936 to help control some sugar cane bug and then 100 of them were accidentally released in Miami at the airport in 1955. And they are poisonous. Not that they would kill humans but their toxins do kill pets. To which I say again, *Heavy sigh.*

The weather man last night said not to expect temperatures in the 50's until late October or early November. Not sure I'll ever want to open windows (because of bugs). Maybe I'll move to the 20th floor of some condo building. Right after I make that million. I will say the lack of bugs in my Pittsburgh apartment never went unnoticed. But the lack of air circulation in that apartment was not unnoticed. Nothing and nowhere is perfect I suppose.

Well, I think it's time to set off a bug bomb in the bedroom. Seems like I've done that bug bombing a lot. I'll just pack a little bag, stay out by the pool (it's not raining yet) and cry. I'm sure tomorrow will be a better day. I'll bounce back. Not every day can be perfect right? Even in paradise.

FRIDAY - SEPTEMBER 26 - FINALLY FLORIDA...FINALLY

As predicted I have bounced back from my woe-is-me day. Typically, I do bounce back quickly or I would be living under a bridge by now.... in Pittsburgh, perhaps the Birmingham Bridge as that is closest to my boy...wonder if he would bring me food...and blankets.

Anyway, a beautiful day today. The sun is shining, it's 75 beautiful degrees. Humidity feels low. This is the Florida I remember; THIS is the Florida I love! Finally! I even had my sunroof open in the car this morning. First time since moving here, I think. I've been up running around, running errands in the sunshine, which helps the mood. Two trips to the High School and then off to Home Depot. I think I might be part man; although that's sort of a sexist attitude. I went to pick up a couple small paint items and all the customers in the paint aisle were women. But anyway, I love Home Depot. I love all the gadgets. I love looking at all the different paints, and tiles, carpets, I mean even the faucets. I limited my visit to what I needed today but still I just love it. I love the whole vibe. I remember remodeling my house and how fun it was.... maybe not "fun" but the process of remodeling is very creative and fulfilling. Especially when it looks nice. Does anyone remember when I was married to Dennis and he hand made those beautiful cabinets for our kitchen and painted them red because I wanted them to look like Jerry's cherry cabinets in her kitchen? And then I HATED it. I remember crying and crying because I felt bad that he worked so hard. But then he painted them white and we absolutely loved that kitchen. When I was painting my dining room in the Fair Oaks house, I remember buying green paint and it wasn't quite right and in the end dumped two gallons together to make my own color and voila...loved that room color too. Then when moving out of that house I had to paint the boys back bedroom and I just pulled whatever colors I had left over in the basement and did some sort of faux painting with a double roller to use up the paint and cover the imperfections. The boys loved it. And I thought it was a hack job. Anyway, good memories go with home improvements and we are doing that here too, even though we are renters, we still "live" here. We are going to keep painting the downstairs this weekend. It's going to be something though because these rooms are furnished. We're going to keep going with the color that we have because we bought so much of it but for the hallway we're going to throw some white in it and brighten it up. I am sure it's going to look beautiful. The biggest concern will be keeping the dog out of the room.

I'm meeting the BF for lunch today. Very exciting. I love having a lunch date with my man. It's like a mini date night. Time alone, away from the house and kids. A little slice of heaven. I get to drive across the bridge and see the water on my way there. Sometimes all I need is to see the water to remember that I'm in Florida, finally.

OCTOBER 2014

WEDNESDAY - OCTOBER 1 - HUMP DAY

You know there's a lot of a nutty crime in Florida. Nutty is probably not the right term. Tragic is a little more like it. There's the man who shot a car full of kids because the music was too loud. Said he feared for his life? No one in the music car had a weapon. Remember the man who shot someone in the movie theater for texting? I guess there are tragic stories everywhere, I know there are. This morning there was a "noise" and the dog perked right up. I wasn't afraid but I was certainly happy to see the dog become alert. I often comment/complain about that dog's powerfulness but today I'm feeling pretty good about it. He can't keep the squirrels away but perhaps any possible intruder will think twice. Thankfully, the noise turned out to be nothing.

Let's see, yesterday we met with Jasen's math teacher. She said he is a JOY to have in her class. Always participates and is typically correct. Pete thinks he has a "bad" kid. I had to dig up Jimmy stories. Mainly Jimmy/Jeffrey stories. Jasen just seems to have test anxiety. He's not talking incessantly to his neighbors, he's not-not paying attention, and we haven't even had to pick him up off the floor of Thrift Drugs wrestling with his friend. He is not a bad kid. Jimmy was not a bad kid either. But not sure I would ever try to pass him off as being a good kid in school. He's a good kid in general but school, it's not for everybody. However, hearing that report on Jasen was great.

After the meeting I went downstairs and did my volunteer stint in the front office. It's okay. I don't love it but it's okay. I think I'm just too new and don't know who anybody is and heaven forbid I have to use that stupid walkie-talkie, but I know I will at some point. There's always some physical plant type person coming in that wants to find Ernesto. Ernesto is only available by walkie-talkie.

After my morning there I headed to St. Petersburg for an interview. Does anybody remember the blog where I was torn between applying for jobs anymore and having that application open before going to the volunteer meeting? Well anyway, it's that job that actually called me in for an interview. Just an interview, but still first one I've had since the first week I moved here. It would be a good fit for me, except that it's 25 miles one way, one hour with *no* traffic. Logistically a nightmare. A far cry from walking two blocks. But we won't go there yet. The campus is beautiful. It's on the water. Point Park is on/near the water (the Ohio River). But the boats are quite different.

Yesterday was busy. Up and dressed, like actually work dressed, new outfit and all, sitting in an office from about 9:00 to 3:00 – stopping at Costco, coming home unloading and then out to get thank you cards, by way of Pier One, Ross Dress for Less and then finally Publix. I picked up these cute plates. How could I resist? This is why I need a job. I mean income...I don't really need a "job" (incase God is listening and wants to grant my wishes) But whatever.

The weather is hot and humid today. On Sunday we are supposed to be down in the 60's at night. The weather predictors say our rain will be over after Saturday. We shall see. Right now, it's like a swamp out there. Sam ran outside when I was throwing a bug out the side door. I didn't get to the paws in time.

Time to get the girl. We will get to the Y and then it's date night. Someone in the house is having their 16th birthday this weekend so it's actually mall night for our date. That's okay too. There will be a nice dinner in there I'm sure.

THURSDAY - OCTOBER 2 - I THINK I CAN. . I THINK I CAN

Guess what I did this morning? Go ahead guess. My sister (Kerry) hates when I do that because really what's the point of asking the other person to guess. I get it. I'll tell you. I LYMED. Yep I did, and I might get back to it after this update. My book, *The Boys in the Boat*, that I've been reading over a month is due back this weekend. I have been lax at reading it even though I love it. Even this morning I read a bit but still

I fell asleep. I can't help it. I'm going to power through and see if I can get through it by Saturday. I guess I could renew it but it's a goal that I've decided I must achieve.

I don't have a lot of goals these days. I'm going to the YMCA and a good goal would be to lose weight and fit into *any* of my old clothes, ANY one of them, but I'm okay with buying new. I know it's bad isn't it? I know to lose weight I have to quit eating a lot of the food that I've fallen back into eating. Bread and dessert, not to mention eating out. I can't believe how I eat these days. It took me years to eat like a good "foodie" and only months to fall back into making and *eating* brownies, because well the kids need a treat. It's bad. There is this one sweater dress (yes sweater dress in Florida) in the window of New York and Company at the mall and every time I walk past it I say my goal is to wear that, and look good in it. Did I pass on dessert on date night? Nope.

I made this big pot of soup last night and nobody ate it. Jasen said he was sick of soup. Really? Dam kids. I accidentally left it on the stove all night. I'm going to eat some now and if I don't get poisoned I'll freeze it for another time. If only I would reach for the soup instead of the cookie.

We had a nice date night, as usual. We went to the mall to play Birthday Claus for the girl. It was fun. They opened a new massage place and offered a 1-minute sample. I went for it. It was great. Next week for date night I'm begging him to get foot reflexology together and then I want to see the movie *Gone Girl*. Anybody else seeing it? I can't wait. It looks creepy but since I read the book I'll know not to get tooo creeped out. And I like Ben Affleck. I don't know why he has such a bad rap. I like him.

The house needs cleaned as I'm not totally sure if we're having company tomorrow. I am surprised that I am reading (and blogging) instead of dusting, but sometimes you just have to be in the mood to clean and I'm not. Maybe after the YMCA I'll feel motivated but around 4:00 today I am leaving the house. We had a major breach this a.m. Zoë took Jasen's potato chips to lunch with her. Figures the one day he wants to take lunch she took them. I expect a full-on blood bath when he gets home. I've decided to let them kill each other. It's above my pay-grade. Perhaps I could negotiate combat pay but I'd rather go shopping. Maybe I'll take myself and get my own reflexology. Then come home and clean up the aftermath.

Wish I had something insightful to share but I got nuthin. Well wait, I did have another call for a phone interview for next week for a different job. Look at that. Two calls after months of nuthin. That's not nuthin, not particularly insightful though. Since no one is beating down my door, or sending me frantic emails to write for them I have hopes that something will come about soon. Preferably lottery winnings but Di, you'll be happy to know, I'm not really living in my head anymore. Sort of living in the moment these days. I'm not sure what I like better. It's just that when I was living in my head the possibilities were endless. I have most of the things I dreamt about, a good boyfriend, living in Florida, I'm not starving (obviously). Honestly I think all those years of living in my head has burned me out for more living in my head. Besides as I've said ad nauseam, who would have guessed that my life would be what it is. Maybe what I've learned is to just let it go and see what happens. Because really I would have never dreamed this up.

On that note, I'm going back out to read. 200 pages by Saturday. Can I do it? Can I? Biggest decision of the moment is do I read inside or outside by the pool?

MONDAY - OCTOBER 6 - A TINY GREEN TOMATO

My friend Larry once said to me it was like I had two lives. One pre "me" (the Miami lost days) and then there was me the mom/single mom, living in Fair Oaks, with those boys I often speak about (and the dogs). I guess now I'm on life #3. I often talk about how much I miss my boys and although the sadness is getting less and less there are days when I can't stop crying because I miss those days, that house, those boys, those dogs very very much. And I miss my neighbors Mike and

Frieda. I have always had some good neighbors. I had the Dullias who lived next door when I was married to Dennis; Donna, Bobby and the girls lived next to us in Victory Terrace and Mike and Frieda in Fair Oaks. One of the things that kept us close, what we had in common was what grew in our yards. I had raspberries that Mrs. Dullias and I shared over the fence. Mike and Frieda in Fair Oaks shared our love of our gardens in our tiny postage stamp sized yards. I will never forget Frieda's delight every spring when she planted the garden and then later when the beans would come in or she got a good tomato. It was always reason for a screech of great delight. She was happy and I was happy for her. My kids probably remember (hopefully remember) when I would make dinner and always specify if something was from the garden. It was mac and cheese and *green beans from the garden*! I actually grew corn back there too. Corn right off the stalk is sooo good. One particularly good year I was out picking broccoli with a flashlight around Thanksgiving. I have lots of pictures of my garden back then.... if only I could find my pictures.

Living in Florida, in the summer, with no farmers market is a huge transition. Gardening is really in my blood. From my grandparents who had a huge garden and canned everything to my mother who was always mad that we didn't help her in her very large garden, to every house I've ever had I've always had a garden. Living down here in the summer when produce should be abundant, and is not, is quite the transition and leaves a bit of a void. Bigger than I would have thought. However, just the other day I was driving down the street and saw someone planting a garden. Then I overheard a couple of people talking in the grocery store about having time to get their plants in and then today I found a tiny green tomato on our tomato plant.

The void of the summer just may possibly be filled with the abundance of the Fall into Spring in Florida. Just as the northern farmers markets begin to wind down, the St. Petersburg farmers market started this past weekend. I've been there several times on previous visits and can't wait to get back there. Maybe even this next weekend we'll try planting seeds.

We all have bad days and today was another one for me but after I saw that green tomato my whole demeanor changed. Maybe today's lesson for myself was to remember what really matters. Maybe it's about the possibilities, maybe it's about the start of growing season, maybe it's the start of my growing into my life #3 or just remembering Mike and Frieda and the best of Victoria #2, I don't know but I'm loving that tomato. I'm used to the growing season being in Spring. Now I have to get used to growing season being in the Fall and Winter. Hey, maybe it's symbolic about me being in the Fall of my life? Maybe there's a really cool transition growing season coming up in my personal life? It's a lot to read into a tiny green tomato. But what the heck, it's the kind of mood I'm in. Just imagine what I could read into our lemon tree coming back from the dead.

TUESDAY - OCTOBER 7 - BELATED BIRTHDAY POST

If I write my update/posts in the evening and I know most of you don't read it until the next day do I then wait and post in 2 days? Or should I keep writing at night? What are the rules? So many decisions. I think I just need to do it when the mood strikes, and when I have time.

I'm half watching *Jeopardy* and Vanna White as I write this. Can you imagine having Vanna's job for as many years as she has? and *still* looking that good? The longest I've ever had a job is 8 years. I don't know what that says about me. It actually doesn't say much since 90% of my jobs ended in reorganization and/or just plain businesses closing. I started to think I was a jinx as any company I worked for went belly up about 2 years after I started. Typically, I was there until the bitter end which is actually a cool process in itself, but I am jealous of those people who stay with one place for 30 years and retire. There are people younger than me doing that. RETIRING! It's heartbreaking that retiring is something that I will never be able to realize this life time, well I mean I'll get social security but you know, not like *retiring* retiring. But then again, that's pretty rare these days anyways. So is hitting the lottery. I can rule out retiring but I don't have to rule out hitting the lottery.

Speaking of work, I had another interview today. Phone interview. Got a follow-up to last week's interview too. Also tried another couple of income revenue ideas and volunteered at the school this a.m. I'm already feeling a little more comfortable at the middle school. Taking messages, running around. Next week I'll be Principal. Okay that might be a stretch. But something is going to happen. I can feel it.

Other than that, all is status quo. Florida kids are good. Weekend birthday celebrations were lovely. We now have a 16-year-old. She hasn't gotten her permit yet. What's up with that? Down here they can get their permit at 15. Not like my boys who were in line the morning of their 16th birthday. She'll get on it I'm sure. She went to a friend's 16-year-old bday party at some swanky place over the weekend as well and had a wonderful time. All in all, I think she's pretty happy. We got some more painting done in time for a couple of birthday get-togethers. I actually started painting Saturday at 2 in the afternoon and ended at 11:30 that night, without help. I mean that's a long time isn't it? Sometimes I wonder if I'm just the hired help. If so, I need a raise.

MONDAY - OCTOBER 13 - PICTURE DAY

The weekend was nice, as usual. The girls back home in Sewickley, Skyped me in on Friday night for Bunko. That was a lot of fun. I really felt like I was there, getting caught up on almost everyone and just listening to the B.S. It was a great idea. I was exhausted afterwards. I haven't been around that much activity/chatter since I moved here. Even if I did just sit there the whole time from 1,000 miles away.

On Saturday my boyfriend woke me up and suggested we go to the beach. WOO HOO! And we did! I redeemed my transgression of the snack wrap from McDonalds from the night before with a delicious and hopefully healthy breakfast from this French place we like to go to. Quiche and fruit crepe. Yum. Then we walked over to the beach, just steps away from the restaurant. A couple of minutes in the water, because it's already cold, at least cold for Peter, a nice long walk and that was it for the day. Then we drove over to pick up Zoë in South Tampa where she had spent the night at a friend's house and then back home by like 5:00. It was a long, hot, sunny, Florida kind of day.

On Saturday night we went to downtown Palm Harbor for Rocktoberfest, featuring Michael Allman who is Gregg Allman's son. I was hoping for a surprise guest appearance by Gregg but he was a no-show. Michael Allman lives right near here in New Port Richey and his band does mostly cover Allman Brothers songs. They were good. They weren't the Allman Brothers, but they were good. Then we walked up to our favorite little café that I've previously mentioned, Witches Brew, and listened to another band before calling it a night. It was a long lovely night added onto our long lovely day.

On Sunday, when I wanted to rest from the long lovely Saturday, Peter was digging out, and rediscovering a lot of Halloween decorations. He's quite the Halloween enthusiast/decorator. After dinner him and the girls made houses from kits I bought them at Michael's. It was craft night. Pretty darn cute. I painted a magnet. And we haven't even put out Marcus the Carcass yet! I can only imagine what the pumpkins will be like. He even has a smoke machine somewhere.

I cleaned Jasen's room a little. I know, I know, but really he's not even fully unpacked yet. I was trying to work some magic in there. Slowly we'll get there. Then the girl and I are going back to the "club", i.e., the YMCA. Well, "I'm" going back there with or without her. We took the entire week off last week. Me because of my back and her because of my back. Time to get back on the wagon. She just told me she's not going...will I be disciplined enough to go without her? Will I? Will I?

TUESDAY - OCTOBER 14 - AWAITING INSPIRATION

I was reading Facebook while waiting for my inspiration to write my update today. I saw a great video of a groom and his groomsmen dancing at their wedding – A little boy dancing to Dirty Dancing and doing all of Patrick Swayze's moves – Lots of sayings about Today, God and Botox being great; dumping those that don't love us; we should put pedophiles who harm children to sleep like we put dogs to sleep that harm children; and not a whole lot nice about Obama and Ebola. The funniest today is Ellen inserting herself into a commercial with Matthew McConaughey. She's funny. Facebook has become what? I can't even put a name to it. I'm not going to unsubscribe though because I still love looking at everyone's pictures (and really some of the stuff is very funny). Jimmy posts some pics, Evan posts the babies sometimes, and look at Lucy getting married! ! But since I don't get on there often I miss a lot, like I was a couple of weeks late learning about Tony and the murder thing. I mean that's pretty serious. Murder and all... I should post more but since I have this blog I feel like posting on Facebook would be repeating myself. I mean really I get tired of rambling on about myself and I'm really not going to do it twice. Looking through Facebook sure is a way to waste a day, and not get your blog done.

Right now, it looks like the end of the world out there. It's DARK, it's pouring and bad storms are coming (at least they are coming here) and we have a chorus concert at 7 when the worst of the storms should be going right over us. We will be soaked walking into it. I am learning what shoes I can and can't wear. Flip flops will kill me as they are too slippery. Everything else will get ruined. I know, rain boots! I better go dig them out and then maybe add some new ones to my wish list. I dropped Zoë off two hours earlier as they have to rehearse. The rain was blowing sideways. She has two hours to dry off.

That's it. I'll report on chorus concert tomorrow. I'm looking forward to it!

WEDNESDAY - OCTOBER 15 - VIVA MIAMI

Leslie brought over a couple of pumpkin bread loaves the other week when she came for Zoë's bday. They were delicious. I ate with abandon. Or is it "without" abandon. In any case I just kept eating it, with cream cheese. I asked the BF if he liked Zucchini bread, knowing that I have a good recipe for that, and I don't want to repeat or try to compare to Leslie's pumpkin bread. And he said banana. Dam men. Well anyway, I thought I'd blog today about how I love my cookbooks and I have many favorite recipes in those cookbooks and even though I didn't have a banana bread favorite I was going to find one, dammit, in one of my favorite cookbooks. And so, I'm making banana bread, with a recipe I found on-line, because I couldn't find one good recipe in my cookbooks. And then for dinner I'm going to make this veggie fritter thing that Jasen made in some cooking class in school that he liked, again not in a cookbook. And *then* I'm going to pick up a ready-made chicken at Winn-Dixie to complete the dinner. But I really wanted to talk about my cookbooks and how much I love my old tried and true and trusted recipes. Now if I was making meatloaf, Quiche or the aforementioned zucchini bread I would be digging them out and boasting about the lost art of cookbooks. I think Suzanne is the only other person I know that reads a cookbook cover to cover, which I used to do. I used to start in the back though. Isn't that weird? I used to start in the back with magazines too. I don't do that anymore. I wonder what that says about me. I'm kind of sick of cooking the same old things, although they are different from what I used to make my kids for many reasons. But it's starting to feel like the same things. Jasen is great at asking for certain dishes, which I always welcome because who knows what to make every night? I made grilled cheese one night and he asked the next day if we were going to have a real dinner? Guess he doesn't consider grilled cheese a real dinner. These kids like sushi too. I mean really, they eat a lot of things my kids would never have considered touching. Their mom was a really good cook, and of course Nina is an executive chef, but I think I hold my own. At least I know they like my cookies! This month's

Food and Wine (thank you Jean) has a lot of Thanksgiving recipes that look doable. I might try a nice Thanksgiving dinner with those recipes (before coming up to Pittsburgh for Thanksgiving). Usually, *Food and Wine* is too far out and I wonder if I would even eat the stuff the print in there let alone if the kids would eat it.

Last night's chorus concert was just lovely. First of all (most importantly) I looked pretty cute in my rain boots. And was sooo hoping it was going to be pouring rain when we came out (as it wasn't when we went in) but it didn't rain then either. I still looked cute and walked through the mud just because I could. The chorus concert was wonderful and Zoë looked super pretty.

Although it's date night I believe we are skipping a big date due to the fact that we are headed to Miami for the weekend! WOOOOO HOOOOOO!

We're staying in the Grove (that's Coconut Grove) and I just can't be more excited. First of all, it's alone time (longer than a date night) with the BF which we haven't had since we got here in May. I think we're due. When I first met him I had said something like we need to be together a lot so we can try to get sick of each other. Something like that. He thought it was the weirdest thing he'd ever heard (men, sheesh). I mean isn't that like a common comment? Even Sandy said that to me once that I needed to spend more time with him to try to get sick of him. Then it became a joke to get him to take long weekends with me so I could see if I got sick of him. Not that I had to ever convince him to spend time with me. After over a year I still haven't gotten sick of him but it never hurts to keep trying. I think a nice week, alone, would be a good test! Like in Costa Rica, the Caymans, or maybe Vienna. Well anyway, we'll start with 3 days in Miami. Fortunately, or unfortunately, I have already talked to my Miami friends and we are seeing them possibly both Friday and Saturday nights and then one of his old college friends on Sunday. It's only unfortunate if we overbook ourselves, so we will make our visits short. I can always go back, right? I mean it's a short drive, well shorter than living in Pittsburgh anyway.

The weather this weekend is supposed to be beautiful. Miami is quite a bit different from when I lived there 32 years ago, but my friends are still there and I'm sure something will look familiar. I told Doug I didn't want to hear ONE word about my weight. And he said he won't say anything if I don't say anything about his. We'll see if he'll live up to his word. Saturday the plan is to go see Lisa and David and Karin. BBQ at their house. It's been 25 years since I've seen them.

Since it still is date night I'll make grocery shopping, just the two of us, a good substitute, and then maybe just go for ice cream. We need to stock up for the weekend for whoever is here. I'm sure there will be a house *full,* but I'm more focused on what to wear and pack. I'll let Peter do the worrying over that. Between the kids staying here, who are adults, and the neighbors, and the dog they will be fine. I say leave them $50, turn off our cell phones and let's go!

Time to go to the "club" and hit the treadmill so I can fit in something over the weekend. That's how it works you know. Work out one day and get those jeans zipped (yea, right).

MONDAY - OCTOBER 20 - HAVE WRENCH WILL TRAVEL

OMG did we have fun. First of all, last Thursday I started my morning at 7:30 a.m. going to the dentist (Jasen) then got my nails done (heaven. . as they include a neck massage while your nails are drying), then got the oil changed (being responsible) and then the car wouldn't start. Just dead. The oil changing people sent me to the auto parts store. Auto parts said there's nothing wrong with the battery or the alternator and sent me on my way. Used the car all day, got a haircut (cute as anything), went to the store, picked up the fam, went out to dinner, dropped off children, went to Winn Dixie, went to get gas, boom.. car won't start. Eff...Pete had a premonition between kids dropped off and Winn Dixie, put one of those battery jumping things in the car. We used it to jump the car to come home. He decided to put a charge on the battery overnight, we'd be good to go in the a.m.

We got all packed, cleaned the house, blah blah, Monica comes we're good to go, out the door, car won't start. CAR WON'T START! After charging the battery all night. Soo, we take it back to the parts store to get a new battery and then they tell us nothing is wrong with the battery (or alternator) but there is something draining it and who knows what it is.... sooo, we decide (he decides) to buy a wrench and every time we stop the car we unhooked the battery cable so it wouldn't drain. Genius/Hoopies I know. But hey we were NOT missing this trip... off we went. Once the car is started it's fine and we got to be quite the team of hooking up the battery and me pushing the button to start.

To end that story, when we got home last night I suggested we keep the cable *off* the battery overnight just to see what happened. What happened? It started right up this morning. It started up 4 times. When I have to take Zoë to the dentist at 1:00 it better freaking start. Now we're wondering if it's a loose battery cable connection. Who knows. Mechanic can't take us until later in the week. Tomorrow is Jury Duty. Hope it starts then too.

But anyway,

Off we went with our wrench to Coconut Grove. My dreams of stopping in Naples for lunch were foiled by the fact that we got an hour or two later start then we had anticipated and we couldn't turn off the car. We drove through Burger King. I know. But anyway, here we go, going into Miami.

Our hotel was right in the Grove. Not like downtown but right off the highway, on the Grove side. We had dinner plans with Doug, no time for sex. Ya know? Like I'm looking forward to this alone time with my man and off we run to dinner. But I was looking forward to seeing Doug too, not as much as looking forward to sex, but...

Friday night we walked to the corner and met Doug and his wife and then the four of us walked to some place called Scotty's where the band was too loud, but we were on the water, and we screamed over the loud band to each other all night. We walked all around the Grove until after midnight and then walked back to the Hotel. NOTHING in the Grove looked familiar. We were home late I was even too tired for sex.

Saturday morning we finally got some alone time (use your imagination) before heading out the door for more going down memory lane. I found my old apartment building, one block from our hotel. I can't believe it is still there. Still looks pretty much the same (crack house-ish) but the pool is gone and there are laundry machines where the pool used to be. God do I remember that pool. My sister burned the shit out of her chest one year when she was visiting. Probably was 1979. No doubt we used baby oil, in Florida, like assholes. She blistered right up. It was awful. That was the year she told my dad I needed an abortion (I didn't) because she wanted him to pay for me to come home for a visit. Which worked. He paid and then I had to tell him she made it all up. She came up with that all on her own, I just thought he was being nice. Lots of memories came flooding back in at that pool site, now turned laundromat.

Everything in the Grove is different. All the old little houses have been torn down and new apartments or bigger houses in their places. Places I worked or went to are gone...like gone...One place is a car lot; another place is a high-rise. It's a very expensive place to live now. And although there are beautiful trees, which my friends Doug and Dawn have been very instrumental in saving, there really are no yards, everything is packed in there. Zillion dollar homes side by side. We walked by a beautiful dog park and playground. The dog park was Astroturf. HA! My friend Doug has become quite the activist in trying to keep the Grove as "the Grove". Good job Doug!

I then took another ride down memory lane, this time in the car, down Bayshore to Rickenbacker Causeway to Key Biscayne. We ended up at Crandon Park and sat on the beach for a little. There are no waves in Miami. None. But that has not changed. There never were.

After that I kept going on my memory tour and found the old grocery store (stayed in the car to keep it running) and then I think I found my old house on the other side of the highway (not in the

Grove) and then remembered the drive to Jackson Street where Karin Arrow and John Brown lived. The house where they lived is gone, but I remembered the route. Fun and sad.

That night we went to Karin and John's new-to-me house (which they bought in 1988) and Lisa and David live there now too. John passed away 3 years ago. Several of the people I hung out with there are now passed away. I'm just happy I'm not in that category. We had a lovely dinner at the Browns (Karin, Lisa and David) Looked at lots and lots of pictures. A lot of "do you remember this person?" and mostly the answer was "no". A lot happens after 25 years, brain cells diminish and what not. You lose track or they're dead.

On Sunday morning we met Doug and Dawn for breakfast. We told old stories, talked about our old friends/roommates Junior, Richard and Stanton and laughed till we cried, I still can't believe that they're all dead. I'm sure Richard and Smitty were sitting somewhere close listening and laughing along with us. Those years were "lost" years and only two of us made it out alive. Literally.

When it was time to say goodbye I was teary again but hopefully the visits will be before another 25 years passes and more of us die. The Gove is only 3+ hours away. My guess is either "we" or "me" will go more often. Plus, Lisa loves to fish and I have my pole (and fishing license). We can wile away the hours like we used to, although not like we used to.... If you know what I mean.

One of the things about Miami is, it's like you're in a different country. That hasn't changed since I lived there. It was like that then too. It's not like that in Tampa, at all. But in Miami there are people who wait on you at various venues that really don't speak any English. It's fun feeling like you're in a different country.

On our way home we decided to stop at South Beach. That's not a different country that's a different world! OMG how much fun we had. We spent 3 hours walking around, looking at people, and cars, went in a couple of stores. I mean I could have spent all day just sitting there watching people, and I guess I did sit there all-day watching people.

And then home. The kids were great. Everyone happy. House was clean. No complaints from anyone. You know what that means? We can go again!

FRIDAY - OCTOBER 24 - STARTING OVER...STILL

When I'm ready to slit my wrists (or someone else's) and/or cry and convince myself I'll never see my kids again I know it's time to exercise. I ventured out on this beautiful Florida day and hit the streets, instead of the "club", to try to jog. First of all, I know that transitioning from the treadmill to outside is a rude awakening. After trying to run a half a block I knew I had to start over and I did. I tuned the IPOD to the "easy" workout of running 1 minute, walking 1.5 minutes. I did that for about 30 minutes and then walked the rest of my 40ish minute workout. I believe I went for total of 1.60 miles. It's a start. I feel better. I am not averse to starting over; in fact, I love the idea, in theory.

Like living here, I don't mind the tremendous changes; as long as I get my visits in with my kids I'm good. The main reason I panic about money is how it may possibly affect my ability to visit them. Then I panic. While it would be nice and I'm sure appreciated for me to contribute monetarily to the Clark household, and believe me I try every stinkin day to find something, it's only when I think I'll never see my kids again that I know it's time to run (as in exercise).

Music helps soothe my anxiety too. Running with the IPOD and listening to the same playlist that I listened to when I was training myself for those 5Ks is comforting. I hear the songs my sister Kathy suggested, I hear my Thor songs, I remember running across that finish line and that makes me feel better. Right now, I'm listening to the same playlist that I listened to in my office at PPU. Believe it or not that's comforting. It's familiar.

I think starting over is exciting but I think it should go the way I want it to go. Like I should have gotten that job at McKinsey when I got here and traveled and built up those miles and perks and banked my checks. Or my accidental blogging would have somehow taken off and that would be a nice surprise but apparently there must be something else. Lottery?

I know I'm getting better with change as when my 40-year-old Jade tree fell over and split in half I did not cry. I simply stuck it in a bucket of water, am going to get a new pot, a bigger pot, and replant it. I'm going to start over. I've restarted that thing many many times in the 40 years I've had it. I can restart it again. This time it'll be bigger and stronger.

MONDAY - OCTOBER 27 - MONDAY MONDAY

So here we are. It's Monday again.

As for the weekend, Friday night was a bust as after my 4-hour trip back and forth from dropping the girl off at her old place I went right to bed. I almost fell asleep driving. Not sure what was up with that. While sleeping Pete made this delicious smelling dinner and was all proud of himself for cleaning up the kitchen afterwards. When I woke up there was (were?) no dishes, and no food. I had an egg sandwich. Jasen assured me the stuffed pork chops that his dad made were delicious. That's how the weekend started.

Saturday was spent at Home Depot spending money on stuff for the house. Then we went to dinner (with Jasen) to Red Lobster. After that we went and saw the movie *Fury*. I figured Jasen sees worse than that on his own so whatever. He loved the action. I think he may have missed the "war" part but anyway, we all liked it. It was a really well-done movie, if you like war movies.

On Sunday we got to putz in the yard for a little. The weather has been beautiful. Low humidity, low temperatures. This is when every-one should visit. It's nice out. I think we're supposed to get hot again for a couple of days this week but then back down to low 80's.

We putzied and then had to drive back up to get the girl. The GPS says it's 26 miles, but my car odometer says its 36 miles (one way). Wonder why the difference? Sunday without traffic only took about 3 hours up and back. And I made it back in time for more than ½ the Steeler game. Zoë had her Steeler sweatshirt on – I wonder if she'll understand when I make her wear it every week.

It seems like all I had to do was whine a little more than usual about not working and I got three job referrals. Zachary sent me a link to work at home typing from audio dictation and Sandie, who previously got me the interview at McKinsey, sent me two more referrals. Sunday after the game I spent time trying to research more about the jobs.

Today I forced myself to clean bathrooms. It seems like I just did it and again they are dirty. Then I cleaned the hallway. Taking advantage of the fact that Pete is home working on his car and had the dog outside with him. Too bad it only lasts until the dog comes back inside. I spent the morning cleaning, going to hop in the shower and then go get the girl. She really needs to get her license.

Tomorrow is volunteer day at the middle school. Maybe something exciting will happen at the school? For the blog's sake I sure hope so...

THURSDAY - OCTOBER 30 - GETTING TO MY TO-DO LIST

I am becoming that person sitting at the computer looking for pictures of Angelina Jolie and Brad Pitts wedding. Also is Bruce Jenner really turning into a woman? And Jim Simmons, did I go to high school with him? He has nice eyes. I don't remember him from high school. I went and got out the yearbook. He's a year ahead of me. I think he played trumpet. Funny how we remember people by what they played in band...well some people.... those in band I guess. These are the things keeping me from my to-do list.

We have a Soccer game on Saturday, and every Saturday from now through February. And in February Lacrosse for the girl starts. I know you are all jealous that I will be back on that sideline. Jimmy played soccer for a couple of years. Not his best sport but I don't remember him being bad. I remember Hayden being a good goalie and that the goalies got to wear crazy clothes. That's about the extent of what I remember.

I still have the chair I used on the sidelines in those days, 10 years ago. I will be reusing it! A good investment for sure. I think it was $6.

I'm not really a good sports mom, I think I push the kids too hard, at least subconsciously. I'm sure they would concur, maybe not subconsciously. I was watching Jasen practice last night and on the tip of my tongue I want to yell "get in there Jasen" but he *was* in there so I didn't say anything. I then did some deep thinking about how I need to let it go and just let him play. I think my biggest fear is that they'll be made fun of somehow. I hate kids to be made fun of. I'm just too protective maybe? The girl was funny talking about sports. She said "oh we suck at sports" and just laughed it off. She just likes to be part of it and do the conditioning. She is a smart girl. We wanted to pay her for her A's (as really motivation for Jasen) but she doesn't want paid. She said her reward will be getting into a good college and hoping for scholarship money. She said paying her for her A's would ruin it and said that's what she's supposed to do, get A's. She's too smart. That's why I didn't pay my kids either. They are supposed to get A's.

Jasen's report card wasn't bad. He didn't get anything lower than a C and got good marks for being a nice kid. When I mentioned that his grades weren't that bad he said "I know, I bet if I did my homework they would be even better!" What a kid. He knows he's lazy. He just doesn't care. This is a great story though...the day we were in the car leaving for Miami I got a call on my cell from the school about Jasen. We weren't even a block away and I assumed that we were going to have to go pick him up, and that he was sick or he did something wrong but after a minute when they said this is a "good" call I put them on speaker so Pete could listen. They were calling to say that Jasen did this wonderful thing by going to sit with a kid that was all alone in the lunch room, he bought him ice cream and made the kid feel better. Both Pete and I were teary. They gave him a "good citizenship" award. When I complimented Jasen at home he said he had bought cookies and cream flavored ice cream and he didn't want it. His comment "Why would they make cookies and cream ice cream? That's disgusting" – and he had to ask the kid about homework. He down played it but I know he's a nice kid. But then he wants to know if he gets something for being nice (he's relentless) and suggested Disney. I suggested that he did not save someone from a burning building; only gave him ice cream that he didn't want. He got dinner and movie instead. Not everyone is a straight A student. Thank heavens for those little ones that give you ice cream that they don't want. One man's junk is another's treasure. That saying fits this scenario too doesn't it? Zoë got almost all straight A's. Almost…They both got additional notes of having excellent behavior, good attitude and excellent performance. Instead of Jasen being good at home and bad at school he's good at school and bad at home. He's not really bad, except to his dad and Zoë. But then again, he's a teenage boy. They are all PIA's right? Do I get an Amen?

I have a to-do list today. And the afternoon to do it again. The girl has after school activities. I really need to vote. They have early voting down here but every day I forget to go. Today's the day, I'm going. Will I or won't I vote for medical marijuana? Maybe that will be our family business? Babe? What about that idea? And, I have to go look at marble or granite to replace the top to the buffet that got broken in the move. We priced a piece of granite. Only $300ish. I was expecting more. We both liked this dark green but I don't know. I don't love it. I need to keep looking. If only Penske would have reimbursed us, it would have been easier to justify the cost. Bastards.

Pete met another neighbor last night. Neighbor Linda hasn't been back since day one when she showed up with cookies for Pete and was visibly disappointed that I wasn't Pete and that I was even here. I just found out that her husband died over a year ago. I assumed he was still living over there. Now I know why she was disappointed. She may have wanted "my" man. Well, she can't have him…. yet. JK. . She waves to me now. Maybe she's getting over her disappointment.

Hey this weekend is Witchstock in Palm Harbor. That might be fun, if we're not freezing. They're giving out prizes for costumes. One of the prizes is for "Best Medical Marijuana Costume." Yep this is the town I live in. Pete suggested dressing up. I suggest we observe this year. Maybe next year we'll join in the fun. Maybe...

NOVEMBER 2014

MONDAY - NOVEMBER 3 - ANOTHER HALLOWEEN, COME AND GONE

Whoever said Florida doesn't have seasons never lived here. We are in Fall baby. And perfect timing. The day after Halloween seems like when it should be getting on with Fall. October has been pretty nice with low humidity and pleasant temperatures but this weekend we were cold! It was great. At Jasen's soccer game on Saturday all the parents were in their chairs with blankets. I didn't have a blanket but then again I did have a warmer jacket and I'm not *that* much of a sissy.... yet. Plus, the sun still shines at 60°and it's still warm!

Friday night was Halloween. I finished decorating (last-minute yes) and Pete finished with the pièce de résistance, a smoke machine and music. We were ready to go at 6:00 pm. Think we got 12 kids, all middle school age, and I only saw 3 of them. Around 8:00 pm Pete and I decided to walk around a couple of our neighborhoods to see decorations. We missed about 6 kids. I think our driveway was too dark. Next year we will plan accordingly. Today my self-imposed job is to take all the decorations down. Figured I'd get this update out-of-the-way first so I could continue without interruption (HA! . . like that ever happens). Marcus the Carcass was a huge hit, but only to me mostly. Marcus (since we forgot to take pictures) he is a head, feet and hands that light up and stick out of the ground. You bury wires under the ground and then he lights up and he looks like he's coming out of the ground. Best Halloween purchase ever. Pete did a great job of burying him and making him look authentic. I've had Marcus for 10 years.

Saturday was Jasen's first soccer game (well first here in Palm Harbor, he's played before). They tied, we sat in chairs, perfect Fall Day. In the evening Pete and I went into our town, ate at Thirsty Marlin, decided it's a good place to take any out-of-town visitors, then ended up back at the Witches Brew in time for the costume contest, had our hemp brownie, which cures cancer, and back home. We had to SHUT windows it was cold. See? We're getting in alone time. It's nice! But those kids (and dog) and responsibilities are never far from my mind. I'm not sure about his mind but I'm always wondering about who's been left at home, what they're doing and when we should get back there. When we've been out of town I don't think about it but out on date night or just out for whatever I think about them...a lot, he would say too much.

Last night Monica came for a visit, we watched some TV together, in front of the fire in our fireplace (cozy), and then I hibernated in the bedroom to watch the rest of the Steeler game. What a game! I don't know what's going on but I think it might be the sweatshirt that Zoë's been wearing on Steeler day that's helping the Steelers win. And yes, I hibernated to give them alone time. Not sure who I was giving alone time to – them or me...maybe both. Monica and Pete have a very close relationship and I'm not gonna lie, there's something about it that makes me feel uncomfortable... I act accordingly and walk away rather than trying to figure it out. I love Monica and she is great with me but there's just something there. I mean think about it – I am brand new to this family. I'm the one that's the stranger. I feel it, so I excuse myself. It usually makes Pete mad but oh well. I still do have my own mind.

Other than this mindless chattering there is nothing new to report. It is life, as is becoming usual, in Palm Harbor, Florida.... . where I live......finally!

TUESDAY - NOVEMBER 4 - FAST FACT TUESDAY

So as not to delay you from your right to vote, I have just a few fast facts for today:

- Pulling the fire alarm is a federal offense (as per the Principal's announcement this morning after the fire alarm was pulled)
- There are 70 cameras at the Palm Harbor Middle School. Someone's child is in a lot of trouble.

- Just because you break a tooth doesn't stop you from being hungry. It does make chewing and eating less enjoyable however.
  - Breaking a tooth can change your whole mood and put quite the damper on your day.
    - When you have bad teeth to begin with you should never, I repeat NEVER, eat caramel.
- Sometimes, even when it's supposed to be 78° it just feels cold enough to sit in front of the heater, on the floor.
- Sometimes I don't feel like doing the dishes and I'm perfectly fine leaving them there.
- I suspect I will never tire of putting my face in the sun which may be a problem in the premature aging department.
- I'm not a fan of the Green Bean Casserole – doesn't have much taste.

And the last fast fact for today:

- CVS charges twice as much as Staples for headphones. TWICE as much.

WEDNESDAY - NOVEMBER 5 - WAITING WEDNESDAY

Today I'm waiting.

My dentist appointment is not until 1:30. The worst thing about the broken tooth is there is a very sharp edge that cuts my tongue if I talk, eat, drink and/or breathe. However, sleeping last night was good.

I decided to make banana bread again because it seemed to go over okay. Zoë and I both loved it and now we have cream cheese. But only 2 of the bananas are over ripe. I have to wait until tomorrow for the third banana to be over ripe. Tomorrow I'll make the banana bread.

Florida voted NO on the Medical Marijuana issue. I thought for sure it would be a landslide YES, being Florida and all. And really it's not accurate to say it was voted "no". 58% voted YES and 42% voted NO.

Even though it sounds like a win there had to be 60% of the votes to say YES. Interesting. All very interesting. My vote for Governor didn't win either. My candidate lost by 1% point. ONE. My Attorney General won though. I've only been here now what, going on 6 months? , and I have "my" candidates already. As far as the overall Republican turn out, guess now we have to wait and see what happens next...if anything. I like to say I hate politics but really I think the whole back and forth is both maddening and fascinating. I'm thankful for Professor Firestone's class that I audited on American Government. Gives me a better appreciation that we as a country have been nuts for a long time and have never agreed. It's just fascinating to watch, from a distance. My Jimmy has always hated the news. Even as a little kid he would make me turn it off. I see his point mostly. I do like the weather forecast though.

I'm watching Sam, the dog, chase squirrels in the side yard. I'm waiting for him to knock the fence down.

Seems like a lot of my life has been spent waiting for something to happen next. I'm here now and settled in and just waiting to see what happens next. Maybe this is it? I shall work on accepting the status quo, which ain't bad at all.

THURSDAY - NOVEMBER 6 - THRIFTY THURSDAY (I DON'T KNOW, JUST GO WITH IT)

A late day entry today as the plan was to get some chillaxing, nee Lyming, in before blogging. It semi worked. I got maybe an hour in, poolside. The sun is just not there over the pool anymore, its path has changed. And believe it or not it's chilly in the shade.

Otherwise, a normal day, laundry, dishes, bathrooms (no floors) – hey did I mention how yesterday I used baking soda and vinegar to clean out the clogged bathtub drain? I think it may have worked. It was pretty cool watching the bubbling going on. It's supposed to work as an alternative to Drano. It's a slow drain to begin with and then add two kids with really long THICK hair, well it's doomed from the start. But I was pretty proud of myself. What did we do before Google eh?

Have I talked about the Dry Cleaner? It's a drive-through? First of all, having 6 or 7 shirts laundered and pressed for under $20 is like a God-send. Not only do they do that for you but it's a drive through. You never have to get out of your car. I mean who would have thunk it?

There are Dry Cleaners and Nail/Hair Salons every block. I don't know how they all stay in business. There is every kind of store imaginable down here. It's hard to discover them all because they are on either side of an 8-lane highway. Well actually that's just ONE place they are. There's all these other streets that we haven't explored that could have hundreds of more shops. For instance, I took a side street today to see where it would end up and passed a garden nursery. Now who knew it was even back there? Ya know? And although it's nice having all these stores everywhere there is something to be said for walking "up street" in Sewickley and knowing where everything is. It's just different here. Which is good because I wanted different.

Tonight is date night. We had to switch from Wednesday nights because Jasen has soccer practice now on those nights. Tonight, we might try going into the city for Tampa Bay Design Week to see what that's all about. At least that's the "plan". I saw it advertised watching a Tampa Bay news show. Perhaps I will have something fun to report on with my next update.

I'm counting down the days for my Pittsburgh visit. Very excited to see the boys, the fam, and the friends. Not sure about that cold but I guess I can suck it up for a week. At least I know it won't last. Last year we lived in Pittsburgh and came to Tampa for Thanksgiving week and I froze in Tampa. See? You just never know.

FRIDAY - NOVEMBER 7 – TGIF

Date night was fun. We went downtown and walked around briefly. I "thought" there was a free event at the museum but it was by invitation only but still it was cool to see Tampa's downtown and their waterfront park.

And then we went to Ybor City. Ybor City was founded in the 1880s by cigar manufacturers and was populated by thousands of immigrants, mainly from Spain, Cuba, and Italy. Sort of reminds me of what New Orleans might look like (not ever having been there) and a little like the Southside of Pittsburgh – old Southside. We need to go back during the day. One highlight was seeing this long line of people waiting to get into a nightclub. The outfits were unbelievable. One woman we passed had a long dress, side slits up to her waist, no underwear. Why? Anyway, it was a nice night.

No weekend plans again. I like the no plans weekend because you never know what might happen. Well other than the soccer/lacrosse commitments which take up our Saturday morning/afternoon. Maybe we'll plant our seeds in the garden.

But right now, I'm going to meet my man for lunch. I get to see the water too. Love them both!

TUESDAY - NOVEMBER 11 - THEY CALL ME MRS. HUWIGGINS

T- minus 20 minutes and counting until a Skype interview. I am sure that in exactly 20 minutes when the Skype call comes in, the pool man will ring the door bell, the dog will bark, both phones will start ringing and my computer will automatically reboot. But in the meantime, I have 20 minutes to compose myself. Nothing like blogging to allay some of that nervous energy.

Soo, where did I leave off? The weekend? I can't remember...let's see, oh yes, Pete put the plants in. He's dug up and out a lot of the plantings here, hope they don't care, and we are looking forward to very healthy eating soon. He put black netting around to keep out vermin. Sam immediately ran through it. He will just have to pee somewhere else for the next few months.

We went and saw *Interstellar* Saturday night. The only reason I had any idea what was going on was because I live with a bunch of engineers who talk about different dimensions and gravity and time and I had at least an inkling about what the heck was going on. The family debriefing after the movie helped.

Tampa decided to show golf advertising on CBS during the Steeler game on Sunday. Probably because they want everyone to watch Tampa Bay. I decided to go to the local bar, Peggy O'Neills, and watch the game there. I didn't get there until the third quarter. I thought we looked good but then WTF with the missed field goal and well anyone that cares knows the outcome. But that was something new for me, going to the bar, alone, watching the game, with my ice tea and French fries. Can't remember why I went alone now but my sister called and we chatted while I was there. It didn't really feel like I was alone. It was like I was with my sister at the bar, eating French fries and drinking ice tea. A lovely afternoon for sure.

Then we had a full house of Clarks for dinner. Nina brought and cooked it all. I made the desserts. I love when she visits. She whips everyone into shape – makes them help clean up, just like the mom figure she was used to being. I appreciate her help more than she knows. I am happy to give her a break from being that mom figure that she is way too young to have to be. Those Clarks come with a lot of responsibilities and she's been the one in the past (before there was a me) trying to hold it together. I'm happy to be able to let her be a "kid" (at 24) – but again I really appreciate the break. And everyone listens to her.

Yesterday was total chillaxing. I mean total. I slept late; I only emptied the dishwasher. No laundry, no cleaning, nothing, just gave myself a mental break.

5 minutes until the Skype interview...I just put the dog in the music room and shut the door, put a note outside on the doorbell telling Steve (pool boy) to go on back (he's fixing something with the filter today), I took both phones and threw them in the bedroom and shut the door. I put on a bra, mascara and earrings, just little diamond studs. I'm ready

right? Have the computer facing a blank wall. 3 minutes to go. Meanwhile she never confirmed who was calling who(m). She's supposed to call me right?

MONDAY - NOVEMBER 17 - IT'S ALL ABOUT THE FOOTWEAR

Hello, it's me! ! I know I've been off-the-line lately. Just not a whole lot to report. I'm getting too bored with myself. The weather has been beautiful, like really beautiful, but today it's very cloudy and windy, and if feels like it's 100 degrees although it just must be humidity. I have two weeks of Pittsburgh weather coming up to get through. Well maybe 10 days or so. Thus, the packing dilemma begins. Different from summer packing, I'm thinking of taking 2 pairs of jeans, wear a sweater, bring a sweater and throw in a hoody. Those are my outfits for the visit. The number 1 goal will be to stay warm while holding my brand-new baby nephew. Kai Richard was born Sunday morning weighing in at 7 lbs. something. He's 3 weeks early but apparently ready or not. How fun will that be to hold a new baby, while the other two wild things (2- and 4-year-olds) jump on me?

The weekend was pleasant. Jasen had a soccer game. I sat in the sun – like pure sun for two hours but didn't get sunburn. What's up with that? It's Florida, shouldn't I be at least pink? Also, the footwear is an issue. I am paying attention at the game to the various footwear. We have everything from flip-flops (my shoe of choice) to boots. I mean there were women there with boots on, snow boots. They're crazy but hey I want to fit in. Should I wear my snow boots when it's 70 and not a cloud in the sky? I think I need some new UGGs. Saturday night we went to a Seafood Festival in Tarpon Springs. I wore a long skirt and boots. I don't know, I guess it was an okay look. We had Greek food at the Seafood Festival. We eat seafood all the time. We weren't talking. I can't remember why. I guess that's a couples thing? Where you're mad but you still go out together? One thing about this whole relationship stuff between us is that I have no experience in relationships...not really..and he was married for 26 years. In my experience when you don't get along or fight or whatever it is you start thinking about ending the relationship. I guess when you're married you just know that you're going to stay together anyway? I think we think very differently when it comes to "spats"...Although I'm getting better at not packing and leaving. Because really where would I go? And now I'm really entwined in this family. It would be really complicated. Best to just make up. Maybe that's how people stay married. It's just less complicated.

TUESDAY - NOVEMBER 18 - BABY IT'S COLD OUTSIDE

It's cold. I hope you northerners are happy about my misery. And it's getting colder tonight. Now when I say cold let me qualify by saying I'm wearing a light sweater and no coat; however, I think a light jacket is necessary. It's 48°. Down in the 30's tonight, but I've already shared that. I guess it's a little preview of what I'm in for next week during my Pittsburgh visit.

I worked (as in volunteered) at the middle school this morning. I have a couple 7th grade girls out to get me. One of them forgot that I am the adult. Guess she wasn't real happy with being reminded. Dam kids. Middle school work study students are quite a bit different from our college age work study's at PPU. I'm pretty sure I'm not allowed to strangle any of them at either school.

I made shrimp scampi last night – I thought it was delicious, and really that's all that counts right?

Thinking of pulling out some homemade chicken broth today so it smells good when children come home in the cold. I'm just not sure about that broth though. But we'll see. If anyone gets sick then I'll know for next time not to wait so long before freezing.

WEDNESDAY - NOVEMBER 19 - YOU SAY TOMATO I SAID COMPLIMENT

Welp, I'm not as good at grammar as I had hoped and the work at home job (from last week's Skype interview) is not an option. I'll tell you this though, I'll never confuse compliment and complement again. But I will probably always confuse populous and populace. Oh well, I'd say it wasn't meant to be but that's just what people say when they don't want to slit their wrists. The results from the grammar test came at the same time the dentist was telling me I need 8 crowns at about $2000 each. I guess I'll become one of those toothless unemployed people. Not a good day.

So, the job search continues. In the meantime, I'll just extend my stay up north by a couple of days for the sheer purpose of driving my sister crazy. That will surely give me some satisfaction.

Today is packing for my trip up north day. I shall see how many warm clothes I can stuff in my suitcase.

I guess that's about it. I won't be blogging while up north, cause well I'll be there. So finally, Florida doesn't seem appropriate, and I don't want to lug my computer with me. When I come back here to Florida perhaps I will have renewed appreciation for my geological change. I'm already looking forward to coming back and getting out of the cold. I haven't been gone long enough for me to get excited about being cold...again. I don't know that I'll ever be gone long enough for that. And the last time I came home (back from Pittsburgh) my BF (that would be Peter) took me straight to the beach for the best welcome home ever.

Perhaps something similar will happen upon my return.

DECEMBER 2014

THURSDAY - DECEMBER 4 - I'M BAACCKKK

And the fair-haired wayward girlfriend returns to the nest. I must say my hair is longer and Jasen is taller. And I was only gone 10 days. But really 10 days is a lot. And it was just enough. Thanks for missing my blog Sandy. And here is the travel blog. It's long – 10 days of catch up.

It was a whirlwind trip starting with arriving into freezing temperatures like I've never experienced. Like biting cold temps. Spent lovely time with son #1 in Pittsburgh, played Bunko at Di's house and got to see the girls, spent Saturday with the babies taking them to the farmers market, dinner at my sisters, then off to Columbus to see son #2! Had a great time visiting with son #2 stayed the night and then off to Virginia in the morning.

I spent 5 days with mom in Virginia then drove back to Pittsburgh on Friday. I rented a room for Friday and Saturday night with a kitchen so I could make birthday breakfast for Zachary and have my kids all back together with me for at least one day. The babies came over to the hotel too for cake. One more day in Sewickley with friends and then, finally time to come *home*. By Monday I was really missing "home" and couldn't wait to get back to Florida. While I was in Pittsburgh I completely enjoyed myself and when it was time to come home I was completely ready and I am sooooo happy to be HOME.

I have absolutely embraced my new surroundings/geography and my new living arrangements and new family. I love it here. I love them and I really feel at home here in Florida, with them. And I loved my visit back home/North. I did a lot of visiting and a lot of traveling. I put over 1000 miles on my little rental car. I'm going to try to make it until April this time before I come back (go back) up. I can do it. Especially if we can get those boys down here before then. Then maybe by April I'll be ready for another 1000-mile trip. Who has April Bunko? It was a great visit and I got to spend just enough time with everybody. Maybe next time I can drag my boyfriend along. Shouldn't he be spending time with my family too? I think so!! Next trip!

Now it's on to Christmas decorating. Can't wait to get started. Neither could Pete apparently. The tree is up (without ornaments) It's cozy already.

FRIDAY - DECEMBER 5 - HEY, I LIVE IN FLORIDA!

Have I mentioned how happy I am to be living in Florida? Have I mentioned it lately? Last night, date night, we drove to Indian Rocks, had dinner at a lovely little place called Guppy's, then walked across the street and walked on a beautiful moonlit beach. The moon was bright you would have thought there were lights on. We walked on the beach awhile, under the moonlight and then drove back home, traveling up the coast, looking at all the Christmas decorations. I mean an absolutely beautiful night.

Today has started off well. Up at 7:00 a.m., walked with the BF, and I've been going ever since. Not like *going,* but I've been awake at least. I thought I'd pound this blog out and then just head to the Winn Dixie and get gas. Big day, right?

Zoë has been bringing her group over from her Physics class. I need to stock up on the snacks for them. They are working on a catapult. Due Monday. They had one built but are now rebuilding because it has to shoot/throw a water balloon 30 meters... for those of you that have no idea how far that is, like me, it's far. It's like 30 yards. The group, i.e., mostly Zoë, is working her butt off trying to get it to work. They're out there with drills, saws, etc. I keep thinking that her brother Jasen would put it together in 10 minutes but I could be giving him too much credit...I don't know though.

So, guess what? We have to rake leaves. The leaves are changing colors and dropping off. Just like up north. Pete said this is unusual and they usually don't fall off until the spring when the new leaves push the old leaves off. In any event there is yard work to do this weekend.

And our garden is growing, and our tomatoes are red. BLTs for lunch tomorrow! WOO HOO!

Then I will be moving the fall Mums to the land of the dead and replacing with Poinsettias. We can plant Poinsettias outside. I mean how cool is this?

Maybe for Christmas we will be harvesting our garden. I am loving this climate,

and lovin life....

MONDAY - DECEMBER 8 - NAVIGATING CHRISTMAS

The girls came over last night for dinner and helped their dad decorate a little. Monica mostly slept. I think that's a complement, no it's a compl*i*ment, dammit, that your kids feel comfortable at your house that they sleep. I made a delicious dinner. White Chicken Chili, rice, a delicious salad with tomatoes from our garden and corn bread. Oh wait, get this, you know I try to be careful when Nina, the star chef, is coming. First of all, I don't want her to have to cook when she visits. She deserves a day off too, right? And I want them to just be able to visit with each other. I made White Chicken Chili and instead of putting in 1½ tsp of coriander I put in 1½ TBS of coriander. Ya know? What an idiot. But, I will tell you, it was delicious anyway. Turns out coriander is effective in lowering both blood pressure and blood sugar. We were all Zen last night. Monica apparently more Zen than the rest of us.

Pete has a big family and they have A LOT of stuff, as I have mentioned, and Christmas is the season of "stuff" isn't it? I think more than one of them in this family have been collectors. I don't know that I would have been any different had I had the space or finances but it's quite a task to try to make sense of it. We've gotten through Halloween and Thanksgiving quite well. I've organized those bins for next year and yes we have four bins just for Halloween and Thanksgiving. What can I say? I like fall and pumpkins. Really, I have no room to "judge", but I do have to make some sense of it. Trying to find places for everything will probably help me take my mind off of not being with my own family.

The trouble with combining families and combining traditions is well one of has to make concessions. I make concessions with being without my family and he makes concessions with his money enabling me to visit my family as much as I have. I am thankful to have had the 10 days over Thanksgiving which encompassed a lot of visiting and Zachary's birthday. I know Christmas is only one day but it's an important family day. I have warned the BF that this is going to be a very very hard year for me but I don't know if he really appreciates how hard. The fact that I cried all day on my birthday this year should give him some idea of what's to come. But I shall remember that even though I can't be home for Christmas with my kids that should not and will not negate all the good stuff about being here. Jimmy has already come up with the idea of him and Zach getting together and skyping me in for Christmas breakfast. Maybe we can plan breakfast together and they can be with this family while I am with them at the same time. I LIKE it!

Another milestone and passage in this personal journey of mine is about to take place. For 32 years I have built traditions and events around the holidays; always of course around my boys. Certain decorations are always out that remind us of years past, pictures are on the wall, certain music we always listen to and then of course the different meals all with matching plates.

The good news is I have place settings for 8 with all those dishes and maybe this year I'll get to use all of them. And there are new traditions that I get to be part of this year, like we're going to go, as a family, to help with Toys for Tots. Something Leslie is organizing. Zoë has a chorus concert this week and I've always loved those. It's all good. We will figure this out.

WEDNESDAY - DECEMBER 10 - TAKING CARE OF BUSINESS

It's 1:30 ish, I'm exhausted, and I'm not even out of my p.js yet. Well, not exactly p.js but sweats. Same thing.

The only thing of relevance to report today is that I've been on the phone ALL morning juggling dentist appointments, getting new insurance and subsequently a new dentist. And I think I've found a new doctor. She graduated from OU (Ohio University, Jimmy's alma mater). Go Bobcats!. That's taken up all of my day so far.

I have my heater on today. It's 60 and sunny. I could probably go sit in the sun and warm up, our house is pretty shady.

Christmas decorations are coming along nicely. Peter put some more lights up outside last night. They look beautiful. We're sorting through the stuff inside as well. He has "promised" (okay not promised but I'm hopeful) that we can have a yard sale. There is a lot of great stuff in these bins that someone else will have to have. Maybe we can do that in like February? Maybe we can get the neighborhood involved? Lots of possibilities. That will give me something to do after the holidays.

Yesterday I volunteered at the school in the morning. We were really busy. Lots of kids leaving school yesterday. Then I met the BF for lunch and then he gave me a to-do list. I stayed pretty true to the list other than the huge poinsettia I just had to have. And now I just walked out to get the mail and it's beautiful. I think I'll go for a walk.

THURSDAY - DECEMBER 11 - WHERE'S MRS. WILLIAMS?

Last night was our girl's Christmas concert. I love high school Christmas concerts. It was quite the extravaganza. First was the jazz band. About 25 piece. They were good. They performed 5 songs. Then the full choir came out and performed 3 or so selections, then the orchestra about 3 pieces. We then had intermission. I don't think my high school ever had intermission. Then after intermission it was the Women's Choir (Zoë is in that) – then, let's see, the Advanced Mixed

Choir, then the Symphonic Band, they were fabulous, really good sound and then the Women's Choir again. But wait that's not all.... The Grand Finale was another grouping of the Symphonic Band who did Sleigh Ride (Leroy Anderson) and it sounded wonderful. Such a good job. Then the choir and the band joined together for the last two pieces. Wonderful. All Christmas music.

While we were seated in the 800-person auditorium I'm looking around and I realized I'm not going to see Mrs. Williams. I've been seeing Mrs. Williams at Christmas concerts since I was in junior high school. That's a lot of Christmases. Then I realized I wouldn't be seeing anyone. And then, unlike seeing Mrs. Williams, I thought about that uncomfortable feeling you get when you see someone you've known all your life but you don't know whether to say hi to them or not. Why is that? Why do we say hi to some people and then other people we either walk down another aisle or just act like we don't know them at all, when actually we (in Sewickley anyway) have known them, their siblings, and their kids all our lives. Is that just a Sewickley thing? I understand not wanting to run into certain people who will detain you from your quick errand but really. Well, none of that here in Palm Harbor. I'm turning over a new leaf. I saw Dolly, who volunteers with me at the middle school, and we did say hello and I introduced her to Peter. Then the husbands (my pseudo husband) shook hands. Like friends, ya know? I think I'm going to try something new, like saying hello to everyone that I've met. Wonder if I can do it. That Sewickley snobbery runs pretty deep. But actually, I don't even know if it's snobbery it's just easier to get through your day without having to chat, but really is a "hello" and a smile too much? I shall make it part of the new me. Being friendly and all.

Tonight is a one-act play thingy at the high school that Zoë is in. Another family night. Love family nights. We're only staying for her one-act though. We don't know anybody else. Hmm, if I start saying hello to people does that mean I have to stay and watch their kids?

TUESDAY - DECEMBER 16 - I SAW SANTA!

It's Payday and there are 9 shopping days left. I got an early start, but really more errands than shopping. I saw a couple of things at Michael's over the weekend I just *had* to have. I went back today to get them. The over the door thing doesn't fit over the door, the bulbs that I wanted were sold out, I decided I didn't really need this one particular book that was on my list anyway, and the whole errand was kind of a bust. Then just got gas and food to get through the day and then got back to cleaning. I believe there was a comment at Bunko when I was up north in November that I do a lot of cleaning. I am backing off a bit but it's all about the dog hair. After Max (my dog) died I realized how much dirt a dog makes. It's *unbelievable* how much dirt a dog makes. A 110-pound dog makes 3 times the dirt and hair that Max, a measly 35 pounds, did. But anyway, it's all good. The windows are open, it's a beautiful day and all is well in the Clark/Bench household.

I believe we are done decorating; I believe. We are both very happy with our *stuff*. Outside looks beautiful all lit up. He did a great job. Only one other neighbor has lights out. But around other neighborhoods there are lights galore. I just read an article that talked about "us" here in the south not needing snow. We have LIGHTS! We do have cold, but not *cold*. We have had a fire in the fireplace for the last 3 or 4 nights. It's been sooo cozy. But today the windows are open.

On Saturday Jasen had a soccer game at the crack of dawn (9 a.m.) I ran around to a couple of garage sales first to look for bookshelves, no luck, and ended up getting to the game for the second half. They put Jasen in as goalie. I was like *why*? The worried pseudo parent that I am, afraid he's going to disappoint himself and the team. I mean he is pretty small, but then we have 8-year-olds on the team too. Anyway, the score was 4-0 when I got there (we were losing) – after they put Jasen in the other team didn't score any more goals. He stopped them all! He was the star! One of his teammates said to him on the way out "great save Jasen, best goalie we ever had." How happy were we? How relieved was Jasen? A good Saturday as well. After that, we just putzied the rest of the day. We hit up a couple more garage sales. Got 2 tennis racquets for 50 cents each. Do we play tennis? No, but we might someday. Maybe we'll have guests that want to play? You just never know.

There was a parade on Saturday. I was able to walk to where it was and watch it. The boys (Pete and Jasen) passed on it and Zoë was at a friends. I went by myself. I had to see Santa or I wouldn't be able to sleep. I fought some of the kids for candy, got one beaded necklace and three pieces of candy for Jasen.

Yesterday we (Pete and I) went to the beach. Not a cloud in the sky. We put on our sweatshirts and walked on the beach for a couple of hours. I even put my feet in the water. The air temperature was around 62 ish – water temp about the same. What a beautiful day. We stayed for the sunset, clapped when it went down (as is tradition here) and then somebody played taps. It was something. Do I miss the snow? Do I? HECK no. I love it here. I love driving around with a sweatshirt on, and only a sweatshirt, looking at the lights, sitting at the beach and looking at the greatest decoration of all, the sunset. We really are having a great time.

THURSDAY - DECEMBER 18 - THE ELVES ARE BUSY

Blogging at the holidays is no easy task, so I will let you know I'm alive, and very busy with the holiday madness. I will be chattier later, I'm sure.

FRIDAY - DECEMBER 19 - WAITING FOR GODOT

I'm making progress, but now I must wait. Pete remembered he had a 50-inch TV at his daughter's house, that they were not using, however, it is part of some recall and they are coming out today to fix a part. There are two things wrong with it and they will only fix one of them, for free. The other item will cost $600. We are choosing NOT to fix that since we can get a new TV for $400. Ya know? Anyway, I'm waiting for them now to come and fix the one thing. I then have to run to Target to get just a couple more things, run home, throw those couple of things into boxes, run to the Goin Postal store (it's a franchise post office store) and get these boxes in the mail. Then I have to run back home and Zoë and I have to run to the airport to participate in this Toys for Tots volunteer day thingy. I'm worried about my feet holding up as they are hurting just thinking about it, and Jasen isn't allowed to participate in the Toys for Tots event because the rule is only 16 years old and up. I'm not really wild about leaving him out.... but it'll be fine. Right?

Last night I made cookies for Pete to take to work for a cookie exchange. I made those melt in your mouth peppermint balls that I made for a couple of Sally's cookie exchanges. And they really do melt in your mouth. We shall see what he comes home with.

I'm starting to plan Christmas Eve dinner and Christmas breakfast. I think I might have to vary from tradition with both meals as both meals will entail a bigger crowd and then of course there are different palates. I made a disastrous dinner the other night. Both kids spit out the fish. Pete and I ate it. We'll eat anything. Probably not a good thing. I don't know if I can redeem myself or not. Anyway, I make okay stuff. Zoë barely eats anything but apparently she loves African and/or Indian food her mom used to make. Maybe what I make is too boring.

No stupid TV repairman yet and time is a ticking. I am going to be behind with everything now. Grrr....

Tis the season, eh?

After 6 months I am quite settled in, I have friends even sort of, I mean they are work friends but that's okay too. Now I have people who I might see at the Winn-Dixie or Publix or the pizza place or soccer game. I have friends that I meet at the mall and I have a friend in Miami that is looking forward to my next visit so we can go fishing! Life is good.

TUESDAY - DECEMBER 23 - DR. SEUSS I AM NOT

Twas the day before the day before Christmas, and all through the house, the cookies are eaten, but not by a mouse. Ole Peter was up and a' popping those kisses, while Zoë was downing the cutout blablishes.

So now I've decided to make the last batch of various choices that no doubt have to last. The children and friends arriving tomorrow and with no sweets to feed them there will be certain sorrow. I'll hide this new batch from Peter and Zoë, I fear Jasen could care less, for sure keeps him leaner.

The dinner is planned and most shopping is done. There'll be ham and a turkey and I need one more run. The dining room not ideal for a crowd, but I'll make it work always, someway and somehow.

There's cleaning to do that I've sworn to pass off. My feet are too sore and my will is a farce. I'm cooking, I'm wrapping, I've made such a clatter, will someone, just someone pick up the dirt matter?

It's hot here today, a high 76, humidity's bad, it's not helping my schtick. I wonder how this will affect all my cookies, my ham, and my broccoli, my hair and my schnookies. I'm running out of words that will rhyme with my verse, so I must dash away, to Winn-Dixie, with nary a curse.

Merry Christmas to all and a blessed fort night,

I miss you all

MONDAY - DECEMBER 29 - MONDAY MORNING COACH

And the frenzy is over! I know the holidays are a lot of work but I still think it's worth it. And really thank God it doesn't last any longer. I mean Christmas night are we the only ones passed out? My sister-in-law always entertains Christmas night. It makes me tired just thinking about it.

Recapping,

Christmas Eve dinner was here , I cooked – Ham (delicious) Turkey on the Grill (DELICIOUS) Kale and butternut squash lasagna (I thought it was delicious but think I was the only one) Broccoli casserole (eh. . Pete loved it) I think it went okay but Jasen was wanting mac and cheese. Which is what I *usually* make but I thought I'd mix it up this year since we had more adults coming. Turns out I'll probably go back to mac and cheese next year.

My Christmas Eve table was okay but not as impressive as the breakfast table.

My boys called (Skyped) at the same time breakfast was being cooked and the kids here started opening their presents. I got out of cooking since I had to watch them all open their presents. I made nothing. That was kinda of nice. Wouldn't mind *that* being a new routine.

After breakfast cleanup Pete and I opened our pile of presents to an attentive audience. It was fun. I got some good stuff. Yes I still like stuff. What can I say? I have even acclimated quite nicely to all of his "stuff" and we were able to combine quite nicely our various decorations. I mean how can you not love this?

I bought another set of dishes before Christmas. I guess you can't take the Martha Stewart out of me forever. I was even on Ebay this morning looking for more place settings for my Christmas morning set. My cute dishes and even my fine china dishes are both discontinued, of course, because I get everything on sale. I used all 8 place settings of each set this year and that's without my kids being here. It's not the dishes so much as the placemats and napkin holders. Well anyway, my kids have good memories around my "stuff" – that's really all it is, memories.

Yesterday was a lovely day. Pete and I walked up to Starbucks in the 70-degree weather, drank our (my) ice coffee, sitting outside just talking. It really is nice to have someone to do things with. Diane and I used to say that if we ever met someone he has to be better than "nothing" because we really like nothing. And well I have to say Peter is much better than nothing.

After our morning walk, we went to St. Pete Beach to visit Stephanie, then went to Frenchy's on the beach to watch the Steeler game with Lori and her daughter. We had a nice time.

Then today, back to work, back to blogging, back to trying to put stuff away and make room for new stuff.

Tomorrow the girl goes to Disney for her Candlelight Processional bit. We, however, are not going. With admission being $100 a pop we have to pass. Maybe someday. I'm sure we'll have another chance next year.

Temps in the 80 all week. I think it's time for a beach visit don't you? I think I need a final 2014 sun burn! I LOVE Christmas in Florida.

TUESDAY - DECEMBER 30 - ICE, WATER, STEAM OH MY

It's a dreary rainy day. Our girl is off to Disney, in the rain, for the choral performance. The rain is supposed to clear up a little later. I'm hopeful for her to have a fun experience. The boy is still in his room. I'd still be in my room too if I didn't have to get up. It truly is the calm after the storm. I was busy getting ready for Christmas that I think it's catching up with me and I'm just a little tired these days. The rain doesn't help. Well, it helps with feeling cozy and allowing myself to take naps, but it's not helping me perk up. I think at this stage of my life it's okay to take naps, whenever I want.

My one errand I was compelled to complete today, other than dropping Zo off at the school, was to take something back to Target then I could get one of those Tupperware bins to store wrapping paper. OCD? Crazy? I think not. Just mature enough to know that NEXT year I want to know where everything is so when we start pulling bins out we will know what's what. Unfortunately, there has been a lot "lost" in this move of ours. Mostly my stuff, or at least it's just that I know which of "my" stuff is missing. Maybe if it's more clearly marked it won't be lost in the future. I think it's a good plan.

Other than that, I started weeding through my emails which led to Facebook, the time suck for sure, then found an email reminding me that I blog. I momentarily forgot. I mean seriously I forgot today was a blog day. Anyway,,,,,,I signed up for this Blogging 101 course and today our assignment is the following:

- Play on the rule of threes. Are the past, present, and future versions of ourselves similar to the different forms of water? (Ice, Water, Steam) Tell us about what's stayed the same as you've changed.
- Tell us about one of the forms of yourself, whether they be con-current, a previous version of yourself, or one that is yet to be.
- If the past, present, and future are the trifecta of time, explore the possibilities. Is time linear, does it overlap, or does it repeat in an endless loop?
- The New Year is a time for self-reflection and improvement. Write about the future self you're going to develop over the next year, or years.

Say what? Kinda doesn't fit with my blogging about nothing theme. It's a lot of writing and a lot of thinking. These types of assignments make me feel like I'm back in school/college, not the dreaded high school, but the Carlow College years I loved. Not to mention it gives me something to do, rather than look at Facebook, or clean. I can answer those questions and still make it about nothing, right?

When have I been Ice, Water, Steam? This might be even a little too out there for me. I guess I've had an icy personality at times. Before moving down here when nothing was happening between 2009 and 2014 that would have been like ice I guess. I was sort of frozen in time. I think now my career is frozen or what my career is supposed to be is frozen. Everything has changed for me now but the changes are not unfamiliar, (man, geography, kids, eh not *sooo* different) but that career frozen thing is something. But is that a version of myself? or a version of the times? My head already hurts.

When things were flowing, like water, I'd say was when I went to Carlow College and other than extreme restricted income, I had pretty much everything I wanted. Loved those years. Going to school full-time, working part-time in the city, a little travel with work, being a sort of stay-at-home single mom. I was doing it. I loved it. Does that qualify as water times? Cause I was just flowing along?

What would constitute Steam? Like Vapor? My past? Cause it's like gone?

I don't usually go back very far in reminiscing because I honestly don't really remember much. The memories that are the strongest are the "mom" memories and the "friend" memories. Those are what tie me to the past. I remember my friends through the years. I love all my friends. The people who I've stayed friends with, people who I knew from various jobs, my friends that have stayed in my life as I've changed. That answers part two of question 1: what has stayed the same as you've changed? My friends (most of them). There are other parts of me that have stayed the same but for today we will focus on friends.

Pictures are the best. When I look at the pictures I remember the people and then I remember how I know the people and then I remember what we did. Ties baby, ties.

Do photo Christmas cards that I've kept through the years answer the question: *If the past, present, and future are the trifecta of time, explore the possibilities. Is time linear, does it overlap, or does it repeat in an endless loop?* I don't know. I just like looking at the pictures.

Tomorrow is more apropos to answer: *The New Year is a time for self-reflection and improvement. Write about the future self you're going to develop over the next year, or years.*

I need time to think about that one. But not now.

WEDNESDAY - DECEMBER 31 - MY YEAR IN REVIEW

It's the last day of 2014! I don't know if that deserves a WOO HOO or a *"damn"*. This year really flew. Everyone else is reviewing so I will too:

JANUARY – living in Pittsburgh

- Had a boyfriend.
- Rented a storage space in the Southside. Why is this mentioned you say? Well, it was a step to getting my independence back from storing stuff in his place in Baden. I didn't think this relationship would last. Plus, for some reason it was kind of fun wandering around that huge building. I've never seen anything quite like it. Jimmy helped me move stuff into storage and was sure it was a place where dead bodies were/are kept. He's probably right. Hundreds of locker spaces, small enough for 2 boxes, large enough for cars. It was an "experience" for me.
- Working and living downtown Pittsburgh. Loving my two-block commute. Loved living in the city. Learned that CVS charges 17 times as much for a broom than say anywhere else. Learned how to navigate the downtown Pittsburgh, where to shop.

FEBRUARY

- didn't have a boyfriend, had to figure out what to do with all my belongings in his house in Baden
- Continuing fun in the city. I believe I had my 6 person Bunko that month with girls over for dinner in my apartment. Loved that. Where was the camera?

MARCH

- Trip to California to visit brother – sister-in-law and sister Kathy. Great trip. Didn't have a boyfriend at the time.
- End of March and I'm back with the boyfriend who is now moving to Tampa. Will I or won't I go? Was there ever a question?

APRIL

- Housing search in Florida has begun
- Still living in Pittsburgh keeping the move on the down-low...somewhat. . waiting for the other shoe to drop or housing in Florida – what will it be?

MAY

- Still waiting for my life to change.
- In the meantime – a Jimbo graduation from college
- And then I got the call – soon to be my home sweet home in Florida and the frenzy began. Goodbyes, packing and moving. While some of my friends were in shock that I was actually making the move, others weren't surprised at all. My brother in for a visit the very weekend I moved. We both stayed at my sisters for the weekend. Spent my last day with him driving around the neighborhoods we used to live in. Zachary helped move me (again) and Jimmy came for a visit and then we were off.

JUNE

- The Blog is born – JUNE 2, 2014
- getting to know my new family and my new hometown
- June also had a quick trip home to Pittsburgh

AUGUST

- It was HOT
- Another trip to the Burg

SEPTEMBER

- New Schools for the kids
- New Schools for the guardian (that's me)

OCTOBER

- Visit to Miami
- Reconnect with old friends

NOVEMBER

- Fall/Autumn in Florida
- Home for the Thanksgiving and Zachary bday holidays

DECEMBER

- Christmas with the Clarks

It's New Year's Eve – I should be getting dressed but I am trying to knock this blog out first. Please forgive any typos I'll catch up later.

And now here's the answer to today's Blogging question: *The New Year is a time for self-reflection and improvement. Write about the future self you're going to develop over the next year, or years.*

The reason I posted the boyfriend breakup and uncertainty in the beginning of the year is because we really never know what is going to happen. I thought it was going to go one way and planned for that (staying single) and then we just decided to go for it and do the couple thing. Ya know? I could have chosen to stay in the city, work the new job, live in the apartment and been happy seeing my boys more, seeing the babies more, but in the end I chose a new adventure. I just went for it and well here I am, in Florida, with the strangers who are now my family. I'm not going to even guess what the new year will bring or the new me will be. I'm just going to watch it unfold. You are all going to watch it unfold with me!

JANUARY 2015

MONDAY - JANUARY 5 - HAPPY NEW YEAR

And here we are. It's 2015. Seriously, 2015. That's like way in the future isn't it? We don't have flying cars, airplanes have pretty much stayed the same since they were invented, but we do have an awful lot of gizmos that we stare at and type on. In our house I am truly seeing where the slang "idiot box" came from for the TV. At least we used to turn it off, didn't we? The TV is on much more with these kids home and shows are so freakin stupid. I think if I have to listen to one more day of the *Simpsons*, or the BBC show *Top Gear*, and now *Street Outlaws* I'm going to lose my mind. Then there's the cooking shows, and the "pimp my treehouse" shows. These shows make everything so dramatic, and they have this music that denotes like a life and death situation when in reality the situation is "will the tree house fit between the two trees?" Ya know? (PS. he turned it off. See? what a good boy)

Our kids have their faces constantly in the cell phone. Jimmy is the worst. Jasen is usually on his cell phone playing games while watching TV. Although that's not too different from me reading magazines while watching TV. The girl stays in her room all day on her gadget. Me personally? I am now back to using a flip phone. The pre-used "smart" phone finally just died yesterday. We found a plethora of phones in the house but only one of the old flip phones will work with my SIM card. Is a new cell phone on my list of anything for 2015? *Maybe.*

What *is* on my list for 2015? As is consistent with 95% of the rest of the population I want to eat right and exercise more. I slept through water aerobics. I'll try for yoga tomorrow. My sister must have told my mother that my weight is up, so every day now my mom asks me if I'm doing something to exercise. *Mom's.* Pete and I decided one time that we were going to walk every day before work. I think we went once. We suck at motivating each other.

I bought some good organic lettuce yesterday at the farmer's market so I can start my new year with good salads. I wonder if I can put Hershey kisses in my salad.

Backing up a bit, for New Year's we got all gussied up and went to Ciro's where Nina works. We left there before 9 pm. We had the 6 pm seating. After dinner we walked through Publix grocery shopping in our finery, talked about Angelina and Brad in case anyone thought we were famous, then home in jammies by 10:00 pm. Both Pete and Jasen were asleep by midnight. There were fireworks everywhere around us at midnight but the trees were blocking most of it. I tried walking to the end of the street to see them but it was dark making me a little nervous to be by myself and by then real smoky from all the fireworks. Didn't hear anybody banging pots and pans. Guess it's different in a state that allows fireworks. We're kind of like an old couple now – he's asleep with his kid before midnight. I'm walking the streets by myself...hmmm.

Today my goal is to start putting some of these decorations away. We started taking stuff down outside yesterday. We were going to go to the beach but Peter started in the yard. He loves to putzy in the yard so we cancelled our beach trip to work around the house. Here's the thing, we (or I) can go *anytime,* so deciding to stay home one day to work around the yard is no big deal. Isn't that cool?

In 2015 though, I do have some goals. I want to learn how to drive a power boat and take sailing lessons with Peter. I also want to find a riding stable and get back on a horse. Also, in 2015 I will win the lottery. My horoscope says so. Horoscopes are always right, aren't they?

I believe it's time to move, as in get off this chair and away from the computer. I have a couple of items at Winn Dixie I need to purchase, then to the post office, then back home and start packing up Christmas shit. The temp right now is 60°. Yesterday at this time it was 80°. It's time to break out the UGGs.

TUESDAY - JANUARY 6 - AND ANOTHER THING

As I was going through the checkout on my daily run to Winn Dixie, I saw a picture from the movie *Titanic* on the cover of this magazine. I can't believe it's been 20 years since this movie came out. Di and I saw it *at least* 3 times at the theater, and of course numerous times since then on TV. I have finally stopped crying at the end, although I still get choked up when she jumps off the lifeboat back onto the big boat because she can't leave Leonardo/Jack. What a great story. Anyway, more nostalgia, and quite timely as I'm driving down to Punta Gorda to see Diane tomorrow. I bought the magazine for her. I might as well read it first. Right? It's always hard to believe we've done something 20 years ago. Especially when 20 years ago we were old then too. Well, I guess not *that* old. We're really not that old now either come to think of it. I watched something the other night on TV and the story was about how you don't start living your life until you're over 50. I get it. I'm living a completely new life.

Something else I read today was about how blogging is exploding. A lot of people out there write about their lives or some random subject. For those of us rattling on about ourselves we have given up all sense of privacy. *The Internet is redefining the concept of self in such a way that there is no private self, there's just a public self. Anything conveyed via the Internet is presumed to be public, whether voluntarily, by surveillance, or by hacking. One's private self becomes a mass media event.*

The WordPress site I use published these statistics for 2014:

Total New Blogs: 18,300,771 (that's 18 million) - That's 49,997 new blogs per day!

Total Posts: 555,782,547 (555 million) Or more than 1.5 million per day.

The top new bloggers have *at least* 10,000 followers and more. How do they do that?

Here are some of my stats (they supplied an annual report – isn't that cool?)

I had 96 posts in 2014, starting June 2

My most viewed blogs:

- 1 Have wrench will travel... 174 views – October 2014
- 2 They call me Mrs. Huwiggins...143 views – November 2014
- 3 You say tomato I said compliment...136 views – November 2014
- 4 I saw Santa! 134 views– December 2014
- 5 I think I can. . I think I can. 132 views – October 2014
  Highest comments and commenters:
  My most commented on post in 2014 was Dr. Seuss I am not
- These were my 5 most active commenters:
    ◦ Ja Nel 18 comments
    ◦ Debbie Bench 18 comments
    ◦ Scott Bench 14 comments
    ◦ Mary Ann 4 comments
    ◦ Liesa 3 comments

I had a total of 5,300 views.

So there ya go. What does it all mean? Mostly it means that I can't make a living doing this but I am happy to entertain my 26 followers! (up from 24!) I am a blogger... whatever that means. My life is out there for everyone to read about. So maybe a good 2015 goal would be to find a "niche" to write about.

I could continue to go on about the weather and my love life,

I could continue to talk about my new family,

I could talk about what we eat,

I can always talk about my boyfriend...still and always the best.

THURSDAY - JANUARY 8 - OLD FRIENDS SAT ON THEIR PARKBENCH LIKE BOOKENDS

I had my first "friend" visitor yesterday. Okay she didn't really visit "me" but I tagged onto a visit she was having with someone else. I'm counting it and I'm going to count on it yearly. It seems appropriate that my first sitting-on-the-beach-with-a-friend would be Diane. She wanted to remake a picture of the two of us that we took in Miami back in the day (1980) when we were leaning against my Ford mustang. Wasn't that a great idea? But we forgot. As I was looking for that old picture I now understand why Diane is anal at keeping her pictures in order. 30 years later she can find them. Who knew? A cautionary tale for young people. But how will they keep all of those cell phone pictures? Diane also forgot her Titanic magazine.

Loved having a day with a friend. Also loved having a day with a friend *on the beach*. Not that it's that much different from sitting on her porch in the summer or dinner at the Sewickley Hotel, but it's the beach and it's Florida so really it's a lot different. She said she's been meeting this other friend for lunch, in Florida, once a year, for something like 10 years. Isn't that something?

You know what else is something? I have to go get the girl and get her permit. I have to gather my proof of residency...in Florida.

FRIDAY - JANUARY 9 - IT WON'T BE EASY, BUT IT'LL BE WORTH IT

A true tragedy of sorts has occurred. My space heater has died. On this, the coldest day of my Florida experience, died...dead. What are the chances I'm going to find another one at the store? It's 48° and an overcast Pittsburgh, grey grey grey day. I turned the heat up a bit, just a bit Peter, but you know the vents are in the ceiling so I can't sit beside them and get warm. I could put some socks and shoes on but I just got my pedicure. I know if I put something on these feet too soon it'll smoosh. Perhaps I should have thought of that before the pedicure you say? Well first, I didn't know it was supposed to be this cold today, second, I didn't know my space heater would quit on me, and third, I didn't know it was supposed to be this cold today (said twice for emphasis.) I know it's relative as up north is literally freezing but still, I'm cold. I have reverted to the hair dryer trick. Just a little warm air blowing on me for just a bit. If I blow it on my feet maybe they will dry enough to put on some warm socks.

Last night was date night and I did wear the UGGs that I got for Christmas, and a sweater top with one of those duster sweater coat thingies and my big wooly mittens. We went to a local Thai place for dinner. It's fun to keep trying and discovering new local options. We have yet to try an Italian place; otherwise, I think we're knocking them out pretty well. We had an early dinner, to Publix to buy some firewood and home to sit in our jammies in front of the fire. No wild and crazy dancing for us. I'm afraid I've lost my boyfriend to Sudoku. He can't wait to come home and work on it. Santa put a book in his stocking and well he's addicted. It could be worse. And I'm getting caught up on my magazine reading as well. It's all good. Still reading *Pillars of the Earth*. I think I started that back in October. I'm on page 787 – only 186 more pages to go. I should knock that out by Spring right? Sheesh.

Yesterday I took the girl for her permit and they said I don't have the right authority. I had stopped in the day before with my guardianship papers and they said it was fine, but the woman yesterday said no, after waiting 50 minutes. However, her dad took her this morning so our girl got her permit. Woo Hoo. Not sure who's going to take her driving but at least it's a step. I don't mind taking her but I want like a deserted area. I think we should get her one of those driving instructors. I won't ever be brave enough to take her on these highways. Not that I think she's a bad driver, or will be a bad driver, but these roads are crazy big and crowded. How did I go through this before? And why is it that I'm going through this again?

I had someone ask me the other day for dating advice, yea I know "me" .. what a joke. But the question from her was should I "run" from someone who has kids. Funny asking *me* that, don't you think? My answer was run if you don't like him for sure, whether or not he has kids is irrelevant but if you like him, and truly like/love him then you will probably like/love his kids too. Even though she thinks she hates kids you never know if that kid will make a change in your life that you could never have imagined or if my friend will be the best stepmom ever. Most people make comments to me, about my situation, as if I'm making this big sacrifice to raise kids again, let alone someone else's kids. But I gotta say I don't know who is saving who here. I'm sure I bring some stability here but I am getting an awful lot out of this experience too. And as the fortune-teller told me, many times, "it won't be easy, but it'll be worth it." I'd have to say she's right on the "it won't be easy" part and every day I'm closer to "it's worth it." Basically, I'm already there.

I got my yearly update from my friend Ellen yesterday and I have to admit I was, and am, super jealous because how much would I love to be living on a farm with a husband who likes to puzty around with excellent projects which is her life now? And then I wonder how many people would love to have *my* life? Okay not many with the kids, but really it's *good* stuff going on here. My boyfriend also loves to putzy around our tropical jungle yard. He has a shed that he hides in at times, organizing for his next project. And we have a garden. I believe our lettuce is ready for salads on Sunday to which we will add our radishes from the garden. Still working on that lemon tree, but we'll get there. We have a great life, we live at the beach for heaven's sake, he has "nice" kids that are great with me. And here I am blogging, which I like doing.

No dear young friend, do not run away from someone with kids just because they have kids. Maybe you should run *to* them!

MONDAY - JANUARY 12 - WHERE DOES THE DAY GO

Where has the day gone? I'll tell you. At the dentist and in insurance hell. New dentist today using my new Obama care dental insurance. Promised to be no more than $285 per crown. Well, this dentist said TEN crowns, plus stuff and I can't get a regular cleaning, I need a deep cleaning which isn't covered by insurance. But now that they've "prescribed" a deeper cleaning it's against the law to do a regular cleaning. I have to pay over $100 (they started out at $251.99 – which included a $90 electric toothbrush? Seriously? *SERIOUSLY?*) Oh, and instead of the promised $285 per crown they said my insurance only covers up to blah blah and MY portion is $925. At least down from $2000 per crown. I told them that something is wrong since the quote is a lot different from what my insurance said to expect so the rest of my morning was spent on the phone getting clarification. But before that, wanting a cup of tea I went in the kitchen and turned on the tea kettle, decided to unload the dishwasher while waiting for the tea. Dropped a glass on the counter top and it shattered everywhere, like *everywhere.* Had to clean that up – clean out the toaster (which was sitting there) clean out the tea kettle, noticed the scum on the bottom of the tea kettle, think *omg gross,* have to clean that out with vinegar, can't get the spout screen back in place, have to go find the extra tea kettle to figure out how to put that in place. There goes another hour. Got a very nice person on the phone at the insurance company and she said "well that makes no sense, they have to abide by the rules of the insurance, otherwise why do you have the insurance?" to which I say "amen" but apparently, it's up to me to call them back, which I do, and then they mentioned something about "hidden" costs. We'll see about all of that. No sense in going to yet a third dentist. I'm just going to have to fight it out with this one and the insurance company and see how it goes. Obviously, I need a lot of work. Eight crowns, 10 crowns, whatever. Not a great start to my week but again...whatever.

Then I applied to two jobs, talked to Diane for an hour or so, made brownies, but still have not had any tea. And now it's 2:00.

Weekend was nice. Friday night I took myself to the movie "Into the Woods". It was good. Sadder than I remembered. Hit a little close to home I guess. Saturday was a soccer game then Peter and I went to the Dunedin Arts Festival. It was fabulous!

Nina came to dinner on Sunday. Really it was a very low-key day. I finally washed my car. I haven't found one of those $5 drive through places yet and believe it or not the car gets very dirty down here. Like dusty, plus there's no garage and I'm parked under trees. And you know how you dream about getting a boyfriend who washes your car, gets your gas and takes care of all that stuff? You think one day…, well, let me tell you, I was out there washing it all by myself. I will admit Pete has shaken out the mats a few times when he has used the car, and he used to get the gas when he used the car, but I guess I'm on my own for car washing. I did a good job, as usual. And it's exercise right? Pete asked if I was going to put my bikini on. That's probably the last time I hand washed my car, when I fit into one of those. That should give you an idea how long ago that was.

We had a nice early Taco dinner with the birthday girl (Nina) and then Sunday night are my shows. I'd force the family to watch my shows with me but sometimes you just don't want to hear the heavy sighs.

I think this is enough for today. I need to go pick up the girl. Did I tell you I took her driving on Friday? We went over to the beach because it was cold and deserted so she drove all around Honeymoon Island. Her dad let her drive a bit Friday night and her sister took her yesterday. Only 361 days to go before she can get her license.

WEDNESDAY- JANUARY 14 - THAT'S WHAT HE SAID

Again, I did not win the Mega Millions. I'll have to reread my horoscope. Maybe I have the dates wrong.

I'm sitting here waiting for a call or a person to show up to fix our hot water heater. Backing up, yesterday I was relieved of my usual Tuesday morning volunteer stint at the school due to some staff meeting so met my BF for lunch. We went to Cracker Barrel. You know you can spend hours in there just browsing. They have some fun stuff. Anyhoo, after a leisurely lunch with my man, I went straight to the school to pick up the girl. After taking one of her friend's home, I let her drive me to the Dollar Store, over the beach road and back home. She's really doing well. Really well. She started singing along with the radio while driving. THAT makes me a bit nervous. We were/are having a debate whether it's better to learn "with" distractions or learn "without" and then add distractions in later. I'm feeling it should be with*out* although she has a strong case of with. In any event we didn't get home until later in the afternoon and came home to a leaking water tank.

A may day situation for sure. After much ado and a scramble to find my channel locks, I was able to turn off a valve that did absolutely nothing to help the situation. Luckily Pete came home shortly thereafter. I was assuming I'd be cleaning up water all night. But he got the water turned off. After more much ado (yes I know, grammar) he fixed the leak, but the heater never turned back on so we still have no hot water. He went to the YMCA for a shower this morning. Had to dry off with a washcloth size square towel as he forgot a towel and it really is not a country club. Oh well, at least he's clean, right? Nobody wants to be the stinky guy at work. Unless of course you're Steve Jobs or Brad Pitt.

Here I sit awaiting the maintenance man. I have some ideas of what to do with myself which I will then be able to report on tomorrow

THURSDAY - JANUARY 15 - IT'S JUST PLAIN UNAMERICAN

Who doesn't like pasta? You know, spaghetti? The Clark kids don't eat spaghetti. It's like they're communists. They do like fettuccini alfredo which I have made on quite a few occasions (and they love, who doesn't? said my thighs) but sometimes you just want the marinara ya know? I used to make sauce back in the day, but then with Nunni (Jimmy's grandma) sending us home with her sauce every Sunday I thought why bother. Zachary actually said he missed my sauce back then. What a good boy. Nunni pasta is a staple in Jimmy's life. I looked in his freezer when I was there visiting him in Columbus and it was FULL of frozen pasta sauce. I'm in the mood for pasta. I suggested it the other night and the kids said to just leave their noodles plain. I didn't make it. I can't remember what we ate. They had plain noodles but I think Pete and I ate something else. Maybe it was salad, with greens from our garden. Yea, that was it. Had no taste. I was so excited and it tasted like nothing.

Today is another grey day. I'm starting to feel like the Pittsburgh weather has followed me here. Other than the temperature difference. But I still have the heater on, so not that different. Okay, okay, it is a lot different. I took something out to the garbage today in my t-shirt and thought it was a little chilly. Just a little

Tonight is date night. We are going to go to a new place, called the Living Room in Dunedin. Not "new" but new-to-us place. The menu looks good. I think we need to go every date night until we have tried everything. I'm half tempted to buy something new to wear tonight but after cleaning out my dresser drawers this morning I think I can probably find something I already own.

Yesterday the water heater guy came, finally, and it was a broken element. We have hot water again. The no hot water was making every-one cranky.

I picked up the girl and we went to Lulus for lunch. Every time I go somewhere I think "when anybody comes to visit we can go here." No matter where it is I'm always thinking of taking a visitor. Anyway, going to Lulu's today was my attempt to have Zo eat less fast food and well I was hungry too. Then I let her drive home. I had her practice pulling up to the mailbox when we got home pretending she was going through a drive through to order food. She did not take off the side mirror. She's doing great.

FRIDAY - JANUARY 16 - TGIF

I got a text from Jimmy saying "who doesn't eat pasta"! Apparently he reads the blog. He has followed up with *when* he visits he is making pasta on Sunday and making everyone eat it. At least I'll be happy. Hope he can get some of his Nunni's sauce on the plane.... and maybe some Mancini's bread?

Last night's dinner on date night was delicious! It's a split dish kind of place so we ordered mango/brie quesadilla, *omg* good, and a beet salad with spinach, bacon, mandarin oranges, red onion, couple of pecans...yumm, it was really too big for two people, but we managed to stuff it down, and then Korean BBQ flank steak lettuce cups. We were so stuffed we didn't even order dessert. That was a first.

And the best news of the day: My boyfriend is home today! We are going to go out into that sunshine and act like we live in Florida. Unfortunately, the temp is only around 60° but it's Florida 60°. Which either means the sun will feel warmer or it'll feel cold cause 60° in Florida is cold. We have errands to run then taking the girl to her old neighborhood and then stopping at the Casino on the way home. Two date nights in a row? Can life get any better than this?

TUESDAY - JANUARY 20 - GOING ONCE, GOING TWICE...DO I HEAR $750?

Ever have those nights where sleep just eludes you? Like until dawn? And then you have all this time to think, which I need like a hole in the wall, cause I don't already think things to death. Lately, however, I have been productive with my middle of the night thoughts. Last time I couldn't sleep I thought of a way to get myself a new smart phone, woke up and ordered it (yet to be received but it should be here very soon, can't wait to take pictures!) Last night, in my restlessness, I made the decision to sell my couch. I can hear Suzanne groaning. I mean really, how long did it take me to decide on that couch? I agonized. But here's the thing, that couch is not family or dog friendly and I am sick of worrying about whether the kids or Pete are going to spill on it or the dog's going to get on it, so in my fit of non-sleep last night I decided I'm going to try to sell it. I got the idea after our busy busy weekend buying a dining room table at Pier 1 and then looking all weekend at various consignment stores for chairs.

The Consignment store said they'd sell my couch for $550; they get ½. I put it on Craigslist for $700. Why so much you say? Because that's what I want. I will take that money, if sold, and get myself a new marble top for the buffet that's never been fixed. Then I think the Clarks will let out a huge sigh of relief because they are sick of me getting mad if they eat/spill/etc. on the couch and it's constantly covered with stuff to keep the dog off. Plus, it's just too small for this Clark bunch. I told Zoë about it already and she seems relieved. She wants something they can allll sit on. I will get my stuff out-of-the-way. Then he can buy new stuff and it will be more suitable for this family.

Now, if you've been following along with my posts, you will know that this whole issue/subject and the final separation of another thing is going to make me cry. Most of you will remember all the money and decisions and fun I had a buying all that new stuff after I sold the house, spending all that money. I had to buy so much new stuff when I moved into that apartment. First it was to make sure that the guest room/Jimmy's room was welcoming enough for him for when he came home from college. I made sure I got nice sheets and comforters, curtains, nice rods, TV shelves, desks. Remember all those pictures framed of their stuff and family pictures? Remember how I wanted them to feel at home? Instead, what happened? Jimmy took the bed to his own apartment and left the beautiful sheets and duvet – but took the down comforter. I never really got a replacement bed other than the one John was throwing out, which was a different size and we propped it up with books cause the leg fell off. I couldn't redo the sheet/comforter look any more. Zachary called the replacement bed the prison bed because he could feel the springs coming up through it. But surprisingly he said it was comfortable. In the end Jimmy probably stayed there twice, Zachary maybe three times in the three years I lived there. I did have a few visitors in that guest bedroom in the apartment who seemed to appreciate it. I had Evan and crew there for a little while, that was nice. My brother visited once and my friend Janice was a great roommate for a couple of weeks. Actually, after meeting Pete that became Jasen's room on the weekends. I even let Sam sleep on the prison bed! I'm not a total monster.

Then I downsized to the city apartment which really was way too small but I hung onto my last few items with claws screeching down the chalkboard, and well now it makes sense for my new family, for me to part with that couch. It served its purpose as we've been getting settled but sadly it's worn out its welcome and needs a different home. No one is happy with it here. I don't even sit on it. There's no room. So, I've commandeered my chair.

A few of my friends have said "just don't lose yourself in all this new adventure with new family" – well, I'm losing furniture that's for sure. Most of my photos that I had framed are broken in a pile, my buffet marble top is broken, I still have my TV but it's in the guest/music room which I don't get in very often. Am I whining? It sure sounds like it. I know again and again they are just things and believe me I will be super relieved when I don't have to look at this couch anymore. The stress to myself and this family over trying to keep it nice is not worth it.

It shouldn't come as a surprise to anyone that I'm always waiting for that other shoe to fall and for me to once again be looking for my own place. It's certainly been my pattern up to this point. Nothing against Peter, it's really not even about him at all, it's about what my norm has been. And, well, I guess if I have to start over again it will be okay. I'll just have to get a different couch. I mean really, I'm at the beach so I'd go with a beach theme. And alternately/preferably if I stay (*when* I stay) with the Clarks for years and years well then that's okay too and I'll like the furniture because it'll be "ours". He's doing a fantastic job of getting new stuff that is "ours" but I swear, if we ever get a new house I am doing one room, completely "Victoria" style. I do miss "Victoria" style but I am embracing the Clark style too. Guess this is all part of this relationship stuff. There's an awful lot to it. Who knew?

THURSDAY - JANUARY 22 - I'VE MET WITH BEACH SUCCESS

I went to the beach and I got some sun. It didn't look promising at first and I had to cover up a bit with my towel (for warmth) but by the time I left it was beautiful. It was a little sad that I had to leave, however

I believe the skin cancer gods were/are probably looking out for me. I always forget to put on sunscreen because, well, it's cloudy, and even rainy sometimes, and cold! Had I still been sitting in that sunshine, *Florida* sunshine, I probably would be regretting it right now with a full-on sunburn. So, thanks to Zoë and her getting out of school early, my face has been saved.

Now I'm sitting in front of my heater. It's a sickness I know.

We're disappointed with our garden. Everything looks like it's growing but no "harvest" yet. The radishes look great up top, but there are no radishes underneath. I dare not move the tomato plant from the screened in lanai into the garden. We tried moving the banana pepper plant and it died within a day. We had one pepper from it, actually we ate it Christmas morning. We need to try peppers again. I mainly let Pete tend to the garden since as I've mentioned he loves that putzing stuff. Plus, he just doesn't get bit like I do from those damn mosquitoes. Last night I went out in the dark to get lettuce for dinner, and brought a mosquito in with me, attached to my hand, sucking me dry. WTF? I'll never get used to that. Pete never gets bit. I don't get it.

FRIDAY - JANUARY 23 - ONE (TWO) DOWN AND ONE COUCH TO GO

The end tables are gone, already. I'm trying to remember why I sold them though. I know we saw similar models all throughout that one consignment store we visited and thought about what they would give us for ours and then just ended up putting them on Craigs list. It was like the momentum of the inquiry. I'm wondering why I sold them cause there's this big empty area where we used one of them to put stuff on, but then again we've moved around furniture because of the new dining room table and well it just didn't seem to fit in there. Anyway, first call, first lookers and they took them. Full price even. Not sure what I'll do if I get a call about the couch. We really aren't in a position to buy a new one yet. HA! Oh well, we'll cross that bridge if and when...

You know when I entered into this relationship way back in the early days in Pittsburgh, Peter came with no furniture. He had a futon for a couch which was the dogs home as well as the two boys (Peter and Jasen) who ate on it every night. In short it was disgusting – it got thrown out when we moved. He had a dining room table. I gave Jasen bedroom furniture that I had bought for Jimmy's room (see previous post on stuff I bought) and our bedroom in Pittsburgh was his bed but my dressers. I'm not sure if everyone is aware that most of the furniture in this new house is mine. Zoe's bedroom is my bedroom furniture. Everything in her room was mine, even the wall decorations. I am very very happy for her to have it. Pete and I did get a new bedroom set together. The guest room is all my furniture which is how I want it so when my boys come they will feel at home. Jasen's room has some of Jimmy's stuff and the living room is all my furniture. Parting with that couch is making me a bit anxious. I have trouble parting with it. None of it has anything to do with them. What I mean is it was all purchased or has meaning before I ever met them. To make sacrifices with my "things" is probably hitting a nerve about making "sacrifices with *my* things" – I don't know , it's just hard. I have so much of me into this relationship, on many levels.

MONDAY - JANUARY 26 - NO SNOW HERE

Does it help to dream that you're here with me in the sunshine or does it make you hate me? Or are you one of those crazies that think all that snow is beautiful? I know there's a big snowstorm up north. I'm watching ad nauseum on the weather channel.

As for the weekend update. . . On Friday, Peter redeemed one of his Christmas presents from me which was advertised as an Autocross experience driving a Ferrari or Lamborghini around a race track for 3 laps. He chose the Lamborghini and it wasn't 3 laps around a race track, it was in a parking lot driving around cones. However, he still had a big smile on his face. I believe it was a successful gift.

Zo and I went for ice cream. I was being good and drank some ice coffee drink while she ate her ice cream. I'm getting kind of sick of the coffee drinks now. No two places make them the same. Sometimes they are loaded with sugar, other times loaded with milk. Maybe I'll just try drinking more water. Zoë had something to do at the school Friday night. That left the three of us (Pete, Jasen and I) to go to Tijuana Flats for some Mexican fare.

On Saturday, Pete and I tried to get up early and go to the Dunedin farmers market which promised to be big. It was *very* windy. We got there and were initially once again disappointed by the limited number of vendors and no local produce. However, we found out that it had been cancelled due to the wind so the vendors that were there were the diehards or the ones that had already started setting up before they got the word to cancel.

Sunday was the best. Peter wanted to walk into our "village" and go to Lulus for breakfast. I was leery because of my feet but they have been much better these days so I went for it. I loaded the "map my run" app on my new phone and off we went. Lulus was closed (she does that on a whim, damn Florida people) so we walked around and ended up having lunch at Thirsty Marlins. I got lobster quiche, so Floridaesque. There is no other breakfast joint within walking distance. Anyhoo, at the end of the day we had walked 3.85 miles and were gone about 4 hours. The weather was perfect. When we got home, as soon as I walked in the door, Zoë wanted me to take her driving. I did. And then our big Sunday night dinner was pizza from Pizza Hut. Does that make me a bad caregiver? Tonight is meatloaf. I hope to make up for my shortcomings over the weekend.

I am trying to get engaged more in my surroundings down here. I am scheduling a few things to make not only my life more interesting but maybe even the blog more interesting. I mean seriously, how much longer can I dribble on about weather, food, teens and dates? Although, I realized today there are 20 years between my son Zachary and Pete's son Jasen. I don't know what it means but I think it might have something to do with sainthood for me. And quite an interesting tid-bit to think about. At least for me.

WEDNESDAY - JANUARY 28 - LITTLE SMUDGE HERE A LITTLE SMUDGE THERE

There are not enough hours in a day, especially when you sleep through too many. I think our bed is possessed. I can't seem to get out of it in the morning. We both have lots of dreams and then this weird thing happens to me too. In the very early morning, I will think that I've slept for an hour and I look at the clock and it's been 5 minutes. Then Pete leaves for work and I think I'll sleep for 5 minutes and it's an hour or two. Isn't that weird? I think it is, and then by the time I get just my normal wake up stuff done another hour is gone. I decided to smudge with sage. Do you know what smudging is? *Smudging is an ancient ceremony in which you burn sacred plants, such as sage, to allow the smoke to clear and bless a space* I thought I'd try it to get the juju out of the bedroom so I can get up in the morning. That's it right? Not that I'm lazy. It's bad juju. Now the house smells like sage. You may think it's a nice smell, kinda like incense, but I have a headache. Go figure.

Date night has been switched to Tuesdays due to Lacrosse practices so we went to dinner last night. Tried out another place in Dunedin, which name already escapes me, and then just came back and watched TV in front of the fire. I started the evening on the couch watching a movie and ended the evening there too. Not that I wasn't productive yesterday. I worked at the school in the morning, then to yoga, picked up the girl and a friend from school, and then I was on the phone with AT&T for an hour (but felt like 4 hours) getting my phone to work properly. Then I did my taxes. I have to wait for my W2 from the ice lady, remember the 2 days I spent schlepping snow cones? She's holding me back.

This dog, this dog we have is a very nice dog, and very smart, mostly. I mean he's a *nice* dog. When people come to the house he may greet you with a jump (and subsequently slam you into the wall) or he may ignore you completely. For instance, when strangers from Craig's List came to look at the end tables to buy, they walked up on to the porch and they were strangers you know, and well, not a peep from that dog. Not one peep. He looked out the window and just walked away. Today, he's upstairs sleeping on Jasen's bed, everything is quiet and all the sudden he starts this vicious barking, runs down the stairs like a bat outta hell, hair standing on end and is jumping at the window. I'm shaking thinking someone is coming to kill me. Know what it is? The neighbors got a new puppy. PUPPY! They have two dogs now, a little Roxy dog (I think that's its name) you know one of those little things, and now this adorable puppy which I think might be a lab mix or some bigger breed as the puppy is already the size of their older dog. I don't know about this dog of ours. It lets strangers onto the porch no problem and wants to go through the window to protect the world from the menacing puppy? Pete took him to the vet and groomers a week or ago and he did just fine they said. Growled a little at some dog but then was ok. They kept him separated from other dogs, but still. I had to put him in the bathroom this morning, where there are no windows so he couldn't see the menacing puppy, until he calmed down. Apparently smudging didn't calm him down.

Another goal I have today is to plan a weekend jaunt with my boyfriend. I feel like we really need dedicated time together to reconnect. I don't know if he feels the same but it's almost like going through withdrawals and although I love date nights, it's just not enough. I need my BF time. I told Pete I'm planning this one and he can plan the next one. That might be fun. I have my budget and I know what I want to do so I gotta get on it. It's a surprise where I want to take him. I won't be able to blog about it until it's complete. That will be a fun task though.

Tomorrow is horseback riding. That should be fun too! Pray that no rattlesnakes jump out at us. That's a thing down here you know, rattlesnakes. I am very used to the lizards now but rattlesnakes are a little different. Fingers crossed.

THURSDAY - JANUARY 29 - I'M BACK IN THE SADDLE AGAIN

I was truly back in the saddle today. One hour, western, walking on the nature trail. I did a little trot which was enough to remember that you don't post western. It was beautiful. The weather was perfect. The trails were really pretty and all sand. We went through a creek and the horse didn't even balk. The lead horse balked at the water but Cracker, my trusty steed, went right on through. I remembered my training and kept him going through it so he didn't get the idea that he was going to go swimming or lay down. Anyway, it was fun and great to be back riding. I didn't get any pictures but believe me it was beautiful and an hour was plenty for my butt and knee. Wonder how sore I'll be tomorrow. Perhaps I'll use that massage Groupon I have tomorrow.

Since coming home, smelling of horse, I have been stoked to get back out there on horseback and have already found a riding stable, closer to home, English riding, and affordable lessons. I think next week seems like a good time to start don't you?

Tomorrow is hair cut day. Erin (old horseback friend) would be disappointed to know that I've finally got the pony tail thing going out the back of my riding helmet and now I'm going to cut it all off. Sorry Erin. But I did get one ride in with my pony tail. If I remember correctly, hair style has nothing to do with riding ability.

I glimpsed a little bit of myself today. That was pretty cool.

FRIDAY - JANUARY 30 - I GOT NUTHIN

I have this big non-compact printer (there should be a better word than non-compact) ,...okay big honkin printer. I got it for Jimmy when he went to college in 2009, he didn't want it because first of all he couldn't figure out how to hook it up and second it was too honkin big. So, I inherited it, hooked it right up and have been using it ever since. The very best thing about it was it was wireless. One night it just stopped working. Just like that. Yes I know, not a major life loss, I'm just saying, I miss my wireless printer.

I had this dream last night that was really stressful. I dreamt I woke up and I was living back in Pittsburgh with this odd group of people. I woke up stressed.

It's the weekend and I'm *not* going to Miami because Jasen has a game tomorrow.

Okay I have nothing inspirational or exciting to share. This is my life...printers, dreams and soccer games.

FEBRUARY 2015

TUESDAY - FEBRUARY 3 - DEAR ABBY, PLAY BALL!

There are a few people who ask me for advice. I give good advice. Today, not to embarrass him or anything, my Jimbo asked me for some mom advice. As usual I gave him the best I got (which is really all one can do) but here's the thing, today I decided I should listen to my own advice...which is...we never know what we're "supposed" to be doing even when we're doing it. The best we can do is keep doing what we're doing and wait for that inspiration to come, or that phone call, or whatever it is that is supposed to happen next to happen. In the meantime, do what you do and when in doubt go to the gym and play basketball!

And with that I called the horse place, signed up for lessons starting next week, and then dragged my ass to yoga. I'm feeling better already.

I don't talk much about my job searching anymore. It's depressing at best, although ...I continue to apply to at least 3-4 jobs per week. *At least.* Sometimes there are really perfect, work-at-home jobs, or part-time ones, or even a good career job (as opposed to just a job-job), I apply to them all. While it is true that I would prefer *not* to have to work a 9-5 or 8-5 or anything to 5 job, 5 days a week, in an office, putting on makeup every day, I am hopeful that at some point I will get something that provides an income. So, I continue to apply for 8-5 jobs, even though I don't want them, just because I feel like I should. If I was my child or friend asking myself what in the world is going on I would have to say that it's not meant to be right now and just keep doing what you're doing and whenever the right thing is ready for you, at the right time, then it'll be right!

As I await my next inspiration my life this month consists of Tuesday morning volunteering at the middle school; next week I start horseback riding on Wednesday mornings; and starting this Friday morning, for a month, I will be attending hospice "volunteer" training and in-between there I'm going to try to fit in a yoga or two, oh yea and clean the toilets when necessary. Needless to say, I am not bored I just have to figure out how to manage the guilt. It's not that I feel like I don't deserve this life I'm living, it's more like I don't know how to process it. I mean who knew *not* working would be so difficult.

So, Jimmy, keep doing what you're doing, and I'm going to start doing more than I've been doing and well, just do it more. And then, we will both have to see where we end up next. Until then, he needs to come here for a weekend warmup. Sunshine can cure most anything. It sure is working for me.

WEDNESDAY - FEBRUARY 4 - HOW ABOUT A CUP OF COFFEE?

Today was another sticker day. I met a friend for coffee. I know! Look at me. But now I'm behind with my day. My friend is Lori – she's a Sewickley person – there's something about being from the same home town that makes you better friends. Here we go, she shows up in her tight-fitting (nice fitting) leather pants, adorable shoes and dressed to the hilt, and here's me in my blue jeans and superman t-shirt and winter clunky shoes. This face rarely sees makeup but I did shower! We had a very nice morning. She's moving here in a few weeks, actually moving "back" here as this is where she lived for 25 years prior to moving to NYC... Anyway, now I'm going to have to fit a friend in every once in a while. The pressure! I came home to having to clean up after the bad dog, someone didn't lock the garbage can. Probably me. I'll probably be cleaning up dog throw up later. Then I booked our vacation weekend. I'm very nervous as it's nonrefundable. Hate that, but he said do it so I did it. It's still a surprise for him and there are a lot of factors that involve us doing things on schedule or things could go wrong. I know very ambiguous, but that's because he reads this and I want this to be a surprise for him. Probably because if not he'd icksnay everything...but I'm hopeful.... *so* hopeful... that it's going to be a fabulous time and well it's a weekend alone, so that's always fun. Happy Valentine's Day to us!

I also am printing out papers that I need for the hospice volunteer training. And yes, I have a new printer. I guess all I have to do is write on this blog things that I want (within reason) and he comes home with a new wireless printer. It really is so so so convenient. My job is to hook the rest of the computers up to the wireless printer. That's on my to-do list. (he ended up doing it)

Last night was date night. We went and looked at cars just for the fun of it. I'm getting the itch for a new car. We both have silver sedans. I feel like there should be an SUV in the family. But he says he's going to fix the Land Rover (we all know he'll never fix that thing). I'm just looking. I like my car – I *love* my car, but do we really need two silver sedan type vehicles? Don't we need something else? I go between something sporty (not particularly kid friendly) to the SUV and throwing all the kid/beach stuff in there. But if he really does fix the Land Rover that takes care of that. Do you see the dilemmas I am faced with? It was fun looking at cars (the lot was closed, no sales pressure). One of our first dates was looking at cars at the Porsche/Audi dealer in Sewickley (on a Sunday when it was closed) and I would make him guess the prices. I have to say he is right about 95% of the time. It's fun. I know nothing about luxury cars. He's rather knowledgeable. It's a fun thing to do for some reason, maybe because it's so foreign to me. After that we went to Rumba's for dinner. Rumba's is one of the restaurants where we first went when we moved here. Got the same booth even. I probably got the same thing. I love it there; I love it here in Florida.

I'm going to have to go pick up the girl, I need to think of dinner possibilities and I was thinking about cleaning that upstairs bathroom. Ughhh... Tonight is a lot of running around with kids. Zo goes to LAX practice at 6:00 – Jasen goes to soccer practice at 7:30 – Zo gets picked up at 8 – Jasen gets picked up at 9:30. How does one even fit in dinner? Saturday is Jasen's last soccer game – Sunday is Zo's opening Lacrosse "jamboree" – We have to drive over an hour to the field where she has games from 1:30 - 5:30 (they play 3, 20-minute games throughout the day). We are sure to be miserable. However, I have signed up to learn how to do the stats (statistics) for the LAX games. I know nothing about Lacrosse so I thought it would be a good way for me to keep up. I used to keep stats at Jimmy's basketball games? I started back when I was 19 years old keeping stats for softball teams. Anyway, lots going on down here.

Weather wise I was complaining to Lori that I was cold this morning, it's only in the 50's, no sun. She said she was loving it. But she's flown in from NYC. Know what I mean? She'll be complaining soon enough.

THURSDAY - FEBRUARY 5 - WHAT AM I DOING AGAIN?

Sometimes I really have to do this blog on the go. I'm on the go today but I'm not sure where it is I'm exactly going. I had a lunch date with the BF so that was a hurry up get up and get going kind of thing. Then a lovely relaxing lunch and then hurry up and get home to pick up the girl. I had two police SUVs pass me while nearing the school and I wondered if they were on the way to the school. Sure enough, seconds later I get a call from Zoë saying they're locked in the school. I started to cry...damn kids. But within 10 minutes they were let out. There are cops on every block and a helicopter. Do we know what's going on? No. Nada, but it doesn't appear that it was something at the school. Maybe they're looking for someone? Or Obama's passing through? Not sure.

I have errands...as usual...but not real comfortable leaving this girl here alone. Although the dog is here. I mean it's not like a high crime area, but it is Florida. Nutty people seem to flock to the warm weather. If you look at the map of sex offenders you would think *only* sex offenders live in Florida. They are *everywhere*!

FRIDAY - FEBRUARY 6 - USING THAT DEGREE

Well today was exciting...so far. This morning was volunteer hospice training. Suncoast Hospice is a big company here in Pinellas County. They serve 69% of the dying population in the county, 1800 patients and family each day and have over 3000 volunteers. Interesting statistics. The orientation class today had at least 20 of us with ages ranged from college students to retirees. If I wanted to just do office work I would be done with training and I could start answering phones or other work non-patient related. However, since I want to work with patients I will go for four more weeks and maybe even more training after that depending on what I choose in the long run.

There are many choices. Backing up a bit, when I went to Carlow I had all those theology courses (my minor) and somehow ended up focusing on death and dying courses in my psychology track and combined the two and did spiritual hospice care for my internship. I never have used my college degree in practice, so to speak, so how exciting could it be to possibly get back into spiritual hospice care? And get this, Suncoast Hospice also has a pediatric care team. I could possibly combine my baby-care (Children's hospital) training with the hospice training. Or:

- Caregiver relief/respite sitting
- Companionship
- Transitions companion vigil
- Or even Palliative arts (pet therapy, energy work, music, etc.)

Our trainer said both the pediatric team and the spiritual care team are very selective and require a lot more training and hoops to jump through. I like a nice hoop. I will probably try to do whatever is the hardest to get into just because of the challenge.

But for now, I will just get through the next four weeks and then I will discuss what to do next. She advised that we plant the seed and see where we end up. I like that "seed planting" analogy. I had a professor at Carlow who called herself the "seed scatterer." I gave Jimmy that advice just yesterday. Told him to pick a future scenario and just sit with it and see how he feels going forward. I did that with Pete and this move. Found out about the move with him in March, came down for a week in April and looked at houses, and then just sat with it until I got the "we have a house" call in May. At no time did I not want to make this move.

We will see where I end up in the hospice thing. I need more information obviously. I really just like to sit with the patients and let them talk, or just sit there to sit there. When I did my spiritual care during my college internship my only real experience was a patient (young – like 40) talking about her fear of dying. Is that spiritual? Or is it just talking? She was scared to death to go on (i.e., die) and helping her find that peace was very rewarding for both of us. She never came back to haunt me. I assume she's ok. But I don't know if that would be labeled "spiritual" or just companionship? Those are the things I need to work out. Babies leaving this world would be heartbreaking to be with the families but I think very peaceful to be with the babies.

On another note, Jimmy booked his trip here February 27! I'm SUPER excited! I hope it's a warm weekend. And now I have to go get the girl.

MONDAY - FEBRUARY 9 - A RAINY DAY IN FLORIDA

What a great day. It has rained all day long. ALLL day. Not only did I get a chance to wear my new rain boots I got caught up on *Downton Abbey*. I only had two episodes to catch up on. I'm a bit disappointed that I don't have any more to watch. I might go back and catch up on Season 2 and 3. Other than that excitement that was it for today.

The weekends are typically so busy that I need a Monday catch up day. Saturday morning started early with me going to "stats" training to learn how to keep stats for the girls Lacrosse games. Then to Jasen's soccer game, then a big lunch and a terrible toothache (still not fixed). And the biggest news is I found another set of dishes that match. Now we have service for 8. I seem to have reawakened my dish fetish. I was tempted to get the last box, having service for 12, but really who needs

12 mugs? They should repackage those dinnerware sets. More dinner plates, less coffee mugs. Maybe even no coffee mugs.

Sunday was an all-day Lacrosse jamboree day. Beautiful weather and by the third game I was feeling like I got the hang of the stats book. Plus, I remembered my sunscreen and hat. Our girl did a wonderful job her first day out ever playing Lacrosse and she's even in the book (the Stats book!) She looked pretty darn good out there. After that long day, another dinner out, we then came home to a quiet night in front of the Grammy's. Usually I don't watch them as I don't think I will know anyone, but surprisingly I knew a couple of the performers and winners. It was a nice night and nice ending to a lovely weekend.

On the agenda for this week is volunteering at the middle school tomorrow, horseback riding starts Wednesday and continue with hospice training on Friday. Tomorrow's date night should be fun. We're doing one of those painting nights. I have absolutely no artist talent when it comes to drawing/painting etc., but it should be fun nonetheless.

WEDNESDAY - FEBRUARY 11 - HEELS DOWN, CHANGE YOUR DIAGONAL, SIT UP STRAIGHT

Today was my first lesson, back in the saddle. I rode Remi. He's 24. By the time I was done riding I was exhausted. I had to concentrate on getting my legs to move one in front of the other so I could get back to the car.

First of all, I had to tack the horse up. Anyone that's ridden with me knows that's my *least* favorite part, but then get this, I'm supposed to pick his feet...me. *REALLY?* Why do we have to pick a horse's feet you might ask? Exactly my question as well. They are just going to need picked out again after I'm done riding, right? Why can't the next person do it? Apparently, horses can get stones or just debris stuck in their hooves and it can hurt them. They can't pick it out themselves. A flaw in their design apparently that I will discuss with God someday. Well anyway, I'm supposed to bend down, get the horse to pick up their leg, you know because a four-legged animal naturally wants to stand on 3 legs, and then use this pick and scrape out any debris I find. WTF. It's just not natural I tell you. There's going to be trouble there. Can they not tell that I'm the baroness? I'm pretty sure I'll be slipping little Kaylen (one of the horse girls) a couple bucks to do it for me.

Anyhoo, Remi is a nice-looking older horse (can't tell he's older) and by the end of the lesson I was back posting on the diagonal, I walked, trotted, cantered and I was even doing a 2 point over some logs and that horse actually cantered over a tiny jump. It was great. Just great. She (my instructor) was very complimentary. It was all coming back to me. I mean I'm going to have the usual issues with keeping my heels down and legs still but perhaps this time around I'll get better at it. The dirt down here is sooo soft but it doesn't seem to trip the horse up. My teacher, (another Katelyn – not to be confused with Kaylen the stable girl) said the ground is soft that it doesn't hurt when you fall. I'm hoping I don't have to experience that because I assure you no matter what she says it *will* hurt.

Katelyn has 10 of her own horses and a total of 34 horses at her place. I just love horse people. They are so dedicated to their trade. She said she owned 3 horses by the time she was 14. She's been doing this awhile. And not yet 30. I also saw 3 full-grown dogs and one adorable puppy. At least 2 cats (I'm sure there are more) 3 chickens, 4 cows, and a parakeet in a cage.

To go on a trail ride the horses have to be trailered to a nearby park. Not as convenient as jumping on and going from the barn like we used to do in Sewickley. But since they trailer the horses to the trail they are already tacked up when you meet them at the trail. That's what the baroness in me likes! I've already scheduled a trail ride for when my sister, Kerry, is here. It also costs twice as much to trail ride as take a lesson. A lot of these girls do barn work in trade for horse lessons or boarding. Perhaps I could offer some office work? Wonder if I could do that for a lesson? She'd probably rather have the money.

Other than this wonderful morning so far, the rest of my update is that yesterday I ended up working at the school all day. The afternoon volunteer called off. They had to put their dog down. How sad is that? I stayed all day. Just like a real job. I even wore real work clothes and I might have had mascara on. And then I came home and got ready for date night.... which was soo much fun. We went to the paint night things. They encourage and expect a lot of drinking. In our small group, the only one pounding drinks was the instructor. It was fun though. The only trouble, we now have two of the same pictures to hang. They should give you an option for one family member to do one design and the other family member do something different. But we will manage and find prominent places for our seahorse paintings. They do look different from each other. We have different styles!

I am hoping to continue with some motivation today and get a few windows washed, screens cleaned and a couple of things done that I've been putting off. We shall see if I go forth and prosper or I sit down and then can't get back up. Posting is a lot of leg work you know. It's also "back" work. Do I have to use my legs or my back to wash windows? What about my arms? If so, I'm thinking it's going to have to wait. Sitting here writing this in front of the heater is pretty cozy.

THURSDAY - FEBRUARY 12 - JUST SAYIN

I'll just say this for today, because the day got away from me, what with the pedicure, talking on the phone to Zachary, running the never-ending sequence of errands, I didn't get a chance to blog. Today I just want to say....

I love my boyfriend. .

Happy Valentine's Week!

MONDAY - FEBRUARY 16 - IT'S WARM – I'M SORRY

I am just learning of a big winter storm across a lot of this country of ours! I am completely unaffected...It's 70° and sunny. This coming Wednesday and Thursday it will only warm up to the mid 50's but I bet most of you northerners would be happy with that. However, our weekend started off coooolld.

Friday night was our first Lacrosse (LAX) home game – I kept the stats and my hands were frozen by the end of the night. I had my blanket but forgot my gloves. It was cold enough that we could see our breath. That's cold isn't it? Then Saturday morning at 7:30 a.m. we had to get Jasen to his soccer tournament. We had blankets again and I was in a turtleneck sweater, it was only about 40°.

Something I noticed over the weekend is where up north temp says 10° feels like -25°; here it says 60° feels like 65°. Just another thing to love about Florida. No matter what the temp, the sun feels good.

I thought I remembered my sunscreen but after two soccer games Saturday, one soccer game Sunday morning and one LAX game Sunday afternoon I'm pretty much looking like a tourist with my sunburn. I don't mind sitting at those games. It's sitting in the sun and how bad can that be? I think we're done with soccer now (season is over) now only have the LAX team to follow. I don't know what we're going to do with ourselves come May. Sleep maybe?

Other than the sports filled weekend we had a lovely Valentine's Day. Having the best boyfriend ever, other than the 2 dozen roses I got earlier in the week, I also got surprised with a pearl bracelet. On our first date (after our initial meeting) he brought me pearls, fake ones, and he meant them as a joke, but I didn't care that they were fake. I still loved them (honestly, I can't tell the difference) but anyway, the bracelet in that fake set broke so I got a new pearl bracelet! And some candy, which of course my teeth and waistline need, and I've eaten all already. Also, after the second soccer game we went to test drive a couple of cars. I drove a Mercedes GLA. They're new for 2015 and slightly affordable and really stinkin cute. Unfortunately (or fortunately depending on your point of view) I didn't love it. If I'm going to drive a Mercedes I want to love it. From there we went to the Volvo dealership and I drove a Volvo xc60. Now that one I did love. But at the end of the day, I don't think I'm ready for a new car. New cars are such an expense and I still pretty much love my old car. But it was fun. It took me a long time to find my Nissan too. I'll probably end up with something but it's good to take our time. For sure.

We had a nice weekend. We're counting down the days to our weekend away. I don't know who's more excited about it. I think it would be hard to beat my excitement. The weather looks like it will cooperate. He still doesn't know where we are going which is making it more fun -watch he'll hate it- but he better not, cause the main event is each other. NO kids.

TUESDAY - FEBRUARY 17 - GO NORTH YOUNG MAN

Pete and I (or probably just me) read an article about the way you sleep effects (or is it affects) your moods and your dreams. Remember I said I have weird dreams? Our bed faces East. According to Feng Shui the best sleeping is if your head is to the South. And I've noticed that when I'm taking a nap without him my body completely turns with my head facing South! We're doing an experiment and trying two nights facing each way. When we were facing South I slept the best (so far) and he slept the worst. He likes sleeping West (which was last night) and I was miserable this morning. One more night of West (poor Pete) and then tomorrow night we end with North. Doesn't this sound like fun? At the end of the experiment I'm not actually sure what we'll know, but no one can say we aren't a "fun" couple eh?

This morning I worked at the school (I volunteered but isn't that the same as work?) Only excitement is some kid had his bike stolen and the kid that stole the bike on Friday brought it back to school today as if it is his bike, so the kid that it originally belongs to put his lock on it too. Should be an interesting end of the day. Too bad I'll miss that part.

You can only take the bus if you live 2+ miles away. Otherwise, they expect you to bike or walk or get dropped off. There are lots of bikes at this school. Quite a few skateboarders too. We used to keep the skateboards in the office but the Principal said no more, because there were too many. The kids told me they throw the skateboards in the woods now, to hide them until the end of the day. He told me no one would steal them because it's an unwritten skateboarder's rule that they don't steal each other's skate boards. I asked if the same applied to bikes and he said "no, nobody cares about bikes". Who knew?

Now home trying to figure out what I should do first. Laundry? Dog hairs? My schedule is off because the kids were home yesterday (or at least I'll blame it on them) and now I don't know what I'm supposed to be doing.

Tonight is date night. We're meeting some Sewickley people in Dunedin. Just can't shake those Sewickley people (JK, it'll be nice). Lori is back now, all moved in I believe. We live about 5 miles from each other.

Tomorrow is horseback riding day. I know, I have a nice life, don't I? Oh, and wait, I just remembered I get a facial tomorrow too. I'm treating myself so I can try to look "good" for my weekend escape with my BF. I'm hoping it makes me look younger. Hoping....

I'm sorry that this dribble is getting more mundane. I mean it's a nice life, not like "work" mundane but you know, it's just routine now. I'm hoping that something inspirational is going to happen here soon, something worthy of sharing, but in the meantime I'll continue with the routine of writing the updates (i.e., blog). The addition of Hospice might add something. But that's another 4 weeks of training. In the meantime, I'll just provide you with these daily escapes so you can live vicariously through me. Who knows, perhaps tonight you will face a different way in your bed and see if you sleep better?

WEDNESDAY - FEBRUARY 18 - SO MUCH TO SAY, SO LITTLE TIME

First of all, last night was date night and I must say it was very nice. Not that all our date nights aren't nice but this time we met up with other adults. I mean how nice was that? We met in Dunedin at The Living Room (our favorite restaurant) and had dinner with 3 other adults! We really had a lovely evening. I apologized to Pete for all the "Sewickley" talk, and those of you that know this syndrome know how annoying it can be. Pete said his wife and her friends would talk in foreign languages (she spoke 7 languages, fluently) so he was just happy to understand the conversation. When Sewickley people get together all we talk about is other Sewickley people and/or memories of Sewickley things. We all do it. I will say though last night we did talk about other things too. Florida things, boats and fish and beaches and how much we all love living here. Anyway, it was fun. I had a really nice time and there was a great band playing there as well. We sat in the back and were able to talk without screaming (don't you hate that when it's so loud?) and then moved to the front to listen to the band before leaving. Great musicians. I've been talking with a few people who happen to be musicians and I'm just waiting for Peter to get that guitar out and start-up a new band. Wouldn't that be fun? Just have to get him to practice. Maybe I could do what my mother used to do to us, lock us in the room for a ½ hour and make us practice. I'll lock him in the music room.

This morning was horseback riding. I had to laugh when Katelyn (my instructor) said to dress warm. She's all snuggled in her sweat-shirt. It's 55° and sunny. I'm like "are you kidding me? " Perfect riding weather (other than the wind). I rode Remi again. He's a nice horse, but it was/is windy today and you know those damn horses get spooked at nothing. The wind was an issue and then he spooked at something and jerked (I stayed on – YAY). My back is for sure going to be killing me tomorrow. (I've already called for a massage appointment – thank God for Groupon) I was squeezing as hard as I could with my legs to get him to keep his trot but that horse was pokey today. I was slow trotting and posting and bouncing and ugh. My feet kept falling out of the stirrups, (we finally raised the stirrups, it helped) my legs were pinching against the stirrup straps, I really need boots or the pants with the leather insets. I think I'll order them today. It wasn't a really relaxing ride this morning. I was exhausted just trying to keep that horse moving. He did canter pretty easily but then I was nervous that he was going to spook while cantering so it just wasn't a very good day. She's got all kinds of things in that ring that look spooky even to me, and then the wind, and added to all that was the mud puddles that he just wasn't' feeling like going through. But get this, when we were done with the lesson I walked him (while riding) around the ring 3 or 4 times and I sang to him so he would stay calm (was my intention anyway) and then when I said OKAY let's go in he walked right up to the mounting block and stopped so I could get off. Now how cool was that? Last week I jumped off. I think he liked my singing. At least that's what I'm going with. I'm already getting better at the tacking up and untacking but that picking their feet thing, I don't know. I don't know that I'll ever be comfortable doing that. I mean I guess they can't really kick you if you're holding their foot up but I was actually shaking I was so nervous doing it today. He even picked his feet up for me. Oh well, I'll try it a couple more times I guess. Why can't they just shake off their feet like the rest of us?

This afternoon the girl wants to go to Chipotle after I pick her up from school, then I have that 3:00 facial, then I take her to practice at 5:30 – then I have to think about something for dinner. I made spaghetti the other night, remember me saying that? It was delicious. Even Zoë ate it. Jasen stuck with his butter noodles but Pete, Zo and I were very happy. I froze a bunch of sauce because....both boys are coming next week!

I'm so excited I could puke. Zachary finalized his plans yesterday. Jimmy will come in Friday afternoon and leave Monday morning (early) – Zachary is coming in Sunday night and leaving Wednesday afternoon. I believe everyone will be here for dinner on Sunday night. ALL of us. We need someone here to take a picture. I hope I make enough food.

We also need a couple more chairs. I might even have to go back for that other box of dinnerware. I'm really *soooo* excited.

That's another thing I have to do, pack. I'll have to do that tomorrow morning. Zoë and I have to leave at like 5:00 pm for a 7:00 pm game and we won't be home until probably 11:00 tomorrow night. Why can't they have busses? Eh? What about Jasen? He can't sit there all night in the cold. Dam kids.

THURSDAY - FEBRUARY 19 - CAN YOU BELIEVE IT?

You know how when you're going away you have all these things to do prior to going? I feel that way today. I'm trying to make sure there's enough food for those left behind. I'm washing everyone's sheets for some reason, I have to wash my own clothes to wear to the LAX game tonight too, my warmest outfit needs washed (I wore it horseback riding). The temps tonight are going to be in the teens with wind chills. Can you believe it? I mean *CAN YOU BELIEVE IT?* And you know I wouldn't care so much if I could just stay home in front of the fire and watch *Grey's Anatomy*, but noo, I'm traveling an hour + to go to Zoë's game, to sit out in the cold and possibly keep score for these poor little girls who are going to be so cold they won't know what hit them. I think they should cancel the game. I think we should all just stay home. Thank God there's no rain in the forecast or we would be staying home staying off the black ice. I guess one reason it is going to be extra cold is that it is a clear sky. I don't know, these weather people are all nutty.

If I had more time I'd get some yard work/planting done. It's time for spring planting you know and I've already bought some flowers to put in the pots. But I don't think it's in the cards for today. We have to cover plants tonight because of the cold. I've already brought in my jade tree.

I took the car to my regular oil change place and they're closed. I bet it's too cold for them. I could take it in the morning but it's still going to be cold tomorrow too. I guess it can wait until next week. See what I mean? My head is spinning with what needs done. Meanwhile I'm only going to be gone overnight. Something is wrong with me.

And now I'm not sure what to do with myself. Should I start something here? Should I plant the flowers? Should I go find another place for the oil change? Should I pack for tomorrow? Hmmm, I think I'll pack, then plant, then get the girl, then maybe I'll get the oil changed.

I need a personal assistant.

MONDAY- FEBRUARY 23 - DA PLANE BOSS DA PLANE

This past weekend was Peter's surprise get-away weekend. It was beautiful and a huge success. We went to Cabbage Key. Peter did not know where we were going and the only time he totally dropped his excitement was when I said we had to take a flashlight. He keeps saying he likes camping but when he thought we were going camping he got a little leery. I think it's a safe bet that I will *never* book a camping trip...unless there is an RV involved. Off we went around 10 a.m. Friday and pulled into Pineland Marina about 2:00 pm – we were early for our water taxi ride.

He had no idea where we were going and even after I told the charter guy that we were headed to Cabbage Key it really didn't tell him much. We made a couple of water taxi stops on North Captiva and then got to our island "home" about 4:00 pm. The taxi dropped us off right in front of our cottage. We forgot money for tips and Pete assumed he would get cash out at the resort – we both would have assumed that. HA! Not this resort. The water taxi people were very happy with their $20 tip.

We rented the Dollhouse Cottage. An adorable cottage right on the water with our own private dock. The water taxi ferry dropped us off on our private dock. We walked right into the cottage, doors unlocked, and made ourselves at home. Then we had to figure out how to check in. There were no signs, and no way to know what to do next. We just headed to the biggest building (not the private home beside us) and that was the answer!

The weekend was filled with absolutely nothing. There is nothing on this island other than a walking trail, a water tower to climb up, a restaurant and a marina. There are no "resort" amenities. (and no ATM for sure) You're even supposed to bring your own water as the tap water is "well" water and it does taste pretty nasty. We needed the flashlight to get from the restaurant back to our cabin. There are no lights between places. There are no cars on the Island (obviously) – it's only 100 acres. There are a couple of golf carts and there are residents on the island. There is the owner with a lovely house right beside our Dollhouse cottage and then a random person who has a beautiful house, (for sale now for 1.7 million) at the tip of the island. Also, the staff lives on the island, imagine that?

The Island was originally purchased by the family of the author Mary Roberts Rinehart for their winter vacation home. The Dollhouse was originally built in the early 1930's for the Rinehart children as a playhouse. It has been remodeled from its original playhouse and has two rooms, a powder room bath in one room and a shower and sink in the hallway, a large front porch and the dock. We had a TV in the bedroom. It got about 3 channels. It was great! The walls had seashells and driftwood and coconuts all around where people had left their names and little sayings on each. We added our own personalized coconut.

The bar/restaurant is known for its "Bill Bar". The walls and ceilings are lined with dollar bills. They estimate $70,000 to be on the walls. It started back in the day when a fisherman taped a dollar bill on the wall and said he knew he would be able to eat there again if he ever came back. It's progressed from that. They say approximately $10,000 falls off every year which they donate to charity.

Another "claim to fame" story is that Jimmy Buffett wrote his song *Cheeseburger in Paradise* at this bar. Although I think that's just an urban legend. I also read somewhere that it's not uncommon to see famous people here as it's certainly a place to get away from it all for sure. There are no phones on the island but cell phones do work. I also read how the owners' son grew up on the Island and took a boat to the mainland every day for school. Now he lives on the mainland and comes by boat to the island everyday to work at the "resort". I mean really you have to use the word "resort" loosely. It's not like a resort-resort.

Here's what we did on our vacation. Sat on the dock and watched boats come in. And there were some *big* boats. When we went to dinner Friday night there were about 10 people at dinner. At breakfast, there were 4 of us. When Debbi (our waitress) told us they were expecting about 600 for lunch I'm thinking, yea right, but the parade of boats in and out of there all day was spectacular. I mean it entertained us all day. We had rented a skiff for the day but it was too windy in the morning and we said we'd come back around noon. At noon the dock guy said it was too busy and he couldn't get to us so we were content to just sit and watch the boats go by. Everyone waved. We felt like the welcoming committee.

We also went for a walk, we climbed the water tower and watched the sunset, we played backgammon (he won) we played 500 rummy (I won), we went to meals. There was sex, it was alone time. It's what I love.

On Sunday morning, after I snapped out of my depression of it being over tooo soon, I sat out on the dock and soaked in the quiet. I mean *quiet*. With no cars, traffic, nothing to make noise it was beautifully quiet. The water was like glass, smooth and did I mention quiet? I heard this blowing sound and opened my eyes to see a dolphin swimming close by. Also, an egret flew down and landed on our dock and kept me company.

Then we got on the water taxi to leave, I went kicking and screaming.

On our way home, we stopped at a great town called Matlacha. It's soo colorful with all these little shops – everything is painted bright bright colors – I mean BRIGHT. So, we stopped and shopped. Each place was unique with different artists displays and different art styles. We stopped for lunch at the Blue Dog where I had the best coconut shrimp wrap ever. I mean EVER.

It was a beautiful, hot day. A perfect way to end the perfect get-away weekend. We had a lovely time getting reacquainted with civilization in

Matlacha, and then headed home. I didn't cry too much. I have a busy week this week getting ready for the boys to visit next weekend. I'll just focus on that.

Cabbage Key is the kind of spot that when I start my book I'll go and stay a month or so. I mean how kismet is that? Writing a book on an island where Mary Roberts Rinehart wintered...and she was born in Pittsburgh and lived in Sewickley! Holy Moly. . It's meant to be.

She's famous for starting a book with "had I but known"...I think that's how I'll start my book...

TUESDAY - FEBRUARY 24 - THOMSON NEWSPAPERS, VICTORIA SPEAKING

It's hard to follow yesterday's blog. I'm trying to hold onto the "island" feel but it is slowing dissipating. I know I should be all caught up in the boys visit this weekend, but wouldn't it be nice if the boys were visiting us on the Island? Oh well, just a little more dreaming. Dreaming got me this far, guess it doesn't hurt to keep it up.

It's a blah day here in the south, although at least not cold (even though I have my heater on.) I'm trying not to focus on the weather for the boy's visit but it's hard not to. It looks like Jimmy might get in one good Florida day, and Zachary is going to get perfect weather for his 3 days. I've got to quit looking at it, it's bound to change anyway. And really we still are 60° warmer than it is up north so it's going to be okay no matter what.

I know the first thing we'll do on Friday is go to the beach. Even when the temperature is only in the 60's you know when you're visiting you want to see the beach. It's funny how acclimated I am already to this climate. I think it's cold. I rarely get to the beach (because it's too cold).

All the things I thought I'd do once I lived in warm weather, like walk every day and stay active have gone out the window. Although I feel like I'm active every day, I rarely go for walks. Rarely. And you know how you think once you're not working anymore you'll have all this time to exercise? Well, yea, not so much. I'm getting activities in here and there but not like what I thought. Thank the Gods for Pete (for many reasons) but if it wasn't for him I probably would be getting even less activity. He's usually dragging me out the door on weekends to go biking or walking. I don't know about you all but I find that I am rarely right about figuring out my future self. Other than the fact that I am here now in Florida, I don't think I've gotten anything else right.

I've been thinking about work. Everyone pretty much knows how much I didn't ever want to work in office work, I think I made that pretty clear. Although there were times when I did some tasks that were rewarding and granted my meeting planning life was good. Meeting planning at Thomson was fun, rewarding and paid well. But I was over it when I was over it and was ready to move on. Maybe it's because I thought I would have done "more" at my next job. But as much as I hated the office is it really over? And if it is, what did all those wasted work years mean? Just a way to eat? Barely? I don't know. It seems a little odd that it could all be over. Something seems unfinished. I imagine when you retire you look back on all these years of hard work and look forward to not working. But with me I thought I was getting out of one place and going to get back into another. I don't feel closure on that part of my life. I need closure. I am *happy* to have closure there, but I don't have it yet. Ya know? I don't feel spoiled by not having to work, although Pete might disagree. Maybe I need to embrace being spoiled and be thankful that those office days are over. Maybe it's all about accepting that they are over, or maybe they aren't over. I mean I want them to be over, don't get me wrong, it just doesn't seem like the right timing. It feels unfinished. Is this a mid-life crisis thing?

Time now to go get the girl. Then I think it's a BLT day. Then it's also date night. For date night I think we're hitting Costco. Gotta stock up for the weekend. My boys apparently want me to cook. Dam kids.

WEDNESDAY - FEBRUARY 25 - LOOK WHAT DAY IT IS

I'm already jumping a cross rail. How about that? A very low jump but still. Can't get that horse to keep a trot to save my life but he canters pretty well and he seems to know when there's a jump to go over to keep the pace. I don't think I'm doing anything. That horse is trained enough to know what to do. But he really doesn't like to keep a trot. There are many things in this ring, like chickens, another horse, a donkey, lots of props sitting around, a tractor. I mean WTF? I guess it helps that the horse doesn't shy away from these things but at the same time he's cautious wondering what the heck all this stuff is in the ring. Do you blame him? We stopped for a drink of water and there was another horse on his tail. Like where did this horse come from? Oh well. Maybe one of these days I'll get my feet digging into his sides just right, and I'll be fearless and then maybe he'll be more fearless. At least this week he didn't spook. Thankfully there was no wind. I was very close to cancelling this morning and thought of Erin who would have been calling me yelling at me to get my lazy butt out of bed and get my ass on that horse, and so I did. I don't know why I get lazy like that. I was a little better at the feet picking thing today. I didn't shake with fear as much, but I'm still not ready to do it myself...probably ever. As I was leaving there were a couple of kids grooming a horse beside me. One little girl the size of a peanut with a very big horse, no fear. Those girls are brave. After a couple more lessons I'll get out on that trail again. That's what I really like, trail riding. I just need to get my confidence back up. There's a woman there who cleans stalls and stuff. I asked her if she still rides and she started telling me horror stories about her and her sister riding and how bad her knee is and how her sister's horse bucked her off and broke her leg in several places. Really? *REALLY?* The answer was no she does not ride, but she seems to be okay with picking the feet.

After riding I met Lori at her new place. She's already ordered new kitchen cabinets, bathroom tiles, new appliances. I mean this is a woman on the go for sure. It was a nice visit. Then off to get the girl, and now home to figure out what to do. I'm waiting for tomorrow to do the big cleaning. I'm washing a bunch of bed stuff for the guest room. We bought new sheets and pillows last night at Costco. The sheets are so soft. I think I'm going to have to go back and get us some too. If I was motivated, I would work on some curtains. But I'm not. Maybe I have a bug. It's possible I have Island fever. Is there such a thing? Post-Island fever maybe? Tomorrow is going to be the big push to clean. I'll start drinking caffeine as soon as I get up!

Date night was spent at Costco and then we just came home. Not a big date night but I like Costco too. We were checking out the 80" TV. Can you imagine? 80"? We didn't get one. I don't know what our next big purchase is going to be. Maybe a car for me. I need to get out there and drive some more to see what I want (and we can afford). Honestly you'd think I have all this time, but it fills up fast.

THURSDAY - FEBRUARY 26 - AIN'T IT THE TRUTH

Nothing like having company to get your house cleaned". Ain't it the truth? I got up at the crack of dawn, beautiful sun shining, birds chirping, a lovely lovely spring day in Florida and I started with the cleaning. It's 10:38 pm and I'm finally done cleaning. I think I did 16 loads of laundry, cleaned the hall floor twice and actually never even made it upstairs to clean. However, I also got a mammogram, my knees x-rayed, an oil change and my car washed, took Zoë to practice, picked her up, went to the grocery store 3 times. I should sleep good tonight...should.

Jimbo comes tomorrow. I'm nervous about his plane taking off because of the stupid cold. I think it's going to be -1° tomorrow morning in Columbus. The trouble is he's on Allegiant Air and they only fly one flight a day to Tampa. If it doesn't take off that's it I guess. Well, I trust it's all going to go well. Zachary doesn't come until Sunday. We won't be cleaning again. The truth is neither kid cares if there are dust balls in the corner, or dog hair. They grew up with dog hair. To them it's just a way of life. But there's just something about company that makes you clean, clean, clean. And I'm grateful, on many levels.

In other news, running through Publix the meat man noticed me, in my shorts, with firewood in the buggy. He commented "only in Florida do you see someone in shorts buying firewood". HA! Another ain't it the truth moment? I was getting my oil changed today when my sister called. I went outside to talk to her, with my t-shirt (no jacket), the sun was behind clouds and I was freezing. My sister said I had no idea what freezing meant. Ain't it the truth? The temperature has been really hard to dress for. When the sun is out it's hot. I mean it feels really good, the air is "chill" and the sun is hot. But when that sun is behind clouds, or behind fog as has been the past couple of days, it gets cold. The jacket is off, and on, and off. You're in shorts buying firewood. What can I say?

Tomorrow morning I go to hospice training and have to cut out early to go pick up Jimmy. I missed last week too due to surprise Island weekend. They said it's no problem and that I can make up the missed days. I hope they're not kidding. This weekend is going to be really busy. Jimmy comes in at 12:30, Zoë gets out of school 2:00, we both go to the LAX game around 5:00, I'm keeping score. Jasen has an 8 a.m. game on Saturday at a field an hour away. If he wins they play again. We are praying for a loss. Zoë wants to go to the mall Saturday afternoon and then to her friend's house in Safety Harbor. On Sunday she has two Lax games (I'm not volunteering for either of them), and somehow I have to fit in Jimmy. Then Zachary comes in Sunday at 5:45 pm. I'm cooking dinner for 8-10 people Sunday night. I mean busy. I will take this opportunity to say have a good weekend.

Wish me luck getting all the kids together. I think it's going to be fun!

MARCH 2015

MONDAY - MARCH 2 - EIGHT IS ENOUGH

We need a bigger house. We had all the children last night and I want them all to live here. Of course, I'd probably change my mind after a day or two, but what a nice weekend we had.

Jimmy came in Friday around noon. It was pretty chilly but still warmer than Columbus, *much* warmer. We went home to "check in" and then I took him on a neighborhood tour on the way to the beach for lunch. Pete and Zo met us and we all ate at the beach. It was freezing. Okay not freezing freezing, but even the Beach Hut had the side thingies down keeping the wind out. We were the only ones there. We still had a lovely time. We walked on the beach after eating and picked up some nice shells. Lots of ocean (Gulf) debris was washed up on shore after some storm that I apparently didn't know about.

After that we headed to Zoë's LAX game. She had gotten the game ball for the previous game and this game they didn't put her in at all. Go figure. I kept stats. Pete and Jim sat on the sidelines. Jimmy said it felt like a fall night at a Football game - it was pretty chilly. Out to dinner at our neighborhood Pizza place and then I made cookies! It was a great first day.

On Saturday we got up at the crack of dawn and drove an hour to catch the last 20 minutes of Jasen's soccer game. I wanted to drive back up the coast so he could see the sites but it was raining hard, so we just drove home.

It rained allll day. Jimmy spent most of the day sleeping on the couch but the day ended with a trip to the mall. Jimmy wanted some new clothes so we went to Old Navy and the mall and he got a ton of stuff. He was very pleased with his purchases. I had intended on making meatloaf that night but it got too late and we ended up eating at the food court. I felt like a real bad mommy. He came all this way and ate

Wendy's for dinner, but ya know, I can't do everything. I mean I *can*... but I didn't.

Saturday night we ended up seeing a late showing of the movie *Kingsmen*. We didn't love it. It's very violent, like graphic violence which means not a great "mom" movie but I hung. It was okay.

Sunday was a beautiful day. After a home cooked breakfast, Jim and I took off for the beach.

Zoë had two LAX games. The first game nobody went to because I was off to the beach and Peter was trying to catch up on stuff. She played ¾ of the game and they won and she played really well. The second game I was picking Zachary up at the airport so Jim and I didn't go, but all the Clarks went and they didn't put her in. High school sports.... they make you crazy.

Backing up, Jim and I went to Clearwater Beach where I proved what a bad mom I am. I don't know what I was thinking but since he missed all of Saturday due to rain and had no sun he (we) decided that it wasn't the end of the world to skip the sunscreen. OMG. I almost killed him. First though we had a lovely time on the beach. It was very crowded, pretty hot, and the water was freezing, so really there's no cooling off on days like that. But still it was nice. When we got home he exploded with sunburn. I mean *exploded*. If he was younger CYS probably would have cited me. But today I think he was looking pretty bronze. The good news is it kinda worked. He got a lot of sun so he looks like he was in Florida for the weekend.

We picked Zachary up at the airport and headed home and then everyone got to meet each other. Then we had a darn good dinner, if I do say so myself, and the evening ended up with all of us on the pool patio playing guitars. Even Peter was playing. It was nice, I wanted to cry. Monica got a picture of all of us with her fancy new camera but I'm not sure when I'll get a copy of the picture.

We all stayed up too late and after a very few hours of sleep, Zach and I took Jimmy to the airport. It was sad. But we have broken the ice now and he sees how easy it is to get here, relatively cheap (relatively) and of course who wants to be in snow and ice when you can come here and have your mom make you peanut butter and jelly sandwiches, at the beach? Who?

Zachary and I went to a very early breakfast (dropped Jimmy at the airport around 7:00 am) and then we headed to the beach. It was foggy but cleared up very nicely by the time we got to the beach. We walked for 5.5 miles. My feet are killing me. Took 4 hours. He never took his shirt off and again no sunscreen (I wore my 50 spf on my face). I don't think either of us thought we'd walk that long. We just lost track of time. Anyway, I may never walk again.

Then we picked up the girl after school and went to lunch. They both had ice cream for lunch (I had chicken salad) See? Still a good parent.

Tonight I'll try and get that meatloaf together and then hoping to take him to the beach for sunset. That should be nice. Tomorrow he wants to go back to the beach and "sit" (thank God). I will make sure he wears sunscreen.

You know this constant entertaining is tough. I mean I have to make so many beach trips. Do we walk on the beach? Eat at the beach? Lay or sit on the beach? Then do we go for ice cream? Shop? I mean so many tough decisions.

WEDNESDAY - MARCH 4 - TOMORROW IS ANOTHER DAY

In about an hour I'll take Zachary to the airport. Right now he's playing the piano. I think I've mentioned before how much I've missed hearing music in the house. Zoë plays sometimes now, which also makes me cry – you know like happy cry – to have music back in the house.

The past 6 days have been pretty darn fun, and full for sure. I think I've mapped out my life pretty good so that when one thing ends, I have something else going on. Like when Zachary graduated from high school. I remember my sister and mom staring at me thinking I was going to lose it and start crying. However, Jimmy was soo bad at Zachary's graduation ceremony, jumping all over the place, that I couldn't even focus on Zachary, therefore didn't even think to cry. When he went off to college I still had Jimmy home and well it just felt like he was gone at his dads for a week. Actually, I was away on a business trip when he went to college. I didn't even get to drop him off.

When we dropped Jimmy off at the airport on Monday morning, Zachary was pushing me to keep going to go out to breakfast and start his vacation. I didn't have time to get teary. Today when Zachary leaves I have to rush home and get ready for a bonfire tonight for Jasen's soccer. I'm going to make cookies. No time to cry later. I thought I'd cry now.

The great thing is that the combining of families has gone off without a hitch. I mean seriously, no hitches, at least from my side. I'll get the debriefing from the Clarks but they sure were nice enough. Jasen even let Sam sleep with Zach last night, much to my chagrin. I felt bad, and Zach did too, that we couldn't spend more time with Jasen. Jasen was begging to skip school yesterday and go to the beach with us. I was close, but in the end I stood firm and said NO! Zachary is hoping to come back in the summer when Jasen is not in school and do more stuff together. This was a great trip for both of my children to get the lay of the land, see that their mom is being taken care of, living a good life, and one that they both hope to visit more often. Zach will be crying about waking up to 18° tomorrow in Pittsburgh. I mean who wouldn't cry waking up in 18° weather. He's also getting home right as the snow storm hits Pittsburgh tonight. Maybe it'll help him decide to move south, with his mommy.

Tomorrow, it's back to normal stuff. I'm going to have to keep busier than normal for a couple of days. I predict the boys will be back, sooner than later. A free place to stay in Florida, with their mom. Who can beat it?

THURSDAY - MARCH 5 - DEEP CLEANSING BREATH

I slept good last night. When I was a meeting planner we would work on an event for months, then the last month before the event was last-minute busy, and then when the actual event was happening it was hit-the-ground-running type stuff. I was up and *on* for 3-4 days and then when I'd get home it would take about 2 days to recover. All the planning and the event madness just caught up with me. I don't know how people do it when they don't get time off after an event. I was always so exhausted. Anyway, that's how I felt last night. Such a build up for the kids coming. Getting the room ready, planning events and family time, and although the event itself wasn't stressful, lots of sleeping on the couch with kids and sitting on the beach, I have to say after Zachary boarded and the tears came, I was exhausted. I was very grateful that my boyfriend met us at the airport and kept things moving for me so I didn't totally collapse. Honestly, I really don't know what I'd do without him. It's like he had some 6th sense to know to meet me at the airport (and say goodbye to Zachary) and keep me going.

I made cookies for Jasen's bonfire; I think only 2 were eaten. It was dark, nobody could see. Pete took them to work today. I didn't stay long at the Bonfire as I bugged out to pick up Zoë at practice. But I could feel the tired just washing over me. Needless to say, I slept really really well last night.

Pete and I had a lunch date today which was very nice. And now I'm back to shopping on-line for a new comforter, looking for flights to and from Virginia for my next trip, tickets for a Pirate training camp game here in Florida, and then going off to a doctor's appointment. Not a lot of time to be sad. Honestly, I'm not sad. I'm going to see them again in one month so there ya go. All is well. We have 11 days until our next visitor arrives (Pete's mom). Maybe we'll (and when I say we'll, I mean he'll) paint the bathroom before his mom gets here. Maybe we'll have our pool refinished by then. Maybe the flowers will start blooming. Who knows what fun things we have in store to happen next.

The boys may be gone but they sure perked my heart up and are making this whole relationship thing even better! Their visit and integration into my new family make me feel even more complete. Zachary is suggesting activities to get Jasen into, Jimmy is just wanting to come back, everyone loves Sam and well it was just a great milestone to get over with.

FRIDAY - MARCH 6 - MMMMM...BACON

I had my hospice training today. It was the class's last training, although I have a makeup class that I have to do next Tuesday. Remember I missed one training class during "Island" days. Going to the Island was sure worth missing a training which now I have to make up on a date night. Maybe we'll go out for a later dinner. Actually, Jasen's soccer practices are over now which were on Wednesday nights. I wonder if we should move date night back to Wednesday. Oh wait, never mind, Zoë has Lax practice.

I booked my trip up north in April. I'm a little worried about how she's going to get everywhere while I'm gone. For some reason Pete doesn't think taking Zo to where she needs to be is a priority. It's a really weird and a not so endearing quality. I better start getting to know some other moms better, throwing in a cookie tin here and there or something. I'm missing a couple of things in April (like the banquet and a couple playoff games) that had I known about I probably would not have booked the trip during this time, but oh well, another lesson learned. Next year, no trips until after Lacrosse season.

Anyway, back to hospice, I have a couple more steps to go through until I decide where I'll end up or what I'll be doing. I've also put out there that I'm interested in getting the Reiki training (offered for free!) and working with the babies. Reiki is a form of energy healing. Does that sound woo-woo to you? Well, I've always been interested in it, always,,,and I don't even know for sure how it works. But if I get the opportunity to train for it I'm in!!! We shall see what happens next. I'm thinking I'll keep to Friday mornings for hospice work since I've already put that morning aside.

I think this concludes my reports for the week. It's a nice lazy cloudy day and I think it could be a good day to catch up on some shows. I believe there is a *Downton Abbey* waiting for me...

TUESDAY - MARCH 10 - LET'S GO BUCS

The weekend was nice. Zoë's Friday night LAX game was cold again. Turns out a cold front came over and stalled right on top of us during the game. The coach "started" her but took her out right away because she was limping. I took her to a massage therapist today, stayed in the room with her, and heard that there is something about her SI joint being out of whack. From Google: The **sacroiliac joint** or **SI joint** (SIJ) is the **joint** between the sacrum and the ilium bones of the pelvis. She has some exercises to do, some ice therapy and no playing for a week. Poor thing. I'm sure she twisted it playing the game, not like something random. Hopefully she'll figure out how to strengthen herself. It was painful to watch them push on her sore spots. Zoë claims she got the joint to pop back in on her own. She's going to take the week off of practice and playing her games. You know what that means? We get to take the week off of games too! I don't even have to do stats because the games this week are away. Hopefully she'll be back in the swing of things soon.

On Sunday we did end up going to the Pirate spring training game in Dunedin. That was fun but *hot*. I was very good in remembering my 50 sunblock on my face but never occurred to me for any other part of my body. I got my first real sunburn since moving here. Nothing hurts but sheese-a-louise how stupid am I? Peter got a lot of sun too. Jasen was with us but no sunburn for him. Anyway, other than it being really hot it was fun to see the Pirates. And we won! I think this might be the year for the Pirates. I'm feeling it!

WEDNESDAY- MARCH 11 - JUST LIKE MOTHER TERESA

It's Wednesday and Wednesday is horseback riding day. I got to don my new riding hat and half chaps. I look stunning. Okay not really but they do fit. Peter bought me this book last year, like when we first met, called *Zen Mind Zen Horse* (by Allan J. Hamilton). First of all, what a nice boyfriend right? I didn't start reading it until this week. Last night I was reading up on grooming. The author says grooming should be like the tea ceremony. Full of love, ritual, bonding, blah blah. Anyone who has ridden with me in the past knows that my experience with the horse I road at the time, Shawndiz, during the grooming stage was anything but loving and bonding. Witch horse (may she rest in peace). But once I was on her she was great. GREAT. Well anyway, I am the first to admit that I am a scaredy-cat around horses when I'm *off* of them. I think I'm good *on* them, but all that man handling I need help with. I read the book and today I was ready to face the love. Me and this horse, Remi, we're going to bond. Right? I read it in a book so it must be so! I get there and he's just been fed. I go in the stall and he's snorting and you know scaring the shit out of me. Now understand, he's barely moving or snorting but in my head he's going to kill me. I decide I'll reason with him. I'll let him eat a little, look him in his left eye, with love, you know like the book said, and then he's going to drop that cud and walk right over to me. Yea, well, I stopped someone and asked them to get him. I felt like an idiot. Anyway, this dude grabbed him like he was a kitten and I took it from there. I put the bridle on and led him, all by myself, back to the grooming area. But now he knows I'm a wus right? He's pounding his feet a little, swishing that tail, dancing ever so slightly (again in my mind it's the same as rearing up) but I stand my ground and brush him. Big brave me. Then comes those damn feet. I was determined.

Zachary gave me some pointers about feet picking those horses. He learned to do feet picking with his dad when he was growing up, who knew? I also got some pointers reviewing the book last night. Taking what I learned, I leaned in towards the horse, ever so gently, pushed him off-balance, slid my hand down his leg, squeezed in the appropriate spot and nothing. He didn't budge. I tried 3 or 4 times and gave up. One of the barn people was walking by and she did it for me. I mean it's embarrassing. *However*, I am good with the bit now. (the thing that goes in their mouth) I put it right in there and right over his head all by myself. I mean you'd think I was an expert. I think back to the days when I was afraid to do that so I know I'm going to get this feet thing down. It might be another 10 years, but I'll get it. I better keep reading the book.

All that grooming work and I'm already emotionally exhausted, that's all before even getting on. Then, the first half of the lesson I couldn't get him to trot again. I don't know what it is. My legs are too weak maybe? I'm supposed to be squeezing and sticking him with my foot and well it just doesn't seem to matter. He barely trots and then typically walks at the corners. It's extremely frustrating. I mean like enough to make-you-cry frustrating. But then we cantered. And there was love. He cantered great, I was feeling great, we jumped a double jump (cross rails, not like jump jumps) he would go from a canter to a great trot, I was feeling great, keeping my diagonal, keeping him going, keeping my two point and then the lesson is over - just like that. I feel like I just get him going and she says, "you can walk him now." Seriously? That was my morning. It should not take nearly as long to get him out of the stall and tacked up. I really need to work on that. I think today I was a couple of minutes later than usual and she had just fed him. Next week I'll go early before she does that. Then, I don't know what I have to do to get him to a comfortable trot. Maybe start out with a canter? He is old. He's 24. Maybe it takes him that long to stretch? Maybe he's just tired and has been ridden too often by years of inexperienced riders that he can tune out the heels in his belly and do whatever he damn well pleases. I'm pretty sure the cantering is less about me and more about him knowing what comes next and probably knowing that it means the end of the lesson. The one thing that is "spiritual" about it, is that I am totally focused on what I'm supposed to be doing. It's the only time of day or night when I'm not thinking about what I need to be doing, who needs picked up, what appointment I have coming up, I mean I think nothing but trying to get that horse to move. Anything that clears that constant chatter in your mind is said to be spiritual. You know how I love my spiritual stuff (or for those of you who don't know that, I do). The *Zen Mind Zen Horse* book promises that a lot of spiritual stuff should be happening between a horse and rider. I'm not convinced but I'm going to keep reading and keep going!

Speaking of spiritual, I had my last hospice training class yesterday. I need a TB test and I'm good to go. I have to wait a week and do another, just to be sure it's not a false negative. And *then* I'm good to go. We shall see what happens.

THURSDAY - MARCH 12 - LIVING HERE

In one month I'll be back in Pittsburgh. That's coming right up. I remember the last time I was there, over Thanksgiving, I had said I wouldn't be back until April. Some people were skeptical and said I wouldn't last that long but honestly I've had no problem lasting that long. The winter of course has a lot to do with it. And some random visitors, not to mention visits from my boys have helped me not to be homesick. I've been gone from Pittsburgh now 9 months. It feels like we've been here longer, like forever. And I mean that in a good way. It's home now.

I was putting something in the trunk of my car yesterday and thought about how differently I pack my trunk now. Well, first of all my trunk needed cleaned out badly. In my trunk I have my soccer/lacrosse chair that I've had in there for 10 years. Now added to that are two beach chairs, a Frisbee, a deflated beach ball, two beach hats, my horse hat and chaps, my yoga mat, an umbrella (I had 5 of them until I brought most of them into the house), a blanket, a scarf and a sweatshirt and now I must always carry my beach bag. This is all in addition to actual car stuff, a tire air pump, a battery charger, bungee cords, some

Armor-all wipes for leather. What an assortment don't you think? Like if I was on "Let's Make a Deal" I think I might win.

More evidence that this is home, last night we went to dinner at a local place we hadn't tried before and guess what? We saw Joan. This is the second time we've seen her and her daughter at a restaurant when we've been out. Remember when I said I used to scan the crowds for people I knew and realized I knew no one? Well, we know people now. I mean we *live* here now. I saw someone I know at the Pirate game last Sunday too. And these aren't Sewickley people! We're like members in our community and stuff. Not real active members but hey, people know us. I even know some parents from the Lacrosse team. One big step that has yet to happen, I'm not yet known for my chocolate chip cookies. Remember when I tried baking cookies for the soccer team at that bonfire? No one ate them. Jasen was cute when I gave them to the hostess she said "oh you brought cookies" looking at the table full of store-bought cookies. Jasen said "yes but these are home-made" What a good boy. Still, no one ate them. Perhaps there is a Lacrosse event in our future that will require us to bring something and I'll try again.

I've gotten my man to walk with me the last two nights. Last night we had a cat follow us home. Many of you know the cat and Sam (the dog) story. For those of you that don't, Sam is a cat killer. Literally, he killed one of their cats so it is important to keep Sam away from cats. Last night Pete had to distract the cat while I ran in the house to put the dog in the bathroom, then Pete could get in the house without the dog busting through either of us to run outside and get the cat. It all went pretty well except the cat came onto the porch and although we got into the house safely it just curled up outside the door, sending Sam into a frenzy, which should have scared the cat away, but it did not. That cat was still sleeping on one of our porch chairs this morning. I haven't seen it yet today but it's a concern for sure. Zoë is panicking a little. She witnessed the other killing so she's having some sort of PTSD.

I have some errands and a possible friend visit on the agenda for today. I've planted some flowers in pots and I want to add just a little bit of blue to come over the sides of the pots. I also want to see if I can find a shamrock for our door for St. Patty's Day. I am part Irish. If you have one Irish member of the family then we're all Irish, right?

I'm off to do errands for the day. I hear it's quite balmy up north. Hope you are all enjoying your warm up. We are warmed up here too. I love it, but it's also a little too soon for summer. I think we're going back into the 70's next week. You know, a cold front.

FRIDAY - MARCH 13 - A COUPLE OF MINUTES

I've got 35 minutes. Which means I really only have 15 minutes to blog because it takes me that long to review and correct mistakes and well, it takes longer than you would think. However, if I was writing a book I seriously could write one page a day and you know in a year's time I would have 365 pages. Not a bad size novel. But I need a subject, other than myself. I guess I could use myself as a basis and then make myself into someone else. Would I make myself an heiress? Homeless? Single? Married? Maybe I should be a teenager. They sell a lot of books. I would be down with writing a page a day, no pictures. Posting pictures is also time-consuming. Getting them from my phone to the computer, or camera to the computer, or finding them on the computer, no easy task. If only Jean's husband Larry would organize them for me. I think he has all their pictures digitally organized. That's such a major task. I guess I should be doing it as I download them but right now I'm just happy they're saved by date. I'm happy I know how to download at all. I mean I used to be really on top of all the computer stuff.

We are half way done with painting the bathroom. It looks great, beautiful color. In the middle of painting the bathroom my side of the closet fell. Zoë is having a friend over this afternoon. I have to pick them up at 1:30. This afternoon, after I pick up the girls and take them to Chik-fil-A, do I take all the clothes out of my side of the closet? And if I do where do I put them? I have no closet? Or do I start to finish painting the bathroom? I think it's going to be the bathroom. The sooner we get that done we can work on the closet. Pete says the rod can't handle the weight of my clothes. I guess it's time to purge. I think it's time to get rid of all of those work clothes that I thought I might wear again someday.

Yesterday I was successful with my errands but as soon as I pulled into Lori's parking lot to have tea, Zoë texted to pick her up. I ran in to say hi to Lori anyway and to say I couldn't stay and we made a plan for breakfast today. We went to this very Zen place, Consciousness Blossom. As soon as she ordered she got a call that someone was at her door trying to deliver her countertop. Cray cray. But they figured it out and we had a lovely breakfast. Consciousness Blossom, is located in the middle of a strip mall on a busy road. We sat outside but outside is the parking lot. I'm starting to realize that everything down here – okay not everything – but a lot down here is in strip malls and parking lots by busy roads. I'm kinda missing my mom's right now. I think I need a dose of trees. Or maybe I could sit in my back yard for 10 minutes before picking up the girl. That's what I'll do. I have trees and it's quiet here at my house.

On Monday I believe we are taking the girl on a college visit which means no blogging. You get a three-day weekend off from my blabber. Maybe for a weekend assignment someone can come up with a book idea for me? Anyone?

TUESDAY - MARCH 17 - HAPPY ST. PATRICK'S DAY

Erin Go Bragh! Ireland forever. I wore green and orange so not to offend my protestant brethren in Ireland. Isn't that diplomatic of me? Actually, my dad was raised Catholic but I was raised protestant, and then went to Catholic college, so really I am an orange and green Irish mutt. Today was a work-at- the-middle-school day and we were all lovely in our green. I also wore my shamrock earrings that I've managed to hang onto for all these years. Jasen was REALLY green today. He wore green shorts and a green shirt. He looks good in green but I'm going to bet that he gets a bit of teasing today and then of course *I'll* feel bad because I bought him the clothes.

Grandma Clark comes today. I have successfully completed all the cleaning I wanted to do. I didn't touch Jasen's room. I warned him for weeks now to clean it but oh well. She may never go up the steps anyway. Let's hope not.

Yesterday we went on a college tour with Zoë to University of Florida in Gainesville. GO GATERS. It was 9 years ago that I went on a college tour there with Jimmy. *NINE* years ago. It's hard to believe that much time has passed. I didn't do college tours with Zachary. He said he wanted to go to Penn State, sight unseen, and so he did. Anyway, Zoë was a little, let's say reluctant, to go initially. Maybe thinking she didn't know what was going on or why she was going. I was thinking it's best to get one out-of-the-way then she can start thinking about what to expect on college tours. Maybe it was too soon but there were other sophomores in the crowd. Anyway, end of the story is she LOVES it there. Now we'll see. Every future college visit will be measured against Gainesville Gators. I suggested she apply to one "dream" college and thought about MIT. Even if she would get in it would be too cold for her, but still, she should try. And I definitely think a college visit to Berkley (California) is in order. Don't you? Again, we have more than a year but it's good for her to start thinking. I predict she will be recruited (maybe recruited isn't the right word) because of her interest in Science and Engineering and being a girl and all. I could be wrong but what the heck, let's dream big. She is #1 in her class in the traditional tract. Plus, she's got all the stuff going on, girl scouts, key club, science club, drama club and Lacrosse. She told us in the car yesterday that she might be interested in teaching instead of engineering to which we both said NOOOOOOOOOOO! Not that there's anything wrong with teaching, she just has a gift with this science stuff, she should think bigger. Like discovering something. Is that bad to say? I just can't get over that I'm back doing college tours again and the realization about how many years between doing them. She'll be starting college in 2017. That's 8 years since Jimmy graduated high school and 16 years since Zachary's graduation. Shouldn't I be dead by 2017?

Pete was a little nostalgic about being in college but I was a little nostalgic for work. I miss the atmosphere, although there is no comparison size wise to PPU. UF has 50,000 students. FIFTY thousand. They mentioned 9,500 faculty. I wonder who does their contracts? FIFTY thousand! !

That's going to have to be it for today. Grandma is here!

FRIDAY - MARCH 20 - STILL HERE

I've had a busy week with Grandma Clark here. All is going well. She's just like "us" sun worshipers and wants to sit in the sun mostly. We went to a movie yesterday and saw *the 2nd Best Exotic Marigold Hotel*. I loved it. We watched the first *Best Exotic Hotel* movie before seeing the new one. They are both good movies. I don't care what the ratings say.

I also had a horseback riding lesson this week. I've noticed that my spine is stronger now. The first lesson and first canter I felt like my back was jello but now I'm feeling stronger. I was on a different horse this week. He was a little feistier for-sure. And the dam horse shied at a jump, but I stayed on. I liked him for his feistiness but not crazy about horses that shy away from jumps. You can get hurt that way! Not feeling any more Zen-like but I'll keep at it. Next week I'll be out-of-town for the day so no horseback next week.

I'm feeling writer's block. I know, even after not writing for a few days. I'm just constantly on the run and I have a lot of running around to do this afternoon... maybe just a 15-minute lyming/resting session will revive me.

MONDAY - MARCH 23- SPRING CLEANING

It seems my blogging has gone to the wayside, but really I'm on schedule since I posted on Friday. It just *feels* like it's been a long time.

Our house guest is still enjoying the sunshine. She's out there every day getting her sun. I remember when I used to do that. You just can't get enough of it when you don't see it for 3-4 months at a time. I do not typically join her but when I do I stay in the shade. Everyone tells me how tan I am. I can't help it; although I don't sit in the sun purposely I am outside enough that I stay tan. I do have to work on getting rid of those tan "lines" however.

On Wednesday I'm meeting Maryann in Sarasota. That will be a beach day; although not happy about putting a bathing suit on in front of someone I know. I've gotten myself a hotel room for the night too (down the road a bit from Mar). I'm taking a mid-week break from the Clark household. I've notified Zoë that she needs to find a way home from practice on Wednesday but I'll be back on Thursday to resume my chauffer duties. Hopefully they won't fall apart one day without me. It's good practice for when I go to Pittsburgh in April. Zoë has already commented they she's going to *die* when I'm gone. No guilt there eh? Zoë ended up walking home from school last week when I was at the movies with her grandma. She's still nursing her blisters from walking. Dam kids.

Speaking of walking, we went to the Pizza place in town on Friday night with Pete's mom. We parked Pete's car in a lot beside the bank. It was after hours. Came out of the pizza place and the car had been towed. Jasen and I walked home to get my car – about the same distance Zoë has to walk from school. It wasn't pleasant. Actually, the walk was quite pleasant but the reason why we were walking was not. But I got my mile walk in and a little bit of bonding with Jasen.

On Saturday morning Pete and I walked over to the middle school and ran around the school track. ONE lap for me thank you, which honestly I was surprised I could still do one lap. Pete wants to run in a 5K at the end of April. I think I'll watch and cheer him on. But while he trains I'll walk over to the track with him and walk around it (wonder how long he'll keep this up?) After we got our hearts pumping we then proceeded to do a lot of pool clean-up work. I scrubbed the railings and screens and chairs to get the pollen off, he tried to get the weeds out of the screens. I must say it's looking rather good! I also cleaned/skimmed the pool for a while. Spring cleaning – Florida style! Jasen got *in* the pool - a sure sign that pool time is coming back.

We had Jasen's birthday dinner yesterday. He turned 14. I'm just going to say this... Fourteen-year-old boys should be sent away until they are 45. That's all.

WEDNESDAY - MARCH 25 - TODAY I'M A WRITER

Today I'm practicing being a writer. I started off my day today packing my bag and leaving the house on my day away adventure. I met Maryann and Bobby (friends from home) who told me all day "no blogging." We sat by the pool at the Sarasota Ritz Carlton for a couple of hours and then went on to the beach. They treated me to lunch at the Ritz and the best fish tacos EVER. After that we sunned and lounged on a nice private beach area, a lot of gabbing, and a good time was had by all. I have found that when I reconnect with an old good friend I really do feel re-energized. It was really a nice day. I dropped them off around 5:00 and the plan was to come to my own room and sit here and write, you know, like a writer. I had to catch up on the blog so I knew I had at least something to start with.

Well,,, I have checked into my small but comfortable room, not the Ritz, but it's really kind of cute. After checking in I saw that I was minutes from Siesta Key. I've always wanted to see Siesta Key. I took advantage of the fact that I still had on my beach clothes and took off to explore. I found the beach! Free parking, nice walkway and onto the beach for sunset.

Then I come back to the room and discover that I am right beside a shopping plaza with Winn Dixie, Starbucks, a really cool drug store (the old-fashioned kind with "stuff" in it...I'll be exploring tomorrow) and a Panera. Off to Panera's it was for dinner. Then back to the room and more time to get the computer set up, eat, skyped with my boyfriend, turned the TV on, can't stop thinking about that nice clean bathtub and the book on the bed that I could read, in the bathtub.

I am a true writer. I have writer's block. See? You can't have writer's block if you're not a writer so I *must* be a writer. I thought blogging would help release those creative juices. I thought a day at the beach with friends away from the daily grind, then some meditative time at a sunset, well that should do it right? Admittedly the TV should not be on. But really, I think the answer is a week at Cabbage Key. If I could finance myself, I would finance a week in seclusion to see if I could come up with an idea. One week, at the beach, alone. Should I have a TV in my seclusion week? I don't ever have it on during the day when I typically blog so I probably shouldn't have it on now. But I like my shows, and staying in a motel room well it's almost a necessity. This is not your typical hotel, it's a "motel" and there's a lot of noise out there. I'm not sure what's up with that. I guess it's not really writer friendly here. But I get the overall idea. I like this pretending I'm a writer thing. I think I might start living in my head again. It was a nice place to be when I was in Pittsburgh. I dreamed for 5 years or more of moving to Florida and look where I am. I remember one time telling Jimmy about my dream of being a writer and he very wisely said "you don't want to be a writer; you just want that lifestyle. " Hmmm, dam kids. He's right though, I do want the lifestyle, but I really do want to write too. He's not 100% right. Now that I've been blogging (almost a year) pretty consistently, practicing my writers voice. I like the blabbing. It's fun! It's me!

When I was at Carlow, in one of my English classes we were promised extra credit if we wrote a play or story. I wrote a play about us Bunko girls. I had had the idea for a week or so and then I sat down one night at the computer and it poured out of me. At that time, and for that assignment, I was a writer. That's what I'm waiting for. That inspiration again. I want Pete to walk into the bedroom when I'm typing and I don't look up to talk because I'm engrossed in my story, I want him to go to bed and ask me when I'm coming to bed and I don't answer because I'm deep into Chapter 5 and have to finish the scene. I want papers to be crushed up and thrown all over the room as if I was on a typewriter (I'll have to just stage it since we don't actually have a typewriter), I want to forget to make dinner because I have the characters at a critical juncture that I have to finish while it's in my mind. I want to make everyone I live with mad and frustrated just long enough for me to finish. And then when I finish we'll all be happy and everyone will let out a huge sigh of relief and I'll make cookies again.

And then I want to send that book away to 10 or 100 publishers and have just one say ok. I just need one to say I'm a good writer, here's $84,000 to finish (I had a dream a few weeks ago that Pete brokered a writers deal for me for $84,000) Is this so much to ask? Well, true to my profession, I'm going to go soak in the tub and read a little of the *Circular Staircase* by my sage, Mary Roberts Rinehart. Maybe after a couple of chapters I'll start to channel her. I mean we are like twins from different eras. Okay not twins but we both lived in Pittsburgh, Sewickley and Florida. That makes us geographically connected sisters.

In the morning I'm going to pretend I live at the beach and possibly go for a walk on it before heading home back to the real world, where I can also walk on the beach daily, if I wanted to. I really do have a great life. I'm happy I moved here. And I'm so happy I have the best boyfriend who supports me and all my crazy dreams. See? I already have my dedication page.

APRIL 2015

SUNDAY - APRIL 5 - I'M HERE, I'M HERE!

Happy Easter!

It's been a while hasn't it? I have a lot to update you all on and it's late and although I had two ice teas and a diet Pepsi after 4:00 and will probably not sleep at all, I still feel like I need to keep this relatively short. Let's see, where did we leave off?

Pete's mom was here for a visit for 2 weeks. I believe she had a nice time. She sat by the pool daily, the weather cooperated nicely for her. One day we went to Dunedin for the Highland Games. Dunedin is a Scottish community and they are very proud of their heritage. Bagpipes and kilts everywhere. Let me tell you, I had no idea men in kilts were so handsome. Pete also has Scottish roots (and he's thinking of wearing a kilt next year too) and his mom had a great time tracing her ancestors.

And then on Grandma's last night we took her to dinner at Nina's restaurant for her birthday. A nice time and delicious food was had by all. Then we had a few days to catch up before my sister, Kerry, came today.

One day we took the kids go-kart racing. I came in last. Pete came in first. Zoë liked it a little too much. I said we better get a slow car cause I have a feeling she's going to have *too* much fun driving. We also went mini golf – I did come in first there. I redeemed myself

In my time off from blogging, I have found my next car, and it's not slow at all. I actually have been looking for a car for a while. I had my sights set on a Nissan Juke. They're cute. Zoë saw one though and called it an ugly-bug-of-a-car. Since we share the car I started thinking maybe I shouldn't get it since she didn't like it. I drove several of those Jukes but in the end I got a Mercedes.... *What???*

I know I know; *I need a job*. But it's a nice car, fer sure. When I test drove it I cried (and when I say cried I mean I got water in my eyes) I took that as a sign it was the "one", and it all worked out. Also, it was the exact same price as the Juke. A couple of years older but whatever. We like it. Not entirely practical or family focused but Pete says it's "our" car, not the "kids" car so I'm goin with it. Who am I to argue? Right?

In other news, Kerry, my sister, is here today. She is happy to be in 80° weather. I picked her up in the new car, we came right home, she got settled in and then we went for Pizza. We also walked to the water from the restaurant to see the sunset. We were kinda late for sunset but she got to see the water, then for ice cream, home for the new *Outlander*, dyed a couple Easter eggs and I made my beautiful Easter cake for tomorrow. I believe she's enjoying sleeping in our beautiful guest room without a bunch of babies (her grandchildren whom she lives with) jumping on her. I'm looking forward to a few fun days with her before driving up north. NOT in the new car, we're renting one.

We are expecting the big girls (Monica and Nina) tomorrow at some point. Nothing fancy for dinner. Pete wants Sloppy Joes. Not your traditional Easter fare but I like it! Hoping to get to the beach or at least the pool. It is my duty to make sure our guests get tanned while they're here.

Hope everyone has a Happy Easter, if you celebrate it. If not I still hope you have a very lovely peaceful and warm sunny day.

WEDNESDAY - APRIL 8 - AND I'M OFF

I swear I have no idea how to pack lightly. I will be gone awhile but seriously there has to be a better way. Then, to top it off, my tooth is really bothering me. I think it's broken through to the whatever bad thing there is, so now what? It just seems like there's so much undone stuff that I'm leaving down here. Can we talk about the Island again where I'm all alone?

I used to have this routine down to blogging after I had gotten some things done in the morning, such as empty the dishwasher, put things away, wash any dishes, do laundry, start blog, pick up Zoë, finish blog, day over. NOW? Well, I'm all messed up. I'm out of schedule, out of sync. House guests will do that to you. You just can't disappear for too long when you have company although I try to disappear at least for a little while every day. I think I will get back to that routine soon. The past couple nights I've been waiting until late to blog but as I'm clicking away 100 miles a minute on this laptop, Peter is getting more and more annoyed as the clicking continues as he is trying to sleep. This time of day is not going to work. I have to go back to the morning blogging before getting Zoë.

Am I whining? Sorry. I try hard not to do that.

Good stuff today? My sister and I went riding. One hour on the trail. Our butts hurt. I'll probably try to find a group to trail ride with but the weather is getting pretty hot. I'm not sure how much I'll ride during the summer. We'll see. Maybe I'll get out there earlier in the day during the summer.

That's it, I need sleep.

FRIDAY - APRIL 10 - A SHORT STORY

I'm in Pittsburgh visiting the fam. Other than the fact that I am tan, I don't feel that different. I mean I don't have a home here in Pittsburgh, but I've been there before.

TUESDAY - APRIL 14 - ZOË. . QUITE THE CHARACTER

A blogging assignment - today's Prompt: A Character-building experience – Who's the most interesting person (or people) you've met this year?

Two years ago, I met Pete. Then Jasen (his son) also about two years ago, but this last year is when I met Zoë. I had met her briefly at Thanksgiving in 2013, however, we didn't spend time together until I moved to Florida when we were thrown together, like it or not.

Zoë is Peter's daughter. Peter is my boyfriend. Me, Peter, Zoë and Jasen all live together, you know, like a family. They would be considered step children if we were married but since we are not, I refer to them as my children if I absolutely don't know the person I'm talking to, my step children if there's a little acquaintance with the other person, otherwise I just use their names, Zoë and Jasen. They refer to me as their dad's girlfriend.

So, about Zoë. Pete and I moved to Florida May 26, 2014. We had a couple of weeks together, alone, in our new house getting settled before he had to go back up north to drive Jasen down from Pennsylvania. Zoë already lived in another part of Florida but still had a couple of weeks of school to finish before she could come to the new house. I will always remember that even though her dad went up north she still came to visit with just me the very first chance she had. No stranger-danger there. We spent the whole weekend together. Just the two of us. She wanted to get to know me. She was up for anything.

The first thing we did was go eat at the beach at sunset and then we walked on the beach. Eating, walking and watching sunset on the beach has subsequently become the way we welcome all our visitors. We also went to a movie that weekend (*The Fault in our Stars*) and shared an Icee (my first one); we went to a neighborhood street fair where she bought something for her new room; we sat with our feet in the pool and talked and talked. We became fast friends. We became fast friends because she was open to it. She was then, and has always been, very welcoming and accepting of me in her life.

Zoë is a pretty little thing. Sixteen years old, a size 4 ish, about 5'4. She has beautiful dark hair that is long and curly. In this past year I've already seen her mature. Sometimes when she gets extra dressed up for an event it brings tears to my eyes. You'd think I'd known her forever. She loves getting dressed up, at least I think she does. Never having a daughter before I have not experienced shopping with a girl. Girls take a long time trying on clothes. I know I'm a girl too, but I usually grab stuff and take it home, and then take it back when it doesn't fit. Being a size 4 it's easy to look cute in just about anything, and she does. It's fun to see her get dressed up and go to parties or banquets or whatever. One event that she went to this past year she was able to wear her mother's earrings and use her mother's purse. That seemed like an extra special night (her mother is deceased). It is hard not to get caught up in her enthusiasm and feel the sadness when she knows her mom is not there to see her.

I typically pick Zoë up after school. It's about one mile from our house. When she throws herself in the car I ask how her day was. Since she's so smart I rarely understand what she's talking about, at least when it has to do with school work, and when she's done filling me in she'll ask about my day. We talk about everything. Sometimes after we get home we sit in the car for another 30 minutes and keep talking. We talk as if we've known each other our whole lives. But since we haven't known each other our whole lives, there's more to discover and talk about.

Sometimes we don't feel like talking at all. You know 16-year-old girls can be very moody. So can 56-year-old girls. Not talking seems just as comfortable as talking. Zoë is an amazing young lady. She is very intelligent, interested in the sciences, a math and chemistry whiz, she plays guitar, ukulele, and piano. My sister and I were playing duets on the piano the other day and she sat down and sang with us. When there is a gathering of family she has no qualms about bringing out her guitar and playing for us. She's in drama club at school, key club, national honors science something society (I can't keep up). She does volunteer work, she's in the Girl Scouts, she completed a Dale Carnegie course, and this year she decided to start playing Lacrosse. She is the most motivated child I've ever met. If she wants to learn something she attacks it with her entire being. Just like getting to know me, she was all in.

Did I mention that her dad and I moved her from her childhood school, where she had attended for 9 years and made her go to a new school? She begged and pleaded with him but he stuck to his guns. Once she finally accepted it she cried a few days and I watched her pull herself up (figuratively like by the bootstraps) and accept it. She then made a plan to use her Dale Carnegie skills to meet people. She now has many friends at both schools!

Zoë is starting to be interested in boys. This is something I am familiar with. I am not familiar with being first in my class, Chemistry or Physics. I am hoping that the boy interest doesn't get out of control. Getting out of control is also something I am familiar with. I am hoping we can go back to the "boys have cooties" stage until she's safely graduated from college.

Zoë is also now learning to drive. She's a good driver but we have found out that she likes to drive fast. We took the family on a go-kart outing. She came in second place and, well, I decided we should buy a slow car. We actually did purchase a new car after that. She was really attached to the old car (a Nissan Altima) and I wanted her to like the new car (a Mercedes, an old one). The first few days we had the new car she acted like she didn't want anything to do with it. I made her drive it. The first day she drove the new car she was very quiet. She was concentrating (and nervous) but when I looked over at her she had this smile on her face and I knew she was hooked. Then after she figured out that memory seat thing we were both screaming (it's so cool). Unfortunately, the new car is fast.

I think this is where I should say that her parents did a great job. But to be perfectly honest I believe Zoë is who she is because she has had to do a lot on her own. Not that she hasn't had some good people in her life but I feel that it is "she" who has made the very smart choices in her 16 years and has chosen to stay upbeat and positive. She is often met with disappointment, not to mention losing her mother when she was 12 years old and has been shuffled around a bit, but amazingly she carries herself onward, and in my opinion, always upward. She is remarkable.

Zoë always tells me how grateful she is to have me in her life. I'm not as good as she is with sharing my feelings with her. I think I'm afraid I'll scare her. I feel like I don't deserve to say "I'm proud of you" or have the right to get teary when she looks so beautiful or look at her and think "our little girl is growing up" but I assure you I feel all those things. I am super proud to be part of her life in any way I can. I love going to her Lacrosse games and being an obnoxious parental figure when appropriate and I'm super sad when I'm not there for an event. I will never forgive myself for missing her Lacrosse banquet this past weekend. She deserved to have me there beaming with pride. She deserves a good life. Everyone deserves a good life; she just deserves it a little more than most.

TUESDAY - APRIL 21 - I'M BAAACCKKK

I'm home...in Florida. YAY. I'm so out of touch with blogging. I had big plans on my trip up north to be secluded and blog but as usual, the best laid plans...

I missed getting to see some people who I had hoped and planned to and I felt guilty when I did run out on the babies to get in my adult visits. I managed to see Zach and Jimmy pretty often which was wonderful of course.

Today I was back at the middle school working then looking for a dining room chair, then buying and delivering lunch to Jasen then wading through the 558 emails that have been accumulating. Laundry, dinner, errands, applying for jobs and blogging.

When I dropped my rental car off in Virginia I had logged 1661 miles (I did all the driving) and I love love *loved* visiting everyone, I hated leaving those babies, I love love loved being at my moms, and everywhere I was, I felt like I could stay there. I could move back to Pittsburgh; I could stay at my mom's...*BUT* I'm so so happy to be back to my not-so-new family and routine. Soo happy. Life is good.

THURSDAY - APRIL 30 - A NORMAL UPDATE...FINALLY

What have you been missing?

- A good horseback riding lesson yesterday. I'm riding Zipper now. I think we might be bonding. First time back in the saddle after my trip up north. Still can't pick the feet.

- A good birthday dinner last night for Monica. She likes vegetables and no dairy. LOVE that. We had a nice healthy dinner and then deliciously bad for you bday cake. All Clarks plus somebody's boyfriend (in addition to mine) were here. Very nice night. The kids (without Pete and I) went to the beach together and flew a kite. Just a nice night all around.

- Our pool is resurfaced. I would not recommend these guys but they did do the job. Some of their equipment is still here. The realtor said they're supposed to come back every day for 2 weeks. Haven't seen them once. I don't think we'll ever see them again. The regular pool guy didn't come this week. I don't know if we can swim in it or not. We had to refill with the hose.

- Pete and I went to the beach last Sunday. We got burnt. I say this like it's a good thing. I know it's not but we had so much fun. There were fun waves. There was a rip current warning. Now we know that's the time to go when there's waves. There was a storm somewhere. I didn't see one boat on the water. At least they were heeding the warning. The beach crowd had an eyeful when my bathing suit top would come off, also Pete's favorite part. It was fun and exhausting. I'm hoping it counted as exercise.

- School is winding down and we're thinking of summer activities for the kids. Zoë is doing a summer LAX league and a trip to Toronto for a family wedding (on her mom's side) with her sisters. We'd love it if she could do a Girl Scout trip to Costa Rica. We're thinking of setting up one of those "go fund me" pages. She'll be busy. Jasen is probably thinking about his TV lineup for the summer. Not sure what to do with him.

- I'm still thinking of work. I really want to be employed by the summer. I can't believe it's been almost a year and I've gotten nothing. *Nothing*. I mean not even an offer to turn down. It makes me feel bad about myself so I try not to dwell on it. Instead, I take it out on Pete and am a bitch (but not always) I just don't know what to do. I wonder what he's thinking? Probably thinking he didn't sign up for this. A year! I mean WTF. Good thing I didn't come down here 5 years ago and try to make it on my own like I was close to doing. Sometimes I wonder if I should move up with my mother and relieve him of his duties of taking care of me, because sometimes I just feel like a burden. Would I be able to get a job there? I mean if I can't get a job here there's no reason to think I can get a job anywhere. It's just a new life experience that I've not had before. I have never *not* been financially responsible for myself. Never. I don't like it and I don't know how to process it. It's the fact that I'm looking and not getting anything. It would be different if I would just accept the status quo but I feel like I should be doing more and herein lies the quandary. I mean it would be fine if I didn't care, then I'd just get on with my days. I don't know. I guess I just need to accept it. I guess I'm not feeling totally accepted here. I'm not sure why I can't just relax and settle in and forget about it.

Well, these are the things on my mind. Things I haven't been rambling about. And nothing new really but it feels like something is changing. I think maybe I'll go get a pedicure in my Mercedes (HA! . . see what unemployment does for me?) My feet hurt, it's payday (for Pete and by extension me), and I need to reward myself for a good show (dinner) last night. A pedicure and a piece of leftover birthday cake. Sounds like a plan.

MAY 2015

MONDAY - MAY 4 - JUST ANOTHER MANIC MONDAY

I'm finally getting back into a routine after vacation. I know it's been two weeks since I've been back, right? Yep, I just checked. Exactly two weeks ago. Funny how long it's taken me to feel back to normal. There have been a lot of factors involved though.

I have my week pretty scheduled these days. Tuesday is Middle school day; Wednesday is horseback riding day and Friday is hospice day. Granted those are only morning activities but since I pick the girl up at 1:30 to me that's the day. That leaves me Monday and Thursdays to hang out. Today my hanging out is going to be replaced with cleaning, because that's what I do too. Sometimes it's nice to do it after the weekend and sometimes it's nice to do it on a Thursday before the weekend. Guess it all depends on who's coming on the weekend.

Speaking of weekends, Pete and I did next to nothing this past weekend. We saw two movies, *The Water Diviner*, which I highly recommend, and the *Avengers* movie. Unless you have children I'd skip right to *The Water Diviner*. Beautiful story.

On Saturday Pete putzied in the yard. I took myself to the beach with my new book called *At My Pace*. It's a collection of essays written by women ages 30's to 80's. It's a great book to read at my own pace, one person's story at a time. I've made it my beach book. Also, my friend's story is published in there. I read her story on Saturday. It happens to be entitled "Overcoming Writers Block" It's sure to be a good read and will help me see how my life is turning out just as it's supposed to be. We don't see it when we're in it but looking back it will all make sense. Right?

On Sunday we rolled out of bed and went right to laying by the pool. We eventually managed to get dressed and went and met Lori at a Tiki bar very close to our house. We didn't even know this place existed. We saw a great band – although very loud – with people our age. No kids allowed…*YES!* So that was something different. The band is called The Black Honkeys. They are really good. I loved seeing the old people out there dancing, and when I say old, I mean 50's and 60's.

Then home to watch our Sunday night TV line up.

Ok, just looking at the time. Dust bunnies await. You know sometimes when I "feel" my life, it "feels" like I'm trudging through mud or against a hard wind. I'm pushing against something. Aren't we supposed to feel like we're being pulled or floating or something? I am pushing myself through my days. When I moved here, I was being pulled here for sure. I wonder what I'm supposed to be doing that wouldn't make me feel this resistance. Maybe getting a housekeeper? Just sayin.

TUESDAY - MAY 5 - AND ANOTHER THING

I could not let the day go by without mentioning another Cinco de Mayo come and almost gone. Tacos all around for dinner. I'm stuffed.

But we all know the true meaning of the day, right? It's Diane's birthday. It's today that Diane turns one year older than me. I'm sure most of you know the story but for those newcomers, back in ought 6 (really it was 1979) Diane turned 21 before me. I'm a little confused why this was such a big deal because I think I was living in Miami where the drinking age at that time was 18. But anyway, she flaunted that in my face like nobody's business. And now 36 years later I continue to remind her how much older she is than me.

Di and I have a lot of birthday memories. I remember turning 30 and going with her to Froggy's the night before my big day where I learned the expression "this. . the last day of your 20's." It was my family that had a bday party for me when I turned 40 but Diane that organized the dinner for me when I turned 50. My favorite was when she turned 50 and I had the whole Bunko group wear shirts I had made where I ironed on pictures of Diane through the years. I thought it was hilarious. Pictures of Di everywhere. I think she was a little in shock but I also think she thought it was funny.

Di and I were talking today about how many of us are the same age now. Like 50 to 65 and we say "our age". When you're in your 20's, someone in their 30's is old. 40's and 50ish, same age. My mom, who is now 83, is starting to separate by age again. Someone is now older than her who is 86. Age is a funny thing. Seriously, no kidding, I had to pull the calculator out to figure out how old Diane is today. We are at the in-between time of our lives where who the hell cares how old we are anyway and I sure don't keep track. I mean I went from steps away from retirement to raising kids, in middle school again. I'm sure not going to think about my age because it makes no sense.

The only age that we are now looking forward to is retirement age. Diane is counting down the days to retirement. June 2020. I am super jealous. She will probably throw that in my face...I hope she does. She deserves it. I'll give it to her.

But the turning 21 before me, that memory she apparently will never get to live down. Although it's getting harder and harder to find "you're older than me" birthday cards I still look for them when possible.

So, Di, for 35 more days, enjoy being older than me. And remember I am the baby of the crowd.

WEDNESDAY – MAY 6 - LIKE A RHINESTONE COWBOY

Isn't being home during the week a little like sacred or something? It is so quiet (except when the neighbor's gardeners are mowing). There's a stillness during the week, when everyone is in school and work, like no other time of the week. The house is quiet, the dog is sleeping. I can hear the water pump for the pool but if I go outside or to another room I can't even hear that. I just hear birds. We're on a cul-de-sac so we don't have traffic either, I mean just peaceful. This is why I wish I was a morning person. If I could drag myself out of bed I would have much more time to enjoy this quiet, instead of sleeping through it.

Even though Zoë is super not-here even when she is here, it's still different when she comes home. I know she's here so my thoughts are different. I listen for her, I'm more aware of what I'm doing in relation to her. Of course, when Jasen comes home, well that's the end of the day anyway. Kids are out of school, people are coming home from work, time to think about dinner or snacks. The first words out of Jasen's mouth *every* day is "what's for dinner?" and/or quickly followed by "there's nothing to eat here, can we go to McDonalds?".

Right now, other than my clicking keyboard I am realizing and appreciating the quietness. I love quiet. I don't know if I've always been like that. Probably not. I like music too. But mostly I like quiet. I have noticed when I'm at my mom's I will get up early (not every day) but I want to get up early to go sit on the porch and breathe in the quiet. Also, you need to get up early there to beat the heat in the summer.

Today was another horseback lesson. We had a good canter around the ring at the end of the lesson. I mean twice around at the canter and I was done.... dammit. I suggested that maybe we start with the canter and then I could see if I could get him to slow down, instead of always trying to get him to pick up the trot. I'll get a good kick in there and he might start off ok but then he's back to like a slooowwww jog. It's gotta be my heels. I can't seem to dig them in the right way. I like what she has me doing though. She has me doing patterns. Like an obstacle course, sitting trot around these poles, posting trot this way, over this pole, over that pole, stop at the rail, back up, trot over that rail and back to a stop. Stuff like that. Getting me to remember what to do is part of the lesson. I mean it's exercising my mind too. We're good at everything except the posting trot. It's a problem.

But I like the horse, I love his canter, and he's friendly. So, there's that. And, knock on wood, the heat is not bothering me, at least while I'm riding. Next week I might start going a ½ hour earlier. Like 9:30 instead of 10. Once I'm on the horse I barely think about the heat. Now, once I'm off and untacked, have put everything away and get to my car, well by then I think I'm going to have heat stroke. Like seriously, I need to watch that. I remembered the SPF on my face today, but forgot water. It's a process. Next week I'll hopefully have it all together.

There's much to remember. It's not like I throw on my shorts and go. I have to wear tight jeans, a shirt that comes over the belly, I gotta find socks and my boots, when I get there I have to put the chaps on, (you know, like lift my leg up when I can't breathe with the tight jeans on) put my purse in the trunk, dig out the money, put my keys in my pocket of the jeans that are painted on my body, then I have to go get a horse, figure out the bridle (sometimes that takes me awhile to figure out how to put it on), get the saddle, the tack, brush the horse, beg someone to pick his feet for me, tack him up and finally get on. After the lesson it's much easier. Take the shit off, hose him off, and put him away.

I think I'm going to make some banana bread. Everyone likes it and I don't like to throw away the rotten bananas. I'm finally not sweating anymore; it takes me awhile to unheat after the lesson. Maybe I'll wash the car first, THEN make banana bread. Hmmm.... so many decisions.

Well, that's my day. More nonsense but that's what I blog about. Nonsense. Zoë doesn't come home until about 2:30 today. That gives me a little more time to regroup. She's practicing today for a talent show that she's in on Friday. I'm nervous for her! Stay tuned!

Tomorrow I believe I'm going to start lyming again. I haven't read a book in a long time. Like a novel book. I need to start something. I still haven't finished *The Circular Staircase*. I know, right? It's a little book too. That can be my goal tomorrow. Finish that damn book. Remember part of being a writer is reading. I'm a writer right? I mean a starving unpublished wanna-be writer, but I do write. I better read too. Just to keep up with my craft.

THURSDAY - MAY 7 - I GET IT

I planted some new flower pots. I think it's time to redo some of the pots. I'm still learning the environment. It's hot, #1, but also I need to be more vigilant with the watering. Diane's plants look so good and she waters every night. She said her grandpa used to say "you drink water every day, they want water every day" or it went something like that. Grandpas are the best...Anyway, I need to start over here and move some of the pots to the dead zone.

Our front flower garden is looking a little pathetic too. I am wondering if maybe we need to water twice a day. Again, it is hot and I'm planting flowers I used to plant up north which may not survive here in the south. It's a learning curve.

I remember when I lived in Victory Terrace. After 4 years living there I had a pretty nice flower garden. It just takes time to get there. This is where I should post a picture of that flower garden shouldn't I? Wonder if I can find one. Ahh, that would be a no. I looked. But I know I have one because I liked those flowers and I remember it took 4 years to get them to where they were pretty. Someday I'll find that picture and then I'll post it. I'll have a random picture day. Now if I can only remember to do that.

Along with summertime heat, it's the return of the Texas size bugs. I think Texas size bugs should stay in Texas.

Last night I was awakened by thumping in the bathroom by Peter (I am quite familiar with the sound of trying to kill something.) Another spider he said but much smaller. *Suuurrreeee (*liar, he just doesn't want to scare me) I know a number to an exterminator. One more sighting and they're getting called. We haven't had any bug sightings since I can't remember when. Last fall I guess. Luckily, I have a can of spray by my bed and a plethora of shoes.

I've declared tonight date night. We are way out of the practice ever since his mother came. We had guests, I was away, things were going on and there goes date night, BUT I am declaring Thursday nights date night again. Kinda wish *he* would have declared it but at least he didn't argue against it. Now I have to think about what to wear.

FRIDAY - MAY 8 - I'M NOT FOCUSED...

This morning I visited with my old lady (hospice) – she's 96. Very alert and pleasant. Also, they called and asked if I would be interested in a "peds" patient (baby), and I'm like yes! I know, what does that say about me? Well, maybe that's why I'm good at this. I don't get sad. But the bad news is they need me in the middle of the night. Ugh. Stay tuned. I think it might start next week.

In other news last night was date night. We resumed our practice. I love date night. Probably because I love my boyfriend. I think any couple that really likes each other needs a date night every week, especially if you have kids. It also sets a good example for the kids (in my opinion.) I'm so excited to get out of here on date nights that I run out the door. Since I haven't had this experience before in previous relationships (having date nights) I am all about it. It's nice for these kids to see us want to be together and have fun. Last night was dinner at a usual eatery, The Living Room, and then we just walked around Dunedin. There was talk about a billiards game but we didn't make it there. Usually after we eat we just want to come home and sit on the couch. Maybe we need to play billiards first, then eat.

Sunday is Mother's Day and I won't be with my boys. Surprisingly I am not crying! How about that! I consider that progress. But I will miss them, just like any other day.

Okay, this is the best I can do for today. I'm just not feeling it. Zoë has her talent show tonight. That will be exciting. Maybe I'll have some fun things to report on Monday. Stay tuned, and Happy Mother's Day!

MONDAY - MAY 11 - MONEY WELL SPENT

And how was your Mother's Day? Mine was lovely. I heard from the homegrown boys (Zach and Jimmy) talked to my mother and then the Clark boys took me to dinner – my choice – so I picked Frenchy's on the beach – and after dinner the boys played in the ocean (I mean the Gulf, but it still looks like an ocean to me.)

I just sat in the chair on the beach and chillaxed...big time. We stayed for sunset and then home for ice cream. And then today I got a new jade tree from Jimmy in the mail.

How sweet is that boy? (yes Zachary, how sweet is that boy?) I understand he has sent a card too (yes Zachary, a card too.) Jimmy and I were reminiscing about walking in the Relay for Life event on Mother's Day in Oakland. He always hated getting up so early (who doesn't?) but then loved the walk itself. That was a nice tradition, even though it was short-lived. After our Relay walks we would meet Zachary for brunch somewhere. Those were nice times. I've always been a proponent of *making* my kids spend the day with me. I had hoped to continue that tradition down here with the new fam, but no such luck. Jasen is always up for a meal and whatever his dad does. But I wasn't so lucky with the girl. She opted out to study. That's the difference. My kids it was mandatory. Here they just say no. In reality I am not their mother. Is Zoë exhibiting some passive/aggressive boundary line? Making sure I know that I'm not her mother? Because if it's either of them that gets the crux of my time it would be her. Dinner out with us shouldn't be too much to ask. But then again it's just dinner. I know Pete was embarrassed by her not coming with us. Dam kids.

In other news I feel like confessing today. I need to admit, I have a guilty pleasure. You know for some people it's chocolate (but that seems too common and boring to fall into that category). I'm thinking it should be more like Hostess Ho-Ho's or Burger King (for food items), or other types of guilty pleasures? How about foot rubs (like the kind you pay for?) or maybe something really kinky like porn? Anyway, my guilty pleasure is that I like to go to Psychics. I always have. My mom got me started actually. From an early age we went to Astrologers. Then she treated my sister and I to a "dream" class taught to us by a woman who was an astrologer/psychic and well it's like a habit for me now. According to some it's also a sin. I can see both sides.

I think the reason I like it so much is because I have this obsession with wanting to know what is going to happen next. It is very rare that I'm happy with the way things are. And even if I am happy I always feel like something has to happen *next* and if nothing is happening fast enough for me well then I find myself drawn to these Psychics to tell me what is going to happen so that I can prepare. I will tell you that 90% of the psychics that I have gone to have been dead wrong. WRONG. My entire life has been spent waiting for things to happen that never came to pass. That's probably where the "sin" part comes in...maybe. I mean why waste your life waiting for something instead of focusing on what's going on under your nose? There's actually a funny movie about spending your life looking for what a fortune-teller says (*Only You*). Me? I get frustrated, or I get bored, or I get stuck. Instead of spending thousands on a therapist to talk me through why I'm stuck, bored or frustrated, I'll spend $50 on a Psychic. They may tell me complete bullshit but for a while it will calm me and I'll think "ok, this is going to happen so don't get anxious..." And then I have a lot of time to build up my tolerance for when it doesn't happen.

Well anyway, why do I bring this up today? Because I treated myself today to a psychic. Pete and I both went to her before I actually moved down here. I got an email on Friday saying she was going to raise her rates starting in June and then as a surprise I got $50 in the mail so I thought it was Kismet and I should go.

I spent $50 for a half hour. Although I ended up being there for an hour and a half. The most interesting thing to note of the day? She saw nothing. She said she was getting "nothing". How about that? Well, not nothing. She did say since she wasn't getting anything to "just keep doin what you're doin." (that's my motto!) She also said Pete and I would be together for good (something like that), both these kids would do fine, both would go to college, both are smart and are going to do good things. Oh, and maybe we'll start looking to buy a house next year. But for me personally? Nothing. She said that's never happened to her before. I think it's fascinating. I said "well either I'm going to die or there's something else going on." Since she mentioned being with Pete for 20+ years I don't think I'm kicking the bucket, but for the first time with me going to one of these places I got nothing. Should I have saved the $50? No. Just sitting there chatting with her was relaxing. We sat outside on her deck and it was so peaceful. I ended up asking her how she got into the business, what her background is etc. I find what people do for work is really interesting. Like how do you end up where you end up? How does someone even become a psychic?

Even though there is no lottery winning in my future, no dream job (no job at all actually), no future so to speak I still had a lovely couple of hours sitting on the porch with my friend Caryl, who I met during our first week together down here when we were looking at houses. It's been a year since our first meeting. She said back then that she saw me moving down (at the time of my visit it still wasn't a done deal) and it would be fast. Those of you that remember my departure will agree. I gave a two-week notice to both work and friends and we hit the road. She got that right didn't she?

Well anyway, that's my confession for the day. Sometimes I keep going to others until I find someone who says something I want to hear, but today I feel satisfied with nothing.

TUESDAY – MAY 12 - SUMMERTIME, AND THE LIVING IS EASY

The trouble with being a smart ass is that many times I feel bad afterwards. Turns out my eldest, and today favorite son, Zachary, did not forget me and I received a lovely M-day card today. In my defense the card said I taught him to be a smart ass, so there ya go. Anyway, I'm taking this opportunity to publicly apologize. I'm feeling worse than usual about my faux pas. Motherhood comes with a lot of guilt. We dole it out and we feel it. It's one of the downsides for sure.

We're signing a lease here for another year. Since we're staying I think it's time for curtains. I'm thinking some valances. That can be my next inside project. The front door needs painted too. I'm going to start thinking about that stuff. I need a new bathing suit too. I haven't gotten a new suit since 2010. I'm due. These are things I must think about today. I think I'll look through some catalogs. Better get busy with it,

THURSDAY - MAY 14 - AS WE GO ON, WE REMEMBER

Let's see. . we had the end of the year Chorus concert for Zoë. She warned me that I might cry because they were singing a bunch of growing up songs for the seniors leaving, etc. I knew I wouldn't cry because I don't know a single soul, other than Zoë, at that school.

Which brings up another interesting tid-bit. Both me and my kids (my kids and I) went to the same high school. Zachary actually had a few of the same teachers I had. I mean that's just weird, isn't it? We all knew each other; the parents, the kids, we all were connected in some way. Now I know *nobody*. I mean I just find that interesting enough to note. Not one person. Well, I didn't know one person when we moved here, I know a couple now.

Back to the chorus program. I recognized 5 of the girls in the chorus. I have given each of them a ride home at some point. That's progress. They don't know me, but that's beside the point. And when we sat down there was Joan (the new Mrs. Williams) who we see everywhere now. At restaurants, at school functions, around town. However, her grandson is a senior so we probably won't see her again. Dolly, another work friend, has a son in the chorus and I saw him there, but I didn't see her; although I know she was there as we were comparing notes earlier in the day about going. Just like a friend thing. Look how much progress I've made in a year.

The chorus concert was so good. There were a lot of solos by the seniors and they were blow-your-mind good. And well I teared up, a lot. Turns out I don't need to know anyone to tear up. I'm sure you probably figured that out.

Also, the talent show was Friday night. Our girl did really well. It was a good show. Not sure why more of the chorus singers weren't in it but it was a nice mix of talent. Dancers, a magic show and this kid that stacked cups. I've never seen a cup stacker before. He was really good. Not that I'm partial, but I think our girl was the best!

What else...

Horseback riding yesterday. Good grief it's hot. I need to get there earlier. Not a great lesson. I almost went over his head one time when he stopped when I wasn't ready for it. It is such a workout plus the added heat, I should be dropping weight in heaps and bounds, but alas....

Tomorrow is old lady visit day (hospice) and then breakfast/lunch with Lori! I know, a *friend*! Then we have a free weekend I believe. It might be time to plan another weekend get-away with that boyfriend of mine. We are coming up on an anniversary! Next week it will be one year since we moved here. ONE YEAR! I don't know if it feels like more or less. I think it just is what it is.

THURSDAY - MAY 21 - ENDINGS...NO WAIT, BEGINNINGS

Did you watch? Did anyone watch the last Letterman? I've been trying to stay awake for it the past 3 weeks or so. Once they started advertising the end was near I started making a conscious effort to stay up for it. I will admit I had about a 45% success rate. I remember specifically wanting to see Julia Roberts and frumphph (sound effect) as soon as he introduced her out I went. Last night we stayed out in the "big" room (the living room) so I had a better possibility of staying awake and I am happy to report that I made it through. I'm feeling a little like I've lost a friend today, not ever losing a friend, I'm 100% sure that it's not the same, yet I'm feeling a loss of some kind. Another end of an era. All these endings make me think about how long I've lived. Letterman was on for 33 years. My son Zachary is going to be 33 this year. I mean his entire life time (so far) Letterman was on.

I visited my old lady today. I asked her if she watched it. She said she'd *never* seen it. It was on too late for her. She said she never saw Johnny Carson either. Never. That seems hard to believe. What else is there to do at 11:30 at night? When I walked in her room today I asked if she was busy and she said "no, just thinking." I bet she has a lot to think about in the way of nostalgia. She has 96 years to think about.

This weekend marks one year that we have lived together, in Florida, in this house. One year ago, I was packing and still working at PPU up until the bitter end. Jordan (my work colleague) walked me home with boxes and we cried and cried. One year ago, Sally showed up at the last-minute and helped me with my kitchen or I would have never gotten out of there. One year ago, we pulled out of Pittsburgh and although I always *look* back, I don't know that I'll ever *be* back, permanently that is. We all know that I come back to visit. But visiting is not the same as living there. I have limited time, lots of babies jumping all over me and boys that I need to catch up with. And then I'm gone again. It's my mother's fault. She should have a house there still that we can all come "home" to and crash for weeks at a time. But nooooo, she has her home in Virginia where we all crash for week*ends* at a time. Although I'm starting to stretch out my time in Virginia too.

I've got a roast in the crockpot on this hot-hot spring day. It's in the 90's all week. No end in sight. It's not horrible but it is hot. It's Florida, I'm happy. We will be looking for a Memorial Day parade this weekend.

MONDAY - MAY 25 - YOU'RE NOT THE BOSS OF ME

Here I am writing on a Monday night. It's a holiday, I'm supposed to give myself weekends and holidays off from blogging so I can feel like I'm doing a real job. I know I know I give myself off other days too, but still. I try to maintain at least a little bit of a schedule. I remember the days when I worked out of my home and every Sunday night I would work. I'm telling you, working at home you do a lot *more* work. Sunday nights I would go through whatever it was I had to go through so I could start the mornings fresh on Monday. I remember starting at PPU that way too. But I soon found out there that nobody else was working Sunday nights so there really wasn't anything to do. I mean nobody even checked their emails over the weekend. Totally different from what I was used to. It was a hard transition. I liked being busier for sure.

In light of that, I should be happy that I'm too busy this week (or at least tomorrow) to blog and so I thought I'd get one in tonight. Tuesdays used to be my volunteer at the middle school day, remember? Did I tell you that last week after I was there an hour my afternoon relief showed up? When I teased her about reading her watch wrong she said her schedule changed and she was working at 10 am now. So now I even lost my volunteer job. I know, right? I can't even give it away. Oh well, so that opens up a day to have breakfast with Lori tomorrow. Then I'm picking Zoë up and we're driving Monica back to Davis Island. Monica, daughter #2, was here visiting for the weekend but is *moving in* next weekend, just for the summer we think. She's pretty much a God send with Jasen. She makes him help after dinner and he listens. Wednesday is horse day in the morning anyway, Thursday is volunteer luncheon and visiting old lady day because Friday morning is my second Reiki training class.

Say what? I know, how cool am I? Because I'm a hospice volunteer, Suncoast Hospice offers free Reiki training to the volunteers because it is used so much with the patients. Free training. Our training is done by Reiki masters too. It's not like we're being trained by lackeys. I'm very excited about it. Ever hear of it? It's very hard to explain. Here's what I found on Google for an explanation:

a healing technique based on the principle that the therapist can channel energy into the patient by means of touch, to activate the natural healing processes of the patient's body and restore physical and emotional well-being.

After week 1 we are to practice on our family and pets. Sam (the dog) is getting a lot of attention as is Pete. Pete says it's very relaxing. Sam doesn't say much. Florida has a law that you are not allowed to practice Reiki for a fee. Something about massage therapists being "licensed" but Reiki people only have certificates. No charging in the state of Florida. It's okay, I'm not in it for the money. I just thought that was an interesting tidbit. And I'm very excited about being able to do this. Especially if I'm at all effective. The one girl in my class said there is a huge need in the Care Center here by my house. Maybe since I can't get full-time work at least I could go to the Care Center during the days and be useful. A paying job would be nice too. There has to be more to life than cooking and sweeping up dog hairs, oh and bathrooms.

That's my biggest news. Although another child moving in is pretty big news too.

In other weekend news, Pete and I were back on bikes. We had a lovely bike ride. Stopped for breakfast and then onto the junk store where we bought a new chair and Dave the pig. Yes Dave is made of tin but I love him just the same. We love this one junk store; well, I call it a junk store but really it's called Antiques and Uniques.

Tonight for dinner we had a ribfest. (not related to Dave) We made two different kinds. Two marinades, two different ways of marinating, two different style rib meat and cooked one in the oven and one on the grill. I like the grilled ones. Love that burnt sticky stuff. Mmmmmm. Tomorrow it's back to salads. We've been doing pretty good with our diets.

And I think you're caught up now. Our year living in Florida anniversary kind of came and went without fanfare. Zoë helped me make a framed photo collage for Peter of our first year here. Although he didn't seem impressed I still think I will do one every year. I got nothing from him. I guess he's not totally perfect. I think Monica moving in has thrown him. Zoe and I talked about it knowing she was coming. We talked about how it will change the dynamic. But she is his daughter (and Zo's sister) and there's no way I would ever say that one of his children could not move in. I don't have that right do I? She needs a place to say and we are her family and this is now her family home so where else should she go?

But that said, it's definitely changed the vibe here.

WEDNESDAY - MAY 27 - A LITTLE CROP HERE, A LITTLE CROP THERE

I finally got the horse to move. What is the secret? The crop.

I remember when riding in the woods with Erin we used to reach up and snap off a branch from a tree and all we had to do was let the horse see it and they would behave. I never actually used one. But even them hearing the snap of the tree they figured they'd better shape up. Well, the same thing happened today. Where my legs and personal cues seem to fail miserably, a tiny little crop held ever so lightly against his withers, bouncing on his shoulder, and he was the best horse ever. Well maybe not *ever*. It was hard to get him to stop. I also almost fell off cantering at the bend in the ring. I leaned in too much, but I was able to recover and we were able to laugh. Shiiiittt. Not so much laughing had I fallen but anyway....

I am thinking there is a life lesson in here somewhere. Something to do with when we can't do something ourselves after giving it our all, we need to call in reinforcements. My legs squeezing as hard as I can and me kicking in which I can't ever feel anyway was useless. A little crop on the neck and I can actually now have a lesson. I don't think that makes me a failure. I think it make me serious, and I think it lets the horse know I'm serious. Honestly, I kick as hard as I can, and I get nuthin. It is soo frustrating. I'm much happier with a little tapping and a flick of the wrist and don't think I won't hit a little harder if I need to. God bless the crop.

I am super tired today. I don't sweat much as a rule but today getting that horse tacked up I had sweat pouring down myself. While on the horse I don't notice the heat as much, plus I think there might have been a cloud that was helping but oh my is it hot. My new horse friend (which is a big stretch to call her a friend) says she rides in the middle of the day when it's the hottest. She said she's built up a tolerance. I don't know about that, but if I can feel like I'm dropping a few lbs. while sweating then maybe, just maybe, this whole horse thing is worth it. Best $25 ever spent.... maybe.

I had to take Monica back to her temporary home. She'll be moving in this weekend I presume. She doesn't have a car. Wonder how this is going to affect my chauffer duties?

THURSDAY - MAY 28 - IT COULD HAPPEN TO ANYONE

There are several reasons one's phone might fall into the toilet. What's important is the one that caused *my* phone to end up in the toilet. It was in my back pocket. I was not playing a game, or checking emails, it was in my back pocket and I had my painted-on jeans on and well it just popped out of my pocket into the toilet. I heard it plop and it took less than a second to say *"NOOOOOOO"*. There was only water in the toilet for those of you going eww. Now I had to figure out what to do with that stupid phone. I think I'm going to be okay. Zachary said "this is why we can't have nice things." I'm starting to feel like he's right. The AT&T guy tried to tell me my phone is old. I'm like "are you kidding me? I just got this phone." I don't know what is "old" about it. I think all this old phone/new phone stuff is a racket. Can I call? Text? Email? Take photos? Then it's not old. He also told me that you can't take the back off these phones to get to the battery so thank goodness I didn't try harder. Thank heavens for small mercies. Of course, the jury is still out whether or not it's going to work again. Stay tuned.

Today was a busy day. I visited with my old lady this morning. She's telling some good stories of her youth. I love listening to her. She told me I could do the talking next week, but I have nothing interesting like she has. I enjoy listening to her. Then onto my Volunteer thank you luncheon. It was lovely. Then Zoë and I ran errands trying to fix *her* cell phone issues, then I had to take her to LAX practice because the coach couldn't pick her up, and then home by 6:30. It was a long day. I know, when would I work?

Tomorrow is my second and final Reiki 1 class. I'm looking forward to it. Summer is definitely starting next week with the last day of school on Tuesday. Zoë is actually already done except for one final she has to take on Monday. We will just have to wait and see how this summer shakes out.

JUNE 2015

MONDAY - JUNE 1 - A YEAR IN REVIEW

Happy June! Happy unofficial start of the summer. My second summer in Florida. How about that? I had to remind Peter the other day about how far we've come in a year. I'm not sure what is going on with him. Sometimes we can't see the forest for the trees, or is it the trees for the forest? Anyway, in one year, Zoë has been oh so successful in switching schools, making new friends, in new committees, in the drama program, in a talent show, *and* playing Lacrosse. Jasen brought his grades up dramatically and continues to be a good kid. Although even this morning said he prefers living in Baden and Baden school district over this one. That's kinda sad but maybe next year he'll meet his best friend for life. It can happen any time.

Me, I haven't worked (as everyone knows) but I volunteer and am back to riding horses. I think that's good progress. Jasen challenges me daily with my cooking skills and Zoë keeps me young by having me drive her hither and thither and letting *her* drive hither and thither. Although I think letting her drive might be adding to the grey hairs.

We've made quite a few purchases. two cars, one of them a Mercedes, an older one but still fun to drive for sure. A new dining room table and several chairs to go with it, new bedroom furniture including the king size bed, a piano and our most recent new chair purchase! We found the 55-inch TV set he previously had so we're good on TV's. I got myself a new smart phone (although perhaps shouldn't go there because I'm not sure it's recovering from the toilet episode), and lots of new clothes and shoes and jewelry. We are Floridifying ourselves and our house. I'm constantly cleaning out old stuff. My sister(s) have done well with my hand-me-downs.

We've had his mother, my sister and my two boys as house guests. I visited with Diane and Mary Ann when they were in Florida and re-connected with Mary Love and Mary Pat from Edinboro who are both

Florida residents. I've also reconnected with Lori, a hometown friend, who has moved back to this area. She's my coffee (breakfast) buddy and she's been very helpful in navigating the area. I've only seen Stephanie and Rick once. I hope to see both of them more in the next year.

I visited Pittsburgh three times and my mother twice. Am getting ready for another Pittsburgh trip next week. A quick trip, but still touching base with the boys is the goal. I don't think they feel abandoned. Honestly it's harder leaving all those babies (my great nieces and nephew) than my own children. I see Joan and Dolly around town and could almost call them friends, certainly people I can say hello to. I've made a lot fewer friends compared with my year living in Miami but then again I'm not 20 and waitressing and I'm happy with the people I do have in my life. Besides having a whole new family probably out trumps finding new friends.

We've gone on two weekend trips, one to Miami and one to my beloved Cabbage Key. This coming weekend our plans are to go to Orlando to see Marissa (remember her?) She's in a play. I originally bought tickets for Zoë and I to go together but she is either going to Canada for a wedding or she has a LAX game. I'll have to take her another time. I'm hoping to turn it into a boyfriend getaway. Still loving my boyfriend and our getaways. We really need a getaway.

In review, I'd have to say I am having the time of my life. Sure, there are things we don't have yet. A boat, a house on the water, but really...seriously...those are like vision board goals. In the real world we're still trying to navigate our health care options, pay the water bill and figure out what's for dinner.

Peter has always told me that I want things to be perfect right away and I need to be patient. I had to recently remind him of his own advice. Looking back over the year I really love how things have unfolded. We had no idea how we would ever get a bed, and then we did. Or a car, or, or, or.... and then one day you find yourself with a new chair and you realize that more and more you are setting down roots together, starting over.

We are both starting over, big time, in different ways. We are coming from such different pasts and combining our pasts with our current selves heading into our future selves. I love how we're progressing with each other and our relationship and with our "stuff". It wouldn't be fun at all to have it all at once. This slow and steady pace is much more rewarding. And really, coming from my past it's not slow and steady at all. It's lightning speed with all the sudden several dreams coming true.

Am I going to be depressed because we don't have a boat yet? But really, I do need a new set of summer dishes.

WEDNESDAY - JUNE 3 - BLAH

Does anyone think when I don't post something I'm in a bad mood? There are a lot of times when I'm really just too busy but there are many many times when that is absolutely true.

Today I had an interesting horse incident. That horse picked his leg up in this "kick" position, like way high, and was freaking out when I was grooming him. I've never seen anything like it. I mean it was unsettling to say the least. *Crazy*. The lesson itself was "okay" not great. And it's discouraging not to make any progress and then of course to almost get killed is not good either. And why can't anyone be around to see this behavior? It's discouraging. Oh yea, I already said that.

Monica is being a big help, I think. She is waiting on Jasen and entertaining him. He is pointing out to me that being waiting on is his "norm." Not sure of what his point was. Whatever.

MONDAY - JUNE 8 - STAY CALM...SOLDIER ON

I went to Orlando this weekend to see Marissa. Marissa was great! The play was called *In the Heights*. A story about Latinos living in Washington Heights. Marissa was the only non-Latino in the cast. A lot of it was in Spanish (or is it Hispanic?) but I was able to understand most of it. Marissa was in the ensemble, a great dancer, and was also assistant choreographer. How about that? Very cool for her.

She hooked me up with a place to stay right inside Universal called the Cabana Bay. It's a retro design. I had a nice little suite. The resort is big and has a lot of family type activities. Unfortunately, I was alone (don't ask) and it was raining *hard* when I arrived. The rain down here is pretty crazy. It like dumps buckets of water onto the roads. None of this light sprinkling stuff. So anyway, there were hail warnings and dangerous lightning going on so I stayed put in the room until time to leave for the play.

I met her mom, dad and grandma and another friend of hers at the play. After the play we went out to eat. Stayed out until 2 a.m. First time I've stayed up that late, by choice, since I don't know when. The next day we all met for breakfast and then I came back home.

Orlando is the worst place to go alone. I remember when I used to have meetings there. I desperately missed my kids every time I was there. I was missing them this time too. There's so much to do but being alone in a place like Disney is the pits. Although I did have a nice time with Marissa and her family. It is always great to see her. I love the atmosphere in Orlando. Makes me feel all excited like a little kid. I mean when you see that Mickey Mouse electric pole it just has to make you smile. Doesn't it?

I saw a really good movie yesterday, *Woman in Gold*. Again, alone. I recommend the movie. Zoë and I went out to dinner last night, just the two of us, and then drove all around to see various sunsets. A very nice night with just the girl indeed.

So, the BF bailed on the weekend with me and bailed on a movie with me and dinner with me choosing instead to spend his time with his daughter Monica, the one that just moved back in and Jasen. But I have my Zo. I'm sure this is just temporary and reconnecting with Monica is just new...I guess(?)

Tomorrow I have two interviews. Woo hoo. Wish me luck!

TUESDAY - JUNE 9 - WE ARE…. Q. V.

The play I just saw with Marissa in Orlando, *In the Heights*, I believe I mentioned was about the Latino experience living in Washington Heights (which I assume is part of NYC). Anyway, the characters romanticized about moving back "home" to their respective countries, Puerto Rico, Columbia, etc. At one point the cast and the audience were all waving flags from their homelands. I read that when the audience did that (or does that) it is very touching for the cast. They all feel this lost connection to their homeland. Not to give the plot away, (spoiler alert) in the end they realize they are home, right there in Washington Heights.

Home has been a subject of this blog many many times. Am I home here in Florida or is Pittsburgh my home?

Tomorrow I am coming "home" to Pittsburgh. I feel like the people in the play. Caught between two worlds. Sewickley/Pittsburgh is my "home" and what I know and where my real family is, my blood family, and Florida is my home, and my new family and where I live now. Actually, it adds a bit of dimension to my life. And lord knows anyone from Sewickley needs dimension, or as we like to call it, "getting out of the bubble."

Still, there is something about that bubble that is appealing. Down here, a thousand miles away, I have found that bubble feeling, that "home" feeling, when I am with my Sewickley friends. There's something safe about it and something so familiar. I mean these people *know* you. Not that I don't have several long-time *non*-Sewickley friends that know me (Sandy, Barb, Jean, off the top of my head), but it's something about the Sewickley connection, and sometimes specifically the QV connection that is so comforting.

Today, Lori treated me to lunch for my birthday. I felt so at "home." I've known Lori for 45+ years. I believe I met her when she was in the 7th grade, friends with my sister. It's not like Lori and I were ever best friends, I mean not that we weren't friends, but in Sewickley I don't think we ever met for breakfast or lunch. I know we never did. But, down here, when we meet for our coffee, lunch or whatever I feel totally relaxed with someone I *know*. It's just that there's no need explaining who the various characters in our lives have been or how we were molded in our high school days. We both know that about each other. I love that feeling of "home."

When I left up north for my new adventure here in the sunshine state, I was asked several times if I would miss my friends. I admit I said no. I know, it sounds harsh. But really I was ready for a different experience. I wanted to try this relationship stuff out, and now reminded of the saying, careful what you wish for. Nevertheless, this is what I wanted to try to experience. I jumped "all-in." (Am I using these quotation marks right?) The fact that I don't have all my friends around me I'm sure helps my new relationship because I have to work things out. I can't run out and sleep on Diane's couch or in Warren's room. When your first response is "flight" (not "fight") it's best that the "flight" option is not so easy so when I calm down, it's over, and I'm still home.

When I married Dennis, our minister said we would never make it if we stayed in Sewickley. Our family ties were too invasive into our relationship. And well, obviously, that old Mike Henning was right (God rest his soul). Sometimes you just need to rely on each other and it's easier to do that, away from home.

When I see my old friends down here, when they visit, or when they call (ahem Stephanie), or when we go for coffee, I am so happy to have that connection to "home." On the other hand, I look outside at the palm trees, the pool, hear Jasen ask "what's for dinner" and I know I'm "home" here too. But then again,,,

I am so looking forward to coming "home" tomorrow and making *my* kids spend my birthday with me. (HA!) To know me is to love me, right? A typical day in the life of a Gemini.

MONDAY- JUNE 15 - LIFE IS A BOWL OF CHERRIES

I'm back from my visit. I had a lovely visit. I was very sad to leave this time. I think it was too short. Plus, I had some quality time with friends that I don't usually have. I saw all the babies this time, Sewickley friends, Jimmy, John and Flo (got my Italian fix) and some of the Bunko girls. I mean really, a very nice time. There was a lot of complaining about the heat, to which I say...*Seriously*? But still, it is a different kind of hot there. It just hangs there, so I get it.

I came home to a very nice boyfriend (for a change, it's been a while.) We went to dinner when I got in (yes it was 9:30 pm but that's how we roll) and then a dozen beautiful roses. On Sunday we slept and slept and then went to Costco for treasures (and food). I'm very excited about my new Tommy Bahama reclining beach chair that also has a little cooler on the back, lots of pockets and a backpack that is apparently my birthday present. I mean does life get any better? Also, some Ranier cherries a pair of capris and some new moisturizer. Happy Birthday to me.

Then out to a birthday dinner at Rumbas. We tried going to see the new Jurassic Park movie but the theater lost electricity. We tried the next theater but it was sold out. We're going to try tonight again (I think) At least Jasen and I think we are. We'll see how the big guy feels after a day of work. I also had another bday cake. I had 4 bday cakes total. One regular, one burnt almond torte, one white chocolate raspberry thing and one chocolate fudge. I mean seriously, delicious. All of them. And certainly, time to detox now that I'm home. Well after I finish off the fudge cake, *then* I'll detox.

Sam, the dog, had a beauty appointment today. He looks and smells delicious and bonus, he didn't eat any other small dogs or cats while there. He was all in all pretty good.

I got the bad news that my phone is "toast". Makes me very sad. But I'm really just as happy with my $40 phone. I'm embarrassed that I couldn't take care of a "real" phone. Although the new $40 phone is just like a real phone, just can't take selfies and the camera isn't as good. Oh well. . life...and really it's embarrassing to act like this is even a "thing." People are starving for heaven's sake.

Thank you to my boyfriend for having the house all clean and beautiful upon my return. And now with a clean dog, well I probably don't have to vacuum until tomorrow.

WEDNESDAY - JUNE 17 - MY CAR IS NOT RED!

There's nothing like getting a phone call that starts off saying "you don't have to tell me if you don't want" to which I respond "you haven't said anything" to which they ask you if your son has been arrested and is in jail. WHAT? WHAT? And then you feel like you have to justify what you know to be true. Let's see, I was just with my son 4 days ago, I don't remember any shackles or ankle bracelet. It's very unnerving even when it's not at all true. And this person is asking "are you sure? " Like am I sure he's not in jail? Yea, pretty sure that was him I was with and I know where he is at this exact moment. This is the way rumors get started. Who do I have to sue?

What a way to start the day. I gotta shake that off. I remember arguments with other people over things you know but they want to convince you otherwise. As an example, like I'm looking at my car, which is silver, and someone argues with me that I have a red car. And I'm actually questioning myself and looking at my car again to make sure it's not red. Really who's the crazy one here?

MONDAY - JUNE 22 - JUST LIVIN THE LIFE

Hellooo...How long has it been? Here's what's been going on:
Peter decided he needed a vacation day so we decided to go to Sarasota for 2 nights. Me, him and Jasen. The girls are in Canada at the cousin's wedding. Sam went to the Pet Hotel. Sam did okay as they did not call us to come back and there was no mention of us never bringing him back, so that should open up other travel opportunities for us.

The three of us left Thursday night, a short hour drive to Sarasota and checked into the Hotel Indigo which is downtown Sarasota, close to the water (the Bay). We might have been within walking distance of a couple of places but we drove everywhere. The first night we found St. Armand's Circle which is this very cool shopping district, in a circle. We ate at Crab and Fin, a schnazzy place, and Jasen was very happy with his King Crab. Afterwards, after ice cream of course, we went back to the hotel and hung out in the hot tub pools. Instead of having typical swimming pools, they have two outdoor whirlpool pools. One is hot and the other cold. Cold being relative. More like normal, not cold. Both of the pools had jets. Anyway, Jasen had a great time running back and forth between them.

The next day we went to this place called Sarasota Jungle Gardens. Very nice, clean, well-kept place with "rescued" animals. Lots of birds, crocodiles, alligators, snakes, a couple little vermin I can't remember. We watched a couple of the shows. I loved it. It was very small and very clean and very *not* crowded. They also take great care to let you know that all of their animals are rescue animals, not stolen from the wilds, and wouldn't survive in the wilds. A lot of these birds live to 80+ years old. They have one bird there named Frosty who was on the Ed Sullivan show, the same night as Elvis Presley. He rode a bicycle on high wire on the show, and did the same trick for us, at 79 years old! How cute is that?

Then we went to a beach, I decided to go right at Armand's Circle towards Longboat Key. When Mary Ann was here we went left at Armand's Circle to Lido beach, so I thought I'd try something different. Longboat Key is very private. It took a while until we could pull over to go to a public beach. Lots of gated communities. But when we could, we pulled in to a public beach access, with 1 other car, and hit the beach. It was so NOT crowded. It was beautiful. I mean beautiful. A little smelly as there was something dead somewhere, but when the wind shifted it was ok. Lots of dead things on the beach at times. It happens.

That night we went to dinner in the downtown district of Sarasota and saw an amazing guitarist.

On Saturday morning we checked out their famous farmer's market, had brunch and got home by noon. Which was also lovely because we still had the weekend ahead of us. The girls came back from Canada on Saturday. A good time was had by all. They are happy to be home though.

Sunday was Father's Day and quite the doings around here. Kinda like Christmas for Peter. Very different than Mother's Day for me. But it was nice for him. All his children were here. We floated in the pool, I made a lovely dinner for everyone just like the caretaker that I am, and then the long weekend was over.

I also talked with my hospice people today and have another hospice patient to visit. She likes to play cards. I said I hope she doesn't mind if I dust her. And they also are pulling together volunteers for their pediatric program and want me to get involved with that. No Reiki appointments yet though. Guess I'll keep practicing on Pete and the dog.

And now you are all caught up. Riveting stuff isn't it?

TUESDAY - JUNE 23 - I HEAR YOU

I believe I've mentioned that I read a couple other blogs, right? Today I read a very cute and very relevant one. She's twenty-something years old and started off on the blog post thinking her life's a failure because she hasn't "made it" yet. *Seriously*? But in the end she decides it's really the process that counts.

Of course, we've all heard that a hundred thousand times, it's not the goal it's the journey blah blah, but it is good to be reminded at various times of our lives isn't it? Jimbo is about to make a major decision and worried about it. I'm like "Jim, you're TWENTY-FOUR – get out there and make mistakes!" We can grow out of activities but should we grow out of making mistakes? Should we? Maybe mistakes isn't the right word. Maybe the word I'm looking for is "risks." We should *never* grow out of taking risks. They don't always have to lead to mistakes, but if they do, then I think what we're supposed to do is learn from them? Right?

I am pushing hard for more volunteer activities since working for pay is not really panning out (and I believe these volunteer opportunities will be rewarding in numerous ways) but, I have to say, if there weren't three kids living here I think I would be happier than sh*t sitting by the pool reading every day, writing my little blog and/or watching TV in addition to the cleaning/cooking that I already do. I mean I wouldn't be a total bum, although I think laying on the couch would definitely increase. Other than really wanting some income, I'm just restless and well it's hard living with a bunch of people. The jump from 2 to 3 kids is proving to be more challenging than I had anticipated.

For 30 years I pretty much lived with two children part-time and even then the schedules were so that I had a lot of time to myself. Plus being the mom, you can set the rules of the house. I'm not in that role here. I think I'm just here to make sure nobody burns down the house, feed them at least once a day and/or to give them rides to wherever. It's not easy to know what to do with myself. I can't help but feel guilty for not knowing.

On the other hand, I am also thankful for them (those dam kids) for giving me any purpose at all and for keeping me off the couch. They sort of force me to find something to do just by their mere existence. It's a good thing!

I was reminded several times today of various successes that happen later in life and the twists and turns and risks that people take in their life time. Who says God doesn't speak to us? He was all over me today. I am living the dream aren't I?

WEDNESDAY - JUNE 24 - THAT JIMMY

He did it. Jimmy quit his job, without having a job to go to. I couldn't be prouder. It takes a lot of guts to go against the "norm". .

The CEO at his company offered $2000 to anyone that wanted to quit yesterday so he took him up on it! He said only 3 people from his office took the offer but 22 people from another office quit yesterday. He leaves for Nashville tomorrow and a friend there is setting him up with all kinds of contacts and interviews. It's crazy. Only Jimmy. We will see where he lands but he took the risk and it's only day 1 of his unemployment, and he's got prospects out the wazoo.

My Zachary doesn't follow the norm either. Zachary, the one who works 8 days a month has more money than any of us. I'm very proud of both my boys. I like to think they got that pioneer spirit from me (and I got from my mother.) In some respects, I have followed norms (i.e., working at an office job) but in my personal life not so much.

I was one of the first (that I know of) to have week on/off custody when I divorced Dennis. In hindsight maybe not so good but at the time, following Sally's lead, it seemed like a nice fair agreement. Also, although not married to Jimmy's dad we had a great relationship for Jimmy. I think I was one of the first to have a "baby-daddy" - Quite the pioneer I am, so ahead of my time. And I remember saying I wanted to be the first single-stay at home mom I knew, and with working at home (and not having money) I actually accomplished that for quite a few years. The pioneer spirit hasn't gotten me very far financially but I believe it has helped shaped my children into following their hearts.

I followed my heart down here. I don't believe that our hearts ever steer us wrong. Although hearts may steer us places we still have to take the next steps. That's where it gets tricky.

But as for today it's *go Jimmy go!* I know he'll do well wherever he lands. He's just that kinda kid.

That's all for today, gotta go play cards with my new old lady. She mentioned a game I've never heard of but I'm a quick learner. It should be fun. Wonder if I should take some pennies (jk) probably not a good thing to take the patients money.

FRIDAY - JUNE 26 - BADDA BING, BADDA BOOM

I don't know what to do with myself. I'm literally going between walking in circles and standing still looking in the mirror. I went for my walk this morning, you know Florida heat and all, so should probably get a shower. But then I want to take a nap because for some reason last night we were up until like after 2:00. (I'm going to blame the late day ice tea.) I also need a pedicure and I wouldn't mind floating in and subsequently sleeping in the pool. Do you see my dilemma?

I mean I don't want to shower if I'm going in the pool, unlike all the signs we're used to seeing from our youth "please shower before entering pool." Who does that? You only have to shower again after the pool anyway, right? And since I'm so tired I would probably fall asleep floating in the pool, which is sometimes okay but I just don't know if I want to bake in the sun today. Have I mentioned it's hot?

Jasen pointed out to me the other day that I say "it's hot" a lot. He's right. I'm not sure why I do that. It made me remember that when I started getting hot flashes I used to announce them all the time. Marissa and I would be sitting in my office and I would look at her and say "hot flash" – I wonder what she thought. Like was she supposed to fan me or something? LOL. Poor girl. I guess I just wanted her to be aware that I wasn't having a heart attack. Not sure why I mention the heat all the time here too. I think Jasen realizes this is Florida, it's hot, it's *always* hot, why do I have to announce it. Dam kids, so freakin logical.

Back to my dilemma, I could get the shower and then take a nap indoors in the a/c and forget about the pool for today. I do like the idea of a nice pool day on Saturdays so maybe I should just wait until tomorrow. I also need to run to the store to get items for dinner. I've decided to make good old-fashioned spaghetti (these days known as pasta).

Can you believe that this family of mine (the new one) has never seen the Godfather movies? We watched I and II this week. Last night was Godfather II. In some scene they were eating pasta and we all went ooohhh. Today I thought I'd channel my inner Nunni and make some sauce.

In my quandary state I decided to sit down and knock out a quick blog. Quick just to touch base and quick because there is nothing new to report and no inspiration to share and really I just needed a minute to collect my thoughts because I'm over tired and needed to figure out my plan of attack for the day.

And see? Just a little blogging and I've come to my decision:

Shower

Pedicure

Shop (for sauce ingredients)

Make sauce

then nap!

So many decisions yet I'm on it! I mean really, who *wouldn't* want to hire me.

TUESDAY - JUNE 30 - WHAT HAPPENED TO MONDAY?

Where did I leave off? Showers, nails, walking, naps I think. You will be happy to note all missions accomplished. Nails are blue. Not sure about the color but it's kinda growing on me. I made delicious spaghetti sauce last Friday night and decorated the table with oranges. You God-father fans will get that. Let's see what else, a lot of sleeping and floating went on over the weekend, mostly Sunday and I'm feeling all caught up on life, for now.

I have a house full of Clarks today, minus Pete. I'm also trying to clean. I did get one bathroom cleaned and some vacuuming accomplished. Floors will have to wait. Zoë is having a friend stay over and well I don't want her friend to think we're slobs. I asked Zoë to think about that bathroom upstairs and whether or not she wants a friend to see it. She just groaned. I think I'm going to leave it. Maybe their Papa will want to give it a once over later. I cleaned it last time.

Speaking of Papa, we took Zoë up to Aunt Leslie's last night. We (I) let her drive. Peter said if I wanted to let her drive I had to sit up front with her. Dam him. I like sitting in the back relaxing and letting him do the invisible brake, but the trooper I am, I sat up there and we stuffed him in the back of the Mercedes. It's a small car. I really am having second thoughts about that car. I love love love driving it but it's small. The doors are heavy, the driver's seat is low, getting in and out of the back is next to impossible, no Bluetooth that I can figure out either. But I do love driving it. Anyway, we dropped her at Leslie's and headed over to Wiregrass Mall for a date night. What a nice night too. Wiregrass Mall is outside. We just wandered around. I tried on clothes and he got lost in the music store. Then we ended up in the bookstore. Just a nice night meandering. It's been a long long time since we had date night. Things are very different with the new addition (Monica) but maybe that's just what happens when you start to settle into relationships. I mean what choice do I have?

There's movement in the Clark household. Doors slamming, people coming and going. Should I be doing something? I better go check.

JULY 2015

WEDNESDAY - JULY 1 - I'M WALKING HERE

I live in an oven. A moist heat oven. Not quite a steamer but not a dry oven like Arizona. I hated Arizona. Everyone, including myself, thought I would love Arizona because I do love the heat but honestly I couldn't breathe. It was exactly like sticking myself inside a 400° oven. It's not quite like that here. Don't get me wrong, it is hot. So, I've been walking in the mornings. I drive a couple of miles over to the causeway and walk over there because it's more scenic and there's the possibility of a breeze off the water. I've been experiencing all kinds of weather during my walks. One day I could see in the distance all these storms out there over the water and sure enough ½ way through my walk they all converged, right on top of my route. The good news was there was no lightning. There's almost always lightning. But this day I waited it out, briefly, by the bathrooms with some other folks and then, well then I just went for it. The wind pelted me, sideways rain and all, and the thing I was most concerned with was getting across the draw bridge. I didn't want to be picked up by the wind and dropped into the sea. Literally. But by the time I got to the bridge the storm was passing and well I obviously made it across and have lived to tell about it. I thought perhaps Peter would have been worried about me but when I came home he was still sleeping and didn't even know there was a storm. That whole concept there could be some sort of life inspirational blog topic. The fact that you are going through a storm and fighting your way to get back to someplace or someone and that person is oblivious to your fight. Hmmm I say *hmmm.* Can I do anything with this?

No.

I've been very good at my morning walks. Yesterday there was a lovely breeze which helped the heat factor. The thing is when I start out the sun is to my back, it's not so bad, but after my 2 miles down and I turn around half beat, then the sun is glaring at me, full force, on my face and person. When I got back to the car yesterday my face was drenched with sweat, today too. This is a new sensation for me. Sweating profusely and all. Is it good for the pores? Am I getting rid of toxins? It seems a little gross to blog about. How did I go from almost inspirational to gross. Is there a blog in that? Hmmm,

No.

Bottom line is, I'm a trooper. I'm walking here. I did cancel my horseback riding until further notice though which makes me very sad. I can walk at 8 am in the blazing heat by the water with very little clothes on, but I can NOT put on jeans and half chaps and get on a horse.

The issue is not the temperature as much as the "feels like" temperature. You know in the north where you have the wind chill factor? Well, here it'll say temp 86°, feels like 102° or 1,000°. If it was just 86° I would do it. If I had Erin here yelling at me, I would do it, but I don't and it's hot and I'm a sissy. I was hoping my instructor would respond with some options but she has not. Oh well,

What else,,, Zoë had a friend stay over last night and all the kids were here. Somewhere in this house there are 5 children, one dog and me. I have to say it's pretty quiet for all those people. Zoë and her friend made this brownie concoction for breakfast. A layer of chocolate chip cookie dough, a layer of Oreos and a layer of brownies. That was their breakfast. I had bought bacon, eggs, blueberries for pancakes but nooo. Brownies. So as not to insult them I had to try some too. I'll probably go into sugar shock before I end this blog.

That's all I have. I mean it's good. All is well. Life is good. Life with the Clarks. Hmmm, well now. Do I have my first book title? Who will play me in the movie?

MONDAY - JULY 6 - IT'S NOT FOR DRINKING

I think in my next life I might want to stay in the same house from the beginning of my children's life to the end of mine. You know what made me think of this today? Rubbing alcohol. When I moved out of

Fair Oaks I remember packing up 3 or 4 bottles of rubbing alcohol. Why so many? Well, if I remember correctly I didn't have a whole lot of storage so I probably could never find the last one I bought. But when I moved I was finding all kinds of treasures. Lots of rubbing alcohol, lots of scotch tape, many many pairs of scissors, band aids galore, treasures, I tell you, treasures. Imagine the treasures you find when you live in the same house for ever and ever and never clean the attic out and still have all your kid's school papers from pre-school on up.

Now I have one Tupperware bin for each kid, one for myself too. These bins are supposed to hold all our memories. I had to scale down when I moved. But looking back I think I would have liked to save everything in that attic, then, when I died those kids could go through the stuff and pitch it. Ya know? I mean the rubbing alcohol in the house alone would have been worth something.

Today I had to *buy* rubbing alcohol. I looked under our sink and there was none. How does that happen? Where did all those bottles go that I packed up 5 years ago before I began my nomadic adventures? I had to spend almost $2 on it. I remember when it was 89 cents. What in the world is going on with alcohol?

Well, I think I'm back to embracing the "stuff." I went through the clean out and scale down period only to be thrown back into a house with stuff, and now I'm getting back into the swing of accumulating more stuff. I mean the dishes thing alone...well it's hard to shake; although I am happy to report that I held back from buying summer dishes.

Now when we see something we think of buying I say, let's wait for the real house. We need a 5-bedroom house on the water and that will be the end of the nomadic period for both of us. We will fill it with new stuff and keep more stuff in the attic and garage (cars will have to be parked outside). I will embrace the stuff. I mean why not? It's nice to scale down and I proved to myself that I can do it but when living with all these people, and wanting to make room for more to come and go, well scaling down is not an option.

I am officially putting it out there that there will be one more move into our forever home. And it won't be small. Of course, I have no job and at this moment in time, this moment today, this could not happen, but that is not to say that it won't happen ever. Tomorrow we could win the Mega Millions. Tomorrow I could come up with a book idea and a subsequent advance from Random House, tomorrow could bring many things.

But for today, I will stock up on rubbing alcohol for each bathroom, for when the time comes.

WEDNESDAY - JULY 8 - I CAN BE A MERMAID TOO

Going back to 4th of July – well, we almost died. *Almost*. Pete, Jasen and I headed over to Safety Harbor for the fireworks. We were proud of ourselves for finding a parking spot 7 blocks away from the Fireworks spot, not bad, although I have a limp and was dragging behind, literally. We got a place on the ground seated around some Steeler fans from Greensburg, laid down our blanket and awaited the night with hotdogs and cokes for the fireworks event to start. We decided that Steeler fans are loud. Anyhoo, an hour or so before the fireworks were to start the ominous multicolored clouds rolled in.

Once the rain and wind started we got up from the soon to be wet ground and wrapped ourselves up in blankets and towels. Then we thought we'd go out onto the Pier to wait it out. I know, sounds like a stupid idea doesn't it? But down here it really can blow over quickly. We weren't the only ones that thought about the Pier. Also, it wasn't *that* bad when we went out there. But it got bad. Real bad. I was very worried for the boaters out in the Harbor. One kayaker pulled his kayak under the Pier. I mean it got ugly. Lots of lightening and lots of rain. We waited it out. Our blankets were soaked, as were we, from the sideways pelting rain but I have to say our mood was pretty light. It was quite an adventure. I announced that if the Pier was going down it was every man for himself and swim to shore. It lasted a little longer than we anticipated.

Since I'm here to talk about it you know the Pier didn't go down. We left our fellow pier-mates as soon as it started to slow down and headed for the car. We assumed the fireworks were cancelled. However, on the way back to the car we overheard that they would be set off no matter how long they were delayed. Still, we hobbled (I hobbled) back to the car, Jasen was now freezing, and as we started heading home the fireworks started. We were stuck in traffic, in our nice warm car, with a perfect view of them. The traffic didn't move until it was over. I must say. We had a GREAT seat.

So, there was that. .

What else...Oh Peter made a delicious dinner the other night. Stuffed the Dutch oven with rice, then chicken, then veggies. A regular Emeril he is.

Let's see. . the whole fam (Peter, Monica, Zo, Jasen and myself) went to this park called Weeki Wachee known for their mermaids, but we missed the Mermaid show. We caught the River Cruise and then onto the water slides. The water park is spring fed. Very clear water at a constant 75 degrees, brrrrr.

Yesterday I might have mentioned going to Mary Love's house, she's an old friend from my college days (1976). I must say it was one of the most relaxing days I have *ever* had. Her place is so nice, right on the water, and really I don't know how you get anything done when the water is right there and well there is *sitting* to do. We went out on their boat twice. Once before lunch. I got to drive! And then another drive in the early evening. However, we were driving into a storm so we had to turn around and go back.

Let's see what else. My 2:00 hospice patient cancelled for today so I think I might read a little. Tomorrow is a full day with hospice stuff as is Friday. They've asked if I'd be interested in being a doula. I have to give them an answer by tomorrow. Keep in mind that these pregnancies and births would not be healthy or living births, thus the hospice component. Yea, I gotta think about this one. I sure do have a lot of hospice opportunities. I think I'll write to Obama and see if they can make volunteer hours count for health care. Isn't that a good idea?

That's it for today. Not much in the way of inspiration. But it is mindless...for those looking for a distraction.

FRIDAY - JULY 10 - THE LITTLE RED HEN IS ALIVE AND LIVING IN PALM HARBOR

I was thinking of giving my two-week notice today. After sitting two hours with my one old lady playing Sequence and Rummikub, which was fun, I went and picked up Zoë, then drove her through a drive-thru for lunch, I ate there too – see? Sooo bad for me. Then dropped her off at home and went to Steve's for produce, the post office, Winn Dixie and Subway for the other two to get them something to eat. It's hot, I'm hobbling (my feet hurt) and I had more groceries than I've seen in a while (I think I went over budget.)

Did one person help unload the car? No. Did one person help put the groceries away? No. Did either of the two come and get their sandwiches which I made sure were fresh and hot when I brought them home? No. Did anyone unload the dishwasher and then put the other dishes in there? No. See what I'm sayin? There's three grown children here. *Three.* We thought the addition of the older daughter was going to be a help and she's anything but a help. She does nothing! It's frustrating to say the least. I say things to Peter but not her. I'm just hoping (and praying) it's temporary. And then I feel guilty because I know she needs a respite. These kids have been bounced around since their mother died. It's the least I can do to let them all be together again. But really, would it kill her to do a dish? Seriously?

Here's the thing though. If their Dad was here they would all be running out to the car to help, everyone putting things away, you know, like they *should* be doing, they just don't do it for me. I don't think I'm helping matters here. I mean I'm not going to waste all those groceries and leave them on the floor because no one will help. Ya know? I'm not about to yell at them because they're like adults and well I can't even get Jasen out of bed. I thought I'd entice him with Subway but that's not helping either. Dam kids.

Probably 98% of all of these problems are just kids being kids in general, not really having anything to do with anything wrong with anybody or them hating me but here's the thing.... I really wanted to retire and live on the beach and take walks with my boyfriend. And to make matters even worse, I can't even walk because my foot is so messed up.

I was walking everyday but in week three my ankle/foot started to hurt. I kept hobbling along, but now it hurts alllll the time, I hobble allll the time and it *hurts*. It hurts too much to walk. Today it's swollen. Have I mentioned it hurts? And no, I don't have insurance anymore because I couldn't find a job. It was on my to-do list today to see what I have to do next with this health-care mess. I don't think I'm going to get to it cause I'm already too miserable.

I know it's not like me to complain on here but this is all I got today. Maybe it'll help others to know that it's really not always sunny in Florida. I have money problems, I have health issues, I have teenager issues, and it's really hot.

Zoë appeared after all the groceries were put away and showed me where to hide my dark chocolate candy bar for later. So, there's that. And Monica thanked me for her Subway. I guess that's enough for me to stay a little longer.

Maybe I can talk them into playing Rummikub with me.

MONDAY - JULY 13 - WALK AWAY FROM THE PARKING METER

I suppose I should quickly blog to let my 28 fans know that I have NOT taken the bridge. I spent 2 hours on the phone this morning discussing my health care options.

I continue to have three teenagers in the house...wait one is in her 20's but teenager-esque. Pete said he's going to do a PowerPoint presentation on how to load and unload the dishwasher. I'm hoping lesson #2 can be when and how to empty the kitchen garbage. People just keep stuffing trash in there. The main thing that helped is hearing from Jennifer that her kids (same ages as these kids) don't help either. It's not just me. I wonder if "dam kids" could be the name of my book? Hmm...perhaps I'll work on that idea. I remember having an idea years ago when Jimmy was a freshman in college, to start a book about things we take for granted that we need to tell our kids before they go out into the world. The incident prompting this was that his friends picked up a broken parking meter that had been knocked over and were starting to walk with it. The police immediately arrested them (and Jimmy). But really, drunk 19-year-old college students...is that something that we think to tell them before leaving the nest? Don't pick up any parking meters? Well, it's going in the book...as soon as I start it. All charges were dropped against Jimmy by the way, but for you parents with children starting college, when you see that option to pay $7 for legal services – check it!!

Peter and I had a lovely Saturday. He asked me not to give my 2 week notice so I am reconsidering. It's nice to be wanted. We ended up floating in the pool a little on Saturday then off to this restaurant, Jimmy Guana's, on the water at Indian Rocks, looked at boats and dreamed a little, went for ice cream and ate it on the beach during a beautiful sunset. We stopped on the way home to play pool (billiards) – I won, 2 out of 3. He's a good dater. It's worth emptying the dishwasher. It felt like old times again, just the two of us and he's even acting like he likes me again and wants to keep me around! Which is good since I refuse to leave!

On Sunday, Pete took two of the three children (Jasen and Monica) to a movie and dinner. He seems to do more things without me now that Monica is here. I guess they have some bonding to do. I'm glad he's reconnecting with her. Zoë went out with a friend and I laid on the couch! I know!! Home alone! I was so excited I didn't know what to do with myself. I thought of calling Di and talking about nothing, I brought in two books that I had planned on reading in the living room and I also had the TV to myself. I vacuumed before laying down so I didn't feel like I had to clean (actually Zoë helped!!) and well then anyway I ended up talking to my mom, read a few chapters and then watched *Legends of the Fall*. That is such a good movie. I mean you just cry from beginning to end, don't you? The last 5 minutes of the movie the family descended upon me (came back home.) Zoë came home earlier and I looked at her mortified like WTF? But she just laughed, went to her room and left me to my evening of solitude.

Life is back to normal. It's still hot, I still hurt, I'm disappointed about the walking thing interruption, but I went to the beach for sunset you know? I mean this is what we do now. Any day we want we can go to the beach. I miss the farmer's market in Sewickley, don't get me wrong, and the lushness of Pennsylvania in the summer, but really.... I think I'll give it another year or 20 before considering moving back.

FRIDAY - JULY 17 - RAIN RAIN RAIN RAIN

I'm off schedule. I try to get these blogs out during the day so the distraction comes at the right time (afternoon) and I'm failing miserably aren't I? I've been so busy, I'm sorry.

First of all, it's been raining and raining and raining. I mean we have fields in our yard now that used to be gravel. Our pool is almost over flowing and don't get me started on the fear of what's going to be coming out of the ground (snakes, bugs, trees). I just heard on the news that right off the coast where I live they measured eight inches of rain. A lot of that is in our pool. It's crazy. But it is keeping the temperature down. And as it turns out my car doesn't do so good in the rain. It likes to fishtail. Kinda unnerving. And then the traffic here in the rain is another thing all together. So, there's that, that adds to the length of my day. It takes twice as long to get anywhere. But truthfully I like the rain…just wish I could stay home in bed while it's raining.

I've been doing a lot of hospice stuff this week. I've had appointments and meetings. I've picked up an extra day and will start on Tuesdays at the Care Center offering Reiki. I still have my two other people I visit/play cards with and now they want me to shadow some birth mothers and witness several births before going through the Doula training. That is an excellent idea as I just don't know how I will react to this experience. Stay tuned!

We start vacation tonight. Peter is on vacation all next week! It's very exciting. I like having him around. I'm sure he'll be ready to go back after a week of being here with us crazies (i.e., *his* family) but let's not go there yet. We don't have any big plans so we shall see what comes up.

I think that's all I have. I need to take Monica to work and publish this post.

MONDAY - JULY 20 - MOVE OVER

Twice now I'm late getting this out.

Here's why:

Zo and I went to the movies on Saturday. We went and saw *Jurassic World*. I had already seen it but I said I'd go with her. I gotta say I liked it just as much the second time. Anyway…. ya know, Peter, God bless him, gets irritated at the movies when it's crowded and people ask him to move so they can get seats together. And then I get irritated at him thinking what's the big deal? Well, so, Zoë and I went to the theater early and got seats right in the center, first row, where we wanted. And then it got crowded and right before the movie starts someone asks us to move over so they can get three people together. And now I get it. I thought, ya know, we came here *early* because we want these seats, right here in the center, and also there were no seats in front of us so we could put our feet up. Zoë moving down one now couldn't put her feet up. It's not a huge thing but I now understand his irritation. And then, get this, this part *is* a huge thing, the person that sat next to me was so sick. I mean you could hear the flu in her lungs and she was coughing, like a really sick cough, and coughed throughout the entire movie. I wanted to cry. And I'm looking at her like seriously?! *Why are you here?* I mean, the least she could have done was sit in the middle of her group of three and get them sick. What is wrong with people?

The end of this story is, I'm sick. I'm full of whatever it is she was spitting out and well this has been my day. . walking .... nap.... shower...nap.... shopping for someone's birthday tomorrow...then a short *short* blog because? I need another nap.

I hate sick people at the movies and now I get it why Pete gets irritated when people ask us to move when we're late. Pete says the polite thing to do is for the late comers to split up because they're late, not ask people to move. I get it!

THURSDAY - JULY 23 - ON THE MEND

I was just reminded that I haven't posted anything. Yes I'm slacking. I've got a lot of excuses though. Wanna hear them?

First, I believe you all know I'm a little sick this week. Yesterday I was finally able to do absolutely nothing. We went for a walk in the a.m. but then home, shower, bed...allllll day. And it has worked. Today I'm feeling better. Not 100% or even close but I got out of bed so that's an improvement and I've done some things on the computer. Go me.

It's still vacation week for Peter. We've been walking every morning together. That's a nice thing. I've been pretty much a slug after that though. However, he's been doing some stuff. Yesterday he finally went for his massage that he got at Christmas. He was a pretty happy camper. Then he took the entire family bowling. Turns out his eldest daughter is a bowling shark. Perhaps after she gets tired of the executive chef gig she can try bowling as a career. or not. Also, it turns out that Jasen is a good pool (billiards) player. I'm going to have to challenge him. Anyway, so they had a nice time (without me). Also, Pete's birthday was

Tuesday. I'm supposed to be the party planner, cooker, decorator, etc., so I ended up buying a sandwich ring and chicken tenders from Publix. I got out of cooking for a couple of days which has also been helpful in my recovery. And I might add a very tasty decision. I did make a tortellini salad which was delicious. Anyway, all the kids were here for a day or so which is nice for the Papa. I basically stayed in bed.

One nice family thing that happened, in my opinion, was when everyone came home from bowling the two little ones (Jasen and Zoë) came back to the bedroom where I was resting, to tell me about it and check on me. Kind of like what family people do that care about you. That has left me with a warm and fuzzy feeling.

The other reason I'm not blogging is I have a lot on my mind and thoughts just aren't flowing as freely. I watched a cute movie yesterday about writing. Now I forget the name. It didn't get very high ratings...well wait, I'm going to have to look it up. Hold on. . ahh, *The Rewrite*. That's it.

Anyway, it was a cute story about how you can "learn" to write better. That wasn't the lesson of the story but it did have some good tips. I sort of thought it was kismet that I watched it as it was advertised as an ex-Hollywood screenwriter becoming a boozing insulting faculty member. I wasn't expecting a lesson in writing. Just a flashback of working in higher ed.

Do you ever find that when there's a lull or down time or you have a problem that you read an article or see a movie or something happens that addresses this problem? I haven't been thinking of writing these days, mostly thinking of getting foreign matter out of my lungs, but then I saw the movie and wondered if I need to get back on track. I might even watch it again.

I also missed all my hospice appointments this week. I didn't think they would appreciate me sharing my germs. You know, like the woman at the movie theater should have been thinking, so I'm feeling behind in my visits too.

And of course, the never-ending quest for an income. Now I'm thinking "go big, or go home". . meaning to stay away from the receptionist job and focus on getting a real job. Not that I'm really going home, maybe I should say "go big or stay home." It all just makes me want to keep my head under the covers, on top of being sick under the covers, well the blog just doesn't make the top of the list. Oh, and one more thing, I weighed myself yesterday. Those are my excuses? You buying it? You should. The whole weighing myself is really all I needed to say.

Inspiration is not flowing. But when I feel more myself maybe I'll get back on top of my game and come up with some entertaining blogs.

FRIDAY - JULY 24 - 11-12-13

Have you heard the expression about the elevens? Like quit thinking so hard "you're getting the elevens"? I never heard the expression until Janice. But I sure get it now.

I am finding my brow quite furrowed this week and my face frequently in that shape creating the elevens, then comes the hand that starts rubbing the forehead. The hand probably knows that it needs to keep the elevens from forming so it instinctively knows to go up there and straighten them out... or "your face will stay that way. "

I typically find my face this way when there is an issue in my life that I have no idea how to process and so I think about it, and think about it, and think about it and you know what? It doesn't help at all.

Today I was reminded that *"throughout your life journey, there will be many challenges. It is often through adversity that you can make the greatest progress. What may seem like very difficult situations to you can result in immeasurable wisdom and good fortune..."* (Thank you Judy for the Goddess card wisdom)

I was attempting to impart this wisdom to Jimmy today in regards to finances. I was telling him that it can be very rewarding to learn that you can live within your financial means and don't have to use credit cards. And it is! I remember that when I worked at PPU and it was the last week before payday I typically had $5 and wondered how I would get through the week, but then I did and well it's kinda cool. When Pete says "we have no money" I just laugh and say you have *noooo* idea. I'm the queen of *no* money. My point being, for Jimmy, and for myself, that difficulty doesn't always equal failure. Quite the opposite sometimes. In the zombie apocalypse when money is no good I'm going to shine! And as for Jimmy, anyone who knows him knows he will be fine. Probably a millionaire before he turns 30.

This time my elevens are *not* financially related. Not that I don't think about that issue ad nauseam as well, but it doesn't usually cause elevens. Elevens are usually caused by things waayyy beyond my control.

Anyway, I think what I need to do with my elevens is let it go. I have realized that there are certain things in life that I will never be able to figure out how to process or what to do with so I, today, this week, understand the true meaning of letting it go. Just forget about it and see what happens next. Time will tell and all those other clichés are making sense. Let it go, time will tell and leave it up to God. I look forward to *gaining immeasurable wisdom and good fortune* just like the saying says. I'll keep you posted.

In the meantime, we're going to go to the casino. We're even going alone! A true date night. That's what I'm talking about.

Have a good weekend, may God *and* lady luck shine upon all of you,

TUESDAY - JULY 28 - JUST SAY "NO"

Do you think it's possible that our body actually expands with gained wisdom? I've decided to make a personal correlation. I believe that I am now so wise a sage that my body had to actually expand to store all the knowledge.

OR it could be the fudge.

Today was my first day offering Reiki to a couple of patients. They were both very happy so maybe, just maybe, there is something to this. I was only there one hour. I don't know how people do three-hour shifts standing on their feet like that. But maybe I'll work up to it. I was with each patient about 20 minutes. I'm not sure if that's the appropriate amount of time? But that's what I did. Yay for me.

And now, I'm going to yoga. Yes yoga. I think it's been 6 months since last I went to a yoga class. Peter told me I just need to make it a priority (what a concept right?) so when Zoë asked if we could leave today at noon to take her to that place far far away, I said "no"...I know, I was a little nervous. But she just said OK and didn't even throw anything at me. We're going to go at 2:00. I don't believe I'm going to let her drive because of the rain.

This rain is unbelievable. There are areas flooding, and we have a very puddle-ly back yard but enough already. Our pool is less than an inch away from flooding over the side. I really do like the cooler temperatures but the amount of water coming out of the skies is something, really something.

Now I must publish this post and get going or else I'll have yet another reason why I've missed yoga.

WEDNESDAY - JULY 29 - A DAY WITHOUT SUNSHINE IS LIKE NIGHT

I went into the shower at 1:00 pm and the sun was shining, 10 minutes later I get out of the shower and it's night. Like the end of the world night. More rain and thunder. On the bright side (get it?) there was sun this morning until now. Actually, enough that the ponds in the back yard almost evaporated...the pool is even down a bit...and the lawn guy came. Yes, we have a lawn guy again (just for the front yard though.) This guy comes faithfully (except this week) on Monday's. He actually does most of the neighborhood so it's nice to see all the yards looking nice at the same time. There are some tire marks in the front yard from how soft the ground is. I'm sure they'll go away by tomorrow.

Anyway, as the official weather girl, I can tell you this rain is not normal. It's too much. Again though, I don't really want to complain because with the sun out it's like 20 degrees hotter and so freaking muggy. So, there you have it. I don't know what you have but you have "it."

I went to yoga again today. Woo Hoo. It feels good to wring out those muscles and all that *wisdom* (see yesterday's post). The instructor also commented how the rain can effect (or is it *affect?*) those weary bones so, anyway, glad to be going again. We'll see how long I can keep it up.

Today I play cards, well really games, with my one hospice person. Just thought I'd take a minute to check in before going. Not a whole lot to report. Perhaps tomorrow will be more exciting. Perhaps.

AUGUST 2015

MONDAY - AUGUST 3 - WHY?

For today's update, it just won't stop raining. The roads are flooding. It started coming down really hard last night around 2:00 a.m. and kept coming down until about an hour ago. We have gotten 5-7 inches of rain in that time and they are predicting to get 2 more inches by noon. It has slowed down enough for me to get the dog out to pee. He doesn't like to get his feet wet. I'm super worried about the pool but Pete assures me it'll be okay. Don't you sometimes hope they are wrong so you can be validated that you were right to be worried? Although I do hope he's right. He usually is. That's probably the worst thing about being in a relationship; not doing things for myself. When I was alone I just did what I needed to do when I needed to do it. In a relationship, without my own income, I have to rely on someone else for many things. I *hate* it. But I'm assuming this is a growing experience and I am attempting to embrace it. Admittedly I have let a lot of the responsibility go. I mean really I should have learned by now how to work the drain on the pool. I've been enjoying letting someone else share the responsibilities of life. There are pluses to this coupling thing that I *don't* hate. I'm glad I had the experience of installing my own toilet once in my life (long ago), but from now on I'm playing "blonde" when it comes to that stuff.

That's probably enough diversion for today. However, I'll leave you with this, contestants on the Price are Right are *crazy*! One girl practically passed out because she won a camera. Go figure.

PS – the pool man showed up! He's draining the pool. Love the pool man.

WEDNESDAY - AUGUST 5 - A QUICKIE

I'm too busy! What happened to those Lyming days huh? It didn't take me too long to develop my "own" life and apparently there's no room for lyming. There's enough hospice volunteer stuff to do that I can't possibly do them all. I don't have that many patients but they sure do have a lot of meetings. I have two meetings tomorrow that I "want" to go to. Then one on Friday that I "should" go to and then several next week. Now I have to make time for *me*. What a tangled web we weave, right?

I walked today, first time in weeks that it hasn't been raining or cloudy. That sun was blaring down on me. I'm not complaining. Just stating facts. There also was no breeze, absolutely still. But I got in a couple of miles then went over to Lori's for breakfast. Her place is beautiful. She did a little rehab, well a "big" rehab really and it's just lovely. Hard to believe it's the same place. She cooked a very healthy breakfast. Delicious.

I know, this is just a diary-day. No time for inspiration or any aha moments to share. Just running around kinda day. I need to leave to go play cards with my old lady. Then home to make dinner. I think we have a full house tonight. Maybe minus 1. I'm getting pretty good at this meal planning stuff. Not great at proportions yet. I either make too much or not enough and we're very bad at eating leftovers.

Tomorrow I need to go to the high school and get a locker for the girl (she's still away at Leslie's), then to a Reiki meeting, then free for lunch (boyfriend maybe?) then another meeting from 2-3, then I have to go back to the hairdresser for her to fix my hair. Not quite short enough. Pretty soon I'll just ask her to shave it. Wonder if I'd still have a boyfriend after that? My point being probably no update tomorrow.

I'm flying to Pittsburgh next week. I'm looking forward to some down time!

THURSDAY - AUGUST 6 - WHAT WAS THAT AGAIN?

One thing I want to do when we move into the "new" house (yes, living in my head again) is catalog all the books we have. There are bins of books in the shed that haven't been unpacked. I personally have given so many books away after all my moves and now I find myself ordering those same books again. I also have a feeling there are copies of the books that I'm looking for out in the shed in Pete's bins. I just ordered Zoë *Tuesdays with Morrie* from Amazon. I *know* that book is out there in a bin. You know, those same bins that I complained about when I moved here? Well, *when* we move into the new house one thing we're going to have to have is a lot of bookshelves, then I'm going to catalog by textbooks, self-help, medical stuff, novels, I can't wait to do it. Why do we have textbooks? Good question, but you never know when the Zombie apocalypse happens, or worse yet the grid shuts down and there's no more Google, well you never know what we might need to look up in those textbooks.

I've just reordered a book for this workshop I'm taking. The book is called *The Four Agreements*. I know I've read it. Well, I *think* I read it. In a few of these workshops I take (through Hospice) they've talked about this life changing book called *An Untethered Soul;* life changing they say. I decided to order that too. When I looked at the book I remembered I already read it. Life changing? I know I liked it a lot and I passed it onto Zachary. Wonder if he ever read it? But here's the thing, I have read sooo many books like that and when I read them I suck them all up. I mean I turn those pages and absorb all that info like I am a sponge sucking the life out of water. Afterwards? I can't even remember I read them. What does that mean? Well, bottom line is I am a voracious reader of self-help type books, and then can't remember a one of them. I wonder if there's a self-help book for that!

WEDNESDAY - AUGUST 12 - CAREFUL WHAT YOU WISH FOR

Why was it again I thought I needed a job? I think the last thing that I blogged, and had come to terms with was "go big or stay home" and then had very happily decided to embrace the new me, dive into hospice work and forget that I ever felt guilty about not working. If that excellent job came up then I would be happy to accept it thank you. That was just a short time ago that I finally got to that place.

Then the phone rang. On Sunday. It was Eileen. I've never met Eileen. She works for a staffing agency. One of the thousands that I've sent a resume to with no response.

Eileen: Are you working?

Me: Nooo (said with much trepidation as if this was a trick question)

Eileen: Do you know Word, Excel, PowerPoint, data entry?

Me: Yea. *Why?* (as if she's a bill collector, what's her angle?)

Eileen: Let me tell you what I have. A temp job with Hospice. Not horrible pay.

Me: No kidding. Ha! That's funny. Well, yes of course I know where they are located (unfortunately not the location 2 seconds from my house). Well sure, I'm interested, sure go ahead send my resume. Whatev...why not?

Me thoughts: hmmmm, well okay, we'll see. Interesting out of the blue timing, interesting with hospice, don't think too much about it just automatically say yes because that's what you're trained to say.

MONDAY:

Eileen: Well, they want to interview you. What's your schedule?

Me: I'm out of town next week (and as I went to say, the kids are starting school, blah blah she interrupts)

Eileen: How about tomorrow?

Me: Oh yea, well, okay sure. I have hospice in the morning but I can go anytime in the afternoon. Sure. (I've gone on other interviews before this is just another exercise in the" say yes" norm. . Feign interest.)

TUESDAY:

I went to an hour of Jasen's orientation. Pete had to bring me home early so I could get to my morning Reiki work at the Care Center by 10:00 am which was really interesting. I was there over 2 hours with many takers. It was fascinating. It *is* fascinating. Since I was running late there, and then had a low tire, again, what is with me and low car tires? I swear I do not hit curbs, or potholes. WTF? Anyway, ran home to Jasen "can you get us Chik Fil A?" No, I have to get to my interview...Still not thinking it's connected to actually *getting* a job, it's just an exercise. To Jasen, I'll text you on my way home and get you food. Dam kids. Meanwhile, I lost my (Pete's) debit card so I'm like fundless for this stuff. I mean *not* good timing. No gas, no Chik fil A money.

Anyway, off to the interview. Got to the beautiful location, very beautiful location. I've been to a meeting there before. The first thing I do is go into the men's bathroom. Seriously I did that. I thought it was one of those co-ed bathrooms but when I came out I checked the wall just to double-check and sure enough man picture. You know those pictures are hard to read. Thank the gods there wasn't a man coming into the room. Sheesshh...

Into the interview. It's a front desk admin position. A career to aspire to? After 30 years, a bachelors, half a masters, no. Whatever.... Do you know Word, Excel, good with databases? Yea, sure. A lot of phone calls (Phone calls? I don't do phones - Right Di? But I keep that to myself) Can I start next Monday? No, I'm away. How about the following Monday (the first day of school)? What are your hours? 8-5 is that okay? (8 to 5? Who works those hours? How about 9-1? 10-2?) Sure. That's fine, 8-5. See you in two weeks.

Out the door in 15 minutes. Fifteen minutes.

Text Jasen and Zoë, I'm on my way home. What do you want from Chik Fil A (kiss those days goodbye.... Pro and con...and where's that debit card...shit.)

Cue the tears

What the hell just happened? How did this happen?

Pete: Oh, that's GREAT news! I'm so happy for you. Why don't you apply for the job full-time?

Really Pete. *Really?*

Drop off the food, leave to get air in my tire, head to the beach. Sat on a park bench on the Causeway, on the water, called my mom (and sister) and cried.

What about my Reiki people? What about my card lady? My Eleanor? (names changed of course) What about yoga, morning walks? What about my Reiki classes? What about the workshop I'm going to? Who's going to pick those kids up after school? What about when Lacrosse practice starts? What about horseback riding? BLOGGING? LYMING?

Not to mention a career suicide job. It's *not* a career job. Which really I wouldn't care about if it was part-time. But 8-5 is more than half my life. *More* than. It's just humiliating.

What the hell have I done?

My sister insists it's not a death sentence and to quit crying. This coming from the person that's never worked a 9-5 let alone 8-5 job in her life. However, she works 17 part-time jobs to make up for it. I don't wish for that either.

I'll just suck it up. I will rearrange my hospice people and try to visit them after work a couple of nights a week. I don't know about the Reiki as that would have me not being home 3 nights a week. But that's the part of my life I love the most. As far as exercise I can walk and do yoga after work if I *never* want to be part of this family again. I can get up at 4:00 a.m. and try to walk, yea that's not happening. I saw a fitness center on the work campus yesterday. I used to do that at lunch once upon a time. Maybe I'll get them to start a lunchtime yoga class. One thing about hospice is they are very much into self-improvement. At least on the volunteer side of things. I'm going to have to call all my volunteer coordinators and resign from future appointments. Good thing that Doula thing never happened. Guess that wasn't meant to be.

Well, I'll tell you what I am grateful for. I am grateful that I had over a year to "find" myself. I have found out that I don't sit around and do nothing. Actually, before the dreaded full-time job I was sharing with my mom that at least now I know what I would do if I won the lottery. I would do exactly what I've been doing. Hospice, spiritual improvement (with hospice), exercise (loosely), homemaker, dinner cooker, taxi cab driver, pizza/food delivery and blogger. Unfortunately, I was not able to turn any of that into income producing...or get over 28 followers. So now it's back to the grind. Back to figuring out how to keep a life going with the two hours I have after getting home before going to bed. I'm happy to give up the taxi/pizza driver, but not happy to strand both kids after school. If only I didn't care. There are a lot of parents who don't. I should try to be more like them.

Not many people get a year off. I know I've been blessed. But Pete has carted my ass long enough, it's time to cut him a break. He needs to get his own girls a car and I need to carry my own ass...large as it is, and pay for my own car. I'm looking forward to paychecks for sure. I'm looking forward to paying off some bills that have been growing this past year (because I really haven't won the lottery and a lot of this life is on credit). I'm looking forward to new work friends. And because I'm dreading this job so much I will probably end up loving it.

I'm not looking forward to coming home to a mess every day. It's only noon and Jasen has his shit in the kitchen and he's already texted can I go get him a Cappuccino blast. And what's for dinner? These things I will *not* miss. Although I'm pretty sure that dinner question will either be texted throughout the day and again as soon as I walk in the door. Kids...

Well, I will just turn this frown upside down. I'm going to get in as much yoga and walking and lyming as I can before the dreaded first day. I have a visit north this weekend and I wasn't planning on going back anyway until Christmas and now maybe I'll be able to get tires for my car and a vacation weekend to anywhere, because I'll be able to afford it. But here's the thing. This is a temp job. I could be back home without a job in two weeks.

THURSDAY - AUGUST 13 - THE COUNTDOWN

I'm happy to report that I'm already feeling better about things, i.e., w. o. r. k. One of my better traits is that I'm able to turn stuff around rather quickly...usually. You know like I can "hate" something one minute...usually lasts a day...and then the next day I "love" it, or at least I'm over it. Some people are able to get past something quicker, some longer, I'm like a "day" person.

With my day, yesterday, after blogging and sitting with this new/old me thing (work) I started to come to terms with it and now almost...*almost*.... looking forward to it. Looking forward to it might take another day or 5 or never.

I don't know if I've mentioned this before but I really do have the best boyfriend ever. I mean don't get me wrong he *really* has the best girlfriend ever...which he says I never let him forget (because I never hear that from him). Listen to this, last night he comes home and said he had no idea that I didn't really want this job and to call first thing in the morning and tell them no thank you. How great is he? and of course I said NO! I WANT THE JOB! You know, just to keep him really guessing as to my true personality, because heaven forbid either one of us really figure "me" out. I think it's all going to work out with the school thing because we can actually car pool together when needed and "we" meaning "he" can get Monica all legal, help pay her fines, so she can drive again, and then *she* can pick up the kids after school and do the running around that's needed. I mean after all she does live here, she's 23 for heaven's sake, she can help, right? Helping does not seem to be one of her priorities.

As for the Reiki, I will just have to figure it out. And I will. I told my card playing hospice person about the job. She's very supportive and I'll just stop by and visit her after work. Here's an update on this situation though. You know how I act like I've got this hospice thing? Well, my card friend, Norma (not her real name), all the sudden she's not feeling so well and the illness that is causing her demise is setting in. And here's me with this huge lump in my throat thinking, "what do you mean? You're fine, you're not dying, don't die on me" and well really she *is* dying. And I don't think I'm prepared. I'm acting okay in front of her but behind her back I'm not doing so hot. I've gotten attached. Every week we play Rummikub and Sequence. I've bought those games now for our family and we play them here at home. In Sequence, Norma is always the blue chips, so at home I'm always the blue chips and I think of her. In this short time, she's made an impact on me and my family, bringing us closer together with these games. I think one of the lessons I'm seeing is that even in the last days, weeks, minutes of our lives we can have a lasting impact on someone. I've got to tell her that next week. Wonder if I can do it without crying. She's starting to sleep a lot but when I visit she is dressed and ready to play our games. I'm going to miss her. A lot. But this is the nature of it. I originally thought I'd just be sitting with people who were days/moments away from dying and not get attached. See what God does to me? Always throwing me for a loop. I love this work though. Truly I do. Just not sure who helps who here. I want Peter to get into it too. They have music therapy volunteers. He could play guitar for people. They would love that! I'll keep working on him.

I have 4 more minutes until I can check into my flight for tomorrow. I probably won't be blogging until my return from Pittsburgh next week, when I will have two more days of freedom...two more days of blogging, (really Pete I *do* want this job...I do...I just don't want to have to "go" to it)

THURSDAY - AUGUST 20 - AND I'M BACK

I had a lovely visit in Pittsburgh. I got to see many friends. Played with babies. Saw my boys. I had a lot of fun with the boys this time. Not that I don't always but for some reason this visit was a lot of boy bonding. We even played tennis together. Maybe we're on to something. I went to the farmers market, yoga, a luau party, lunch with Zach, dinner with friends, family fun day, played with babies, checked on the progress of Jimmy's (well his dad's) new house, went to the mall.

I came home to flowers *and* a small dent in the car. It's very minimal but major consequences for our little felon Zoë driving without a license driver, because Monica does not have a license. The police decided they were lying about who was driving the car so they handcuffed her. Seems a little excessive, doesn't it? I'm hoping they were trying to do one of those scared straight things. Unfortunately, she told me she won't be able to get her license now until she's 18. Another year and half. Guess who's *NOT* carting her ass around? It was her dad who suggested she drive Monica to work. He really has lapses in parental judgement. Monica was handcuffed too. Monica thinks it's funny that she wrecked my car and is relieved that I'm not leasing the car. Because I am not leasing she thinks now they don't have to fix it. I'm not laughing,

I guess I can never leave Florida again, because all hell breaks loose. Stuff happens, especially when there are teenagers involved. Always an adventure, right?

In other news, my card playing hospice patient died this morning. *This morning!* I mean we just played cards last week. She was out shopping yesterday. I'm sad. I thought we had at least a couple more weeks. Apparently, it's not about me. I visited with my other hospice person this morning. Told her I got a job and that I'd be stopping by after work now. She worked until she was 77. I hope I don't have to go that long, but she sure understands work.

I'm starting to look forward to work. I'm ready for something different.

FRIDAY, AUGUST 21 - THIS IS IT

This is what I'm doing with my last day off:

I went to an advanced yoga class. I really like my *gentle* yoga better. I found out there is a yoga class at the YMCA every night – so that hurdle has been addressed.

I got a letter on August 9 from Humana saying my health care coverage was cancelled. Do I really want to spend another hour out of my life on the phone or do I want to float in the pool? But after today I won't have hours to sit on the phone.

The kids are fighting over doing laundry today. I know this is typical and ordinary sibling teenage behavior, maybe not typical that Jasen is doing his own laundry, but I mean the fighting over stupid stupid stuff. Their father must have had a "come to Jesus" talk with them while I was away. There was a clean bathroom (upstairs), clean bedrooms, dishes are being done…Zoë even cooked dinner last night. I mean it's a little slice of heaven. And now today Jasen is obsessing over getting his laundry done. I checked the wash machine after he put in his clothes and said it was a little full and took out a sweatshirt he told me he doesn't want the sweatshirt anyway and to throw it out. I can't tell if he really wants to throw it out or if since it didn't fit in the wash machine that he thinks the solution is to throw it out as opposed to washing it in another load. I really do need to write some of this stuff down. One day, a while ago, Zoë and I were talking about her getting a car whether she'd ever get a new car, blah blah, and I said who knows what will happen in 6-8 months, we could win the lottery, I could move, let's just wait and see. To which she responded…"wait, if you move will you take your car? "HA! Kids.

Last night we had a "Sewickley" gathering in St. Petersburg. We love it in downtown St. Petersburg. Another old friend (from 8th grade) lives here now so another old homey to hang out with. Pete is very tolerant of our Sewickley talk. We were all cracking up last night at various past antics. Martha was in tears laughing so hard. It was fun. They want to bike ride. Where are the friends that want to just lay on the beach?

I wish I had some wonderful insight here on my last day off but I really don't. I need to figure out the health care, stock up on Advil for my tooth to last me two more weeks, Zoë wants to go apply for a job, I should do something nice for lunch for these kids. I mean I got no time to reflect. Maybe that's because I'm secretly hoping that this is temporary and I'll be back to my daytime routine sooner than later. Maybe because I'll start crying again when I think about having to get up and get out of the house every day by 7:15, which I've never done, maybe it's just so normal for me to work that it doesn't seem to be any different, maybe I'm relieved to get outta here and do something else (other than breakup fights over laundry and run errands). I just don't know. Not that I won't cry today (because we should all know by now that I am a cry baby) but I'm also ready to work.

In the meantime, before I run around with whatever it is I have to do today I think I'm going to float. That pool is calling my name. I'll reflect and get sunburned at the same time.

MONDAY, AUGUST 24 - DAY 1-BACK TO THE GRIND

Not bad. I got through my first work day relatively easy and although I was a little tired at the end of the day it wasn't as bad as I was anticipating. The commute is not bad. About 35 minutes. Parking is free and today I parked right outside the office door. The offices are all in individual buildings; it's a campus. To walk to anywhere you have to go outside under covered walkways, but still outside. One of the perks of living in Florida, you can have outside walkways.

Got home by 5:30 which is not bad. I don't know whether I should take a nap or power through and start dinner. I started the dinner last night, yay me, marinating chicken for shish kabob tonight. I've got this.

TUESDAY, AUGUST 25 - DAY TWO

Today I'm falling asleep. Literally nodding off. Martha, my new work bff, tells me it's from sugar. I had a mini cupcake after lunch and then HR held an event that had food leftover. I should have gotten a piece of chicken but instead opted for the delicious Tiramisu. It was good. But starting tomorrow, protein for snacks only. I'm packing chicken. Martha doesn't want to give me too much work to do. I think that's a mistake. I need to stay busy or thus the nodding off. Oh well, this blog update (that I'm typing at work) has to keep me going for one more hour.

Today we had Audubon day outside of the office's back door. There was a mother duck and her ten chicks and then comes this beast of a bird called a Wood Stork that wanted to eat the baby ducks. One of my office mates said the Wood Storks are aggressive and at some point in her life was chased by one. Creepy. Another office mate (a very brave one) in my office went and chased the Wood Stork away. Martha has been bringing food to feed the ducks so the mama duck must have been up here looking for food. Most everyone in this office is a native Floridian. They are more used to this wildlife than I am. And believe it or not they don't really care about my cold winter stories or the Steelers.

I attempted to do something on my own today, work wise, and Martha informed me it was the totally wrong way to do it. I'm despondent. Okay not despondent but I really thought I was going to do my first independent task. *Not*. She leaves early (she has flex time) so said she'd show me tomorrow. I'm also trying to do some online trainings for myself.

Dinner was delicious last night and then I ended the evening with making cookies, to celebrate the first day of school. It was a little bit too long of a night so tonight is Taco Tuesday OUT. The kids had a good first day of school and today they made it home without me as well. The world has not come to an end in my two days of working. Jasen was surprised however that I have to work *every* day. And then of course immediately pointed out that it wasn't fair being home for Zoë last year and not for him this year. It's more about being taken out for lunch after school than being home. The year is not over. I bet there is a lunch or two in his freshman year future.

WEDNESDAY, AUGUST 26 - AND ANOTHER THING

Day 3 and I can't believe I'm saying this.... . I *like* my job. I know I know...

But it's only Day 3. I helped two whole people on my own today. I was busy until about 3:30 which is better than yesterday when things came to a halt around noon.

The highlight of my day today was that I got to feed the ducks. Martha brought in duck food again. The ducks wait for her when she gets here in the a.m. and then they come back after lunch. I went out and fed the momma and the babies. The momma was a little snarky with me so I just kept throwing food at her. Those baby ducks sure are cute though. People have been counting the chicks every day to see if she's lost any. Kinda morbid but the good news is she still has 10 babies.

My commute has been really good these past few days. Last night I was home in 23 minutes. Pete and I sort of raced to work today. No one was speeding (or was he?) because he has to go further than me and we got to work at the same time. Logistically he should get to work about 10-15 minutes after me. Hmmm, so either he was speeding OR his way is a lot shorter.

I'm going to stop and see my old lady tonight on the way home. And maybe next week I'll see if I can add-on a Reiki night after my old lady visit. The only time I get a little teary about working (remember I'm the cry baby) is when I see something related to Reiki training and can't go because I have to work.

There are a lot of things going well. I'll still wait and see how much vacation time they get as a full-time employee before throwing my hat into the ring. That will be the clincher. I need time for my mother visits and my Pittsburgh visits and what about the spring when people come to visit? Plus, I don't know how long I have to work as a temp anyway. So far so good.

THURSDAY, AUGUST 27 - THE CONE OF UNCERTAINTY

I had no idea the *Cone of Uncertainty* is a thing. Hurricane Erica is in the "Cone of Uncertainty". I think I'm going to use that again and again. i.e., "Do you like your job?" answer: "Jury's out, it's still in the cone of uncertainty." Question: "Are you going to have that hot fudge sundae for dessert?" Answer: "It's still in the cone of uncertainty." Perhaps the response will become CoU for short.

Also seen on the weather channel...*Can you get high by second-hand marijuana smoke*? This question is pertinent because there are wild fires in California burning fields of marijuana plants. This burning question (get it?) is not in the Cone of Uncertainty...the answer, according to the weather channel, is no. I beg to differ. I'd probably go sit close and do some research. Especially today.

Why today? I have a pounding headache. My neck is killing me and my head is killing me. I ended up drinking a Pepsi. I was hoping the caffeine might help the headache. I believe the caffeine *did* help the headache, but the neck pain is not going away. Is this caused by sitting at a desk for 4 days, 8 hours a day, slumped over a computer, after not doing this for over a year? I believe the answer is in the Cone of Uncertainty. stay tuned.

FRIDAY, AUGUST 28 - WEEK 1 AND DONE

I made it through week one! I must say that each day got better and better and now I'm actually thinking of applying full time. I need to figure out the Paid Time Off (PTO) thing. It's unclear how it works. Someone here told me that the offices are NEVER closed and although there is Paid Time Off if you are off on a holiday it counts as PTO. It might sound like a lot of days but if you have to use it to take Christmas and Thanksgiving off then it's really not a lot of time and I need my boys/mom time. If it's too restrictive then I'll probably keep trying to figure out a part time option. As some of you predicted I *am* liking this working thing. Oh, and get this, *most* days this week I was up and made breakfast for myself. I also packed lunch (except for today). Could it be the new me?

I was in charge of the ducks today. She still has all 10 babies. They are bigger every day. Can't wait to see the difference after the weekend. The mom comes right up to the door with those babies and is kinda bossy about getting her food. She will peck on the glass to get our attention. She's a good mom.

The storm and the Cone of Uncertainty is getting higher up on the danger list. Still in the wait-and-see stage and most people are pretty nonchalant about it but it is a concern. I believe the expectation is that it will pass us, probably inland to the east, on Monday...ish...possibly causing a day off. *Possibly.* One of those "if you don't feel safe stay home" things. It's rumbling thunder now too. Afternoon storms are expected around here this time of year. Zoë is afraid once it starts raining it won't stop.

Last night was open house at the high school. Both Pete and I came from schools that were in one building. The most I ever had to do in high school was go from the ground floor to the third floor. This high school here is like a small college campus. Nobody at this school should be overweight. I was exhausted and limping by the end of the night. I followed Zoë's schedule and Pete followed Jasen's. What a school though. It's huge. And I did see a couple of people I knew! Look at that, friends! Dolly was there who I volunteered with last year and I recognized someone else who I worked with at the middle school last year. My how things have changed in a year. Two kids in the high school. Another kid living with us (except she's no kid.) A new building at the high school added since last year. Friends and a job. What's next? A house on the beach maybe?

In sad news my other old hospice lady died this morning. I wasn't expecting that. I am sadder than expected. I arranged for weekly visits now to the Care Center where I can offer Reiki. Those people typically have days to live so no attachment... probably... no talking either. But I did say I would take on another talkative patient to visit.

And now it's time to go home for the weekend, as I've been typing this while still at work. My first weekend as a working girl in Florida. It wasn't bad, wasn't bad at all. Getting paid will be pretty nice too. I think that's next weekend. But for now, I am looking forward to sleeping in tomorrow!

MONDAY, AUGUST 31 - GO FIGURE

Does anyone else have this problem? By the end of the day, sometimes mid-day, I'm taking off my ring, my watch, any bracelets. What is up with that? I tend to get itchy too. I've seen LOTS of little bugs on my desk. Turns out that a colleague has also been seeing these bugs, called maintenance and there is some sort of infestation directly above our desks. See? I don't make it up.

No ducks today. Martha says not to panic and that sometimes they go away for a while. She said we might not see them again until the ducks are full-grown. But just in case I have the duck food.

The weekend was uneventful from what I can remember. Dinner out, just the two of us Friday and then we went to listen to a couple of performers at Open Mic night at Witches Brew under the full moon.

On Saturday, I had to do all my errands, you know the ones I used to do all week-long. Like the post office, food shopping, Dollar Store items. Then ended up going shopping with Zoë. Saturday night I enjoyed another night out with the BF. We had plans to meet friends in Tarpon Springs but the day got away from us and we ended up at Macy's and then a really late dinner. It's bad, shopping, shopping, shopping. It's stuff I need. Think weight gain from the last time I worked. I'm not going to stuff myself in old clothes that don't fit. I got in some float time in the pool Sunday morning for an hour before shopping. I wanted to get a little sun incase the big hurricane hit.

Speaking of hurricanes, we got nuthin. That's not a bad thing. I think inland is getting some heavy rains but here on the coast we're staying relatively dry. We had a little rain but not much at all and it didn't last long. The kids were disappointed that they had to go to school. Now they're saying the storm "might" be trying to reform out in the Gulf. . although that's a stretch. Crazy stuff.

I took Monica car shopping yesterday. For some reason her dad won't take her. She needed to see what she can get for $4000. Not a whole lot. After car shopping we went clothes shopping. That's when I got the cute dress I have on.

That's it...

SEPTEMBER 2015

FRIDAY, SEPTEMBER 4 - AND THEN THERE'S THIS

I like working more than I thought I would. A lot more; although it could just be the novelty of it. I also like my time. Free time, that's something I became familiar with during my unemployment hiatus. When the BF wants a weekend somewhere, well it's my *duty* to go right? I mean who am I to say NO, let's not go to New Orleans? Or tell my blind mother that I can't come see her in this, these final years. Or tell Mya (baby niece) I can't come visit? What if I miss my boys and need a boy fix? I mean there is no clerical job worth that heartache.

But I don't mind being here when I'm here. It's just when I don't want to be here, I don't want to come in. What's wrong with that? Where is the disconnect?

This is supposed to be a vacation weekend. Pete got to leave early today and is home already. I not only *don't* get to leave early; I don't get the vacation day on Monday. This is just wrong on so many levels. I must re-evaluate.

Have a nice weekend.

WEDNESDAY, SEPTEMBER 9 - IT'S HAPPENING

I'm getting busier at work. Every day I'm learning something new and then as these tasks come in I handle the old and learn something new. It's all good except I can't sneak a blog in at the end of the day. I know, it sucks. But still liking the job so that's good.

I got a paycheck – even better; although not much to it. I'll start getting caught up though. Maybe by 2075 I'll get that student load paid off.

I didn't have a holiday weekend since I worked Monday and I was on pain pills all weekend (because of teeth problems) so therefore slept. But I did get out of work early on Monday and my boyfriend surprised me with a few moments at the beach in the rain and then we went to this touristy area called John's Pass. It is a really cute area. Other than being drugged up (combatting my tooth pain) it was a very nice after-noon/evening. This has been a bad week for the kids though. I haven't cooked one night since last week. My nanny duties are very lax.

Pete and I are going to try going to a Steeler's bar in Clearwater tomorrow night. At least try to make it until half time. The bar is on Clearwater Beach so that'll be a plus. If they start stinking we'll just go take a walk on the beach. Although, Jimmy told me today that he expects my full support this season. I promised I'd be there in spirit for the Steelers all season. But I think I might watch Tampa Bay Buccaneers some too. (don't tell Jimmy)

And that's all for this week.

TUESDAY, SEPTEMBER 15 - WHAT IS THAT?

It was 73 degrees here the other morning. The news said "you might want the kids to take a sweater to school" Pete and I laughed...but you know what? It was chilly!

I saw a dead armadillo on the road yesterday. I've never seen that before. They're big. Like the size of a groundhog. Pretty freaky. I saw the dead armadillo while I was walking on the causeway. The good news there is I finally felt good enough to walk and I wore my new fancy shoes. I was prepared to pay $100+ at a fancy walking store but couldn't find any I like. I like these, very comfy. And they were not $100 or even close. Also, I slept like a baby last night. Best I've slept in a looonggg time. I think it was the walk after work.

It's Homecoming this weekend. Pete is out shopping with Zoë look-ing for a dress and getting her hair cut. Good Papa.

I'm tired.

TUESDAY, SEPTEMBER 22 - HELLO THERE

It's the end of another workday, and I find myself with some time on my hands. This new job is very task oriented...like I mean non-stop stuff to log in, count, file, sort. Fun stuff. I still don't mind it. I also got some Hospice aide real mad at me because I gave her the wrong information about a CPR class. I wanted to cry. I hate being new and not knowing what I'm doing. Martha figured it out for me (her). Someday I'll learn it, if I stay here, which I probably will. Maybe.

The reason I have time is because I've run out of steam for the day. My brain hurts. Seriously I have a headache so I'm not starting any-thing...but this blog. In other news the temp agency "forgot" to mail last week's check to me. Forgot...isn't that something?

Pete and I are going on a date night tonight, meeting his daughter Nina for dinner. I guess that sort of counts as date night. I can't remember the last time we had one, can you? We were supposed to be picking Zoë up after a performance at the Straz (a performance hall place) that she was going to with her drama class, but nooooo all these accommo-dations we made so we could pick her up after and then find out the whole thing got cancelled. I feel bad for the kids that are missing out on the performance. But I got a date night out of it anyway. Yay for me!

I'm heading to Orlando this weekend to see my Marissa in another play. I'm looking forward to seeing her and spending a day in Orlando. Every time I see those Mickey ears on the highway I get excited like a little kid. I really need to save money so I can go to Disney at some point. I mean I live right here; I just need to go...now that I'm working. Is the boyfriend going with me this weekend you ask? Don't you need some boyfriend away time you ask? Don't ask.

I have some weekend trips planned so maybe that can be the blog focus for a while. Orlando, *maybe* Miami, going to Virginia at the end of October, but nothing planned with the boyfriend, and that's not *my* choice.

It was homecoming weekend in Palm Harbor. Zoë's dress was too short, so I've been told by anyone that saw her picture. A friend of

Monica's came to the house to do her hair and makeup. Good thing they don't look to me for that.

This was kinda funny... Zoë's friend (she went with a couple of girls) that picked her up for Homecoming was assuring me that they would be home early and home right after the dance blah blah, and here's me "you're not going out after?" Like in a *what is wrong with you* tone? Who comes home right after? They did end up going to Steak and Shake after but were home by 11:00. A good time was had by all. I think she's fallen into a "good" crowd. . . knock on wood.

TUESDAY, SEPTEMBER 29 - I'M MELTING, WHAT A WORLD, WHAT A WORLD

This working full-time thing is for the birds. I have come to the end of the time that thinks this is fun. The novelty has worn off. My house needs attention, cleaned, vacuumed, the dog needs to go to the groomers, the house needs bug bombed, I miss making dinners, I miss sleeping, I miss yoga, I miss lyming, I miss blogging. Is it really such a bad thing to be dependent on someone else? Really? Aren't there other ways to make a living that don't involve being in an office every stinkin day? Day in, day out, and on top of that you have to remember shit? Like how to do stuff? And people ask you questions and I just stare at them because really, I have no freakin idea what they just said. I mean really, doesn't money grow on trees? Where are those trees?

I'm going to go now to offer Reiki to the dying folk. The peaceful me must get centered.

OCTOBER 2015

TUESDAY, OCTOBER 13 - SCARY STUFF

It's been 14 whole days since I last blogged. As I write this what is foremost on my mind is my bed, right behind me, calling my name. I'll be brief.

I was offered the job full-time; I countered the salary, they came in even lower than I thought the original offer was (I misunderstood the original), I turned it down. They said I don't have enough experience. *What?* Apparently, I have a higher opinion of myself than anyone has had since Thomson Newspaper days. My current boss is trying to renegotiate on my behalf but we all know how that goes. I said I'll stay as long as they want me to as a temp. My boss said she'll keep me indefinitely, but again, who knows. I'm still going in every day. I don't mind going, but I'm ready for vacation. There will be something else. I'm not settling. I'm just not.

Last night after work I drove to the beach, just to see how long the commute would be to and from the Hospice job if I lived at the beach, just because. It's more stop and go traffic but I made it there in ½ hour. I know, right? How many people can say that? Had I planned better I would have stayed for sunset. It was a beautiful night, instead I just drove up the coast to home.

We decorated for Halloween over the weekend. Pete brought home this scary clown. I said it was too scary it's got to go. He put it in Monica's room for her to see when she comes home at 3 a.m. When she screams in the middle of the night I'm decking him. Closed fist.

I was at the Care Center tonight doing Reiki and met one of the patient's daughter who is a nurse in Connecticut and also a Reiki practitioner. She said they "hire" Reiki practitioners at her hospital. Like for money. How about that idea? Maybe in 4-5 years it'll be me.

That's it I guess. Looking forward to going to Virginia next week. Wonder how cold it will be.

THURSDAY, OCTOBER 22 - JUST A LITTLE BIT

I work, I race home, and I race through things so I can go to bed and get up and do it all over. Tuesday and Thursday evenings I am still volunteering with hospice, which makes the week even longer. I'm not really complaining, although it probably sounds like it, I'm just stating facts about why I rarely get to this computer. My job is a really busy job too. I have lots and lots of tasks. No time to blog there. One thing I've started is I listen to WYEP (Pittsburgh station) at work, streaming on my computer. First of all, there is no other radio station like it but it's also fun to hear the Pittsburgh news and especially the Pittsburgh weather. Makes me feel very at home, working and listening to Pittsburgh news. But then I go for walks and/or leave work and it's 85° and sunny and then I remember, ahhh yes, I live in Florida, finally.

I have officially turned the job down, have I already shared that? But they are keeping me until the bitter end, which I'm not sure when that will be. I'm feeling maybe mid-December. At least that's what I think will happen. Then I'll throw myself back in the volunteer mode and see what happens next. Something always happens. I like everyone and I don't hate my job so you just never know what could still happen.

Pete and I have been trying to walk a couple of nights a week. The air is soo nice, cooler, and the sunsets are beautiful. They expanded a beach near us (where we walk) so things are really looking up.

Tomorrow I'm going to my mom's. My sister and brother will also be there for the weekend. It's going to be both fun and busy.

Still lovin life. Still lovin Florida.

NOVEMBER 2015

THURSDAY, NOVEMBER 5 - REMEMBER ME?

I can't explain my absence. I take that back. I "can" explain it but when I do then I get accused of whining and maybe it is whining but there's no other way to explain my absence. Working at a desk job just doesn't get the creative juices flowing. However, at my job, I am being quite creative redesigning forms, coming up with new processes, always trying to think of a way to do something better. That's a kind of creativity, isn't it? I do enjoy that and I'm trying hard every day to get to a point where I will feel comfortable leaving, yes leaving (i.e., quitting), which I think I've already shared. My goal now is to get the new processes up and running smoothly, write down the new processes and then get the heck out of there. They are very supportive and agreeable to my help/changes but really dragging their feet in looking at resumes. I get it though. It's the end of the year. I'm busier than hell. I also am paid hourly and I'm not allowed to go over 40 hours. I like this because I *have* to leave at the end of the day. There's a lot to be said for a non-exempt position.

Life in Florida continues to be lovely; although unseasonably hot and the pool is too cold to go in, as is the Gulf. Pete and I went to the beach last Saturday, a new beach (to us) called Caladesi Island. We had to take a Ferry to it. For some reason I thought it would be hokey but I was wrong. It happens, I am wrong on occasion. It is a beautiful beach. A great place to go to feel like we're on vacation on an Island, because well it *is* an Island. We also got some sun which felt good after being locked up in offices for quite some time.

The time change is not good for our evening walks and I'm sad to be giving those up. We had been walking a couple of days a week during sunset and the sunsets were/are beautiful always, but this time of year they seem to be a little more beautiful. There are no street lights on our walk and it's just a little too dark to keep that going. I had high hopes of getting up at 6:30 a.m. to walk because that would be really 7:30 a.m. A little later than my usual time so no problem right? Yea, wrong. I can't drag my ass out of bed ever. I don't know what it is. I have always wanted to be a morning person, it's just not in my DNA I guess.

I got all my hair cut off tonight after work. Not literally all, but quite a bit. As I've mentioned I'm a fan of short hair. I don't know how it makes me look but I like how it feels. I asked for a couple very subtle highlights and well, you can't even see them. I'm hoping they come out more in the sun. I didn't want them to be invisible, just not loud. This weekend, Saturday, I'm headed to Siesta Key to see Jean (and Diane and Maria) and Steph. I'm looking forward to it. More beach time and maybe it'll help the new highlights. Did I mention how hot it is? 91° today and right now at 11:18 pm it's 77°. Some fall huh?

Have I revealed that I eat Sushi now? I remember going to a restaurant with Jasen in Baden and he kept trying to tell me that Sushi was good and teaching me how to hold chopsticks. I didn't want any part of it. Well, I eat sushi now and I love it. I also use chopsticks. I'm not very good at the chopsticks but I'm getting better. Jasen is very patient with me. He really is good with me, that is until I ask him to clean his room, then I'm totally ignored.

We got through Halloween with just two doorbell rings. We were so decorated. We got all the decorations down and put away the day after. We actually bought a couple of Christmas items already. No, they're not up but we did buy them.

Thank you to Emily and Diane for saying they miss the blog. It does inspire me to stay up late and write. Soon, I'll be back on here, soon!

MONDAY, NOVEMBER 9 - YOU MAY CALL ME MADAME VICE PRESIDENT

Jasen is failing. We need help. Our school is failing us and I don't know what else to do other than to start yelling. And now I've locked myself (okay not literally locked) in the bedroom until I quit yelling about bad grades. But really the school needs to help us. They need to be a vital member of the education team. I hate parenting.

In other, better news.... I had a fun time in Siesta Key with the girls. I never realized how much I miss my girlfriends until I'm with them. I just love them. I went to Siesta Key on Saturday morning (an hour and half ride), spent all day on the beach with the girls, went out to dinner and home(vacation home) on the couch to watch SNL with Stephie, the other girls were still out having fun. I fell asleep during the monologue. Not quite the good time I used to be but I still had fun.

And then I became vice president of Equal X consulting. Vice President! Pete started a business today for "us". We were discussing my clients and I said it's going to be pretty hard to get clients when I'm poolside, but nevertheless if I get one I'll return the call. By the way, we have 1000 shares to sell. We'll be happy to sell you one or 100. Get them cheap now before we become really big and have the name of our company on the side of the US Steel building. Don't laugh, it could happen.

Pete's picking out a website right now. I could help him. But maybe I'll hire someone to do that. I like delegating.

THURSDAY, NOVEMBER 12 - WHO SAYS MONEY DOESN'T GROW ON TREES

Alas, I'm home. Only for the day, but still. It's like a big heavy sigh of relief, a little slice of heaven. I slept in until 9. It's only 10 now and I've already managed to make beds, start laundry, look around upstairs (BIG scary mistake), called Jean and sang happy birthday, followed up with one of Jasen's teachers, got my info for tonight's hospice visit, am on the phone with Nationwide Insurance trying to figure out why some consumer agency shows I had an "at fault" accident in 2011. I hate consumer reporting agencies. But my point is how productive is that, for one hour? And look at me blogging, while on hold with the insurance company. Like the multi-task queen I am. I can't access my home emails from work, other than through my phone, and I feel like I get so behind without responding and following up on them. Don't they know my life is connected to my emails? I guess they don't care.

Today is supposed to be an Equal X Day as well. I wanted to start thinking of some ways to get organized. I decided shoe boxes are a good idea for receipts. You know, then we can decorate the boxes with glitter and stuff. But that means I need to go buy a pair of shoes. My question is: are shoes a legitimate business expense? I think "yes" and one pair per month since I will need separate shoe boxes for each month. This month I think I need red shoes. I'm feeling red. Next month will probably have to be sparkly shoes so I'm set for the season.

Turns out our new company name might be already taken so we have to wait now.... and see...and try another name. I can't really get started on the website as hoped. That's too bad because I was going to draw a salary from the company for today. Although that would put us in the red, but isn't that a good tax thing to *lose* money? Should I just take the money from the tree? I can see I have a lot to read up on. Hmm, reading, that sounds like a tie with lyming, which goes with pool. Yep, still a business function I say pay me! I am already exercising my executive authority.

I'm picking Jasen up after school today. He asked if we could go to lunch like I did all last year with Zoë. Except Zoë brought up Red Lobster. I'm like *no*, we're talking drive through here. We settled on Chik fil A – which also happens to be where Zoë likes to go ad nauseam, but she is not going today. She's too cool now and hangs with her friends after school, conditioning for Lacrosse.

I was/am also hoping to get a walk in with Lori today, although I haven't told her that because I'm not sure I have time before the boy pickup. Well, in any case, I'm so stupid happy to be home today back to my other old self. I think I like "this" old-self better than the worker-girl old-self, so better get the company going. No pressure Peter. It's just my happiness in the balance.

WEDNESDAY, NOVEMBER 25 - I'M LIKE A PILGRIM

I find myself with a few moments, watching the clock until 3:00 when I get to go home and the Thanksgiving cooking madness begins. I'm cooking this year for 6. We'll have enough food for 26 but that's the Italian coming out in me. Yes, I know I'm not Italian, but I did give birth to one and so I think the *Mangia! Mangia!* gene found its way to me. Tonight, I'll make the pies, but on the other hand they are so good when they are right out of the oven. I don't know. I have to keep thinking. There's an awful lot of prep work involved with Thanksgiving and I really want to do as much as I can tonight so I can sit with my face in the sun for at least a little tomorrow. After all I am coming up north for a quick weekend and it just wouldn't do to look as pale as everyone else.

I'm having a little difficulty in packing as usual. How cold will I be I wonder? Someone said, shouldn't be too bad, highs in the 50's. You know here we're under blankets in the 60's. Especially if it rains. I'll probably have to buy an extra heater to sit in front of.

Last weekend we (me, Pete, Zo and Jasen) went to a new Sushi restaurant recommended by someone who I work with then drove into Dunedin to walk around. I saw two people I know, one at a distance and one (my boss) got to meet the whole fam. Another time, we went out to lunch and saw someone from my office. We went to the Farmers Market in St. Petersburg and another coworker was there. Don't you think that's weird? Pete works with people and we never see any of them out. Wait, I take that back, one day at lunch we saw someone. But anyway, I only work with 7 people and Pete has already met more than ½ of them. Makes me feel like I know people now. Remember that post where I said I quit looking for people I know because I don't know anyone. Well look at me now. I know people everywhere! Actually, this company employs over 1000 people but my "team" is only 7. Imagine if I get to know all thousand of them! I'll be like the mayor.

I came to the realization yesterday that this job has not improved my quality of life at all. Sort of the opposite. I'm not yoga-ing, I'm not walking (too dark now), I'm rarely cooking for the fam, one of the kids is not doing well scholastically (not that my presence would help, but it *might*), I am still volunteering one night a week with the Reiki, but miss all the meetings that are in the daytime. The other day they called and asked if I could sit with a patient after work who was transitioning (dying), but no, I was at work until 6:30 and I think grocery shopping was next. I might have been actually crying that day from the stress. You may say to yourself "what about the money?" well, it's not improving my life at all. I still scrape by. I can't even afford to come up for Christmas. Really why am I doing this? It should be improving Pete's life but I don't think the money I make (that he is saving) is enough to make a difference. At least not that I know of.

Awareness of my situation is the first step right? Like a Pilgrim wondering the earth trying to figure out life (I know it's a stretch but I'm trying to make it fit the season).

Yesterday my boss said they would like to make me another offer in January. They asked if I would stay on as a temp until then and they are hopeful that they could make me a higher offer after January. I doubt it will be high enough but she mentioned that they would consider a job share if I wanted to try working that out. Sooo, we will see.

I get to see my boys this weekend. YAY! My big boy is turning 33 on Sunday – can you imagine? Wasn't he just born? Wasn't that like yesterday? I'll also get to hug babies, maybe hang out with a friend or two. And in 45 minutes I get to go home for the day! So much to look forward to. Life is good, it does not suck.

I wish a Happy Thanksgiving and moderate eating day to all tomorrow. Just think after this weekend we can start playing Christmas Carols and decorating. Woo hoo!

DECEMBER 2015

SUNDAY, DECEMBER 16 - IT'S A BLOG

Hard to believe next week is Christmas. I'm not coming up again this year. Kinda hard to talk/write about without crying (yes still a crybaby) but I will survive. Airfare just got outta hand. It's cheap to get up there but apparently going from Pittsburgh to Tampa is a pricey option on Christmas day or thereabouts. Guess it's a popular thing to do. There should be two prices. One for residents and one for tourists. If you want to go home you can pay the cheap fare. If you're going on vacation then pay the tourist rate. Don't you think that's a good idea?

Peter and I went to New Orleans last weekend. I *loved* it. We stayed at The Bourbon Orleans, in the middle of the French Quarter. It's actually a "haunted" spot. But we didn't see any ghosts, dammit. We were one block from crazy Bourbon Street so we could walk up/down that, and we did walk on it one night and then I politely asked if we could take a quieter street back to the Hotel. I mean it's CRAZY and lots of crazy shit everywhere there but also lots of other stuff. Lots of art, lots of music everywhere, lots of history. We went on a Plantation Tour to Oak Alley Plantation, went to eat at several different places (I've had my fill of shrimp), saw a wedding procession on Bourbon Street, had a famous beignet (eh) met a couple of Pete's friends, lovely people, saw the Mississippi River which reminded me a lot of the Ohio River and Pittsburgh and Pete gave me some beads without me having to flash my boobs, well not in public anyway (TMI?). I learned a lot about the bead thing and the different sizes of beads. It's a crazy city. The city reminded me of Pittsburgh. Not the occupants, but the views. And we were somewhat lucky at the Casino. I think we doubled our money. The weather was beautiful and even "smelled" like vacation. It's warm here in Florida but it never "smells" like vacation. Not sure what that's about. All in all, just a great time. It was really hard to acclimate back to work.

The New Orleans weekend started off as a great "getting re-acquainted" weekend between Pete and I. We haven't been having such a good go of it as of late. Mostly since last summer. The additional child living here has changed the dynamic and puts a lot of stress on both of us. She does absolutely nothing around the house. Nothing. It's stressful for Pete who does everything humanely possible to deal with her. I mean he's tried everything and she just doesn't care. Well anyway, our weekend away was so nice, but the last day was a bit stressful again. I guess the stress of knowing the weekend escape was over brought him back to reality and he started getting crabby again. There's really nothing I can do about it. I am just trying to maintain my sanity between working and now dealing with more stress from the Clark family expansion and then that makes me retreat to the bedroom more and then I miss my kids more. Things are stressful. I can tell something is up. I assume it's just Monica but I don't know. Seems like there's something I can't put my finger on.

TUESDAY, DECEMBER 22 - WHERE'S REVA NOW

Here I am. Home. Not alone, but nevertheless home. And I might as well be alone. I've heard a couple of doors closing so I know there are people here but they are holed up in their bedrooms. I too am holed up, but I have the door open in the event someone wants to reach out and ask for a grilled cheese. I'm supposed to be at work but I took a day. Actually, I'm supposed to be on my way to Pittsburgh and off for the rest of the week, but alas that didn't happen so I said I'd work. I can't remember the last time I worked through the Christmas/New Year's week, let alone Christmas Eve (which I'm working this year). In one way I don't mind for some odd reason, but on the other hand I think my body just said "enough already" and here I am, in my jammies (or version thereof) at 3:00 in the afternoon. I've still been productive. I've wrapped presents, I'm doing laundry, I'm cleaning exploding corners (a term Sally coined) and I think I'm making dinner too.

Today I watched soap operas. I haven't watched soaps since they took the *Guiding Light* off. But when I hear the *Young and the Restless* theme song it takes me sooo far back. I vaguely know the characters on the *Young and the Restless* and a few of them are from my GL. (*Guiding Light*) At my funeral I want the *Guiding Light* theme song to be playing. When I do my "rounds" at the Care Center for hospice (ha! rounds!) anyway, they always have music on in the rooms. You know those music channels on TV? Sometimes I think it's annoying and wonder if these patients would really prefer silence. I mean, really, doesn't the noise get to you sometimes? Except for those of you that sleep with the TV on all night (you know who you are) – I can't stand the noise after a while. Only one time did I turn the TV off in one of the patient rooms. I felt like it was the right thing to do. Once there was a note that the patient liked classic rock and they had on punk rock. I changed it immediately. Who can die peacefully with punk rock playing? Anyway, I think if I end up in that situation (which I hope not) I want them to be playing songs from old TV shows. Especially the *Guiding Light*, which had like 27 different versions throughout the years. Maybe throw in a *Dallas* theme song and *Dynasty*.

As far as family activities around the house, we're getting there. Seems a little more haphazard this year. Probably has to do with that work thing again and the lost weekend in New Orleans. But Christmas will come and go regardless of who is working, who is in Florida and whether I have the perfect table setting or not. I'm pretty much done (i.e., out of money) – I've sent all the boys stuff this year through Amazon, less wrapping that way. Maybe I should have paid for the gift wrapping for them. I don't know. I am always surprised to learn things about myself. Like this year I've learned I'm a little OCD. I have always had a coordinated Christmas wrapped event. I bought double-sided wrapping paper and one boy had one side and the other the other side. The Christmas stockings were opposite green/red styles – I mean it was coordinated. Last year with this family I did something similar – each kid had their own wrapping paper – but all four piles matched in some way. Anyway, anyway, Pete wants to mix it up and have it all haphazard and says that's the fun of it that it's chaotic. I'm letting him do it his way. After all, it is "his" family and well they are probably okay with it. I might be in therapy for a while after but it's a growing experience for me right? It makes me a little cray-cray. I need to learn to let it go...Who knew I was so OCD.

Have you seen our temps for Christmas? 85° expected on Christmas day. The weather people say that's 20 degrees over what we should be. A record high. It's not bad for me but it is different. Not like you can go in the water at the beach. The water temp is in the 60's. That's cold by anyone's standards. Next house we'll have a heated pool and then will be able to float on these unusually hot winter days.

I just wanted to check in. It's not a real day off without a blog and I'm missing my friends and family and New Orleans.

Hope you're all doing well and ready for Santa. It's like in 2 days. Sheesshhh. Pete, we still gotta get that ham!

SATURDAY, DECEMBER 26 - IT IS ALL ABOUT THE STUFF

I like stuff. I'm no longer embarrassed to admit it. I've come to accept it about myself. I know, I know, when I sold my house and downsized to the 2-bedroom apartment I got rid of stuff, then when I went into the even smaller apartment I got rid of more stuff and was down to the bare minimum. Well, bare minimum for me. But I have to admit it was *too* bare minimum, I was never quite comfortable going down that far. And yes I know when I moved here with the Clarks I complained about all of his stuff. And I mean "stuff" – it was overwhelming, I cried. I thought I was over with the "stuff". However, he loves stuff and I find myself going back to my roots of liking and buying more stuff (but now I buy consciously.) And here's more reasons why I like the stuff:

Every year at Christmas I pull out my most treasured stuff and I have memories of each and every item. Pete is right now gluing back together an item Linda gave me one year. Linda also gave me a Santa blanket which I use every year and tea cups (I haven't pulled the tea cups out yet...I have to wait for when I have girly teas again). I have so many "things" that I have saved from those teas. Remember the cookie tree? That was a gift from Jean. It matches the Christmas dish set we both have. I use the dishes only on Christmas Eve, although this year I didn't. But that was because we had crab legs and well they are messy and I decided I'd use the Pier One dishes that I've had for eons.

I also use the wine glasses every year that Liesa Bracken brought me – one set of 4 – I think maybe I'll try and get one more set of 4 this year because they can also be used for water and they're very pretty. All of my other dish sets are discontinued so they are priceless. All of them. The Pier One, the Christmas Eve and the Christmas day. All discontinued, but I think I saw those glasses somewhere recently. Donna and many others gave me little knife sets. I've got a votive candle holder that Cathy Carroll gave me eons ago that I still use.

A pot holder and beautiful salad tongs from Mary Ann. Sally Johnson bought me a beautiful dish we saw together once at the Hallmark store. It's just beautiful. Whether or not I use it every year I still look at it and remember. Lisa Decker made me adorable stained-glass ornaments when she was in her stain glass phase.

Then there's this tree that I bought from the Dollar Store that one year I decided I wasn't going to struggle getting the tree out of the basement and putting up all by myself because no one cared and Jimmy threw a fit and came home and put the tree up in the middle of the night. How can I get rid of this Dollar Store tree when it comes with *that* memory?

I love the memories of my girlfriends and those days. I'm so happy to have the stuff that reminds me of them all.

And now I have more stuff that are memories in the making. I think the boys used to judge how good a present was if it made me cry. Lots of these memories make me cry.

My boyfriend got me lots of new stuff this year and I must say all stuff I love. I got books that are meaningful, these patio lanterns that we both love, of course bling, a stunningly beautiful ring that we picked out together, a Ninja bullet and a Fit Bit so we can be healthy. Nina got me beautiful jewelry and a dreamcatcher. Monica gave me a Teavana tea set. Zoë a picture of her and I framed (she won for making me cry) and Jasen a new Brita water pitcher. It's amazing in so little a time how well these Clarks get me. They even appreciate all my different place settings and now I have one more place setting to add to the mix. We have Christmas Eve china, Christmas morning breakfast dishes and now that I'm cooking Christmas dinner I added a Christmas dinner setting which consists of new placemats and napkins (purchased last year) and we will use the good china that is Peters that he's had since college days. There is a great story that goes with those dishes, but I won't publish it on here. You'll have to visit us to get the story. Wait, here's a funny story. I put out some appetizers yesterday and ran out to storage excited to find and use plates that I "thought" belonged to their mother so they could all feel "ahhh." Nina said she never saw them before in her life. HA! But they're cute dishes and maybe now that's a memory to go with them.

I hope everyone had a Christmas filled with stuff. Enjoy that stuff while you have it and remember where it came from. Pete and are going to sit out by the pool and read our new books then we're hoping to catch the new *Star Wars* movie. It's been a really really lovely Christmas. Hope yours was too.

JANUARY 2016

THURSDAY, JANUARY 14 - HELP WANTED

Big blog-worthy news...my last day of work in this position here at Hospice is Friday, January 29. I know, woo hoo and uh-oh, right? Do I have another job to go to? Uhh, no. I know I go back and forth between saying I like where I work and I hate my job which I guess both are true. I really like the people I work with, the actual facility is a nice place, the duties of the job aren't bad, I mean I like the tasks, but I just don't like the "job" or especially the offer they have made me. I just told my sister this week that I was going to take the job because well why not, I like the people, it's a job, it's the only offer I've gotten, there's health benefits and I'm in Florida. But when that offer came it made me sick to my stomach. I thought about what advice I would tell my boys (or any human being) if either of them called me and said that a job offer was making them teary I would scream at them to run away from that job sooo fast. I took my own advice. I'm testing my own wisdom. I decided to cut my losses (with the support of the best BF ever) and take my chances back out there in the big wide world. The good news for anyone looking to move to Florida is there is a job opening here. I will be happy to forward your resume. Just keep in mind that you won't be able to afford a condo on the beach with this job but otherwise it's a great job and it is in Florida! Does that make me sound crazy? Well, who cares, everyone who reads this (all 28 of you) already know that about me anyway. I just know this particular job is not my forever job so with that in mind, I need to move on (as do they) and move on I shall. Isn't it exciting? And you all get to go through it *again* with me. All the angst as well as the pedicures, lyming days, maybe even a horseback ride or two before getting that next job. Oh, and most importantly MORE BLOGGING! YAY! ! If only I had a book idea from this experience. Then it would make it all worthwhile.

Pete suggested taking a month off before going back. I wonder if he remembers how long it took me to find this one? But I'm trusting in *something*,,,,not sure what, but something is giving me courage. I remember when I quit PPU and all the promise that was in front of me. It's kind of like that each time I quit something, like jumping into the abyss. Nothing as drastic as when I moved here but I mean anything can happen; from me getting a great job, to a stinky job, to ending up living with my mom (cause my car's too little to live in).

One thing that didn't happen for me this week is I didn't win the lottery. But three people did. I really hate when the media focus on the odds of winning. Of course, the odds are ridiculous but people do win. Just ask the three today that woke up and are now multi-millionaires. We'll probably never know who they are (if they're smart). They (media) also always dwell on all the negative aspects of winning and people who go bankrupt. But poor people go bankrupt too. Just think how much fun the lottery winners have before going bankrupt.

I am all ready to get immersed back into the volunteer aspect of Hospice care again after January 29. I'll now be able to attend more classes during my hiatus. If only the volunteer gig paid. But I shall take advantage of my free time and volunteer more. I will probably pick up a lot of afternoon shifts (when the kids are home from school – ha ha!) My free time might be cutting into Monica's free time now too. Her and I may be competing for the same chair by the pool (not much sun by the pool this time of year). I'll probably acquiesce and let her have the pool chair and head to the beach, with a book. I feel confident this is a hurdle I'll be able to deal with. I don't think she is at all happy with my return to "my" home. Just a little stressful for us both.

For now, I'm looking forward to a couple of weeks of free time, sleeping in, taking walks in the sun and maybe finishing a book or two, after January 29. That's two weeks away. Anything can happen.

FEBRUARY 2016

MONDAY, FEBRUARY 1 - ANYBODY OUT THERE?

To say that I'm in heaven would be a bit of an exaggeration. And although no situation is perfect, day 1 of semi-pseudo retirement and I'm pretty darn happy. My boyfriend took the day off too. We had big plans to go golfing (we actually went to the driving range yesterday, finally, after 2 years) then we both got side tracked with really mundane boring stuff. Me on the phone for 2 hours with the Healthcare marketplace since the 1095 form that they sent me is wrong. Soooo wrong. And it's a mess. And Peter had to go to the DMV to settle some stuff (not at all related to my stuff). So, there was that. But Jasen was happy with a ride home from school (although he walked most of the way) and a drive through Taco Bell. I also washed sheets and towels, made beds, organized a couple of clothes drawers, (did you know there's a book about tidying up and the way you fold your clothes will change your life?) took Zoë to practice, and made dinner. I was very happy to be doing these things again. Not quite sure if the 22-year-old (Monica) who still lives here was happy to see me when she came breezing through so I thought I'd give her space and went for a walk on the Causeway. Got some steps in, some sun, and some quiet time. I like giving her space. Tomorrow, I plan on going all the way to the beach to walk (instead of the road by the beach.) It's the least I can do for her. I am the palest I've been since I moved here. I could come up north and fit right in so I have a lot of sun to catch up on. I like looking like I live in Florida.

I have offered, and they have accepted, for me to continue to work on Fridays after my end date. I think it's only going to be ½ day Fridays just to keep them caught up until they get their new person in place. I'm going to like the one day (or 1/2 day) a week schtick. The paycheck will barely cover the gas but I'll like mixing it up. That might be the ticket. Plus, I like the people I work with so I didn't have to say goodbye.

I started some good routines while working. Making a smoothie every night, and mixing it in the a.m., taking it to work for my morning protein. I was also taking a break twice a day to walk around the campus. Now, I need to try to stay in that mode. I just made Pete a banana split and unfortunately took a couple bites. Maybe I should walk three times a day.

I have promised myself not to look for a job until May. I am thinking about other stuff right now. I feel like I'm on a mission. I'm not sure what that mission entails but until I get it figured out I'm going to be adding more volunteering into my days. If nothing materializes out of the cosmos by May I'll probably ...well I don't know what I'll probably do. I'll worry about it then. My point is I'm giving myself some time to do whatever.

I've got my boys (and Zach's girlfriend) coming in 2 weeks and I'm supposed to be going to my moms for a few weeks to help out this Spring, and I'm trying to get together with a couple of girlfriends for a weekend. I've got the Reiki II classes coming up in March and another girls weekend in May. This is why I can't work.

It's time to go to bed. I have books to read.

THURSDAY, FEBRUARY 4 - HOLA

Today it's raining – at least it is now. I picked the kids up after school, together in the car. There was so much arguing that I told them if they were going to be like this then I'm not picking them up...silence...it's golden. And we didn't even go through drive-through. . although we did stop at Winn Dixie. That's better than McDonalds. I think.

Peter is on his way home, which will take extra-long today because of the rain. Rain down here is like snow up north. Traffic stops, accidents everywhere. It's always something. He wants to take me to this different pizza place tonight. I'm pretty partial to my Fireside Pizza joint but I will give it a try. I'm that nice.

Tomorrow, I go to work work in the morning and then to hospice in the afternoon. Thus ending my week 1 of semi-retirement...again...round 2. This time I'm more determined to make it last. No more full-time office work. I need to say that mantra to myself daily...several times a day. Say it with me....

MONDAY, FEBRUARY 15 - AFTER WEEKEND UPDATES

My folding mission:

I was told by my work colleague (and new friend) that my shirt drawer didn't really look exactly right for the Kon Mori method but I continued on with the rest of my drawers and I have to say I am very pleased but I don't think they're perfect either. I'm most proud of my underwear drawer but I'm not posting it. I also have to rethink my t-shirt drawer. It's already getting unruly. Still a whole lot better than they were.

For the boys (and girl) visit:

Jimmy has come, visited, next Zachary and Rachel came, and Jimmy has gone ...already:

I'm sad and exhausted. Actually, I was exhausted yesterday too. Our only full day of all of us together and I was so tired. I passed out on the beach. Not a bad place to pass out. Today Zach and Rachel are having "their" vacation and I'll take them to the airport tomorrow. Unfortunately, today's weather is not very vacation friendly. Overcast, cloudy and without the sun it gets kinda cold.

After dropping Jimmy at the airport, I met Pete for breakfast and by the time I got back to the house Jimmy had landed in Pittsburgh already. Isn't that crazy? Such a quick flight. I've resisted the urge to crawl back in bed by downloading pictures and updating the blog but I don't know, I have a couple more hours before the dentist and well nap time just might win.

FRIDAY, FEBRUARY 19 – I'M EVOLVING

I'm into gel nail polish now. A few weeks ago, the nail people talked me into it (I didn't know it was $20 more) but it did last a little over a week. At a volunteer training meeting this week they said our nails should always be manicured with no chipped nails or chipped polish because chips hold bacteria. I think I have to keep doing the nails now, you know for the good of the cause. But no one has complimented me on the color. You know what? I don't really care that no one likes it. I'm that evolved now.

You know what else I'm not fretting about? Unemployment. I am so relaxed about unemployment this time around. A few people have asked what I'm going to do. I don't know. I don't really care that I don't know. I'm not worried about it. I just can't get over the fact that I'm not worried about it...yet. I keep myself busy for sure and now I'm mixing it up (unlike before when it was too heavy on the nanny duties.) Now I'm Reiki-ing 2-3 days a week (that would be volunteering), I'm still going to work 1½ days a week and might keep that up until the end of March. After that I'm planning a trip up to Mom's. I also have lots of doctors and dentist appts to catch up on. I still run the kids around like an Uber driver, without the tips, but they seem happy about it which makes us all a little happier. I've even picked up some morning shifts taking them to school since Pete has been very sick (flu-ish) and get this...I'm not even going back to bed when I come home from dropping them off at 7:00 a.m. I'm actually staying awake and getting a little quiet time in. Okay okay, today I slept for 20 minutes on the couch but still, I'm feeling a little bit of a shift. Evolving baby.

The Reiki might be turning out to be a passion, maybe, sort of. That's been an area in my life where I've always felt incomplete, the fact that I'm passion-less. You know the old, follow your passion line kinda stumps a person without a passion. But I think this Reiki thing is as close to a passion as I've ever had. I find it fascinating and I like to keep going (to volunteer) and seeing where it may lead. I don't even care if it doesn't lead anywhere, I'm just interested in it. That's like evolved too isn't it? It feels like it is. I'm putting it in the evolved category.

I'm doing what I'm doing. I'm hanging in and hanging on and to reward myself I went to the beach for an hour today. It's amazing what an hour at the beach at the end of a busy week can do for the soul.

MONDAY, FEBRUARY 29 - PURE DRIVEL. . AS USUAL

First of all, I thought it was "dribble" not "drivel" – didn't you? Thank heavens I looked up the meaning because I would have been so embarrassed to have used the wrong word on this riveting post. Wait how long have I been saying dribble for gawd's sake.

The visit from my kids was beyond wonderful (Have I talk about this already?) Their visits are much too short and I was running around like a lunatic the whole time but I think they still enjoyed their visit. Especially Zachary who stayed with his girlfriend at a beachfront resort. What's not to love there? Zach thanked me for moving to Florida. I think that's a good thing (so he can visit.)

And now I'll just look forward to April when we shall meet up again in Pittsburgh while I'm still on my sabbatical.

I've been busy, lazy and sick. I was bragging to Jimmy that I don't have Kleenex boxes everywhere like we used to (he was looking for them during his visit) because I never get sick and I *never* get a cold. (he had a bad cold when he got here) Florida is not a place where your nose is always running, or so I boasted. And then I got sick as a dog. Not the flu but just so much stuffiness. I caught what Pete had. We blamed it on Jimmy at first but I think Pete got his from work and then shared with me, which is okay because we share everything (right honey?) I've had to cancel all my hospice visits. I did get my nails done today, I guess I don't care as much if I get them sick. They kept bringing me cough drops and she told me to go home and rest. I "feel" okay but I sound awful.

I'm finally on the manicure circuit, after 57 years. Remember a blog last year where I brought up the age-old question.... to manicure or not? I've always been a pedicure girl but in the past manicures just weren't me. And now they are, since they came up with gel that doesn't chip. (as suggested above, riveting subject matter) I did some internet research today on color combos. They say it's not "hip" to be matchy matchy so I went with two colors. I got a woot woot from Zoë. I guess that's good.

And that's enough of that.

Lacrosse season for our girl has started and I'm back to keeping stats. It's not easy. We can't see the players numbers, I don't know the rules, by the time I find the little circle bubble on the sheet to fill in, someone got a ground ball and I've missed 10 other things. It's the bubbles that are hard to find on the page, hard to fill in and well, there's got to be a better way. ...and I'm gonna figure it out.... dammit...

That's it. That's all I got. Unless you want to know that I ordered a new Lacrosse t-shirt so I can show my team spirit (I'm such a resident now), I need to make an appointment on Thursday to get new tires and new brakes, I have blood work being done on Thursday to check my cholesterol and I need a new purse. I noticed today my purse handle is frayed.

MARCH 2016

WEDNESDAY, MARCH 9 - STICKER DAY!

Zoë passed her driving test. She is an official licensed driver now. A happy/sad day for sure. I don't have to haul her ass all over creation anymore, that's happy! But all you moms out there know that a lot of "quality" time is spent in cars with those dam kids. Zoë and I have spent a lot of time bonding in the car. Kids weirdly forget that you are in the car and shit just flies out of their mouth. I don't haul Zoë *and* friends around. It's just her and me. But it is alone time where I have my captive audience. Sometimes. Sometimes she doesn't get her face out of the phone. Anyway, I'll miss that. However, for her to drive her own ass around means she'll be taking "my" car – so then I'm like grounded. Ya know? Not sure how this benefits "me" yet. It would be one thing if I didn't have to pick them up here and there and could go to the beach, to the store, to see a friend for the day, but in order for me not to be the chauffeur it means I'm stuck in the house. Now, don't get me wrong, it's not always a bad thing to be stuck in the house. Especially when the pool warms up and I have a good book so you see, pros and cons. Pros and cons...I'm sure her dad is looking at the "con" of her car insurance. When I added my boys to my insurance it was at a minimal cost. With her, we're talking more than a car payment per month. Good thing he has a good job. I hope he has a good enough job to get her insurance *and* a car.

In Florida you can get your permit when you're 15. Jasen turns 15 next week. Guess who is not going to be his driving teacher. But today it's YAY for Zoë! She waited until she was over 16 to get her permit and then had to wait another year so she has been waiting a long time for this. Plus, she passed with a perfect score! The driving instructor told Pete that rarely happens. Let's just hope she doesn't mix up the brake and gas pedals again, and if so maybe she can do that in her father's car next time.

I have the morning off before I'm back on the road. It's also another hair cut day today. I never know what I'm going to do until I get there. But I'm leaning towards not short. Zoë asked me if I thought it was weird that she never knew me when I had long hair, to which I said "no honey, I don't think that's weird at all, but that question is." Kids, what goes through their heads?

WEDNESDAY, MARCH 30 - GOING AWAY.... AGAIN

Big doins going on here in the Clark/Bench household. When I pack to come to Pittsburgh for a weekend I over pack. Well imagine how I'm trying to pack for 20 days. I actually think I'm doing pretty good although missing the days of the steamer trunks and of course someone to valet for me (you know, like *Downton Abbey*). With any luck I will have shoved a sufficient amount of clothing into my suitcase and will be on my way tomorrow afternoon. I need to pack summer stuff *and* winter stuff. I guess what I don't have I'll just have to buy. *Wait a minute....* . Could that be a way to get new stuff? Because I forgot to pack it? Hmmm, I might be onto something.

Let's see what else. Oh, big news...Zoë has her first official boyfriend. Scary scary stuff. Zoë throws her heart and soul into everything she does. She's been able to balance everything but the addition of boys/ love that's a whole new ballgame. Let the praying start! (or continue) If I could just detach enough to be happy for her and this new thing... I just don't want her to change.

And then the whole boyfriend thing is a little bad timing when I'm giving her my car while I'm away. That's like a couple big things. BIG thing for me, just handing over my car to a brand-new driver, who wrecked it into a building the last time I was away. Lots of trust going on here. Now she has wheels *and* endorphins. Goodness.

Here's something funny and stupid I did this week. I accidentally shredded my debit card, and didn't figure that out until today, the day before the trip. I never have cash (for all you would-be robbers) and now no way to get it either. I've ordered another debit card but who knows how long that will take. It'll have to be mailed to me in Virginia. Pete says I can use the "Sun Trust" account which is sort of like a "joint" account except the only thing joint about it is I *take* from it and never put anything into it. But that's the way it should be, right? Go feminism!

Tomorrow is my last day in the "office" at Hospice (I will continue the volunteering.) I have realized that I am quite nostalgic (or a cry-baby, whatever) I'm pulling out of the parking lot at noon today, the rest of the staff is going into a quarterly staff meeting (like 300 people staff not just our office staff) anyway, anyway, so they go into the meeting and I pull out of the parking lot while this song is playing on the radio: *As if we never said goodbye.* The song is also appropriate because they had my going away party for me back in January when I quit! And I'm still there. Now going away again, as if we never said goodbye (get it?)

Back to the scene/moment, that song is playing and there I am getting a pit in my stomach as I think about driving away while they are starting a new phase without me. My boss is going to introduce my replacement at the big staff meeting. I mean it does give me a little tear as I drive away. It was my first office job living here in Florida. The first time I've felt competent again, in that work world anyway, I made some new Florida friends and so the whole experience is like a big deal in the life of Victoria, finally in Florida. But I'll be back in that office tomorrow morning and THEN drive away for good...I think...unless they call me back when I get home from vacation. Who knows. Well anyway, it was a Hallmark movie moment in my mind with the song playing, me driving away, the sun shining and then off to get my nails done. *And cut...*

APRIL 2016

WEDNESDAY, APRIL 6 - A ROLLING STONE GATHERS NO MOSS

I lugged this computer with me on this trip so I'm gonna use it, by God. I've been here in Virginia for almost a week of my down time and it's been nothing short of lovely.

First of all, did I mention that Pete drove me to Virginia? Sometimes I don't mention that we are *both* going to be out of town. I don't want to announce on a blogsite that we are both away. However, we did go together. It was a lovely, and a much-needed boyfriend trip. Our stop in Savannah was beautiful. Our hotel was beautiful, the historic city is beautiful, the weather was beautiful. Did I mention our hotel was beautiful? (said twice for emphasis) I think it might be one of the nicest places I've ever stayed in. We got in late so we didn't get to see too many sights that night; although we did walk around the park that was directly across from our hotel. We watched the movie *Midnight in the Garden of Good and Evil* before our trip. We recognized a lot of sites from the movie. A fortune teller told me once (remember my weakness?) that I lived in Savannah in a past life, so I was waiting for a vibe. I will say that I stood outside one building for quite a while. Just stood there. And when we walked into the restaurant for breakfast in our hotel I started to tear up. I might have been tearing up just because the trip was so lovely and I didn't want to leave, ever. Maybe I was a southern belle in my past life, what with my obsessions with dishes and all. Our day in Savannah included an Old Town Trolley tour and then we dined at a Vietnamese restaurant. HA! I know, but we were hungry and it was the first thing we found open. We ended our day around 4:00 pm.

Then we drove onto Salisbury, NC and spent the night there, in a normal roadside hotel and spent that day touring where he used to live and work in Salisbury; where Sam used to run in the field across the road and where Jasen went to school. And then we drove onto Virginia

During the 2 days that Peter was with me in Virginia the weather was absolutely gorgeous. Perfect blue sky, coolish but nice temperatures, cool enough to keep the annoying bugs away (but not the bees) and warm enough to wear a t-shirt. Just nice. Our time together at my mom's was just so nice. When we had first started dating, 3 years ago now, while he was still living in Salisbury, before the move to Pittsburgh, he met me at my mom's in Virginia. My boys were soo mad about that. I guess everyone feels like my mom's house is "sacred" and what am I doing bringing some stranger into our personal space? I know, right? But I was so happy to have him there. And with this visit too, he just seems to be relaxed when he's there. Pete loves the woods and there's plenty of it at my mom's. He loved walking down to the creek in the woods and you know he loves putzing outside. I think he sat there and dreamt about all the yard work he could get into if he was there longer. It really is a special place. I was sad that he had to go. I always try and get him to spend more time with me on our trips away but I have yet to get him to commit to more than 3 days.

Last night it dipped into the 20's. As soon as I'm done with this blog I'm going to sit in front of the fire with my feet up and read a book.

FRIDAY, APRIL 8 - GOODBYE CITY LIFE

I am tired. I'd like to blame it on all the yard work, digging in the dirt and housekeeping that I've been doing while here in Virginia but seriously I think it's just all the fresh air that my body is not used to because I haven't done any yard work or digging in the dirt. We haven't gotten to any of the cleaning that I was hoping to do. First of all, mom's been keeping up with the cleaning really well but I had thought I'd take one room a day and scrub from top to bottom kind of cleaning. And so far, nada. I dusted a little bit down stairs but no spring cleaning for me. Basically, we've been entertaining. I guess that can make me tired too. We had Norie the other day and today we had the neighbors. My table was a little prettier today only because today I served a green salad (more color). With Norie it was tea sandwiches (and green asparagus soup) but anyway, so I'm not sure if one gets over tired from entertaining for a few days? I guess it's possible. Even if it is just one or two people at a time. Although I cook on a regular basis for at least 4. *Hmmm...*It's gotta be the fresh air.

Another thing about living/visiting in the woods is I rarely care what I look like. I know many others of you may be saying I *never* care what I look like, woods or not, but when I used to have date night I always tried to look nice. I can't remember the last time we had a date night. They really went by the wayside. When I went to work I wore mascara, until I got a tan then I left that off too, but here I look REALLY bad. Clean, but bad. After our luncheon, which no one dressed for, we're not talking "luncheon" just lunch; anyway, after lunch I got a bath to warm up, then I got cold, then I wanted a fire, then I remembered that this firewood that someone brought mom doesn't burn for shit so I hopped in the car and went to search for fake firewood. I realized half way through the aisle at Food Lion how I looked. I stopped for about ½ second embarrassed and then thought, WTF, I don't know anyone and carried on with my mission to find fake firewood. Which I was successful with.

I remember a time when I was in high school and went into our local grocery store and saw my mom and dad shopping in the aisle. They both looked like they just walked in from the homeless shelter. When they saw me they both started laughing because they knew how bad they looked. I know I used to run to the grocery store as well not looking my best but today I think I surpassed them. The man in the front of me today in the checkout line, with no teeth, probably thought I looked okay. It's the country, I'm with my people.

MONDAY, APRIL 11 - THE PARTY IS HALF OVER

My last night in Virginia...I can't believe it. The time has just flown by. Usually, I'm ready to go after a weekend stay but I wouldn't mind staying another week. It seems like we didn't get nearly enough done, although we were social for sure which we don't usually have time to do. Today we went and got the flowers that I plant for her every year, but with this unusually cold weather they are suggesting not to put them out until next week. I've planted most of them in their pots and left them on the porch for Wayne (mom's helper) to put out next week. One of the pots that I put a flower in every year I noticed had this little squirmy thing in it. Being used to the lizards of Florida I felt quite brave when I took the old pot out ready to replace it with the new one and have the little lizard run out. But alas, it was NOT a lizard. It was a snake. I screamed and that was the end of that project. Wayne can put that plant out there next week. So much for my bravery. The woods are great but there's those other things you have to put up with, like snakes. Well anyway, I'm sad to leave. I've enjoyed my time here immensely and I really like this little room that I've been blogging in. If I ever get a book idea I think I'll do it here, in this house, in this room, at this desk.

Tomorrow I'm off to see my kids. I won't see them until Wednesday but I will see those babies tomorrow. Those babies are my great nieces and nephews. They are adorable and I love seeing them. Hard to believe I'll be gone another week before going back to Florida. I wonder how they are faring without me? I hate to say it, although also glad to say it, but I think they do better without me there. Makes me both happy and sad. Pete took Jasen to the beach yesterday and they had great fun. They went to a movie and probably out for ice cream every night. Zoë has her own car and can come and go as she pleases, in her Mercedes. Ya know? I'm pretty sure they are having a great time without me. Oh well, good news, bad news.

Now we have to decide if we want to use up the firewood that I picked up around the yard for our last fire tonight. It's 60 degrees out. Probably not the best temp for a fire but I really want to use up that wood. It'll probably burn up in 10 minutes. We can always open the doors for cool air.

Off to Sewickley tomorrow. I have a nice place to blog when I'm there too. The fun never stops.

MONDAY, APRIL 18 - WRAPPING IT UP...OR WHAT I DID ON MY SPRING VACATION

Here I sit, on the floor, of my attic room at my sister's house, the last night of my time away. My mother lived in this attic room for 10 years or so back in the day. And now I use this room when I visit. It is a lovely space. But the ladder steps aren't easy on the knees. I can't believe my mother went up and down those ladder steps all those years. No wonder she was always in such good shape.

I'm not sure what to call my time away this past month. Vacation? Escape? What do I call these visits back "home"? Vacation doesn't ring true since the definition in my mind of a vacation is doing nothing, in a hotel, relaxing or site seeing. At my mom's there is a constant list of to do things, not that I'm complaining as there is also a nice relaxing vibe there. Not quite vacation but it can be relaxing and therapeutic as soon as I'm done with the to-do lists.

Here in Sewickley, there is no down time. None. Nada. Well, I take that back a little. I sat at Jean and Larry's who fed me a delicious dinner. I stopped in at Jerry's for a minute and went with her and Janice to Eat N Park. I mean those events were nice and I consider that down time. But the rest of the "Sewickley" time was running from one place to another. Vacation just doesn't seem like the right terminology. Escape could fit but I could use escape either way. Escaping to here or escaping from here. Escape just doesn't sound right either.

Whatever it is I've been doing, away from Florida, has been great. The drive up here from Virginia was absolutely beautiful. I never get tired of the scenery. My Sewickley time, as usual, has been over busy with lots of babies; I also got some friend time in, some Eat N Park strawberry pie in, some wonderful son time in, really good son time this trip, a great weekend with old college friends, I mean it's been great.

There are a couple of people who I didn't get to see that I usually do and that always makes me sad. I never get to see old work friends. I have yet to be able to get into the city for any amount of time to visit with all that I would like to visit with at work. I plan to visit every time I'm here but I am always, *always,* diverted by something. By the time I get this figured out (how to get all the visiting in when I'm here) no one is going to remember me anyway.

I was asked several times if I missed Florida and I have to say every time someone asked me I was like "eh" ... and then I would wonder to myself "does this mean something?" Like should I be worried that I *don't* miss Florida? And after a very short time of analyzing this the answer is "no" I do not feel bad. How could I? I am here with my family and friends who I am with maybe 5 days out of the year now. I am in Florida all the rest of the days. I was also with my two very best college friends, like *very* best college friends who I haven't been with for years. I mean time with them is unbelievably precious. And really I just love being with my boys. I always have.

However, as this evening approached, and my son time draws to an end and I'm going up and down this ladder at my sister's house to try to pack clothes and I missed getting a shower and eating dinner because the babies are all over the place needing put to bed, read to and climbing all over me, well I'm starting to look forward to "home". The dinner missing isn't going to hurt, but the shower thing, well I don't even want to talk about it. Then my boyfriend said he's going to take a ½ day off to spend with me when I return. And that makes me happy. And I'm signing up for a class at hospice on Thursday, planning a day at the beach on Friday with Stephanie, in addition to going to a concert with Pete on Friday night and now my mind is back in Florida. NOW I'm ready to go home...to Florida. I like that I live there. I love living there. But, I'm not going to lie.... I miss my kids. I miss hanging out with them, making them cookies, going to the restaurant Fuel and Fuddle with Zach, sitting on John's deck with Jimmy. I miss them. They (the boys) act like they like seeing me too. I mean it just doesn't get any better than that. But it does make me miss them even more.

I don't know when I'll be back after this time which is a bit disconcerting. My sister says I'm here every 6 weeks. I don't know if it's really that often, but I don't plan on coming back for a while. I'm thinking September. In the meantime, I'm having another girls weekend in 3 weeks in Florida. Sewickley girls are coming down and we're going to spend a weekend at Siesta Key. How great is that? I think there needs to be more of those kinds of visits.

I know that once I'm on the plane I will be super excited to get home, to Florida, and my boyfriend, and my own bed. Plus, there are a lot of unknown new adventures to be had. I mean I don't have a job anymore. Remember that? Don't you wonder what will happen next?

Looking forward to blogging from home in Florida again and getting back to my conundrums there!

WEDNESDAY, APRIL 20 - DON'T TELL ANYONE

I made a list today. Blogging is on it. I've been pretty good going down the to-do list marking things off. It'll take a little while to get a "new" routine now that I'm back to not working. And of course, once I'm happy with that routine it will change I'm sure.

I'm back in Florida. I didn't get excited (not that I *wasn't* excited) until I looked out the window of the airplane as we were approaching and saw the Tampa area all lit up (it was night) it was then that I got really excited. I thought "I LIVE here" and just started smiling. My boyfriend was a little frazzled because I was 30 minutes early but he looked cute and I was very happy to see him. When I got in the house Zoë gave me the biggest hugs ever, I think Jasen smiled too. He might have been more interested in the Sarris candy bars I brought back but I jest. I think they were happy.

Pete and I had a lovely morning off the next day. I felt like a brand-new person looking at all the flowers and the garden he planted.

You would have thought I was gone a lot longer. I'm very happy to be back. I have not lost my love of him or living in Florida. Pittsburgh has beautiful days for sure and I love the city and Virginia and my mom's house are beautiful and relaxing but I *LOVE* Florida. I'm in the right place. If only this euphoria would last longer than a week. Maybe the key is to go away more often. Hmmm...

Sometimes when talking with friends I focus on everything negative. Everything. And then those people think my life sucks. And of course, the way I've described it anybody would think that at that moment. But then I'll tell all the great things about my life and then they're envious. My niece, Evan, thinks I'm rich (meanwhile I can't pay my bills) Some people think I'm some trophy wife...ha haha haha...I mean seriously HA HA HA.... but it's not only the things we say to each other but it's how they are interpreted based on the other person's perspective and their experiences.

On the other hand, sometimes you don't want to share things because you don't want to jinx them. The opposite of telling secrets...you don't share with anyone. I've done that a few times. You know like when you're starting something new and you think if you share it, it won't come to pass.

BUT there are other times when you really need to air things and mull it over with your friends (or the Pizza delivery man.) It can help put things into perspective for you. Someone always has an opinion, of course you need to discern through a lot of those, but it doesn't hurt to know that you are not alone in your perceived suffering and have someone else be interested and sympathetic, and/or give you encouragement. Sometimes you just need to get it off your chest and get it out in the world, then you can forget about it.

That's what's on my mind today. Now I have to get Jasen off the couch (which I never sold by the way, it's still my couch) so I can sweep up the crumbs under the couch cushions that have been accumulating for the past 20 days. This time I'll just keep my thoughts to myself because Lord knows they are not secret and everyone is sick of hearing about it and it doesn't help anyway.

MONDAY, APRIL 25 - WHY GOD WHY

Why are there snakes, lizards and bugs? These are the three questions I will ask at the pearly gates if and when I get there. I went to pick a gardenia, minding my own business, heard a slither which again I assumed was a lizard but then the long black slinky body kept moving. Lizards do not have long black slinky bodies. They run quick and are gone. Why is there a black long slinky bodied snake IN the gardenia hedge? Needless to say, I did *not* pick that gardenia. I screamed and ran back into the house. I stayed at the window to watch and could see his little head hanging there, still as a statue, waiting to see what *my* next move was going to be. Meanwhile I'm inside the house so whatever the move it's not going to affect him adversely, right? I think snakes know when you're watching them. The snake out front in the hedges this morning I could see was little. Doesn't mean it won't bite me but I think it's probably one of those racer snakes which are very common down here and apparently welcome as they eat rodents. This particular snake didn't seem to be racing anywhere though. After our little stare down, I went to get my camera so I could have proof and send pics to Pete (and or to post on the blog) and the little dear had slithered out of camera range. This snake today did not slither very far mind you as I could still make out a tail but it had moved on a smidge. Moving a smidge is not characteristic of other black racers I have seen. I think there is a nest in the hedges.

I had plans to go at least start my car (I'm having car issues) and maybe try to go to yoga. I'm feeling like I should put on some long pants and boots and carry a machete just to get to the car. We actually do have a machete somewhere. I moved it because I was afraid someone would break in and kill us with it. Now I wish I knew where I hid it.

I love Florida but I could so do without this wild life part of it. I like nature, but not so much reptiles. Give me some birds, some water life, you know dolphins and such (no sharks or alligators), I like deer in moderation but that's about it. Maybe this is why the snowbirds go back up north for the summer. The snakes and lizards are kinda slow down here during the winter. They seem to like the really hot temperatures and it's already summer here. I've seen more lizards recently than I've seen in the last two years. Probably has something to do with Global Warming. Great. I finally get to Florida and it becomes the jungle.

MAY 2016

TUESDAY, MAY 3 - NOTHING IS HAPPENING...OR IS IT

Thank God nothing is happening. I know that it might seem to the naked eye that nothing is happening in my life and part of me feels that way too; but on further scrutinization there is a lot going on and I'm glad not to have more...at this time.

One thing I've been trying to do is unsubscribe from a lot of these junk emails. You know when you want to look more at an ad for a pair of shoes and it makes you subscribe before you click on it, so you click on it and subscribe and then never find those shoes again on that website? And then that same website has 13 affiliates and they all start sending you emails. Just because you wanted to look at one itty-bitty pair of shoes. I'm trying to unsubscribe. I've noticed that it usually doesn't work. They keep sending you stuff. But finding the time to unsubscribe in itself is a commitment.

This past weekend Pete and I went to Boca Grande, which is a little island a couple of hours south of here, and we visited with Cricket and her husband for a night/day. A lovely place on the water and a great little town and of course there's nothing like spending time with a friend you've had forever. We were talking about how having kids is just a blip in your life. We were friends for years before kids, we were friends during kids (she lives in Colorado so distant friends) and here we are walking on the beach after our kids are grown. Kids, in relation to that perspective, aren't that important. HA! But the reverse of that is our parents are soo important because they're the only people we know our entire lives. Isn't that a little weird to think about? It's like our kids don't really know us. They live with us for this brief period (if we're lucky/or unlucky depending on your point of view) and then they're off and we're back to being who we were before. It's just one perspective on that subject and well, something to blog about.

So, see? That happened. And traveling takes packing and planning, driving and such so that's not nothing.

My car is in the shop – as of last Wednesday. It's not as ugly as it *could* be...and then again I'm not getting everything fixed, but they've held it hostage waiting on a part. I had to pay extra for expedited shipping to get it back in a week (as opposed to 2 weeks) – hopefully I'll have it this Wednesday. But because I have no car, I'm doing nothing. I don't have to pick up kids, I don't have to take Jasen to some fast-food place against every grain of everything I believe in because there are no options. No rides, no nothing. That could be thought of as nothing's happening, but I'm loving it.

However, I spent the whole day, yes the WHOLE day, cleaning yesterday. This house has a lot of dust – and well you know when you start working in those exploding corners well those corners will suck you in for sure. You look at these odds and ends and think first of all "what the heck is this" and then secondly "why am I keeping it? Do I throw it away or put it back after I dust it in case I remember one day why I am keeping it?" I go 50/50 on that. Keep. . pitch. I have these coffee cups that have been sitting behind the microwave that match dishes that I gave Jimmy that I've been meaning to get to him. I just drove up North. That probably would have been the time to take him the mugs that I'm sure he could care less about. They're coffee mugs, not beer mugs. But because they became such a staple in that corner I didn't even think about it. Now I've put them in a cupboard. Chances are that's where they'll stay until the next move and then I'll wonder, keep...pitch?

And on that note, I should get back to the subject at hand. Banana Bread. The real question is where is the recipe that I always make and why can't I seem to find it? I can't remember do I make the one with the cinnamon or the one with the vanilla? I'm goin cinnamon.

MONDAY, MAY 9 - SPRING CLEANING

Remember me? I'm still here. Busily cleaning up around the house. I'm having friends, yes friends from up north here, for breakfast, on Friday, so we are cleaning. I've always said it's good to invite people over once in a while to get things done around the house. We're having fun getting beautiful. A pressure washer is my new favorite item. It used to be electric hedge clippers. After years of manually cutting my hedges in Fair Oaks I was given auto hedge clippers once and I thought I died and went to heaven. I mean what a difference. I'm sure the manual clippers helped my arm muscles more but OMG the amount of productivity difference. I'm all about this pressure washer now. It cleans concrete, it cleans around the pool patio, it's cleaned furniture, this brick patio in the back of our house was black with dirt and now it looks brand new. I love it. I'm also planting a couple new flowers for the summer. Spring is over. We had some beautiful Hydrangeas in pots but they've outgrown the pots so I put them in the ground. They don't really grow this far south...too hot. BUT we'll see. Maybe they'll like it here. I also repotted my Jade plant...again. It is doing horribly. I'm surprised it's living at all. I'm a terrible caretaker of it. I put it back into its original pot, got new soil and I will try to be more attentive. I mean every day I look at it with love but maybe it needs Miracle Gro instead.

Yesterday was Mother's Day I hear. Gone are the days when it was mandatory for my boys to spend the day with me. I guess I traded the Grand Concourse for Florida. Zachary thinks it was a good trade-off (he gets out of having to spend the day with me) but I don't know, I really really used to love Mother's Day. Instead of lunch at the Grand Concourse with my boys, I worked my butt off all day cleaning but am happy with how it looks (see above info re: pressure washer). I did end up going to dinner with Pete and Jasen and after dinner we went to the new *Captain America* movie. I really did like the movie. I got a text from Zachary, text from Nina that made me cry, text from Monica even. Both Zoë and Jimmy were MIA. I was the first one to call my mom so I got the star in that category anyway.

Zoe is deep into that boyfriend relationship. We went from inseparable to her spending every moment she can with that boyfriend. Even on Mother's Day she went to spend time with *his* mother. I'm not gonna lie. It really hurt my feelings. But so much is different now than last year, our first year (although she never really did spend time with me on Mother's Day before either). But *everything* is different. All the newness, the excitement of being together, no date nights, it's just different. I can't imagine being anywhere else and can't imagine I will ever be anywhere except with this family but something is off. Something is not quite right. I just can't put my finger on it.

WEDNESDAY, MAY 11 - SEE WHAT I MEAN?

Last night Monica came home in tears, like 24-year-olds are wont to do. She was crying about "the stupid boyfriend" blah blah so end result is she is moving back in - she wasn't actually moved out except she has been staying at the boyfriends more or less full time and comes home to sneak stuff out of the house to take back to her boyfriends – you know like pots and pans, TVs, food, tools, oh, and she has no car as of Friday and we're not actually sure if she has a job. So, there's that.

This morning I spent 3 hours in car repair hell. I just got my car back after a week of repairs and took it in today for brakes…I mean I know I had to have brakes I was just trying to space this stuff out…and yesterday I got my new windshield – that was exciting…okay so this morning I take it to a new shop (trying out different places) and this guy (the owner) has been working on Mercedes since 1974 and…drum roll…the owner is from Pittsburgh as is the technician that worked on my car. *GO STEELERS!* The mechanic did a couple of repairs for me…no charge…scheduled me for brakes next week…but informed me that my front tires are bad…so since they are brand new I was happy to take them back to the tire place…Tires Plus. . which I can't say enough *bad* things about. I swear I was going to have a stroke arguing with this guy.

Two hours later I got the new replacement tires on and came home. I was exhausted from the stress and the tension.

Daughter #1 (Nina) was here when I came home from my tire battle and I said "how nice of you to come and support your sister in her time of need." And she says "funny thing, we're both going through the same thing. I left my boyfriend last night and packed everything in my car, which I wrecked and I'm behind in the payments. And so, I'm moving in. And did I tell you I quit my job? "

I'm making steak and chicken for dinner. #2 doesn't eat meat and #1 doesn't eat chicken.

Do you think I was a Nazi war criminal in a past life? Maybe I was Pontius Pilate?

Pete is on-line looking for efficiency apartments – (probably just for him)- I found something on Craigs list for a nudist friendly efficiency. What the hell....

This is my life. . Dam kids. .

THURSDAY, MAY 12 - JUST SHOOT ME NOW

My engine light just came on. I'm on a roll.

TUESDAY, MAY 17 - THE PARTY'S OVER

I have my heater on. I know cray-cray. But I'm cold. What can I say? It's 84° but not sunny.

A great update today after my updates of doom last week. First the car issues seem to be nothing. The mechanics don't know why the check engine light came on so they turned it off and the car is operating beautifully. They checked it thoroughly first, then gave it a clean bill of health.

And my friends came. I have friends. First they came to my house, got to meet Sam (the dog), Monica and Pete (in that order) so that was nice and they liked what I cooked! Pete, the good boyfriend, took my car to the mechanic while I was entertaining, he came home with the good news and car filled with gas, said hello to the girls and off we went on our girls weekend. We were at the beach by 1:00 pm

The girls loved The Cottage I had reserved at the Inn at Siesta Key and that set the tone for the rest of the weekend which was just lovely. Good friends, good talks, good food, lots of sleep, a good book, a lot of steps (37,500) a nice sunset (or 2). . just a little slice of heaven. And the best barometer of all is that we booked it again for next year adding one more day!

Now back to my life. Now, I will see what unfolds. Now, I have no more trips planned. Now, the unemployment might start sinking in. Now, I have to let things come to me. That's a thing you know. Letting things come to you

While I'm waiting for things to pop, I will continue with my chores, laundry, dog hair, dishes and other household duties just like the old days. And then for personal growth I should be doing my morning journaling, meditating, practicing Reiki daily and exercising. Work is much easier than self-development for sure.

THURSDAY, MAY 19 - READY SET MOVE

I'm so good. I got up early-ish (early for me). Made Pete and I smoothies, I wrote 3 pages in the journal, meditated, exercised, tried to bring a dead butterfly back to life (Reiki practice...okay he wasn't Lazarus) and now I'm waiting to cool off from exercise before I jump in the shower. Might as well blabber on my blog.

Here's the update. . my car is *back* in the shop...a different shop but none the less I'm carless again. I took it in for the brakes which is just maintenance. . you know every car needs brakes now and then – the car ran perfectly back and forth to the beach last weekend and it's been running very smoothly since then and I can tell those other tires were bad since now it's nice and smooth. But that stupid engine light came back on and they are stumped as to what is wrong. They have kept my car hostage. I am trying to remain calm about it all – if it takes every last dime of mine (okay of Peters) and all of *my* credit then it's God's will because at this point I just don't know what else to do about it. It's a great car – I love it – so I will just hope for the best and trust that this issue is related to the last issue and once this is fixed I'll be good to go forever... and ever. . amen.

And oh, on top of that? We have to move. Yep. Have. to. move. The leasing company called Pete the other night and said the owners decided they want to sell the house. No, we do not want to buy it. Alright fine, "I" don't want to buy it. I think we can do much better for the price. I mean there is a lot I love about this house – I mean it's *our* house, except it's not. I'm projecting on my mental vision board a 4–5-bedroom house, a kitchen with room for more than one butt (we call our kitchen the one-butt kitchen), maybe a garage even? A real master bedroom with our own bathroom with a real bathtub and walk in closets – maybe even his and her closets? I mean I'm dreaming, why not. Pete wants to be on the water but I'll be happy with closer to the water (more breezes) and I would still like to have a pool and a yard to putz in and of course a fenced in yard for the beast. I refuse to believe God hates me or us and instead choose to believe we will find a better place. Just because we have had the rug pulled out from under us doesn't mean it's going to be a bad thing. We found this place, didn't we? We'll find another and maybe there won't be a snake nest right in the front hedges (PETER! I saw it peeking at me this morning) At least not for the first week. I have reframed and I'm now looking forward to what we will find next. I believe it's going to be even better. Come on everyone believe with me!

That's all for now. I have to get on with my day. Not sure what that entails since I still have no wheels. But I'll get on with it none the less. Seize the day!

WEDNESDAY, MAY 25 - DID YOU MEAN I'M SUPPOSED TO DO THAT NOW?

I'm procrastinating. My mind is obsessed with packing and moving but actually doing it is another story. My goal is to get all of "my" stuff packed in boxes and out of the way so Pete can decide what of "his" stuff we should keep – or keep all of it. There isn't a whole lot of "our" stuff but, *but,* on the other hand he would say it's all "our" stuff. But here's the thing. Okay not *the* thing but here's *a* thing...there are boxes of stuff of "mine" that I've never even opened. Literally "things" that I've never used or even looked at. Does that mean I don't want them? I don't know what it means. I have downsized how many times now since I sold that house in 2010.

Then I upsized when I moved in with the Clarks. Now I feel we must downsize again. Why? Mainly because I don't feel like packing it or moving it. Take for instance these wine glasses I just bought. Just 2 weeks ago at Ross for $5. Are they worth packing or do I just smash them in the recycling and buy more? I mean they were only $5 and I feel they will break in the move (most of *my* stuff breaks anyway) so really do I even bother wrapping and packing? I have a bunch of pictures that never made it onto the walls. Half of them don't have glass in them, they were broken in the move down here. I was thinking of taking them to Michael's today and getting glass put back in all of them but should I wait until after the next move? Surely they will get broken again or maybe I take them now and pick them up after the move. But, who knows if we'll have room for them in the new house anyway. And then what about that marble top buffet piece of mine that got broken in the last move? We've never replaced that marble. How do I ask movers to move that? Do I even keep it? I'll probably just put the pieces of marble in my car and piece it back together at the new location. And then where do we put these boxes after they are packed now. We don't have any-where to move to yet. Pete is supposed to be getting a storage unit but I have a small car. How am I going to get boxes to the storage unit? When I had that storage unit in Pittsburgh I could easily fit 5 or more bins in that Nissan. Didn't think of that when I bought my current car. Didn't think of that at all. And on top of that I'm back to job hunting.

Who knows when we will move anyway. I don't want the place to look abandon while we are still living here. The house may never sell. Our next house might not be found until September. Do you see why I don't want to do anything? I don't even know where to start. And at any minute the car guy could call me to come back and pick up my car.

Life. It sure keeps you guessing doesn't it? I mean seriously. Right now, I'm going into that kitchen and look again in those cabinets. Keep. Pitch. Goodwill.

God help me, seriously God, please help me.

FRIDAY, MAY 27 -THE BIG REVEAL

When I said God, please help me, this isn't quite what I was expecting. Not at all what I was expecting.

First let's talk about this blog (and when I say "talk" I mean I'll write and you read.) This is a long long blog post so if you don't want to read it walk away now. If you do, I recommend getting a cup of tea, coffee, maybe a chardonnay.

To recap, which I often do, this blog was started as like a mass email after I moved to Florida from Pittsburgh. I didn't know who really cared about my Florida adventures so left it up to my friends to "tune in" if they cared to. Then it got to be fun and I kept it up because I like writing, I like purging, and it gave me something to do in an otherwise Clark-filled environment. It still serves as my diary although there are times when I think (I hope) that I have something inspirational to say, typically spurned (wait not spurned, spawned maybe?) by something going on in my life. That's the first thing to keep in mind. Because all of my readers are my friends that I would have to send the following news in separate emails, I am using this same format to advise of an important Victoria update. And when I say it is long I'm talking 3000 words. I mean long...

As author of this blog content, I made a decision early on to remain as upbeat and positive as I could be on my posts. This was a two-fold decision. One, nobody wants to hear my bemoaning, because it's just, well let's leave it at that, no one wants to hear it...okay, I take that back, *some* people want to hear it but in general let's say no one. Two, when I focus on the positives it makes me see the glass as half full (rather than half empty) and in turn keeps me positive and keeps *me* going. It can also act like *a fake it till you make it* scenario. I'm constantly (at least when I'm blogging) looking for the positives to report, making me focus on being grateful. That doesn't mean the negatives aren't happening, it's just that I'm focusing on the positives. And I will admit, full confession here, that I have on occasion made up stuff. Not like actual details of where we went or what we did but perhaps, maybe just perhaps, I may have exaggerated a bit on the wonderful-ness of it all. However, I want to stop right here and say that 90% of this Finally Florida experience has been great, especially the first year. I just want to throw that out there upfront. I can spin it either way but spinning it in a positive light is more truthful.

And now keeping all that in context let me just start here talking about my track record with relationships. Can I pick em or what? Each BF (boyfriend) I have had has obviously had strengths but more often an overwhelming number of weaknesses. When you're in the thick of things much of the time you can only see the positives while *everyone* else is going *hmmm*. And then once you see the *hmmm* basically that's all you can see.

Here's the skinny, let's review. Let me preface this with saying there is nothing wrong with internet dating. Sure, you don't know who you meet on the internet, but you also don't know who you meet at a bar. You don't know who you meet on a blind date; you really don't know people you work with. I mean there is no way of knowing people until you live with them, and apparently not even after that. Backing up, when I met Peter I always felt there was something off. I often said, okay I *always* said, there is something here that I am missing. Then a lot of somethings came up that were missing and I took each one as they came, processed the info and it was my decision to forge ahead. Although always a *hmnm* lingering. But, I was having fun. We always had fun and when those *hmmm* feelings would surface I pushed them right back down and said to myself "Self, I'm having fun." I threw myself into the relationship from the start, which I thought was a welcome throw, and having fun so why not? Then as most of you will remember, early on in our relationship before the move here, there was the breakup, the reveal of some indiscretions but never quite sure whether or not we were on a break and didn't really care except for the "lying" part of it. Keep the "lying" part at the forefront of the rest of this tale. We decided to stick together after that and moved to sunny Fla where the Finally Florida story starts.

About that lying...there is a lying problem in this family. It starts at the top. The top would be Peter. He is a terrible liar. I mean literally terrible, but I would just laugh about it and move on because although I knew the *hmmm* factor to be there I wanted to trust. Trust in everything. Trust in the move, trust in the process, trust in the family and trust in his feelings. You know, trust is pretty important in relationships. I just gave it my all and hoped that the *hmmm* feelings would subside, or that they were based on my own insecurities because that happens too. Sometimes there's nothing going on but because we/you/me have built-in insecurities we make up stuff. Bottom line is I had no proof of anything and we continued to have fun, at least I continued to have fun. Especially that first year.

After Monica moved in there were a lot of changes. No more date nights for one thing. Did you notice the lack of them in the blog? There was no more room (literally she took the room) for visitors (i.e., *my* family) and I admit I was feeling a little pushed out but whacha gonna do? She's his daughter. She has no home. Her father is her home. She needed a place to go. I get it, but it was the start of all the changes, the start of my unhappiness. I had hoped it was temporary, as did he, or at least he said as much (who knows really) and I soldiered on feeling quite stressed most of the time in my own home.

Then I got the full-time job. Personally, I think this was the biggest factor of my downward spiral. I was unhappy. I was able to pick out facets of the job that I liked. I like tasks, I like figuring things out, I like everyone I met, I liked the location, but it's the *lifestyle* that really depresses me. And there was no acceptable salary to compensate for that lifestyle so there was nothing in it for me really. Nothing. Yet I soldiered on until I didn't soldier on and I had the best boyfriend ever that allowed me to quit. Best Boyfriend Ever. LoL

The other thing that the Best Boyfriend Ever (BBE) allowed me to do was go home to Pittsburgh or go to my mom's whenever I wanted. Nice right? Working and having a little bit of income to subsidize those whims did help; although I will say I never made enough and I find myself about $10,000 in debt now thanks to the whims. But Peter allowing me to take these trips turns out to be a little on the "not so BBE" side. It seems like he might not really miss me as self-reported. As a matter of fact, I'm not even sure he is *here* when I'm gone.

I'm going to guess that by now 90% of you know where this little novelette is leading, and 80% of you are not surprised in the least. Some might even be judging and saying things like "I told you" (my favorite) or "you should always trust your intuition which always has said something is not right" – to which I would reply FU to the first and I DID and DO trust my intuition and I always have been on guard knowing that something was not copasetic. Remember when we used to use that word, copacetic? Anyway, anyway, I *have* been listening to myself, I have been guarded and I have been just waiting for the truth to be revealed. In this regard I have never ever felt settled in this relationship. I've always been waiting for the truth.

And then it was... revealed. I'm not sure if it is done being revealed or now that it's opened up I'm going to start being bombarded with all his past (and current) indiscretions but really "dear Universe" I just need *one* proof. I know there's probably many more but really, do I need to know? I'm good with the one thanks, although even since I started writing this I have gotten more. I think the Universe wants to be sure I get the picture. Thanks, I'm good.

In a nutshell he was the creepy guy with my friend while I was out-of-town. And as she pointed out, if he did that with her you know he was doing it with others. And I'm going to guess it went on all the time when I'm out of town. Am I sad? Well yea, of course. Am I mad? Only when he's here. Do I hate him? Do I forgive him? What's to forgive? To forgive implies that he has done something *to* me. He hasn't done anything *to* me, he's just himself. Well maybe he has been lying *to* me. That's true. In that regard I guess I need to forgive him for being a liar that I've always known him to be? The liar lied. See? Forgiveness doesn't even feel like it applies here. He has always been, and I fear always will be that creepy guy that is not honest or...big reveal. . faithful. The cheater cheats. Big Surprise! I admit when it was revealed to me, I wasn't remotely shocked or surprised. I was embarrassed and embarrassed for my friend who was on the receiving end of his texts, *and* forever in her debt for being brave enough to share it with me. It took her 8 months to tell me. The timing is perfect for this reveal. Eight months ago would have been devastating. See? Things happen for a reason. Had we not been told to move I would have had to think about leaving this family, leaving "my" home...again...which I said I would never do and then I'd be both mad and sad, mostly at myself again for taking the risk. But as it turns out we all have to move so it's perfect timing to move apart. Not that I'm not sad about it. I really am sad, and mad, but overall, not too bad under the circumstances.

The forgiving part will come with myself. Do I forgive myself for getting into a situation where I knew, I've always known, that something was wrong? I don't have one regret (as of this writing, let's wait and see next week) I would not have done anything differently. I believe there have been times when he has been sincere in his feelings for me and maybe he's just a sex addict or some weird other thing that has nothing to do with me. I didn't cause his illness (we'll call it an illness) and I'm sure not going to cure it. I don't think he's alone in this personality flaw (and I don't want to know if he has other comparable flaws) so I'm not going to lambaste him as if he's some sort of pariah (big words in this sentence) I'm just not going to continue on in this capacity. I hereby resign as VP of Equal X Consulting, as GF (girlfriend) and unfortunately for the kids as chief bottle washer and chauffer of the Clark household.

Would I do anything over? I would do it *all* over again. I would move here with him. Do I wish I would have trusted my feelings from day one and gotten out sooner? Nope. I think this scenario had to run its course. If you believe in this, it's like our souls had an agreement to help each other out. I have been helping him have the pretend semblance of a family life. I have really helped the kids with a semblance of a family life, running them to and fro, talking with them, cooking for them, yelling at them. I agreed to do what I could here with the Clarks. I'm not remotely saying I did a perfect job. I'm very moody and not always consistent and well I got tired of the constant discipline. I think someone else in this position might be better and have more patience. My values are not their values. I think they *should* be but you can only hit your head against the wall so many times and then say, fine...eat food in your room (among other things.)

Peter's agreement with me was to move me down here, to make me feel like I was a part of his family giving me a purpose for a little while (no matter what he's been doing on the side) – He has mostly made me feel very welcome and wanted and appreciative of what I have to offer to his family. On the surface he's been a good boyfriend (on the side not so much.) He has been super supportive of my Reiki practice, super supportive of my attempt to find myself and quit my job, never yelling about money and we have had a lot of fun on our trips. I really and truly have enjoyed so much of our time together. I'd go as far to say that I've enjoyed 95% of our time. But I have been seeing this end coming, I've always felt it and been feeling and noticing more and more signs and allowing myself to believe in what I'm feeling and then well I got "the proof" so it's time. Time to move on.

Should I stay for the sake of the kids? Are you crazy? But yea, I've thought of that albeit very briefly. I'm not leaving the kids; I'm just leaving Peter. I'm not their mother so there are some sacrifices that someone in my position should not have to make, like staying here with the kids while he's out philandering. I guess that's good enough for some people but I prefer to live a more honest life. I think I deserve better. I'm a good person. I'd rather be with a good person or no one at all. I think no one at all is best for at least the next 20 years.

What I don't know, yet, is *where* I'm going to end up. Will I stay in Florida? Will Finally Florida continue or will I move back to Pittsburgh? Maybe the blog will become "Back in the Burgh" Or maybe "Vegging in Virginia? " To end up back in the "Burgh" with my kids and family and friends is not the end of the world now is it? And to move back up in the summer is the time to do it. However, if I have an opportunity to stay here and can afford a place here I will probably choose that and try to maintain my visiting schedule up north and with my own place I can perhaps entertain guests (i.e., friends and family).

I had been planning on making a very dramatic exit and blind siding him, like in a revengeful way, but in a moment of clarity, a moment of maturity and most important a moment of *honesty*, I decided to advise him of my plan to leave and see if we can tell the kids together. It didn't go very well but I have told Zoë and she's okay. She is mainly concerned with staying in the school district for her senior year and realizes she's going to have to be more responsible for herself. But she has always been her own caretaker in my opinion anyway. It'll help that everything is in turmoil so when the dust settles the only thing missing will be me. I'll wait on telling Jasen when I have a better idea of my move out date and I'll let the big girls know later today incase this affects their move out (or move in) plans.

And lastly there may be one or two of you wondering about me posting all this on a "public" blog. He is *very* worried about it. I'd be comfortable saying he's shitting himself right now. But here's the thing(s), a blog is a like a diary, at least *my* blog is, kinda like a reality show in print with my life as the entertainment. I'm the author. Perhaps a cheater should have thought of that before cheating on a blogger. Ya know?

Consequences. Life is all about consequences. And I am living with mine. Right now. I thought it was okay to deny those feelings. Deny the signs. Well, it's catching up with me big time. My consequences are not too fun. I hope I can remember the fun I did have when I'm living in a box.

I wasn't going to post this until I knew where I was going because the end isn't written yet. This ending is another beginning and the beginning is wide open and well now there's a Chapter 4 of Victoria's life about to start (or end) and the blog will evolve into its next phase (or end). Life with Peter and life after. Maybe there is a book in here somewhere.

I am at the mercy of the Gods. I am hoping that they will smile upon me. I just wish they weren't so big on living a life of poverty. I bet I can make a case of still being a good person and living comfortably in a 2 bdrm condo, on the beach. Thanks for reading...I must get to packing.

TUESDAY, MAY 31 - HOROSCOPES ARE NEVER WRONG – RIGHT?

Daily Gemini Horoscope (I'm a Gemini)

TUESDAY, May 31, 2016 — You are ready to launch into the future right now, and there isn't much that can stand in your way. The pioneering Aries Moon energizes your 11th House of Friends and Wishes, encouraging you to think about where you are going and how to get there. Unfortunately, life is more complicated than ever, making it tricky to get all your ducks in a row prior to moving ahead. Luckily, once the major pieces are in order, everything else should fall into place.

I'm on it!

JUNE 2016

FRIDAY, JUNE 3 - YOU DIRTY RAT (AND OTHER PARTING GIFTS)

Two nights ago, I slept on the couch after a very loud screaming match with Peter. Last night I made dinner, did dishes, did laundry, swept floors, helped Pete move some boxes into storage, came back home from storage and floated in the pool with Pete – it was after 9:00 pm – a hot and humid night – perfect for a pool dip. I listened to him reminisce about his deceased wife for a solid hour and then I quietly got out of the pool. I made cookies for the kids, negotiated with Jasen on a start time for school today (he wanted to go in late), watched TV on *my* couch, then went to bed like a normal family/couple.

Today is move out day for me.

Such is the life at the end of a relationship. I will never again question someone who doesn't leave a relationship when clearly there are signs to go. It's hard. It's *very* hard. You get caught up in the day-to-day routine. Everything seems normal when you're not mad, you cook, clean, float in the pool. It's hard. The fact that he talked nonstop about him and his wife while we floated last night, our *last* night together and this is what he talked about, well it helped not to be too sad today. Although I could have powered through with my blinders on, like I have done so many times over these past three years, I could have easily stayed and just said eff it and continued to live my life here with the Clarks

However, I did not choose that, nor does it seem that the Universe has chosen that for me. If you thought my move down here was quick; this next move is a freakin whirlwind. I have packed up all my stuff away from his possession; like my dishes, all my personal stuff that I've had (and blogged about) over the years. Christmas stuff, books, albums (yes vinyl), piano music, even my wedding dress from 1982 I still cart around. It's all in storage.

I'm moving into a 1-bedroom vacation rental until the 15th of the month and then moving into another smaller 1-bedroom vacation rental in the same little complex. I am super excited which does not take away from the sadness. Okay maybe it does just a little. I can't move in until 7:00 this evening so I'm stalling. I'm sitting here at my desk, like I've done so many other days, blogging for the last time in this house. I was thinking of going back into the pool for a while; delaying packing up the car. It's so blasted hot out there I think my clothes might melt if I leave them in the car too long. I've already done all my running around, 3 banks, the post office (forwarding mail). Maybe I'll wash the car. Get it ready for its new digs.

I can't help but believe it is because everyone has been so kind and thoughtful and people saying they are praying for me that this whole move out has been almost seamless. Well, seamless would be that I won the lottery and moved out in style, but I am very very happy to have found this place, the landlord is kinda cutting me a deal, kinda, I have a two-month lease then can go month to month after that if I choose to stay. I LOVE the feel of this little beach community I'm moving to, the apt is right across from the beach. I can wake up and walk across the street to the beach every day. It is hard to believe that it's not meant to be.

My original thought was to come back (or go back?) to Sewickley; hang with the peeps for a little until I could figure something out. Zachary immediately called and said "we have to talk." Zachary is such an interesting kid. He is very hands off most of the time, hard to get him to chat, rarely calls, but in a crisis he is right there. I mean *right* there. He said that I worked so hard to get down here (with my dreams over the years) that he does not want me to come back. He discussed with Jimmy and they agreed to help me financially stay down here until I can get on my own two feet. I mean it's humiliating and humbling and so so, well I don't know what, but I'm crying as I'm writing this. They are such nice wonderful kids. Zachary has been constantly checking in to see what is going on and how he can help. His comment that sticks with me the most and makes me laugh is when we were talking about Jimmy's contribution financially and I was concerned that Jimmy doesn't have the money; which Zachary assured me he does have the money and said something like "if he can't find the money to help out his homeless mother instead of going to a concert…. " It makes me laugh but also a wakeup call that I really could have been homeless (not that I had to leave here) but my boys were so quick to come to my aid. Ok, Zachary quicker. When Jimmy deposited the money yesterday, I told him I wanted to barf and he said he thought he would too, but then quickly said he thought it was all good and he is very happy to help. When those boys were growing up I had always just hoped they'd split the check when we went out to eat. I never expected this; and I didn't plan for this either which is why I'm in the pickle that I am.

But it is *not* a pickle. There is something happening. Some force that is moving me forward as if life is saying "get on with it…*go go go.*" I have been humbled and overwhelmingly surprised. I don't know the right word so I'll just say humbled by the comments and the support by everyone I know. Everyone. My hospice co-workers on Tuesday night, who I didn't even know if they knew my name, have been calling. The support of my friends, have been truly, truly a blessing. Stephanie in particular, has been on my ass (a little bossy) driving me all over the place looking at rentals, calling people, introducing me to friends and realtors staying on top of everything and offering me help in so many ways. She's the one that found the place where I'm moving to; although she prefers I be in her neighborhood I will be close enough for her to cook for me often. Seems like everyone wants me out of the Clark household. This has truly been a humbling experience. I don't have any other word for it. I am blessed beyond belief.

When I leave today it won't be the last time I'm here. I will come back for my plants next week. I'm not sure how much room I will have at the new place. My permanent place is small but there are decks for extra chairs so we'll see. Anyway, so when I leave today it's not like it's sooo final. My plan is to come back on Tuesday and pick Jasen up from his last day of school, swing by and see my hospice friends and then I suspect that day will be the last time I'm here. I'm leaving my furniture here for the Clarks to use until they move out and then I want it in storage. I went around yesterday and put smiley faces on all my stuff. It's kinda cute.

Anyway, I don't feel too sad about leaving, it's almost like I'm just going on another trip. But that doesn't mean I am not very thoughtful and insightful about my time here. I have been wondering for a while if my time here has been over (and obviously that answer is yes) and to help me make the move I often thought of myself as like Mary Poppins. When I was here the kids loved me (well I hope) and I have hoped that I made a difference but then there comes a time when your time is up and the kids need to take it from there. While I don't know that Peter will ever be as enlightened as Mr. Banks, my hope is that I have made a difference in the kids lives and that maybe I gave them some sort of foundation and now they have to run with it.

I got this quote in my email today, related to hospice work, and I thought how appropriate, so I will share it...and it will make you cry. I don't want to be the only one crying today:

"As people experience healing presence, they change. The shift may be subtle or dramatic. They're likely to open more – to themselves, to others, to the world, to the amazing mystery of life itself. Sensing another's belief in them, and seeing that belief reflected in life around them, they can begin to develop in completely unexpected ways, and to move in directions they have not gone before. Or perhaps they will return to their original path, but with new spirit, new vision, new hope. As they encounter the inevitable pains and diminishments that life will present, they can begin to understand that such adversities can be experienced as more than adversities – they can be known as opportunities for growth, as avenues for moving toward wholeness. (From Miller and Cutshall's book **The Art of Being a Healing Presence.** *)*

This is how I think of my time here with the Clarks. I hope I have been a healing presence.

Oh, and the rat story? (The title of the blog) Last night Sam went out to pee –like dogs do – and when I went to let him in, he quickly turned to retrieve something that he then brought to the door to bring into the house. It was a rat. Not a mouse, a rat. A dead rat. I know cats will do that, bring things into the house, but Sam has never done anything like that before. I am going to have to think of the significance of that. Anybody have any ideas?

Thank you!

This story would not be possible without **Phil, Jorden, Zenah, Tashah, Alyna** and **Sam.** When I read it, I am right back there reliving and loving every minute (almost every minute). I love you all.

To **Diane Hess** for being my blogging partner since the 1970's. All those phone calls, all the emails (once there was email) it was all practice/fodder for my blogging. It truly is all because of her that I ramble on as I do. Not too many people would be that patient (or interested) in what I have to say. She gave me confidence to let it all out there. (Well, most of it is out there, she still gets her "Di" updates).

Sandy Betz Krentz and **Emily Quidetto** were my original beta readers. Thanks to both of them I was redirected on my original attempt to publish a fiction novel and decided to make the blog into a book. I so appreciate their friendship, their time and their honesty.

To **Zachary Kumer**, for reading his mother's blog and always encouraging me and teaching me how to be a better writer. To **Jimmy Munizza** for his motivational "you got this mom" talk throughout the years. I love you both more than I'll ever be able to express.

A special thank you to my cousin **Debbie Monahan** who wins the prize as my top commenter. Her reassuring comments on my life and cheerleading me along while following the blog helped both calm and encourage me.

To the runner up commenter, my brother, **Scott Monahan**, for reading my blog and offering his always entertaining and reassuring comments.

Other thank yous for their comments and encouragement to **Ja Nel Orwig, Barb Buchwach, Jennifer Nugent, Cathy Susko, Peggy Vandenbord, Jan Ryan, Diane Hess, Kris Julian, Amy Sampson** and **Ellen Morton**. Many others sent me private emails encouraging me to keep writing and keep going, specifically **Sue Haywood, Sandy Krentz,** and **Gina Puppo**. I often wanted to quit writing and inevitably I would hear from one of them telling me to keep going.

And to all the Bunko girls (who I haven't already mentioned) that I know have been following along because I hear stories about how my adventures/blog comes up at Bunko –**Mary Ann Rondinelli, Sally Maloney, Suzanne Swegal, Liesa Besong, Donna Cooper**. Without my many reminisces of our friendships I would have had less to blog about. Thank you!

To **Kate Sullivan** of Wordsmitten and our little group of readers. It was when Kate said "this is going to be big" that I was like "alrighty then..." and off I went. Let's hope she's right. Thank you, Kate, for your confidence and encouragement.

To **Peggy Lambert** from the Port Orange Scribes, Port Orange, Florida for so much encouragement and editing help.

To **Melissa Fleming Chapman** for her review, suggestions and encouragement.

A special thank you to **Ellen Green Morton** and another to **Sandy Betz Krentz** for being contributors, you know like *contributors,* trying to keep the *Finally Florida* dream alive.

To **Patricia Churchill** for convincing me to post this myself and not wait for an Agent/Publisher.

There are no words for how much **Stephanie Smith Shanahan** has meant to me. During my darkest days she was my "rock" and came into my life finding me housing, new friends, and helped me get back on my feet, encouraging me to write, encouraging me in life and just being the best friend at a time when I needed her the most. I will never forget her generosity during the month I spent with her and Tim where she housed me, helped me to edit, tweak and print out 600 (or more) pages on her printer. There were papers everywhere. She continued to push my book to any publishing friends she had and then helped me to know that being in Virginia was where I was meant to be at that time. There are no words Steph, but there may be a few oysters in our future. My treat!!

And lastly I want to say a special thank you to **Kris Julian**. As I was saying my goodbyes at Point Park University heading to Florida she came to say goodbye and as she was walking away she looked over her shoulder and said "blog"! And I did.

Based on a true story, however, names are changed to protect identities.

Because I am my own editor I take full responsibilities for all typos.

Most of the grammatical errors are on purpose.

Damn: to be condemned by God to suffer eternal punishment in hell.

Dam kids: pains in the ass (I don't wish anyone to suffer eternal punishment)

Please report all typos and comments to: Lynn Monahan at: finallyflorida2018@gmail.com

Lynn Monahan was raised in Sewickley, Pennsylvania and currently lives in Pittsburgh, Pennsylvania. She has lived in Florida a few times over the years. While she works on subsequent books you can follow her blog on lynnmonahan.net where she shares much of what is going on in her life. *Finally Florida* is her first book.

To read additional blog posts from the original blog of *finallyflorida*, subscribe to finallyflorida.net. If you would like to contact Lynn, email finallyflorida2018@gmail.com.

www.ingramcontent.com/pod-product-compliance
Lightning Source LLC
Chambersburg PA
CBHW031438160726
47994CB00005B/1777